The
Transformation
of the Jews

Chicago Studies in the History of Judaism

Jacob Neusner, Editor

*Calvin Goldscheider and
Alan S. Zuckerman*

The
Transformation
of the Jews

The University of Chicago Press
Chicago and London

CALVIN GOLDSCHEIDER is professor of sociology and demography and chair of the Department of Demography at Hebrew University in Jerusalem. He is also adjunct professor of sociology and Judaic studies at Brown University.
ALAN S. ZUCKERMAN is professor of political science and a faculty fellow in the Program in Judaic Studies at Brown University.

THE UNIVERSITY OF CHICAGO PRESS, CHICAGO 60637
THE UNIVERSITY OF CHICAGO PRESS, LTD., LONDON
© 1984 by The University of Chicago
All rights reserved. Published 1984
Printed in the United States of America
93 92 91 90 89 88 87 86 85 84   5 4 3 2 1

LIBRARY OF CONGRESS CATALOGING IN PUBLICATION DATA ·
Goldscheider, Calvin.
   The transformation of the Jews.

   (Chicago studies in the history of Judaism)
   Includes bibliographical references and index.
   1. Jews—History—1789–1945. 2. Jews—History—
1945–   . 3. Israel. 4. Jews—Cultural assimilation.
5. Civilization, Modern. I. Zuckerman, Alan S.,
1945–   . II. Title. III. Series.
DS143.G615 1984   306'.089924   84-198
ISBN 0-226-30147-8

To Frances E. Kobrin

and

Roberta S. Zuckerman

Contents

Preface

This book is about modern Jewish society and politics. It focuses on all Jews, not their elites; on comparisons of Jewish communities; on Jewish continuity and change in the context of the societies in which Jews are found; on historical patterns, but not on history.

Analyzing modern Jews is the same as analyzing any other group—that is, to study a people who are enmeshed in the social, economic, and political transformations of recent centuries. With Jews, however, it means an examination of a community set apart from others. Most students of Jewish society and politics have emphasized the factors which make the Jews unique. We are not doing that. In our view, the changes that have occurred among Jewish communities exemplify general processes. In order to specify what is peculiar to Jews, one must first place Jewish society and politics in a general context by comparing Jewish communities with each other and with those of other peoples. These comparisons demonstrate that most—but not all—of the transformations that have occurred among Jews during the processes of modernization relate to general forces of social change.

We approach the problem of explaining the transformation of Jewish society and politics as social scientists. Calvin Goldscheider is a sociologist and a demographer. Alan Zuckerman is a political scientist. We apply theories of modernization, political and social conflict, ethnic cohesion and assimilation to the transformation of Jewish communities in Europe, America, and Israel. We focus on communities, in towns and cities as well as nations. We emphasize neither individuals nor ideas and intellectual systems but the social, economic, and political interactions that define Jewish communities. This study is not intended to be a theoretical treatise on modernization, social conflict, ethnic cohesion, and continuity. It neither reviews the extensive literature on these subjects nor does it establish a definitive answer to the relationship among these concepts. Our effort to address issues of general theory follow and derive from the particular analysis of Jewish communities.

Collaborative work by social scientists of different disciplines has been slow to develop. Usually differences of theoretical orientation and methodology impede the effort to work together. We have been more fortunate than most in that we share a theoretical perspective that emphasizes the importance of structural over cultural factors, and patterns of sustained social interaction rather than values and motives. We both view modernization as an open-ended series of processes, not guided by economic, political, technological, or any other single factor. Our disciplines and substantive strengths complement each other, thereby expanding the scope of our analysis and limiting the areas of disagreement. In addition, we share a passionate interest in understanding what has happened to the Jews during the past two centuries. Much of the power of our analysis derives from joining the complementary perspectives of demography, sociology, and political science into a coherent argument. Thus, this study has two senior authors and no junior author.

Our theoretical approach guides our descriptions. We neither examine all Jewish communities nor detail all the characteristics of any of them. Rather, we select examples which allow us to compare variations in the level and rate of modernization and the internal structure of Jewish communities. We tie a comparative analysis of various Jewish communities into a theoretically rich argument about the effects of modernization on Jews.

Variations in the availability and quality of data on Jewish communities also determine which cases we study. We have collected little original information. Instead we have utilized the fruits of other people's research. As a result, some of our comparisons are incomplete, and the general quality of the descriptions leaves room for improvement. There is much work for those who will mine the rich lodes of material on Jewish communities that may be found in various censuses and surveys. Nevertheless, the empirical evidence that we have synthesized is considerable and supports our broader theory of social and political change.

The theoretical goals of social science guide our approach. We seek to analyze the Jewish communities in a manner that is precise, logically coherent, and related to the analysis of non-Jews. Hence, we set forth hypotheses and propositions that are testable, logically related to each other and to arguments applied to other nations and communities. The uniqueness of our work lies in its theoretical scope, the great number of cases which it analyzes, the precision with which this is done, and the testability of its claims, not in the detailed descriptions of particular communities, Jews, or events. We provide a theoretical map that will ease the travels of those who follow us, whether they confirm or negate our claims.

The utility of this approach extends beyond formal rigor to uncover items heretofore overlooked. For example, it leads us to find similarities between the emergence of Reform rabbis in Germany in the first part of the nineteenth century and the formation of Jewish political movements in Eastern Europe at the end of the century. It helps us to uncover similar divisions within the Jewish communities of Eastern European and Israel, and differences between them and the Jews of Germany and the United States. These and many other nonobvious findings emerge from a comparative analysis that is guided by precise and logically related propositions.

We are well aware that our approach differs from those used in most other studies of Jews. Those scholars who emphasize cultural characteristics are especially limited by a dearth of information. We know very little about the values held by contemporary Jews. Few surveys exist to shed light on their beliefs and attitudes. Studies of the culture of those no longer alive are even more difficult to carry out. Approaches that assume the existence of universal Jewish norms reduce an empirical problem to a theoretical assertion. As a result, they are unable to explain variations in the particular characteristics of Jews and their communities. Those scholars who equate the beliefs of Jews with the ideas and values espoused by their intellectuals replace the analysis of Jewish society and politics with intellectual history. There is no reason to assume that the cohesion of Jewish communities, for example, varies with the kinds of ideas set forth by Jewish intellectuals. Those who do not set their analysis of Jewish communities, organizations, or institutions in a comparative context are prone to other equally fundamental errors. To explain the formation of Jewish political movements in Germany, for example, without examining other political organizations in Germany or other Jewish political groups in other countries risks overemphasizing that which is German and Jewish. It unnecessarily limits the scope and, therefore, the theoretical power of the analysis. Traditional approaches have suffered from studies that are imprecise or theoretically limited or both.

Our primary objective has been to reshape the questions which guide the analyses of contemporary Jews and their communities, comparatively and historically. Our central theme has focused on the impact of modernization on Jewish cohesion.

We conceived this study in Eilat and completed it in Jerusalem. In between, we have spent much time in Providence. Several institutions in the United States and Israel have made our joint enterprise possible. Brown University has given us the opportunity to think, teach, and write together. We thank our colleagues in the Program in Judaic Studies for providing an environment that fosters collaborative research across disciplines. We want to acknowledge the assistance of the Brown University Faculty Development Fund and the Department of Political Science, which provided the means to pay for typing the manuscript. Alan Zuckerman would like to thank the Department of Political Science of Tel-Aviv University for providing a home in Israel and the Memorial Fund for Jewish Culture for financial assistance at an early stage of the project. The Hebrew University,

Jerusalem, provided Calvin Goldscheider time to think through and research some of the fundamental issues covered.

We are pleased and honored to thank several friends and colleagues who
gave us the benefit of their critical comments, encouragement, and assistance. Jacob Neusner's theoretical vision allows him to see beyond traditional approaches and academic boundaries, and stands as a model for us.
He never ceased to help us believe in the importance of our work. Ira
Katznelson's comments pushed us to our intellectual limits. He provided a
detailed point by point critical reading of the manuscript that forced us to
confront basic theoretical issues. Alice Goldstein, Joel Migdal, and
Yonathan Shapiro provided important criticisms of the entire manuscript.
Barbara Anderson, Bartholomew Schiavo, Seymour Martin Lipset,
Jonathan Frankel, Tzvi Abusch, Sergio Della Pergola, David Sorkin, Saul
Stampfer, and Gerald Showstock helped us with their thoughts on various
chapters. Lila Weinberg gave us extraordinary help and devoted editorial
assistance. Mitchell Cohen was an able research assistant. Margaret Soares,
Carol Walker, Gayle Grossmann, Susan Cohen, and Marjorie Lau typed
various chapters, and Donna Souza helped us to master typing with the
computer. Without these friends and colleagues, our work would have been
much less enjoyable as well as much less convincing.

Our children, Judah and Avigaiyil, Gregory, Ezra, and Shara link us to
future Jewish communities. We thank them for their strength as we have
moved them back and forth between Israel and America. We pray that they
will have benefited from the travels as much as we have. Our families in
Baltimore, Brooklyn, Long Island, and Netanyah tie us to the departed
Jews of Prussia and Byelo-Russia, Lithuania and Volyn. We trust that we
have accurately interpreted the experiences of these and other Jewish
communities.

We would not have completed our work without Frances Kobrin and
Roberta Zuckerman. They heard the ideas aborning, read each word, and
commented on every line. Each gives the love that makes our careers and
lives meaningful. We dedicate the book to them.

Jerusalem
Erev Tu B'Shvat, 1983

Part I: Theoretical and Historical Points of Commencement

We study Jewish communities as social, economic, political, and religious structures interacting with each other and with the communities and societies of other people. The path to understanding these interactions lies through the use of the concepts of economic development, state building, political conflict, demographic growth, and other ideas associated with the processes of modernization. These forces of change do not arrive all at once but are conditioned by the already existing social, economic, political, and religious structures. To proceed with our analysis we require a theoretical map and a view of the historical starting point.

1 · Modernization, Conflict, and Ethnic Cohesion: Theoretical Issues

Recent decades have marked extraordinary events among Jews, even when measured by the standards of their long and diverse past. A historical heartbeat separates the Nazi massacres of millions of Jews from the establishment of the State of Israel. The United States and Israel became the largest and best developed Jewish communities when the center of Jewish civilization in Europe ended. They are the paradigms of Jewish survival and destruction in the contemporary world.

The Jewish communities in Europe, their destruction, and Israel and American Jewry are products of a cacophony of changes that have characterized Jews over the past two centuries. Religious denominations have appeared bringing Jewish prayers in a variety of languages and theologies in diverse modes of thought. Skirts and blue jeans as well as beards and side curls adorn contemporary rabbis. Jewish political movements have formed espousing socialist, Zionist, religious, and ethnic ideologies. Today, in Israel, they compete as parties in elections; in America, they are pressure groups. In Tsarist Russia, they were once part of the revolutionary movement. Jews have migrated across the globe: at the end of the last century, three-quarters of them lived in Europe, most in the Pale of Settlement of the Russian Empire. In 1980, two-thirds lived in the United States and Israel. Occupation changes marked these decades: from filling traditional roles as middlemen, merchants, and artisans, Jews moved into the salaried and professional classes. They created the nooks and crannies of the Israeli economy, from the kibbutz to the national bank, from the bus cooperative to the building industry. Massive population changes have had extraordinary effects: all the Jews of an average *shtetl* community could fit into the sanctuary of a not especially large American synagogue. At the same time that tens of thousands of young Jews fill American universities, there are many times more students in rabbinical academies in the United States than there ever were in Europe. Each of the recent generations has witnessed staggering alterations in their lives and the content of their Jewishness.

These transformations have given new meaning to the perennial questions of Jewish survival. Wars continue to threaten Israel. Less visible social, economic, and political alterations have eroded the overlap between religion, occupation, language, and ethnicity that long distinguished the Jewish Diaspora. Having been integrated as minorities, assimilation threatens Jewish continuity. The Holocaust, conflicts in the Middle East, and the open society challenge the survival of Jews in the contemporary world.

How does one make sense of these massacres, elections, educational transformations, occupational changes, new religious beliefs, and the other elements of the cacophony of recent Jewish history? Most students of these subjects have assumed the uniqueness of each event. They have examined religious changes without regard to migrations, political changes in one country isolated from events in other nations, educational changes apart from occupational alterations. Efforts to explain a particular event almost always have begun with Jewish values and beliefs. The ideas of Jewish thinkers have been assumed to determine the behavior of all Jews. Generally the Jewish community has been studied with little regard for the social, ethnic, and political contexts in which Jews have lived. As a result, there is a parochial focus on Jews divorced from the actual ways in which they have lived.

Our effort to understand the transformation of Jewish communities departs from the accepted wisdom. We develop comparisons—over time and space. Systematic and multiple comparisons are necessary to move beyond description to the analysis of contemporary Jewry (Lipset, 1970; Shofer, 1979). The ideologies of the intellectual elite—whether cultural, political, or religious—have a marginal impact on the lives of most Jews. The ideas need to be explained and are not sources of explanation. Hence, in order to account for the ways Jews have changed over the past two centuries, we must move beyond particular descriptions and intellectual history. We locate Jews on multiple and interrelated dimensions of social, economic, political, and cultural life, analyzing each with regard to the others. Population growth, changing economic opportunities and educational systems, new political arrangements and religious services, and migrations affect and interact with each other. At the same time, this mode of analysis demands and provides the means of comparing Jews and other people. The uniqueness of the Jews may be a cardinal principle of Jewish theology, but in the study of Jewish communities it serves only to replace theoretical understanding with metaphysics and self-congratulations. The analysis of Jews in a comparative framework is the path out of the mire of random and idiosyncratic research. It is the road to integrating the analysis of Jews with the study of other people within the domain of social science.

MODERNIZATION AS TRANSFORMATION
The master theme of contemporary social science is the social, political, and economic transformations associated with modernization. Industrializa-

tion, political mobilization, and population changes are key elements. New structures and values, new institutions, ways of behaving and thinking, new jobs, residences, political movements, cultures and ideologies as well as new sources of conflict, competition, and inequality appear. Modernization is more than change. It is the transformation of society.

Capitalist economic development and the establishment of the nation-state are primary factors of modernization. They involve the separation of economic activities from family control, the development of national and international markets, and the emergence of industrial labor. Political control moves from local areas dominated by a handful of burghers and nobles to national governments controlled by bureaucrats and politicians. The tightly integrated old order is replaced by new and less rigid forms of integration.

With the expansion of economic activities and opportunities, there occur improvements in standards of living, social mobility, opening up of new jobs and better education, and aspirations for improved socioeconomic status. Concomitantly, values and attitudes emerge which emphasize achievement rather than ascription, the individual and the nation rather than the group, change rather than tradition. Structural, cultural, and personal factors operate to reinforce the overall transformation.

Changing economies, politics, and values entail conflict as well as expansion. People fight over jobs, business opportunities, entry into schools and housing. As democracies develop, political parties organize various sectors of society in electoral competition. Where totalitarian regimes emerge, party, government, and secret police eliminate conflict and opposition. Liberal democracies, authoritarian regimes, and Nazi and Soviet totalitarianism appear during modernization.

The impact of these transformations on the Jews provides the master questions of our analysis: How have they responded to the forces of modernization? How have the transformations and responses affected the cohesion of Jewish communities? Does modernization lead to a world in which Jews are as likely to interact with non-Jews as with other Jews? Does it provide new bases of interaction, tying Jews together in ways different from the traditional community and yet still distinctive? Does it produce conflicts within the Jewish community? These questions guide our general effort to compare Jews with each other and with non-Jews in a variety of societies.

Rates and levels of modernization among societies are major factors accounting for variations among Jewish communities. Industrial development and state-building erode village life, replacing artisan guilds with industrial labor. Population growth and urbanization provide job competition and new economic opportunities. Educational expansion and new systems of transportation reshape communication patterns. These changes vary in pace and intensity, flowing from different political and economic configurations. In turn, they have different impacts on Jewish communities.

Where new cities grew rapidly, where large portions of the population worked in industry, and where governments fostered national integration, there were massive changes among Jews. As the intensity of modernization varied within societies and over time, the pattern of Jewish changes did so as well.

Differences among Jews also reflect the particular structural features of their communities. Variations in population size; economic concentration; residential distribution; religious denominations; strength of communal, social, and political organizations; and scope of school systems help to explain the differential impact of modernization on the cohesion of Jewish communities. The relatively large and well-institutionalized communities of Eastern Europe were affected differently by modernization than the relatively small and poorly institutionalized communities of Western Europe. At the same time, the former contained class and religious divisions not found in the latter.

The characteristics of a particular Jewish community also reflect the interrelationship among local, regional, and national communities. At times, these ties were asymmetrical, with capital cities, like Paris, Berlin, and Vienna dominating peripheral areas. In other places, like the Pale, dozens of relatively similar communities interacted. Currently, the interdependence between Israel and the Diaspora structures relations within world Jewry.

Hence, to understand the transformation of Jewish communities one must examine variations in general patterns of modernization as well as specific features of the Jewish societies, politics, and economies.

In the modernization of the Jews, their religion is transformed. As the old order changes, so do the institutions legitimating that order. These alterations relate directly to the process of modernization, to new political and economic conditions, residential and educational patterns.

It is impossible to analyze the impact of modernization on Jewish communities without examining political anti-Semitism. Much of the contemporary understanding of Jews is conditioned by the Holocaust. How does this catastrophe relate to earlier government policies against Jews, to discriminatory laws, to pogroms, to anti-Semitic political movements? In what ways is the Holocaust linked to issues of state-building, economic development, and the emergence of revolutionary political movements?

The study of societal transformations provides the intellectual means of ordering these claims into an analytically coherent whole. Modernization is composed of a series of interrelated processes. No one dimension—whether demographic, economic, ideological, political or any other—drives the forces of change. Variations on one dimension affect change on others. Modernization is not a curtain raising on a new world. The processes of social, economic, and political change relate to what is already in place as well as to each other. At any point in time, the characteristics of a Jewish community reflect the traits of an earlier period. Change within Jewish as well as other societies is in part autoregressive. The emergence of a Jewish proletariat in Eastern Europe, for example, is tied directly to processes of population growth, urbanization, and industrial development, and to large numbers of Jewish artisans already present. The winds of change work on existing structures as they transform societies and the Jewish communities within them.

MODERNIZATION AND ETHNIC COHESION

The most general theoretical question of our study examines the relationship between modernization and ethnic cohesion and continuity. The pattern of interaction among the members of a community defines the level of cohesion. Where Jews, for example, interact exclusively and without conflict with other Jews, the cohesion of their community is at the maximum. A random pattern of interaction, where Jews are no more likely to interact with each other than with non-Jews, denotes assimilation. The level of cohesion reflects the level of communal interaction. The more spheres in which the members of an ethnic group interact frequently and without conflict—residence, work, school, politics, family, social organization—the higher the level of cohesion. Each sphere provides a structural basis for ethnicity. Whereas assimilation and cohesion refer to a particular point in time, ethnic continuity, persistence, and dissolution indicate dynamic processes.

Initial efforts to understand the relationship between modernization and ethnic cohesion argued that systems of social organization based on religion and ethnicity are poorly adjusted to the requirements of modernity. The spread of a national economy and bureaucracy entails universalistic criteria which cut across ethnic statuses. Ethnic attachments are replaced by social class and purely political cleavages (see discussions in Leifer, 1981; Nielsen, 1980; Glazer and Moynihan, 1975; Gordon, 1964). The maintenance of ethnic cultural forms is partially an attempt to preserve a backward lifestyle. If modernization means progress, ethnic continuity implies resistance to change. While there may be some ethnic remnants who are less affected by modernization, time and institutions, such as universal education, minimize their differences. Over time, ethnic cohesion declines and ethnic groups dissolve.

Ethnic persistence, therefore, is viewed as an aberration, a cultural lag, an unexpected feature of modernity that may be explained away. Some have qualified the theory to argue that the presence of ethnic groups is based on selective political interests, cultural consensus, external constraints such as discrimination and racism, or that it reflects nostalgic cultural traits of no depth or consequence (see the essay by Bell, 1975; and the introduction in

Glazer and Moynihan, 1975). The fundamental argument remains: modernization leads to ethnic demise, except under particular or temporary conditions.

A more recent theory sees ethnicity as the consequence of the overlap between class and communal conflict. It analyzes ethnic groups with the concepts of power and control in the framework of "internal colonialism" (Hechter, 1975; Stone, 1979). Since modernization is spatially and socially uneven, initial advantage is crystallized and new advantaged groups are created. The ensuing conflict heightens ethnic cohesion. The dominant group's exploitation and control over resources are, therefore, the major sources of ethnic cohesion and continuity of the minority groups.

This argument postulates that ethnicity is sustained by disadvantage, particularly economic deprivation. In extreme form, ethnicity is viewed as epiphenomenal. It is not ethnicity per se but economic class conflict that is the core of ethnic continuity. The overlap between ethnicity and social class is, therefore, critical. This is referred to as the cultural division of labor, "a system of stratification in which objective cultural distinctions are superimposed upon class lines" (Hechter, 1975, p. 30). In turn, this is tied to territorial constraints and center-periphery relations.

The dominant group uses the state to reinforce the cultural division of labor. Institutionalized racism and discrimination emerge through policies of differential access to schools, the military, jobs, and housing. The overlap between residential and occupational concentrations gives a decisive advantage to the development of ethnic rather than class solidarity. The persistence of ethnicity is directly related to the continuation of the cultural division of labor. Intergroup contact strengthens ethnicity. Ethnic solidarity resembles class consciousness. The greater the inequality, the greater the cohesiveness (Hechter, 1975; Smelser, 1969).

Both theories predict the eventual demise of ethnic groups. Either ethnicity is a temporary lag, a consequence of the absence of complete diffusion and convergence, or it is class based. When modernization is complete or when class inequalities are eliminated, ethnic groups will disappear.

There is yet another and we think more cogent view. Since the transformations associated with modernization build on and modify existing structures, they do not replace already existing overlaps of language, region, religion, residence, friendship, occupation, and politics. They modify the relationships, sometimes weakening them and sometimes strengthening them. Ethnic groups with occupational specialization in peddling and trade are likely to move together into more elaborate forms of commerce. Those with heavy concentrations of peasants are likely to split into farmers and unskilled laborers. These developments have variable consequences for ethnic cohesion and continuity. As socioeconomic development diffuses over a territory, social groups become more homogeneous, and the cultural division erodes. The distribution of economic and other opportunities becomes similar among dominant and minority groups. As social groups compete for the same occupations, places in universities, and houses, new forms of ethnic cohesion appear (Nielson, 1980; Bonacich, 1973; Leifer, 1981; Barth, 1969). Ethnic organizations, political as well as social, erect new bases for the frequent interaction of group members. The processes of modernization do not necessarily erase all but the links of social class.

In this view, ethnicity is neither an ascribed nor a transitional characteristic. It is a continuous, not a discrete, variable. It emerges in the modern world; it is not the cultural legacy of the past or a fixed primordial quality (Yancey et al., 1976). It reflects many bases of social interaction; the more bases of frequent nonconflictual interaction, the stronger is ethnic cohesion (A. Zuckerman, 1982).

This argument suggests further that ethnicity may be reinforced by a cultural division of labor. At the same time, that division does not necessarily imply disadvantage or economic deprivation. Ethnic inequalities are one route to ethnic cohesion; competition is another path. In addition, the conjunction of ethnicity and occupation as well as social and cultural organizations, political movements, and family and kin networks are further sources of ethnic cohesion. These reinforce bonds of friendship and marriage and, consequently, strengthen ethnic solidarity. When ethnicity does not involve economic disadvantage or competition, these institutional bases and social networks may still persist. Hence, even in the absence of a clear ethnic division of labor, ethnic cohesion may be found.

Furthermore, international links between groups strengthen ethnic bonds. They may take a variety of forms, including threats to the continuity of related ethnic groups in a national homeland or in other countries. Modern technology and communications link ethnic groups across national boundaries. There are, therefore, a variety of bases of ethnic cohesion in the modern world.

The persistence and cohesion of ethnic groups are also closely associated with the relative size of the groups. Small groups lack the numbers to provide enough marriage partners and the resources to build the social, economic, and political institutions that establish bases for ethnic cohesion. Especially large ethnic groups have both many sources of cohesion and conflict. As they approach total societies, they are as likely to contain class, religious, and political divisions as multiple sources of cohesion. Ethnic persistence and cohesion are most likely to characterize groups large enough to permit ethnic homogamy and the creation of diverse organizations and small enough to avoid internal social, economic, and political cleavages.

MODERN JEWISH SOCIETY AND POLITICS

Our analysis of Jewish society and politics draws on these perspectives. Clearly, the prediction of assimilation is confounded by Jewish continuity in the contemporary world. Similarly, economic disadvantage cannot be a necessary basis for Jewish survival. Jews have not always been deprived or exploited economically. There are a variety of sources for Jewish continuity, comparatively and historically.

The analysis of modern Jewish society and politics elucidates general themes of the modernization of ethnic groups. At the same time, the study of general processes of ethnic modernization clarifies issues of Jewish continuity and transformation. Jews, unlike other groups, were located in a variety of places within those areas of Europe which experienced the initial thrusts and subsequent intensifications of modernization. They were concentrated as well in areas of later modernization in Eastern Europe under different regimes. Immigration brought them to America, the first new nation and the most modernized society. The ideal of Zionism and the catastrophe of the Holocaust led them to a national homeland, where nation building and rapid modernization have been conspicuous features.

Therefore, our comparative-historical framework analyzes the cohesion of Jewish communities in Europe in several analytically distinct cases: (1) societies in Europe before the advent of modernization, with Jewish communities of various sizes and levels of institutionalization; (2) societies in Western Europe, characterized by early and rapid modernization and relatively small and poorly institutionalized Jewish communities; (3) societies in Eastern Europe, with lower levels and rates of modernization but large and well-institutionalized Jewish communities; (4) the reaction and fate of Jews under the totalitarian systems of Nazi Germany and the Soviet Union. This is done also with two cases in the United States: (5) the immigrant period in which relatively large numbers but poorly organized Jews came in contact with extraordinarily high levels of modernization; and (6) contemporary America, where a large and stable Jewish population confronts continued social change; and Israel (7) in which the Jewish community exists as a total society characterized by rapid modernization and diverse sources of conflict and cohesion. Our perspective facilitates multiple comparisons: the shtetl community and Israel, immigrant American cities and centers of Jewish urbanization in Europe, and other cases less obvious than East and West Europe or Israel and the United States. It provides the basis for the analysis of the transformation of Jewish communities in comparison with the broader societies where they have been located.

The comparative analysis of Jewish communities focuses on a wide range of conditions of modernization and time periods for different areas. At the same time, the mode of analysis helps clarify the patterns of change and continuity that have affected the Jews during their transformation.

2 · The Jewish Condition in Premodern Europe: External Constraints and Internal Structure

Imagine Europe consisting of small rural communities devoted to agriculture and the constant struggle for economic survival, with relatively low levels of technology, poor means of communication and transportation, and characterized by Christian culture. Imagine, too, the presence of a rigid system of stratification of the society, where the peasantry accounted for the overwhelming majority of the population; and the nobles, landlords, clergy, city burghers, and artisans formed the higher strata. Very few moved between these sharply differentiated and well-ordered social divisions. In this ascriptive world, the family and by extension the local community defined the individual's place. Religion and its organizations reinforced social continuity. These broad characteristics apply to much of Europe, from the Peace of Westphalia (1648) to the middle of the nineteenth century (Blum, 1978; Braudel, 1975; Cipolla, 1973; Laslett, 1971; Rude, 1972; Walker, 1971; E. Weber, 1976; Davies, 1982). We shall refer to this period as "premodern" Europe.

Where and how did Jews fit into the societies of premodern Europe? Specifically, how were Jewish communities special or similar to the Christian communities in which they lived? What was the nature of their community? Jews were a minority group in European society. Was this status associated with a particular social and spatial niche? Is the image of the Jewish shtetl, the small town where social tranquility, family centeredness, religious commitment, and economic hardship prevail, an accurate portrait or a stereotype? What roles did pogroms, anti-Semitism, and other manifestations of discrimination play in the relationships between the Jewish community and the general society?

The answers to these questions allow us to understand the place of Jews in premodern Europe. More important, they allow us to develop a theoretical and empirical backdrop for the analysis of the transformation of Jewish communities. Processes of modernization cannot be understood without attention to the premodern social structure. Moreover, we recognize the diversity of Jewish and non-Jewish communities. Vilna and its Jews were clearly not the same as the Jews of Alsace nor identical to the Jews (and non-Jews) of Rome, Cologne, Prague, or Minsk. Similarly, 1650 was not 1700, nor 1750 or 1800. Enveloped in small societies, many of the Jewish communities shared similar characteristics, but no two were exactly alike. Nevertheless, we can isolate general patterns from which modernization developed.

The theoretical models specified in the previous chapter help identify where to look and what factors to examine. The critical factors guiding our analysis are residential patterns, occupational concentration, population size, political conditions, and the broader opportunity structure and their interrelationships. The search for evidence to construct an overall picture of premodern Jewish life ends with fragments—bits and pieces of the puzzle. Given the relatively small number of Jews in most areas of Europe, many scholars have analyzed those societies with but passing reference to Jews (see, for example, Kann, 1974; G. Robinson, 1972). Those who have focused on Jewish history have frequently omitted all but minimal reference to the general non-Jewish world. And Jewish historians have especially emphasized the idiosyncratic and focused on cultural and intellectual dimensions, minimizing the investigation of the broader features of social life (see the community studies of Freimann and Kracauer, 1929; Grunwald, 1936; Kober, 1948; Zarchin, 1939; I. Cohen, 1943; as well as the general works of J. Katz, 1971; Mahler, 1971; Weinryb, 1973; Ettinger, 1976a). We draw on diverse sources and the theoretical literature of social science to develop a more comprehensive picture of premodern Jewish societies.

THE PLACE OF JEWS IN PREMODERN EUROPE
The Jews occupied special positions in the ordered societies of Europe. They not only composed a distinct social order but they often lived in separate quarters of the towns and cities of Europe, in some places behind the walls of ghettoes. They attended their own religious institutions, were guided by their own clergy, lived by a distinctive annual calendar, and rarely interacted socially with the non-Jewish community. Moreover, because they were forbidden entry into certain fields, Jews had distinctive occupational patterns. They were not peasants, when almost everyone else was. Where Jews engaged in agricultural work, they were estate managers and lease-holders, when no one else had those positions. In many areas, they were forbidden to join the guilds, and where they were in handicrafts they formed their own. Most Jews were merchants; the famous "court Jews" were far fewer in number than the moneylenders, small retailers, and peddlers. The concentration of Jews in particular occupations usually developed into a symbiotic (or parasitic) relationship between Jews and non-Jews. The position of the Jews in premodern Europe may be seen as an example of internal colonialism (see Chapter 1).

Perhaps nothing symbolizes more clearly the position of the Jews than their political dependence upon local authorities for residency rights. These rights were the consequences of complex social, economic, political, and cultural relationships. Whatever the specific combination of factors, the dependency relationship that emerged had major repercussions. Indeed, the control over where Jews could live formalized the distinctive position Jews occupied in these societies.

The rights of residency could easily be abrogated:

The Jew had no legal claim to acceptance or toleration, and if he was admitted, it happened on the basis of a contract between the Jewish community and the relevant political authority. . . . The fact of the contractual origin for Jewish residence was never doubted. Jews at no time used the obscure origins of their domicile in a given place as an argument to prove precedence over their non-Jewish neighbors there. Had this been the case, their right of residence would have existed independent of any concession. [J. Katz, 1978, p. 16]

The residency rights determined where—but not how—the Jews would live. Jews were expected to organize and regulate their communal affairs. Several contemporary sources illustrate their organization. In April, 1800, the governor of Vilna filed the following report on the Jewish communal institutions:

Having established their own administrative institutions, called Synagogues, Kahals, or associations, the Jews completely separated themselves from the people and government of the land. As a result, they were exempt from the operation of the statutes which governed the peoples of the several estates, and even if special laws were enacted, these remained unenforced and valueless, because the ecclesiastical and temporal leaders of the Jews invariably resisted them and were clever enough to find means to evade them. [Cited in Levitats, 1943, p. 31]

Four years later, the Tsar appointed a committee to regularize the place of the *kahals* (the political organizations of the Jewish communities also referred to as *kehillot*). They concurred in this description of Jewish self-government:

Jews have always maintained a separate government of their own. Isolating themselves, as it were, from all general institutions, their constant endeavour has been to leave their civil affairs in the hands of Kahal, and their spiritual affairs to the administration of the Synagogue. All matters pertaining to internal order, including economic problems and the collection of taxes . . . are considered and passed upon by their Kahals. [Ibid., p. 31]

This conception treats political dependency as the consequence of a voluntary act by Jews rather than an imposed status.

It is probably inaccurate and certainly incomplete to argue that the isolation of the Jewish community was a consequence of like-minded persons choosing voluntarily to associate for religious or ethnic reasons. The sociopolitical restrictions imposed externally limited Jewish residences and jobs, creating more intense social interaction among Jews, community consensus, and reinforced Jewish religious culture. Religious norms (the need for minimum numbers for prayers, the requirements of ritual baths, specially prepared foods, etc.) did not determine social structure. Rather, once the residency patterns and occupational concentration were established, religiocultural factors legitimized and reinforced these structures. Therefore, it is the elements in combination which defined the nature of the community. A static description overemphasizes the primacy of religious norms as the source of Jewish social structure.

Jews lived as a distinct social stratum in premodern Europe. Indeed, the society as a whole was structured in terms of strata. The particular political organization of the Jewish community paralleled the mode by which the guilds were run, the nobles controlled the countryside, and the burghers dominated the cities (Davies, 1982, 1:297–306). Like other groups, the Jews lived most of their lives in small communities in which transportation between local areas was exceedingly difficult. The tight bonds of the Jewish community found their counterparts in peasant villages, artisan guilds, and burgher communities. Only those relative handfuls in the exceptionally large cities of London, Paris, and Amsterdam lived significantly different lives, but that was true for both Jews and non-Jews. While Jews were placed in a separate category, so were peasants, bakers, carters, merchants, and all those of distinct orders.

Most people lived with the threat of sudden illness and death, perched on the edge of absolute poverty. Data on infant and child mortality indicate that about one-third of the children born did not reach their first birthday, and almost half died before age five. Although Jews seem to have had somewhat lower mortality rates, they could not escape the overwhelming presence of death (Goldscheider, 1971; Schmelz, 1971; Baron, 1937). "Material life," to borrow Braudel's (1975) concept, enveloped society. The uncertainties of economic fluctuations and the hardships of life at subsistence levels dominated personal and social life in premodern Europe.

POPULATION PATTERNS

These points may be made more concrete by examining the structural features of the Jewish communities. Several points stand out with regard to Jewish population size and distribution. The number of Jews was small absolutely and relative to the size of the Christian majority. Jews were more likely to live in urban places than non-Jews. Where Jews lived in rural areas they tended to be engaged in nonagricultural occupations. As a result of these occupational and residential characteristics, rural Jews were more likely to be located in small towns that were geographically near and had trading relations with larger urban centers.

Out of a world total of 2.5 million Jews at the end of the eighteenth century, 1.5 million (60 percent) lived in Europe (Ruppin, 1973, p. 23). The total population of Europe at that time was over 100 million. Estimates are that there were 800,000 Jews in Russian Poland and Western Russia, 300,000 in the Austrian Empire (including Galicia), 70,000 in Bohemia and Moravia, 100,000 in Hungary, 100,000 in Prussia (including Posen), 40,000 in France (including Alsace), and 50,000 in Holland (Ruppin, 1973, p. 23; Mahler, 1971; Weinryb, 1973, pp. 317–319; Lestchinsky, 1922; Davies, 1982, 1:162, 202–5). In most of these countries, the Jews were fewer than 1 percent of the population. Only in parts of Poland, and there only in the cities, did they amount to as much as 8–10 percent (Weinryb, 1973, p. 115). Toward the end of the eighteenth century, Amsterdam contained the largest Jewish community in Europe (23,000), over 10 percent of that commercial center (Bloom, 1937, p. 31). This was clearly exceptional for this period. Although three-fourths of Europe's Jewish population lived east of the Elbe River, none of the communities in Central or Eastern Europe approached the size of the Dutch capital. Prague, Brody, Lvov, and Warsaw, the largest cities in the densely populated Jewish areas, contained no more than 10,000 Jews each (J. Katz, 1971, p. 12; Davies, 1982, 2:204; Mahler, 1971, pp. 218, 280, 347–48). Other centers of Jewish life in Europe, such as Hamburg-Altona and Vilna, numbered approximately 7,000–9,000 Jews (Mahler, 1971, p. 130; I. Cohen, 1943, p. 33). Frankfurt had 4,000 Jews; cities like Brest, Grodno, Minsk, Pinsk, and Dubno numbered fewer than 3,000 Jews (Soliday, 1974, p. 59; Mahler, 1971, p. 280; Weinryb, 1973; also see Gelber, 1928).

Even these numbers distort the size of the community. The number of children below the age of fifteen may be estimated as about half the population. If we further reduce the size by 10–15 percent to remove the ill and enfeebled, it is clear that very few communities contained as many as 2,000 adults. Also, women had limited public roles in the community. Adult males numbered fewer than 1,000 even for the very largest Jewish communities. Few Jewish communities had more than 1,000 Jewish households; most had less than half that amount.

Jews lived not only in the towns and cities but many dwelled in rural hamlets and villages. There is evidence that in 1764–65 one-third of the Jewish population of the Ukraine (63,000) lived in 6,541 rural villages, approximately one family per village (Engelman, 1973, p. 230). At that time, in Poland, 111 towns had fewer than 100 Jewish residents, 153 had 100–300 Jews, 66 between 300 and 500, and 73 between 500 and 1,000 (ibid. p. 117; see Weinryb, 1973, pp. 115, 318–19; and Mahler, 1971, pp. 279–80).

In areas where there were but a small number of Jews, communal institutions were weak and interactions with non-Jews high (Hundert, 1978).

Poland and the Ukraine were not alone in containing many rural Jews. Before the French Revolution, the Jews of Alsace-Lorraine could not live in Colmar (Alsace's capital) or Strasbourg and were spread throughout the villages of the area (Szajkowski, 1970, p. 51). During the ancien régime, no communities contained as many as 500 Jews (Szajkowski, 1970, pp. 51–54). In nearby Cologne, in 1801, only 124 of the more than 2,000 Jews of the province lived in the city itself (Kober, 1948, p. 329; Cahnman, 1974). In Regensburg there lived 110 Jews, in Augsburg only 56 (Straus, 1939, pp. 164, 235). These are not isolated examples. In the late 1790s, fewer than 8 percent of the Jews of Germany lived in the country's seven largest cities (Engelman, 1973, p. 202).

At the end of the eighteenth century, other European cities that would later be home to thousands of Jews contained none or very few Jews. Berlin had just opened its gates to a small number of Jews. Vienna and Paris had relatively few legally "tolerated" Jews, whose activities were important to the crown (see Mahler, 1971, p. 234; and Szajkowski, 1970, p. 46). Kiev and Lodz simply forbade Jews, and Odessa was not yet a city; fewer than 200 persons lived there in 1800 (Baron, 1976a, p. 67).

To describe the Jews in premodern Europe is to speak of people living their lives in small communities. Jews, as others, rarely migrated, mainly because of residency rules but also because there were few economic opportunities to attract them. The lack of economic differentiation among areas combined with political constraints to produce the relative stability of the Jewish communities. Those who migrated tended to do so either for idiosyncratic reasons, or for reasons associated with marriage or larger relocations of families and communities as the result of evictions or local pogroms, or for short periods of time. Most migrations, therefore, did not disrupt the ongoing structure of the socioeconomic, political, and cultural life of the community.

ECONOMIC STRUCTURE

Economic activities did not usually divide the members of the Jewish community. Censuses taken during this period illustrate the general economic characteristics of Jews throughout Europe. Substantial portions of the Jewish communities, especially in the West, engaged in trade (Mahler, 1971, pp. 132–29; Lestchinsky, 1932). Among the 3,000 Jews of Frankfurt in 1694 and 1703, approximately 400 were listed as employed. Of these, 70 percent were merchants (nearly half as moneylenders and peddlers of secondhand goods; an equal number as retailers of clothes and notions; and the remainder in assorted retail activities, among them tavern and innkeeping); 10–15 percent were professionals, presumably in the employ of the community; fewer than 10 percent engaged in handicrafts and day labor; the remainder were poor or had no known occupations (Soliday, 1974, pp. 60, 181). One hundred years later, Cologne's tiny Jewish community had two teachers, five butchers, one day laborer, and ten merchants (Kober, 1948, p. 329). Jewish moneylenders and peddlers predominated in nearby Alsace, where they had been legally prohibited from all other occupations except cattle and horse trading (Szajkowski, 1970, p. 501; Mahler, 1971, p. 20). Only among the court Jews of the capital cities and among the Sephardic communities in southwest France do we find evidence of Jews engaged in the kind of international trade that would play a central role in the development of central governments and capitalism (Szajkowski, 1970, pp. 515–57; Malino, 1978). Most Jewish traders were poor peddlers and wholesalers.

The occupational structure of Jews in Eastern Europe was more diverse than in Western Europe. For example, there was a greater proportion of artisans among the Jews of Eastern Europe than among those of Western Europe (Weinryb, 1946, p. 262; Mahler, 1971, pp. 280–84; and Ruppin, 1973, p. 111). At least one-third to 40 percent employed in Vilna were engaged in one of the various handicrafts. Almost half were tailors, furriers, and jewelers, and the rest filled the various occupations in what was generally a self-sufficient economy (I. Cohen, 1943, pp. 100–101). In the communities in Posen, one-third to one-half the Jews were tailors (Zarchin, 1939). A census taken of the Jews of Hungary in 1735 reveals a similar pattern: nearly half were peddlers and merchants; one-third were artisans; and the remainder were rabbis, teachers, ritual slaughterers, and other communal officials (Marton, 1966, pp. 32–33). Even among the merchant classes Jews clustered in particular occupations (Hundert, 1978). Jews in Eastern Europe also had occupations more closely tied to the land, in a way not true even for the Jews in the villages of Western Europe. Many served as leaseholders and estate managers for absentee Polish landlords. Others operated inns and taverns, and still others controlled toll bridges (Mahler, 1971, p. 280; Weinryb, 1973, pp. 37–39). In Zhitomir, 1787, a census of the Jews revealed the following occupational distribution: 40 percent kept inns and taverns; 25 percent were tradesmen and shopkeepers; 20 percent were artisans, and the remainder, servants, maids, and the poor (Halevy, 1976, p. 15). Nevertheless, all but a few engaged in a very limited set of occupations in their small communities. Thus, the specific nature of occupational concentration varied between Eastern and Western Europe and among Eastern European communities reflecting societal and local economic patterns and opportunity structures.

There were also political constraints on economic opportunities that involved conflict between the local and central authorities. The more powerful the local authorities, the greater the occupational restrictions on Jews. Where extralocal powers exercised greater control, as in Poland before the mid-eighteenth century, Jews had greater access to economic opportunity (Davies, 1982, 1:127–32, 213, 440–41; Bogucka, 1982). Occupational concentration, therefore, was in part a reflection of the balance of power between the various governments. There is no evidence that it reflected Jewish preferences for different fields of endeavor.

The concentration of Jews in particular occupations had important links to residential, cultural, and political statuses. It had, as well, critical importance for the subsequent changes associated with the industrialization and urbanization of Europe.

The occupational specialization did not usually lead to strains, tensions, and bitter competition within the community. In most areas, communal leaders were strong enough to limit the number of competitors for jobs and customers. Just as non-Jewish guilds and local governments regulated the intergenerational transferal of places, apprenticeships, quality of goods, prices, and shares of markets, so Jews, through their organized communities and guilds, controlled their economies. They allocated occupational positions, controlled the entrance of "outsider" Jews into local openings, and regulated family expansion through controls over marriage and outmigration (Levitats, 1943, pp. 218–22 and 230–38; J. Katz, 1971, p. 60; Weinryb, 1973, pp. 157–60; Davies, 1982, 1:348–50, 440–44). These same structural mechanisms characterized European society generally. The absence of open competition implied not harmony and tranquillity but careful control and legal regulation.

POLITICAL STRUCTURE

The kehillot provided the political organization of the Jewish communities. We shall briefly look at Vilna which, because of its relatively large Jewish population required a complex array of organizations, taxes, and services (I. Cohen, 1943, pp. 114–46; see Levitats, 1943, on Minsk; Nussbaum, 1978, on Posen; and Davies, 1982, vol. 1, more generally). Some communities had no formal political organization because of their small size, and many have not been well documented.

In Vilna in 1750, 120 men were qualified to select those who would run the community's affairs: the thirteen members of the executive board of the kahal and the sixteen others who assisted them as judges, almoners, and heads of other agencies. All of the 120 electors had been married for at least six years; they were also wealthy, belonged to families of good repute, and held the honorary titles of *moreinu* (our teacher) and *haver* (associate) (see I. Cohen, 1943). Given a total population of roughly 1,500 Jewish male adults in Vilna at the time, the electors amounted to approximately one-sixth of the men. They were the elite of the community.

The elections of the kahal's officials occurred each year on the first of the intermediate days of Passover. The community's beadle chose at random five of the electors who in turn selected the members of the governing council. In Vilna, as in other communities, custom and law governed the qualifications of those chosen. Formal procedures barred nepotism and the reappointment of those already serving on the kahal. In Vilna, as in most if not all other communities, these rules were frequently ignored in practice.

The kahal governed the public affairs of the Jewish community. It raised funds and disbursed them to the charitable organizations, educational institutions from the primary schools to the academies, to the hospitals, and to the different agencies that attended to public buildings. The kahal negotiated with government officials and raised taxes to meet their demands. The court (*Beth Din*) carried out judicial activities in ways that paralleled the Russian boards of arbitration and even survived the demise of the kahal. The Chief Rabbi sat at the head of the court. He and the twelve other members adjudicated matters as varied as business transfers, disputes over seating arrangements in the synagogue, the accuracy of shopkeepers' weights and measures, and ritual law. The kahal itself handled breaches of the peace. Political, economic, and religious functions were clearly intertwined.

The Chief Rabbi served as the authority figure for the community. He chaired the court, taught in the academy, and provided religious leadership. He also had political power. The members of the kahal, including the rabbis and judges, elected the Chief Rabbi to a three-year term, and the local Polish authorities had to approve their decision.

Given the centrality of the Chief Rabbi, his religious authority and political power, conflict frequently occurred over his selection. The use of a secret ballot and strict contractual relations taken by the Rabbi and community limited but did not remove competition for the post. These conflicts frequently provided bases for political cleavages within the community, as did the tendency for the Rabbi and kahal to seek to extend authority at the expense of the other. Hence, these issues more than occupational competition were sources of internal conflict.

The dependence of the Jewish community on external (in this case Polish) authorities resulted in another series of conflicts. The power of the local officials and their arbitrary rulings were frequently overcome through bribery. Decisions regarding the formal status of the Jewish community or demands for exaggerated payments to the treasury were the most threatening situations. Wealthy individuals or officially appointed intermediaries (*shtadlanim*) interceded and negotiated for the kehillah. The importance of the shtadlan was reflected in the fact that the kehillah typically apportioned to him a salary second only to that of the Chief Rabbi (I. Cohen, 1943; Davies, 1982, vol. 1).

How did the community support all its activities? How did it pay for the maintenance of synagogues and schools; the salaries of officials; the health, burial, and other functions it ran? The Jews of Vilna paid taxes to the kahal from the dues of their artisan and merchant guilds, from the fees associated with registering marriages, as well as from their business profits and general income. A special board of assessors supervised the annual income tax. Bakers, butchers, and wine makers, traveling merchants, and those who sold religious articles paid a special tax as did those who were members of the kahal and its various boards. As do all governments, it taxed its citizens as much as they could bear. When economic conditions deteriorated and they had no more to give, the kahal took loans from other official bodies, most frequently those associated with the Church. This represented an additional form of dependency.

Smaller communities could not provide as wide an array of welfare and educational services. Those who lived in villages had to manage with visiting tutors or send their children to schools away from home. Many Jews probably provided no education for their children. Solomon Maimon describes this situation in the last third of the eighteenth century, as seen by an urbanite:

My first position as family tutor was an hour's distance from my home. The family was that of a miserable farmer in a still more miserable village. . . . The poverty, ignorance, and crudeness which prevailed in this house were indescribable. The farmer's . . . language was a sort of muttering, intelligible only to the boors with whom he daily associated. Not only was he ignorant of Hebrew, but he could not speak a word of Yiddish; his only language was Russian, the common patois of the peasantry. His wife and children were of the same stamp. . . . My other positions as tutor were more or less similar. [1967, pp. 48–49]

Clearly, not all rural Jews fit this description. The father-in-law of Gluckel of Hameln appears to have maintained his Jewish commitments, despite the rural residence. She describes:

Everyone knows the difference between Hameln and Hamburg. I, a young child brought up in luxury, was taken from parents, friends, and everyone I knew, from a town like Hamburg to a village where only two Jewish families lived. And Hameln is a dull, shabby place. But this did not make me unhappy because of my joy in my father-in-law's piety. Every morning he rose at three and wrapped in talith (prayer shawl), he sat in the room next to my chamber studying and chanting Talmud in the usual sing-song. Then I forgot Hamburg. [1963, p. 33]

Gluckel's family was perhaps typical of a small number of wealthy business people in Germany in the early 1700s. They were unlike the rural Jews of Poland a century later or even most of the Jews of Germany. The poor Jews, artisans, peddlers, even farmers, did not have the wide-ranging contacts of Gluckel's family. The village Jews, whether in France, Germany, Poland, or

Hungary lacked the educational, social, political, and economic opportunities of those who lived in Prague, Vilna, Brody, and Warsaw.

Most Jews lived neither in large cities nor rural hamlets, but in villages, towns, and small cities, where the number of Jewish households did not exceed a few hundred. In these locales, the communal structure was not as elaborate as Vilna, although more developed than in the hamlets.

THE INTERRELATIONSHIP OF INSTITUTIONS

One theme in understanding the place of Jews in premodern European society is the interrelationship among the elements of social life. Family, religion, politics, social status, residence, and economic position were all linked to each other. The place of Talmudic civil law as the basis of court decisions as well as in the activities of the rabbis as judges and the synagogue wardens as court bailiffs illustrate these ties. The links extend to the use of the court and its officials to carry out the ritual decisions of the rabbis. Thus, groups could form new synagogues only with the permission of the rabbis and kehillah. Those that formed did so around the various guilds and associations of the community. They did not form for reasons of ideological difference.

The kahal's formal rules frequently set forth social relations and economic sanctions for the violations of norms. The following applied to those who challenged the court's authority in Minsk, a city with 500–700 Jewish households in the late eighteenth century:

a) The contumacious one shall forfeit his rights to participate in Kahal activities or in those of the associations.

b) He shall be excluded from Kahal membership and removed from whatever office in an association he may be holding that year.

c) He shall be excluded from membership in the plenary assembly or in any association.

d) He shall not be called to stand to the reading of the Scriptures, nor shall he be honored with the privilege of performing any ceremony or ritual whatsoever, whether it be in the synagogue, house of prayer, private chapel, or anywhere else. He certainly shall not be permitted to act as the people's messenger (cantor) during prayer services. Under no circumstances shall a service be halted for his sake, even if only for a quarter of an hour. No synagogue honor shall be sold to him.

e) He shall not be invited to ceremonial feasts, public celebrations, and none shall participate in a feast given by the defiant on any occasion whatsoever . . .

f) No one shall rent from him an apartment or a store, nor lease any to him. However, contracts entered into with him on such matter prior to his being placed under the ban shall remain in force. His wife shall not be permitted to take ritual baths . . .

g) If he be an artisan, it shall be strictly forbidden, on penalty of the ban, to order work . . .

h) All preliminary marriage agreements, as well as betrothal contracts, entered into with him may be broken with impunity as to fine or reimbursement of expenses.

i) It shall be permissible to accuse him publicly of having partaken of non-kosher meat, of having broken a fast, and the like, and to produce witnesses in the matter and subject him to punishment. [Cited in Levitats, 1943, pp. 209–10]

The kehillah sought to place the lawbreaker outside the community. He could have no part of its economic activities and its social life. By forbidding his wife to immerse herself in the ritual bath (section f), the rules deny him the sexual rights of a husband. The sanctions highlight how tightly bound together were all elements of social life. They illustrate the latent power of the community over areas beyond religion.

The kahal also formed auxiliaries who policed the religious behavior of the townspeople. These vigilante committees supervised the continuing conformity of the members of the Jewish community. The establishment of these committees suggests that violations of the rules were commonplace. Nevertheless, individual space for deviance was circumscribed; space was communal and collective, and formal and informal pressures reinforced conformity to the rules and regulations. Only the relative few who had extensive political and economic links to the non-Jewish authorities could withstand these sanctions.

The associations joined religious, ritual, and leisure activities, thus further tightening social bonds. Jewish guilds, like their Christian counterparts, had annual social events. Family and life-cycle events—births, marriages, deaths—religious rituals associated with rites of passage, and cyclical observances on the Sabbath and holidays all tied into community life (J. Katz, 1971, pp. 157–67; I. Cohen, 1943, pp. 124–30).

The Talmudic scholar stood at the head of the religious, social, and political hierarchies of the community:

The study of the Talmud is the chief object of higher education among our people. Riches, bodily advantages, and talents of every kind have indeed a certain worth in their eyes and are esteemed in proportion; but among them no merit is superior to that of a good Talmudist. He has the first claim upon all offices and positions of honor in the community. If he enters an assembly, whatever his age or rank, every one rises before him out of respect, and the most honorable place is assigned to him. He is director of ordinary men's conscience, their lawgiver, and their judge. . . . [Maimon, 1967, p. 16]

As rabbis and judges, the scholars were among the political leaders of the community. This reflected contradictory but parallel developments: access to highly valued posts for those without wealth, and the purchase of that status by the wealthy through marriage. Children who excelled in their studies were encouraged to continue their Talmudic education. Their mobility depended primarily on their intellectual capacities, especially where local communities were wealthy enough to provide students with meals and board. When this did not happen and when the student came from a poor home, marriage into a wealthy family provided the means of continuing one's studies. The wife's father supported the new family and allowed the young scholar enough time to finish his studies. Since the behavioral rule linked the best students and the wealthiest daughters, the marriages tied the religious leaders and the wealthy. Maimon's story (1967) of how two families fought over him is but one example in a vast literature in which the ideal marriage linked young scholars and rich daughters (pp. 20–30). Thus, open access to positions of high status existed alongside the control of those places through the bonds of marriage.

The various dimensions of stratification were generally linked to family networks. Control over when and whom people married was related to the system of power and status within the guilds and kehillot as well as the community at large. They were tied also to the occupational opportunities and local economic conditions (see J. Katz, 1971, pp. 139–44). Marriage patterns reinforced the continuity of these social bonds.

The marriages that linked the religious elite with the wealthy and powerful suggest that corruption of rabbinical positions occurred when the latter sought to buy offices for their sons-in-law and when rabbis found it difficult to rule against the interests and desires of fathers-in-law. Still, this pattern underlines the enormous prestige of the Talmudic scholar in the community. Not only did he symbolize the religious ideal, but the rich spent large sums to have a scholar in the family. In turn, this suggests that scholars were rare. For most people, neither Talmudic scholarship nor wealth was a realistic option. The struggle for physical survival dominated their daily lives.

The interrelationship among institutions was a general feature of premodern societies. The small size and tight political, economic, and social bonds typified the mode by which most people—Jews and Gentiles—lived in places across the continent. In addition, the Jews had unique demographic, economic, and residential characteristics. A greater proportion of the Jewish community, however, lived in towns and cities and were employed in commercial occupations. As a consequence, more Jews than Gentiles had access to tutors and schools and learned to read and write in the local languages as well as in Hebrew and Yiddish. Educational attainment provided a powerful method of social and economic advancement within the Jewish community. In addition, extralocal ties associated with trade and education affected relatively larger portions of the Jewish community. Furthermore, issues of Talmudic law and scholarship sent rabbis calling on their colleagues in other communities. The most important of these links among communities was the *Va' ad Arba Arazot* (Council of the Four Lands) that covered all the kehillot in Poland and Lithuania for two centuries, ending only in 1764 (J. Katz, 1971, pp. 122–31; Davies, 1982, 1:440–43). This organization came closest to providing some form of national administration for the Jews, but its actual power was limited by the independence of the kehillot. Hence, the rate of social and geographic mobility was probably higher among Jews if only because most non-Jews were peasants tied to the land. Nevertheless, most people most of the time, Jews as well as non-Jews, lived within the sharply constrained dimensions of their community.

RELIGIOUS NORMS AND PRACTICES
Most Jews lived in a community in which the observance of ritual law was the socially expected and politically sanctioned norm. Individuals did not have the right to decide for themselves whether they were in the right mood for prayer. One attended the synagogue at prescribed times. When the *Hasidim* raised just such issues agout the requirements of devotion, community leaders branded them heretics (J. Katz, 1971, pp. 231–44; Mahler, 1971, pp. 430–36). Personal and public religious obligations overlapped.

This does not imply that individuals always conformed to the community's norms. It is difficult to imagine a society in which deviations from the ideals do not occur and in which public expectations and requirements determine all behavior. Corruption of rabbinic offices could be found. Ritual obligations were not always fulfilled. Whether for reasons of public or personal exigency, not all requirements could be met. Many Jews lived in villages where there were too few Jews for public prayer. Then, too, one must not assume that the behavior of all persons meshed perfectly with religious ideals. Vigilante committees do not exist where there are no transgressors.

The discrepancy between religious demands and actual behavior may be shown in another way that also sheds light on the marriage patterns within the community. Some scholars have taken the descriptions of marriages between students and daughters of the wealthy, which typically occurred at young ages, as describing the pattern for all marriages. Those described by Solomon Maimon (1967) and Gluckel of Hameln (1963) join children aged ten, eleven, twelve, and thirteen. It can easily be shown, however, that no matter how much people valued this ideal, it was not widespread. To return to Vilna as our example—at the end of the eighteenth century, of the approximately 6,000 Jews in the community, 1,500 were married. Of these, fifty-nine were boys and eighty were girls sixteen years of age or younger. A calculation based on the structure of the population shows that no more than 15 percent of those between ages ten and sixteen could have been married (I. Cohen, 1943, p. 101). In Berlin at that time, most men married in their late twenties and most women in their early twenties (Shofer, 1981, p. 83). Many could not afford to follow the ideal of a very young marriage. The

Talmudic norm of male age at marriage at eighteen years challenged financial necessity and the widespread expectation that marriage required establishing an independent household. Early marriages were exceptions that underlined the norm. The rarity of such events illustrates that knowledge of the society's ideals and values are not the best guides to behavior. The extent and timing of marriage undoubtedly varied more in relationship to local economic and social conditions than to religious norms.

There were other factors which impeded religious deviation in the premodern Jewish community. Few visible alternative ways of behavior existed. Christian patterns were completely unacceptable as they entailed conversion, an absolute break with one's God, community, and family. Charismatic movements were the only source that brought about behavioral changes. While Sabbateanism, Frankism, and Hasidism provided alternative forms, only the last was successful in attracting and holding large numbers.

The small size and the tight social bonds of the communities also account for religious conformity. The political and economic power of the non-Jews reinforced, but did not cause, the cohesiveness of the Jewish community. Shared religious norms, the authority and power of the community's leaders, gossip, social pressure, the fear of ostracism, and even excommunication bound the Jews together. The dominance of the family and the controls over economic and cultural resources reinforced conformity and generational continuity. As elsewhere in premodern communities, deviance carried high social costs. Persistent deviations brought not only personal scorn but threatened one's place in the community and, therefore, the future of one's children. Who would employ someone who violated the Sabbath? Who would give one's child in marriage to the child of such a person? Solomon Maimon describes the difficulty of independent religious thought and behavior in his native community. He and a friend developed ideas that differed from those around them but did not act on them. Rather, they followed the community's expectations:

We were the only persons in the place who ventured to think independently about everything and not be mere imitators. Differing as we did from the rest of the community in our opinions and conduct, it was natural that we should separate ourselves from them by degrees. But we still had to live by the community, and so our circumstances deteriorated daily. We saw where our inclinations were leading us, to be sure, but were nevertheless unwilling to sacrifice them to material advantage. [1967, pp. 45–46]

In order to support themselves and their families, they became tutors, thereby serving as instruments of continuity. The community constrained Maimon. Only in a metropolis like Berlin did he find release from the social bonds and the opportunity to change his religious practice.

The absence of real alternatives and the community's strong bonds usually made the use of the political power of the rabbis—the police and judicial
authority of their offices—superfluous. The beadles, pillories, and vigilante
committees stood as final deterrents to religious as well as other forms of
deviance. Religious behavior in this society was for most people not necessarily tied to deep devotion but to living in tune with one's community. The
struggle for physical survival dominated most people's lives. Poor economic
conditions and the strains of daily life left few to ponder the broader issues of
God and man.

SOURCES OF CHANGE
The highly structured characteristics of this society do not imply that they
were rigid communities as well. There were changes, but they did not alter
the structure of the communities. For example, throughout this period some
Jews moved from town to town, from region to region, as peddlers, scholars,
students, and other circular or temporary migrants. Many others moved in
the wake of Cossack assaults. The Chmielnitzki raids in the middle of the
seventeenth century destroyed Jewish communities in the Ukraine and
southern Poland and sent survivors packing, as did the Haidamek raids a
century later. Both resulted in Jewish migrations within Eastern Europe and
to the rapidly expanding areas in Western Europe, in Germany and the
Netherlands (Shulvass, 1971; Mahler, 1971; Weinryb, 1973; J. Katz, 1971;
Davies, 1982, vol. 1). The newcomers effected new cleavages within the
Jewish community, often establishing their own synagogues, while not
challenging the community's basic structure.

When economic conditions deteriorated, the strength and autonomy of
the Jewish community declined, and the level of internal conflict rose. In
Eastern Europe, particularly Poland, a weakening economy in the last half
of the eighteenth century reduced the power of the Jewish communities
(Mahler, 1971; J. Katz, 1971; Davies, 1982, vol. 1; Levitats, 1943; Hundert,
1978; Nussbaum, 1978; Stone, 1979). When the kahals' treasuries could no
longer cover expenses, they turned for loans to monasteries, churches, and
priestly orders. This multiplied the kehillot's debts and dependencies. Synagogues were closed and buildings were mortgaged in a continuous and
fruitless effort to regain financial solvency. Declining economies forced the
nobles to demand more money from Jews; individually and collectively, the
Jews slipped into even deeper poverty. These developments added to the
political power of the wealthy, since the community increasingly turned to
them for financial help. Not surprisingly, a growth in corruption and nepotism followed, even the purchase of rabbinic positions for the sons and
sons-in-law of the wealthy. This fanned resentment of the oligarchy, fostered internal conflict, and began a decline in the authority of the community's leaders, both rabbinic and secular (I. Cohen, 1943, pp. 164–81).

The rise of the Hasidic movement coincided with these declines in the Polish central government and economy, the political and economic bases of the established order in the Jewish community (J. Katz, 1971; Mahler, 1971; Weinryb, 1973). It drew mass and elite support. By the end of the eighteenth century, the conflict between the Hasidim and their established opponents, the *Mitnagdim*, split many communities. Where Hasidim dominated, however, there were few changes in the social and economic positions of the Jews and in the interplay between communal authority and religious behavior. New leaders took power. Various forms of competition emerged. Yet, this internal conflict did not weaken the core structure of communal life.

The religious leaders fought the challenges of the *Haskalah*—Jewish Enlightenment (J. Katz, 1971; Mahler, 1971). The spokesmen of this new movement argued for fundamental educational changes, decreases in the centrality of Talmud, and increases in the place of Hebrew language per se. As such, these were hardly revolutionary demands. Their challenge lay in two implicit claims. The first was that one did not have to master the Talmud to be a Jewish scholar. This was interpreted as a direct threat to the centrality of the rabbis and, hence, a challenge to the social and political structure of the communities. The second implication was at least as significant. If the rabbis were no longer the sole interpreters of Jewish culture, it opened the possibility of Jewish learning outside their control. Hence, it threatened to replace religious standards. Both threatened the authority of the rabbis and grew in importance as their political bases weakened.

These political and ideological conflicts are illustrated by a story told by Abba of Hlusk (near Minsk), one of those Polish Jews, like Solomon Maimon, who in the late eighteenth century went to Berlin to study with Moses Mendelssohn, a leader of the Jewish Enlightenment. Having heard in Berlin of the Vilna Gaon's scholarship, Abba returned to the East to meet the Gaon. Their conversation ended quickly. Abba criticized Rashi and other traditional interpreters of the Bible, whereupon the Gaon immediately dismissed his visitor. Abba recounts what then happened:

I returned to my lodging. But scarcely had I crossed the threshold when two evil messengers who were there waiting for me summoned me to appear before the heads of the community and their law-court. I went and found myself facing seven greybeards adorned with praying-shawls and phylacteries. Then one rose and from his seat said: "Art thou the one who scoffed and blasphemed against the sages of the Midrash and our master (Rashi) of blessed memory?" I replied: "I neither scoffed nor slandered." Then he said to me: "And what did thou say at the Gaon's" to which I replied: "I stated that the sages in question deviated in their explanations from the immediate sense." The old man thereupon made a sign with his hand, and the two henchmen of the evil one seized and led me out of the courtyard. Then I heard from the lips of the same old man the decision of the court, that on account of defaming the sages of olden times I was condemned to forty strokes, which the two myrmidons administered to me on the spot. But their rage was by no means assuaged by this, for I was then led to the threshold of the synagogue and my neck was enclosed within the iron rings attached to the wall, so as thus to expose me to the people, with a piece of paper on my head baring the words: "This man has been punished for scoffing at the words of our holy teachers." Everybody who came for that afternoon service stopped and called to me: "Traitor to Israel!" But even more: they spat nearly into my face, so that the spittle really flowed in streams. Thou knowest well that Vilna is not Berlin, and that the people there go to prayers in crowds. After the evening service was over, I was conducted outside the city and obliged to depart. [Cited in I. Cohen, 1943, pp. 224–25]

Vilna was not Berlin, even in 1780. How and why that was so and how Vilna too changed entails an analysis of the transformation of the structure of the Jewish communities. The features of the seventeenth- and eighteenth-century Jewish communities represented powerful sources of cohesion. Jews, as others, lived in highly stratified, organized, and distinct small societies. Sustained changes in the structure of those communities and in the place of Jews in the broader societies would have to be enormously powerful to break and transform these sources of cohesion and stability.

Part II: **Initial Modernization in Europe**

The transformation of the Jewish communities was closely linked to structures present before the forces of change arrived. Characteristics of the general society and structural traits of the Jewish community interacted with the processes of modernization to affect the precise pattern of transformation. Hence, the explanation of the process requires fine-grained descriptions as well as general propositions. Our analysis of the modernization of European Jewry proceeds in two parts. The following section studies the initial patterns of social, economic, political, and religious changes. Analytically, it examines the initial stages of modernization. Chronologically, it focuses on the years before 1880. This provides the necessary material for the comparisons of the transformation of Jewish communities over time in Europe.

3 · Political Modernization: The Early Transformation of the Jewish Community

The modernization of Europe overwhelmed the traditional Jewish society and polity. Napoleon's armies, Enlightened Despots, the Declaration of the Rights of Man, the Industrial Revolution, urbanization, and population growth led the forces that altered the foundations of the Jewish community. As the forms of political authority and organization changed, so did the place and internal order of the Jews. As economic opportunities developed and expanded, Jews took advantage of them. As mass education emerged, Jews went to the *gymnasia* and to the universities. As the walls of the Jewish quarters came down, Jews moved out. Modernization transformed the old order and the place of Jews within it.

The forces of change encompassed everyone—peasants, landlords, artisans, burghers, merchants, and of course Jews. Within countries, too, the pace varied. Nevertheless, urban populations and the middle classes were effected earlier than others. As important, the onset and pace of change varied across the continent, occurring first in the West.

MODERNIZATION AS MATRIX AND WINDSTORM
No one force led the way. Rather, the power that altered the face of Europe drew on diverse sources:

Reforming princes, improving landlords, new crops and new techniques, new economic opportunities, noblemen interested in profitable enterprise, discontent with the economic inefficiences of the servile order, new and disturbing ideas about the equality of man and injustice of privilege, and restless sometimes rebellious peasants, all formed the matrix out of which emerged the emancipation of the peasantry of the servile lands. [Blum, 1978, p. 357]

Many of these forces overwhelmed Jewish society, but the Jews unlike peasants and workers, did not settle into one class. Indeed, no single analytic category encompasses the varied social positions Jews occupied. The "proper" place of the Jews in the new society, the Jewish Question, would be asked and answered in a variety of ways.

One metaphor describing this change was used by Rav Nahman of Bratslav in his story *The Master of Prayer*. The great-grandson of the founder of
Hasidism and an extraordinary leader in his own right, Rav Nahman described in 1810 the cataclysm that threatened his world:

There was once a time says the master of prayer when each of us had
gone to his own special place. The warrior, the orator, and all the rest
of the king's men—each had gone to renew his particular strength.
At that time a great windstorm swept over the world. The entire earth
was confounded; dry land was transformed into sea and sea into land,
deserts came to be where there had been towns, and new towns sprang
up in areas where there had been only desert. The whole world was
turned upside down by that wind.
When the wind came into the king's palace, it did no damage at all.
As it whipped through the palace, however, it grabbed up the beautiful
child and carried him away, all in an instant. The king's daughter ran off
in pursuit of her child. Soon she was followed by her mother, the
queen, and then by the king himself. Thus all of them were scattered,
and nobody knows their place.
None of us was there when this happened, as we each had gone off to
renew our strength. When we did return to the palace, we found no one
there. . . . Since then we have all been scattered, and none of us can
now get back to that place where he needs to go to renew his strength.
Since the wind came and turned the entire world around, changing land
into sea and sea into land, the old paths are no longer of any use. We
are now in need of new paths, because all the places have been altered.
Meanwhile, we cannot renew our former strength. We do however retain an imprint of those former times and that in itself is very great.
[Cited in Green, 1981, pp. 248–49]

Rav Nahman's biographer interprets the tale: "It is particularly the courtiers
who make us realize that what we have here in part is a tale of Europe in the
Napoleonic era. The old order (be it that of ancien régime France or
prepartition Poland) has been swept away by the great winds of change. The
Napoleonic wind was bringing with it changes in the religious order as well:
Nahman saw the advent of chaos in the incipient Haskalah, which was now
beginning to cross the borders of the Hassidic 'empire'" (Green, 1981,
p. 249). Nahman's tale depicts more than the inability of the Jews to find
God. It portrays the forces that overturned the traditional world in which
the paths to God had been clear.
   The Jewish communities did not fall like a row of dominoes. Some agreed
with Nahman that new paths had to be found, though most of them did not
search for the way back to God. Others found new Gods. Many erected
walls to keep out the windstorm, seeking to continue their way of life in
defiance of the changes around them. Even more important, the structural

features of Jewish and general societies redirected the forces of change. Eventually the winds reached everyone.

The Jews and the peasants were not the only ones to change. Since they were most constrained by the traditional structures, the winds of transformation were seen as hitting them hardest. Artisans became proletarians; the burghers developed into the bourgeoisie, and the nobles eventually became the antique ornaments of a no longer existing civilization and the socioeconomic elite of the new society.

A matrix of forces—like a windstorm—provides no obvious point of entry. It singles out no primary dimension. In order to analyze the forces of change, however, we begin with the political dimension, which contained some of the first and most conspicuous transformations. The absolute dependence of the traditional Jewish community on the non-Jewish authorities ensured that when the latter changed so would the place of the Jews.

POLITICAL MODERNIZATION

Political modernization has three defining characteristics: (1) increasing rationalization, the growth of the bureaucracy, and rules and regulations; (2) differentiation and specialization of political activities, of the branches of government, and of the modes of policymaking; and (3) greater inclusiveness of sectors of the population in the political process (Black, 1966; Huntington, 1968; M. Levy, 1966). These are long-term and complex processes that interact with social and economic modernization. The development of an ideology supporting the new order was a visible early indication of political modernization. Beliefs in the rights of individuals and democracy defined the ideology. In this chapter, therefore, we examine issues of political modernization and ideologies that legitimized political change.

State builders sought to apply their rule uniformly for all individuals in their societies. Special taxes, statuses, and privileges had to be eliminated. Hence, policies toward Jews had to be revised and their place as a special group had to be addressed. The Jewish Question illustrates the general policy problem. In 1783, the Royal Society of Metz announced a literary competition: "How to make the Jews more useful and more happy in France?" The same question bothered Prussian civil servants and Emperor Frederick II. It troubled government officials in Austria, and underscored Emperor Joseph II's decision to promulgate the Edict of Tolerance some two years earlier. Even Russian officials asked the Jewish Question (Low, 1979, pp. 31–35, 116 ff.; A. Hertzberg, 1968, p. 132; Walker, 1971; Lee, 1980; Kann, 1974; Wandycz, 1974; Greenberg, 1944, 1:9–15; Baron, 1976a, pp. 13–21).

Government officials and others engaged in political modernization posited that the Jews suffered and caused others harm because of their limited rights and peculiar economic status in society (Low, 1979; A. Hertzberg, 1968; J. Katz, 1978). Christian Wilhelm Dohm typified this view. "If this reasoning is correct, then we have found in the oppression and in the restricted occupation of the Jews the true source of their corruption. Then we have discovered also at the same time the means of healing of this corruption and of making the Jews better men and useful citizens. With the elimination of the unjust and unpolitical treatment of the Jews will also disappear the consequences of it, their corruption. . . . " (cited in Mendes-Flohr and Reinharz, 1980, p. 30). Removing the political and economic fetters on the existence of the Jews would improve their lot and that of society in general.

The Jewish Question and the answers proposed reflect the world of Enlightened Despots, seeking to build states and reform and rationalize their nations. They were not concerned only with Jews. Officials posed the same questions about peasants, artisan guilds, and burgher control over cities (Blum, 1978; Walker, 1971; Lee, 1980; Kann, 1974). These new bureaucrats governed enormously diverse societies, which had inherited a confusing array of rules and laws. They sought to rationalize these problems so as to strengthen their own power. The place of the Jews was one of many policy issues which first emerged in Western and Central Europe.

Political change affecting the Jews in Eastern Europe first occurred with the partition of Poland. The issue was not yet political modernization. In 1772, Prussia, Austria, and Russia took parts of Poland. In 1793, Poland was partitioned again, and in 1794, Poland no longer existed as a political entity (Wandycz, 1974; Weinryb, 1970; Davies, 1982, vol. 2). The partitions divided the Jews of Poland, bringing different sectors under diverse political regimes. Nearly 100,000 Jews of Posen came under Prussian rule. The 250,000 Galician Jews entered the Hapsburg Empire. The Tsars, who had barred this rebellious people (in the words of Catherine the Great) from Russian soil, now ruled over 1 million Jews (Wandycz, 1974, pp. 11–23; Mahler, 1971; Ruppin, 1943; Weinryb, 1970; Davies, 1982, vol. 2). In Prussia, state builders led by Frederick II sought to "Germanize" the Jews and Poles (Hagen, 1980; Wandycz, 1974). The leaders of the multi-ethnic empires of the Hapsburgs and Romanovs were less concerned about the ethnic elements. They sought to control the Jews' religious particularities and economic roles as well as Polish political aspirations (Wandycz, 1974; Davies, 1982, vol. 2; Kann, 1974). The empires sought to regularize the place of the Jews without restructuring the total society. The political status of Jews varied across Europe in direct relation to more general policies.

Political modernization specifically affecting the Jews occurred under the Hapsburgs (Low, 1979, p. 17–25; Weinryb, 1970, p. 354; J. Katz, 1978). In 1781 Joseph II announced the Edict of Tolerance, and in 1789 he applied it to Galicia as well. This initial effort at solving the Jewish Question sought to remove them from their spheres of economic activity and integrate them into the society at large. Thus, Jews were no longer allowed to operate inns or to be tax collectors. They were forbidden to send money to the Jewish communities of Palestine. The edict destroyed as well the political power of the kehillot and limited them to religious activities. At the same time, the rules specified that Jews could attend public schools and would be permitted to attend gymnasia and universities. In addition, they had to conduct their business affairs in German, not in Yiddish, and they had to adopt family names as well. The edict did not provide complete political emancipation. For example, it did not remove travel bans and special taxes. Most of these would not be lifted until after the Revolution of 1848, six decades later. Indeed, as radical as these policies were for the Jews, they implied less drastic changes than did government action on the peasants, Protestants, and control over local administration (Kann, 1974, p. 190). For a variety of reasons, the policies regarding the Jews were not fully implemented until the end of the nineteenth century.

THE FRENCH REVOLUTION AND THE POLITICAL STATUS OF THE JEWS
France provides the first example of a total alteration in the political status of the Jews. First for the Sephardim of Bordeaux and Bayonne and the Provence in 1790 and then for the Ashkenazim of Alsace a year later, the revolutionary government declared the Jews equal citizens and symbolized this step by allowing them to take the civic oath (A. Hertzberg, 1968; Szajkowski, 1959, 1970; Malino, 1978; Kobler, 1976; Schwarzfuchs, 1979; Mahler, 1971). The French Revolution is particularly crucial since its leaders sought to build a united rational society. In addition, the Revolution's ideology attacked frontally the society of estates, orders, and corporations and replaced it with individual citizens of equal rights. The emphasis on the individual and the full implementation of these goals contrasted with the claims and activities of the Enlightened Despots. We shall use France to illustrate our argument because the issues there are most dramatic and the implications for the French Jewish community were so conspicuous. As important, the French case highlights the general themes of political modernization. It is a limited case, nevertheless, since French Jewry was small in size and most Jews lived in nations where political modernization did not occur until decades later.

The clear ideological break represented by the French Revolution and its importance for locating Jews in the new order may be seen in the Declaration of the Rights of Man (De Ruggiero, 1959, pp. 66–67). The free interaction of equal citizens forms the nation. The King is out; sovereignty belongs to the people, not to any person or office. The estates, corporations, guilds, the social categories of the old order are dismissed as well. Free persons with equal political rights compose France, These rights belong to the individuals, not their orders and not the state. Indeed, the state represents these individuals and acts to protect their rights.

If all citizens had the right to religious and political liberty, who were the citizens? In dismissing the distinctions of estates and guilds, the French Revolution included all Frenchmen. Were the Jews French? Were they foreigners living in France with the permission of the French government, as would follow from the traditional conception of their place in society? Would the debts of the Jewish communities be absorbed by the state as it took over the obligations of all the guilds and corporations? The revolution's ideological foundation provided answers: the Jews were citizens. In return for disbanding their communities, they would have all political rights. In the words of Clermont-Tonerre, "One must refuse everything to the Jews as a nation, but one must give them everything as individuals; they must become citizens" (cited in A. Hertzberg, 1968, p. 360). Communal debts, however, proved more problematic. Money matters did not always follow revolutionary logic (Szajkowski, 1970, pp. 593–735).

The leaders of the Jewish community relinquished their communal political structure for the rights of citizenship. Berr Isaac Berr, the spokesman for Alsatian Jews, on the occasion of their assuming the rights of citizens in 1791, proclaimed:

At length the day is arrived when the veil, by which parted from our fellow-citizens, we were kept in a state of humiliation is rent; at length we recover those rights which have been taken from us more than eighteen centuries ago. How much are we at this moment indebted to the clemency of the God of our forefathers! [Cited in Tama, 1807, p. 11]

After thanking God once again, praising France as the place of their liberation, Berr Isaac Berr calls on the Jews to "work a change in our manners" so as to become citizens. This entailed a change in the formal organizations of the Jewish community.

But I cannot too often repeat to you how absolutely necessary it is for us to divest ourselves entirely of that narrow spirit, of *Corporation* and *Congregation*, in all civil and political matters, not immediately connected with our spiritual laws; in these things we must appear simply as individuals, as Frenchmen, guided only by a true patriotism and by the general good of the nation. . . . We had the privilege of forming a distinct body of people and a separate community; but this carried with it the exclusion from all other corporations, and the submission to particular taxes, much above our means and our resources and arbitrarily imposed. [Cited in Tama, 1807, pp. 15–17]

In a new society bereft of institutionalized social orders, the Jews would disband their corporations and congregations as political bodies. They would join the French community as individual citizens. Judaism, and its spiritual laws, would be their religion, not their society and polity. The signs of structural differentiation—the separation of religious, political, and economic organizations—begin to emerge.

The relationship between religious and other social institutions, however, could not be so easily disentangled. In the period before emancipation, many viewed Sabbath observance as a stumbling block to Jewish economic and political integration. How could Jews serve in the militia and how could they be farmers if they could not work on their Sabbath and holidays? If they could not work the land, how could they leave their traditional roles of "exploitation" and learn to work with their hands? Did not the new government have an obligation to prohibit their separation? There are instances of Jews being punished for their religious observances during the Reign of Terror. In some towns, they were fined for not engaging in business on the Sabbath. In others, the authorities compelled them to open their stores. High Holiday services had to be held in secret, and in 1799, in Nice, the municipal authorities sent an agent to the top of the church steeple to search for booths used on the holiday of *Sukkot*. Beards and sidelocks too were symbols that demanded shearing (Szajkowski, 1970, pp. 399–412, 785–808). Jewish religious distinctiveness quickly raised questions about social and political distinctiveness and, hence, about the place of the Jews within French society. How much difference could be allowed before Jews were seen as a nation within the nation? What were the boundaries of Jewishness? If the old order enshrined communal distinctions, the structure of government and the ideology of the new order had no place for any social form that stood between the individual and the state.

These political transformations divided the Jewish community as some Jews formed alliances with non-Jews, which moved them out of the Jewish community and away from Jewish religious practice. The French Revolution opened social, economic, and political opportunities to large numbers of Jews and Christians. It held out the promise of a secular society limited not to an intellectual elite but to all those who would join it.

The ideas of the Revolution, however, did not guide everyone's behavior. Most resisted the calls of the rabidly antireligious movements of the Revolution. Many fled to Germany. Jews ignored the specific call to become peasants. Jewish law retained some of its political character, even if it lost the backing of a kehillah. Jews persisted in being distinctive largely because their political organization was not the only source of distinctiveness. Hence, they remained a problem for those seeking to destroy the old order (Szajkowski 1970, pp. 45–52). Again, Jews were not alone. The history of French politics for the next century and a half would grapple with the general issue. Indeed, because they were not alone, their distinctiveness symbolized the problem. Their particularity had to be resolved along with all the others: the peasants, the Church, the language divisions, so as to

maintain the Revolution. Deviations threatened the builders of the new
French state.

Napoleon's rule completed the Revolution's formal restructuring of the
Jewish community, as it pushed on with a series of administrative changes.
He called a meeting of the leaders of the Jews under his rule, pronounced it a
Sanhedrin empowered to represent the Jews. He posed a series of questions,
indicative of persisting doubts about the formal status of the Jews in the new
order:

1. Is it lawful for Jews to marry more than one wife?
2. Is divorce allowed by the Jewish religion? Is divorce valid, although
   not pronounced by courts of Justice, and by virtue of laws in contradiction with the French code?
3. Can a Jewess marry a Christian, or a Jew a Christian woman?
4. In the eyes of Jews are Frenchmen considered as brethren or as
   strangers?
5. In either case what conduct does their law prescribe toward Frenchmen not of their religion?
6. Do the Jews born in France, and treated by the law as French
   citizens, acknowledge France as their country?
7. Who elects the Rabbis?
8. What kind of police-jurisdiction have the Rabbis among the Jews?
   What judicial power do they exercise among them?
9. Are the forms of the elections of the Rabbis and their police juris-
   diction, regulated by the law, or are they only sanctioned by
   custom?
10. Are there professions from which the Jews are excluded by their
    law?
11. Does the law forbid the Jews from taking usury from their
    brethren?
12. Does it forbid or does it allow usury toward strangers? [Cited in
    Tama, 1807, pp. 133–34]

These twelve questions highlight the issues of universalism versus particularism, intermarriage, the legal and political structure of the Jewish community, national loyalty, the ethnic and religious definitions of Jews, and
their concentration in particular occupations. Napoleon's questions remain
the central ideological concerns about the place of the Jews in the modern
world. They have been asked and answered for the last 150 years. Underlying these questions are an elementary misunderstanding and distrust of the
Jewish community. The questions reflect the concern about the relationships among family, economic, religious, and political structures. They
could only be asked at a time when differentiation of structure, reintegration, and political rationalization were beginning to occur.

The Jewish responses to these questions are revealing as well (Tama,
1807, pp. 150–56, 176–83, 193–207). The rabbis and communal leaders

balanced fidelity to Jewish law with the willingness to join the political community of France. Hence, they denied that the rabbis and communities had any police or judicial powers. Their concerns were religious and ethical. Only in the area of marriage did they fail to distinguish sharply between the religious and legal, but they added that they were no more and no less willing to bless such marriages than were the Catholic priests. Even in this answer, the one that most clearly points out the importance of Jewish religious law, the distinctiveness of the Jews was downplayed. The rabbis were singled out as holding this position on marriage, not the communal leaders.

Napoleon's policy reflected the tension between the distinctive qualities of the Jews and their place in the new order. Two years after the meetings of the Sanhedrin, he organized the Jewish community into a nationwide administrative structure (Schwarzfuchs, 1979, pp. 179–94; Albert, 1977). Modeled on the Protestant groups, the Jewish consistories were formed in Paris and in all departments with Jewish populations. They supervised that which remained of the kehillah, that is, the religious and charitable activities of the Jews. Having no political power of their own and representing a religious but not political community, the consistories operated under the direct control of the French government. At the same time, Napoleon imposed restrictions on migration (Szajkowski, 1970, pp. 95–97). Although the Jewish religion was formally integrated into the French state, Napoleon's policy did not treat the Jews as equal citizens.

The treatment of Jews by Frenchmen did not live up to the ideals of the French Revolution. Numerous examples of anti-Semitic behavior in Alsace and in other areas with a Jewish populace have been documented. Resentment and hatred of the Jews remained, less among the political and intellectual elite of the Revolution than among citizens of France (Szajkowski, 1970; Schwarzfuchs, 1979).

The gap between the ideals of liberal politics and ideology and the attitudes of many Frenchmen remained. The Dreyfus Affair, in which political anti-Semitism joined with the forces still opposing the Revolution's child, the French Republic, is the most famous instance of this problem. Jews frequently found themselves in the sector of French society supporting the strong national state and espousing the Revolution's principles of liberty, equality, and fraternity. Despite the conflicts, however, political emancipation of the Jews was never rescinded. Over time, legal equality was firmly established in French law. Migration restrictions were eliminated in 1818, and legal equality was accorded to Judaism in 1831 (Rurup, 1981, pp. 6–7).

Government policies began the transformation of the Jewish community. The consistories introduced French culture and language in the Jewish schools and served as one institutional mechanism for the greater integration of Jews into French society. The absence of legal barriers to Jewish entry into government bureaucracies and economic enterprises further enhanced the incorporation of Jews into France.

VARIATIONS IN EUROPEAN POLITICAL MODERNIZATION

Napoleon's armies spread the Revolution eastward. In Germany and Italy they freed the Jews from the ghettos and established new communal organizations (Schwarzfuchs, 1979; Rossi, 1974; Kobler, 1976). In Italy he was hailed as a "lover of Israel" for having removed the ghetto walls in Milan, Padua, Rome, Ancona, and other cities. Responses in Frankfurt, Cologne, and among Jews of other German places were equally positive. In the rest of Europe, as in France, Jewish political rights expanded or contracted with the successes of political modernization. Civil servants in Prussia and some other German states followed Napoleon's departing armies with laws that maintained new Jewish rights (Low, 1979; Kobler, 1976; Freimann and Kracauer, 1929; Walker, 1971; Lee, 1980; Kober, 1948). These bureaucrats pounded away at the plethora of complex traditional rules. In their effort to build rational governments, they allowed Jews into the guilds and eliminated special Jewish taxes. The place of the Jews was one of many issues in the conflict between the modernizers and those who held the traditional sources of power, the guilds and the burghers. The state builders encouraged Jews to enter traditionally Christian trades and to leave the world of peddlers, real-estate speculators, and cattle dealers. The burghers who controlled the cities and towns and the artisan guilds fought to retain their traditional rights, economic benefits, and political power against the encroachments of state governments.

The civil servants fought for fiscal clarification and rational government. The political condition of the Jews rested squarely on the outcome of these contests. These factors and the absence of national unification meant that the place of Jews varied dramatically across German towns, municipalities, and cities. Nowhere did they have complete legal equality (Toury, 1977a). The victory of the nation builders later in the century led to the legal emancipation of the Jews, first in 1869 in Prussia, then the entire nation in 1871. Legal emancipation, however, did not end the political conflicts (see Chapters 8 and 9).

In the Austrian Empire, the variable success of political modernization and power of the different nations—Poles, Hungarians, Germans, Czechs, Slovaks, and others—affected Jewish political rights. In Galicia, increasing Polish autonomy exacerbated the condition of the Jews (Wandycz, 1974, pp. 220–28). In Hungary, many Jews joined the nationalist movement (Seton-Watson, 1974). In Western areas of the Hapsburg domains, Jews frequently identified with German liberalism. No single revolution, as in France, led to the law in 1867 that formally equated all religions. Here, too, political conflict over the Jews remained after formal emancipation.

In the Empire of the Tsars, legal emancipation did not come until the Romanov dynasty fell from the throne. Russian policy vacillated between forcing Jews out of their economic place in the small villages, encouraging them to take up farming, and locking them into the Pale of Settlement (Greenberg, 1944; Baron, 1976a; Levitats, 1943; Mahler, 1971). It moved between policies of forced military service, the cantonist system, and those that brought Jews into government schools and universities. Policy change in the direction of Jewish legal rights occurred with the abolition of the kahals in 1844, the end of the cantonist system a decade later, and a marked liberalization of the regime in the early 1860s. Twenty years later, the May laws brought a return to a repressive policy highlighted by the Black Hundreds and the pogroms. Tsarist policy regarding the Jews did not lead to fundamental changes in their legal and political status.

Political forces and ideologies favoring modernization competed with those that sought to retain the ordered society of the past. Some sought to retain the principalities, guilds, and burgher-dominated cities, opposing the formation of the nation-state. They legitimated their interests with an ideology which opposed the secular state seeking to build a proper Christian nation, which had no place for Jewish citizens. Others viewed Jews as a social group standing between the individual and nation, a relic of a dying society. The bureaucrats juggled these forces as they pushed on with the efforts at reorganizing government (Low, 1979; Walker, 1971; J. Katz, 1980).

Political change led to the removal of old laws that restricted the behavior of the Jews and the enactment of new laws transforming how they lived. The emphasis on individual rights rather than on legal estates meant the destruction of the kehillot. New administrations created consistories and other forms of Jewish communal organizations. Specific policies fostering Jewish integration affected synagogues and Jewish schools. Legal and political changes by themselves did not necessarily alter the lives of the Jews (J. Katz, 1972, p. 101). Removing the old restrictions provided new opportunities. Whether Jews took advantage of those openings depended less on their political views or the actions of the government than upon social and economic forces. Widespread poverty and the availability of new jobs were powerful sources of change for Jewish communities as for the societies of which they were a part. The conspicuous character of political modernization does not necessarily mean that it was the primary determinant of social transformation. The combination of social, economic, and political modernization transformed Jewish society and politics.

4 · The First Waves of Social and Economic Modernization in Europe

Nahman's windstorm transformed the face of Europe. Not only did it scatter kings and nobles, it turned populated regions into deserts and wastelands into metropolises. The railroads that linked distant places traveled on beds that recarved mountains, and the barges carried goods through canals that redirected waterways. People labored, prayed, and struggled to survive in strange new ways never before seen in the world. In Hobsbawm's words, the industrial revolution "was probably the most important event in world history, at any rate since the invention of agriculture and cities" (1962, p. 46). Once it began, life was not the same.

While the general political modernization and the specific changes within the Jewish community were conspicuous features of European modernization, other changes were no less important. Shifts in the occupational and industrial structure, expansion of educational opportunities, declining centrality of extended family networks, the emergence and spread of technology and new forms of transportation and communication, population expansion, redistribution, and urbanization were among these changes. Together, they transformed the general societies and the Jewish communities. Moreover, these changes implied that the social, economic, cultural, and political relationships between the Jewish community and the broader society were undergoing radical redefinitions as well.

Unlike a windstorm, the socioeconomic transformations associated with modernization were not random. The patterns may be observed within countries and in specific combinations of socioeconomic processes. By analytic necessity, we shall focus on selected illustrations of stratification, urbanization, and population growth. Nevertheless, the overwhelming feature of modernization is that many of these processes were interrelated, which resulted in a transformation of European society and the Jewish communities within them (see especially, Goldscheider, 1971; M. Levy, 1966; Hobsbawm, 1962, 1979; E. Weber, 1976).

Much as France exemplifies the political revolution, Great Britain symbolizes the transformation of the economic world. On the island kingdom, factories first emerged and spread rapidly, journeymen and artisans lost their positions and became the industrial proletariat, farmers left their homes to work in the cities. Capitalists developed not only out of the traditional merchant classes but from skilled artisans as well. Rapid population growth accompanied marked improvement in life expectancies. Expanding national and international markets flourished as capitalists, merchants, and industrialists invested and reinvested their resources. Britain led the way (Laslett, 1971; Thompson, 1968; Hobsbawm, 1962, 1979).

With variable speed and thoroughness, the rigid social order of burghers, nobles, artisans, and peasants gave way, across the continent, to varieties of jobs, social rankings, and political power. New sources of wealth emerged as new forms of manufacture replaced manual labor, as factories took over from home production, and as national and international markets grew. Just as the political power of the nobles and burghers retreated before rationalizing bureaucracies, they were overwhelmed by the newly rising capitalists. A world of stable and distinct estates became a universe of kaleidescopic complexity.

The individual threw off tradition's chains, and the changes opened new opportunities. It is not fortuitous that liberalism—as economic and political theory—is closely linked to the society of capitalist development. The "free-floating atoms" of liberal theory—to borrow Marx's critical phrase (Bottomore and Rubel, 1964, pp. 219-20)—may not have accurately described the individual in society, but the image nicely emphasizes the ways in which the new society made way for mobility.

The crucial achievement of the two revolutions (the industrial and political) was thus that they opened careers to talent, or at any rate to energy, shrewdness, hard work and greed. Not all careers, and not to the top rungs of the ladders, except perhaps in the USA. And yet, how extraordinary were the opportunities, how remote from the nineteenth century the static hierarchical ideal of the past! [Hobsbawm, 1962, p. 226]

The societies of Europe retreated before the matrix of forces that produced an increasingly complex and fluid society and greater personal freedom. Some exploited these new opportunities, while others ignored them. By the end of the century, however, few could avoid the windstorm.

Britain is a generally useful illustration of the modernization and industrialization processes as they first emerged in Europe. It is not, however, a helpful example for the analysis of Jews. The Jewish community there was very small, numbering no more than 10,000 in 1800. Furthermore, British Jewry did not have the highly structured Jewish communal life that characterized those on the continent. Most of the Jews in early nineteenth-century Britain were immigrants or children of immigrants, and they did not build what we have described as a highly structured Jewish society (Endelman, 1979). To analyze the early modernization of traditional Jewish communities, Jews in Central Europe are a better example.

We shall focus on occupational, educational, and demographic changes, for these represent the structural underpinnings of broader community transformations. The analysis of these changes illustrates the differential velocities in the West compared to the East. The objective of this chapter is to identify the first forms of social and economic modernization and their impact on the Jewish community. Since the initial thrust of these processes vary by place and time, we shall be constrained by geography and chronology.

CHANGES AMONG THE JEWISH ELITE

The windstorm first reached the most exposed Jews, the wealthy and their families. In 1848, the Viennese *Theaterzeitung* reported:

There are talented Jewesses everywhere, but the greatest number is to be found in Vienna. It astonishing how much knowledge they possess, how well they are able to engage in conversation, what superior judgments and views they offer, how felicitously they express themselves. Most of them speak three or four languages, sing Italian arias beautifully and support the arts conscientiously. One finds the most important artists at their soirees. They are true patrons of the theaters and concerts. They dress very simply but most tastefully. In conduct and appearance they are most charming and graceful. While occasionally their husbands are heard speaking jargon, they themselves have completely abandoned it. They give their children the finest education. In all charitable undertakings, they set an excellent example. [Cited in Grunwald, 1936, pp. 235–36]

What an extraordinary transformation from the traditional society: well-educated Jews, patrons of the arts and theaters, and not Jewish men but Jewish women! How their world had changed! This mid-century source described upper-class Jews of capital cities. Its description is not especially futuristic. More than sixty years earlier, Rabbi Israel Baer of Amsterdam pointed to similar changes occurring in his city. Jacob Katz paraphrases the rabbi's plaint: "The Jew of Amsterdam, whether Ashkenazi or Sephardi, was dressed and curled to the height of new fashions; men used razors to shave their beards; people went to the theater and to the opera; the daily prayer was neglected and cardplaying was the rage; the Sabbath was not strictly observed and some did not even fast on the ninth of Av, the day commemorating the destruction of the temple; the sons of the rich attended the universities and lived a life of dissipation" (1978, p. 146; see also Endelman, 1979, pp. 207–17). Amsterdam, the early center of the commercial revolution, was also precocious in examples of change within the Jewish community.

Perhaps the most famous and earliest transformation in the social lives of Jews occurred in Berlin in the decades surrounding the turn of the nineteenth century. The friendship of the German poet, Lessing, and the Jewish philosopher, Mendelssohn, led an array of close ties between Jews and Gentiles that flourished in the living rooms of the wealthy. Numerous memoirs describe the meetings and teas, where the children of rich Jews met poets, noblemen, and philosophers. The extraordinary character of these relations—as well as some of the ambivalence held by many Gentiles— emerges clearly in the contemporary sources. "The educated Jews were for the greatest part more obliging and lasting in their admiration of Goethe's personality as well as of his writings than many of his co-religionists. As a rule they show more pleasing attention and flattering interest than an indigenous German, and their talent of quick perception, their penetrating reason, their peculiar wit make them a more sensitive public than, unfortunately, is found among the at times slow and dull genuine and original Germans" (cited in Low, 1979, p. 82).

It is important not to exaggerate the extent of the social integration that took place at these soirees. It is true that many Germans visited Jewish homes, but at the same time many considered their hosts inferior. Some of the ambivalence toward Jews was anti-Semitic. Moreover, only a small number of Jews were involved in such gatherings, at most, 1 or 2 percent. No more than 5–7 percent of German Jews lived in Berlin, Frankfurt, and Hamburg, the centers of these activities (Engelman, 1973, p. 202; Lowenstein, 1976, p. 52; Weinryb, 1946, p. 26). There were not that many Germans involved either since very few attended universities. In 1820, there were approximately 7,300 German university students scattered throughout the country, and almost all came from the nobility and clergy (McClelland, 1980, p. 199). It can be seen, therefore, that salon society included only a small portion of the Jews and Germans.

It would be wrong, however, to dismiss the soirees as the frivolous gatherings of the rich. Jewish entry into salon society illustrates the initial erosion of the barriers between the traditional orders. It further indicates the growing wealth among large numbers of Jews and the increasing distance between them and most of the Jewish population. Those who would have been the political and economic leaders, *parnassim*, of the Jewish communities began to interact socially with Gentiles. Jews with money, resources, and contacts with non-Jews were the most receptive to social, economic, and political changes. Their increasing numbers and the weakening of the kehillot distinguish this pattern from the premodern era.

The Jews who attended the soirees saw a choice between remaining within the Jewish community or entering the seemingly unfettered new society. Many turned away from the traditional world. They rejected what they saw as the backward, uncultivated, uneducated, poor Jews of the provinces. The standards of the new civilization replaced those of the old order. Some, as we have seen in France, distinguished the religious dimension of being Jewish from its political organization. Some applied the new secular philosophies in an effort to reform Judaism (see Chapter 5). Others, and relatively few, left the religious community entirely (Toury, 1977b, pp. 53–60; Barkai, 1981, p. 124). As a result, this movement within the economic elite necessarily weakened the cohesion of the Jewish community (Low, 1979).

Economic Opportunity and Occupational Mobility

Economic changes increased the wealth and importance of the former court Jews and merchants. "In 1739, Jews were allowed onto the floor of the Berlin stock-exchange only to talk to the Christians there. Fifty years later, the exchange did not distinguish between Jews and Gentiles" (Engelman, 1973, p. 92; see also Low, 1979, pp. 27–29). There was as well a marked increase in the number of wealthy Jews, who obtained residency rights in the Prussian capital. Efforts to expand and rationalize the Prussian and Austrian governments required large sums of money (Seeliger, 1958; Lestchinsky, 1932; Engelman, 1973, pp. 91–92). Former court Jews provided much of the funds that fueled the new political order. When, in 1819, the Rothschilds left Frankfurt because of anti-Semitic riots, James Meyer Rothschild complained, " . . . what can be the result of such disturbances? . . . Who buys state bonds in Germany, and who has endeavored to raise the rate of exchange, if it not be our nation? Has not our example engendered a certain confidence in state loans, so that Christian firms have also taken heart and invested in all kinds of securities" (cited in Engelman, 1973, p. 92). In France, Berr Isaac Berr's calls for integration into the general society (see Chapter 3) echoed many who had prospered by supplying material to Napoleon's armies.

The expanding opportunity structure also affected some wealthy Jews in Eastern Europe. In areas of partitioned Poland, Jews moved into the newly developing sectors of the economy. In the earliest forms of industrialization, around 1828, there were seventy-five woolens factories owned by Jews in Russian Poland, producing almost 320,000 yeards of cloth. This put Jewish entrepreneurs in the forefront of the most important industry at that time in the Ukraine (Lestchinsky, 1928a; Dubnow, 1928; Blackwell, 1968, pp. 233–35). Across the continent, wealthy Jewish merchants and investors played key roles in the first development of capitalism.

The new economic opportunities in Germany beckoned the wealthiest Jews and those located in sectors of the economy particularly favored by early expansion. In the South and West, Jews were the cattle traders whose wealth and importance increased in the wake of agrarian reform and agricultural crises of the 1820s. Over time, Jews expanded in this economic sphere (Richarz, 1981; Rurup, 1981). There are examples of Jewish peddlers and weavers in Wurttemberg, Prussia, Augsburg (Bavaria), Silesia, and Thuringia who became entrepreneurs and opened textile factories. More generally, they entered branches of industry that were related to their original trades: tailors moved into textiles, hardware and rag peddlers went into metal and paper manufacture. In all these fields, the possibility of economic mobility provided the basis for social advancement (Richarz, 1975, p. 74). Between 1843 and 1861, the proportion of Prussian Jews engaged in trade and commerce increased from 48 percent to 57 percent (Barkai, 1981, p. 132). The Jews of Frankfurt quickly moved away from a concentration on investment, moneylending, and peddling. In 1824, half of the Jewish labor force were self-employed businessmen. Most were involved in finance and the textile industries (Ruppin, 1973, pp. 110–11).

The rapid change may be illustrated with occupation statistics from various areas. In Baden in 1816, 89 percent of the working Jews engaged in trade. In 1833, one-third of the gainfully occupied Jews were artisans or working in agriculture, the sciences, and the arts, and two-thirds were in trade. In Wurttemberg, the development was dramatic. In 1812, 86 percent of the Jews were described as hucksters; the proportion was 39 percent in 1837 and 18 percent in 1852. At mid-century, 5 percent were engaged in the sciences and arts, 10 percent in agriculture, and 64 percent in the artisan and regular trades (Rurup, 1969, p. 82). The memoirs of B. L. Monasch of Posen detail the efforts needed to survive in the budding world of new industrialists during this period. Apprenticed to a bookbinder, Monasch struck out on his own into printing. He expanded into movable type, printing prayer books, Bibles, and an edition of the Jerusalem Talmud, before succumbing to bankruptcy (P. Fraenkel, 1979). Throughout Germany, Jews moved quickly into new spheres, which were becoming part of the new economic order.

The expanding economic opportunities generated upward occupational mobility. Because of their previous occupational segregation, the location of Jews in towns and cities, and the absence of constraints tying them to the land, Jews in Western Europe tended to be in the forefront of these mobility patterns. They moved to new jobs, however, only in sectors of the economy where they had been concentrated: agricultural credit, service industries, trade and commerce, and textiles but not heavy industry (Barkai, 1981; Toury, 1977b; Shofer, 1981). The greater receptivity of Jews to new economic opportunities was selective. It was the consequence of their economic concentration and the particular form of economic growth around them. The relationship between general economic expansion and Jewish occupational mobility was particular to economic sector and geographic location. There is no reason to suppose that Jewish ideologies or value patterns determined the intensity of the Jewish response, its timing, or variation among communities.

The occupational transformation, therefore, had an additional feature of consequence. There was a greater diversity relative to the fixed structure of the ordered economy in the premodern communities. Jews did not disperse randomly throughout the occupational structure. They moved into jobs in new and expanding areas of the economy, structurally linked to their previous occupations. The rate of Jewish occupational mobility varied with the growth of new opportunities and the expansion of their traditional occupations. As a consequence, occupational mobility resulted in new forms of occupational concentration and segregation among Jews. In the middle of the nineteenth century, half the entrepreneurs in Berlin were Jews (Richarz, 1975, p. 74). Unlike the premodern period, these new patterns of occupational concentration did not imply economic stagnation and deprivation.

One of the conspicuous and most immediate consequences of the first forms of occupational mobility was an increase in wealth among German Jewry. By mid-century, the *betteljuden* (the wandering paupers) began to disappear. Many left for America. Most found places in the expanding economy of Germany (Lowenstein, 1976, p. 49; Bartys, 1972, p. 201; Toury, 1971, 1977b; Barkai, 1981). The income structure of many Jewish communities changed. At the start of the period, most Jews were in the lowest tax brackets. At mid-century, 15 percent of the German Jews were in the upper and middle social classes, 35 percent were in the lower-middle classes, and half were at subsistence level. Twenty years later, 60 percent were in middle- and high-income brackets, with less than 25 percent (and as low as 5 percent in some areas) in the lowest social class (Barkai, 1981, pp. 133–36; Toury, 1977b). By the last quarter of the century, Jews typically paid a share of local taxes far in excess of their proportion of the population (Richarz, 1975).

Many Jews in regions of economic decline, such as Posen, migrated to areas of economic opportunity. Government policy sought to turn Posen into a granary and supplier of raw material for the rest of Prussia. By the 1820s, nascent industries, many owned by Jews, disappeared, and skilled workers began to look elsewhere for employment. The flow of artisans out of Posen turned into a flood by mid-century. Between 1824 and 1871, nearly 50,000 Jews and 20,000 Poles left for other parts of Germany and the United States. The Jewish population of the region peaked in the early 1840s at about 75,000 and then began a period of rapid diminution. Even so, there is clear indication of increasing wealth and occupational change among portions of the Jews who remained. Between 1843 and 1861, the number of craftsmen declined by about 30 percent, while the number of rentiers, big merchants, and shopkeepers grew sharply. Declining economic opportunities moved Jews out of Posen, depopulating and eroding one of the most highly structured Jewish communities of Germany (Bartys, 1972; Ruppin, 1934, 1973; Hagen, 1980 Wandycz, 1974; Shofer, 1979; Zarchin, 1939). Economic factors and general government policies rather than anti-Semitism or the failure of the Revolution of 1848 determined Jewish out-migration from Posen.

Even before the leap in German industrialization in the late 1850s, the windstorm of economic change surged against the Jewish communities. There is evidence that the forces of change affected the Jews more quickly than it did others in Germany. The apparent affinity betwen the Jews and capitalism has fascinated many over the years. Polemicists and scholars, anti-Semites and Jewish apologists have debated the issue. For some, Rothschild stands as the symbol of capitalism; for others, Marx, Bernstein, and the Socialist movement define the place of the Jews. Sombart and others attributed to the Jews a central place in the genesis of capitalism. Others have followed Weber's contention that a people so outside the mainstream of premodern Europe could not have had much effect on the process of industrial development. The sudden visibility of the Jews and the economic success of many of them under capitalism have puzzled many for a long time (see Engelman, 1973, pp. 82–94; Mosse, 1979; Mendes-Flohr and Reinharz, 1980; as well as the original sources).

We are less concerned with establishing the role of the Jews in capitalism than analyzing the impact of economic change on the Jewish communities. The most important effect of early occupational changes and increases in the wealth of Jews was the erosion of the structure of the traditional society. Regular contact between Jews and Gentiles introduced new divisions within the Jewish community as it created bonds between those who heretofore had been members of distinct orders. The primary determinants of these occupational transformations were structural rather than cultural. The emerging economic structure altered the Jewish communities and their relationship to the general society.

To the extent that new occupations were generated by economic expansion and growth, Jews took advantage of these job opportunities without generating competition and conflict with non-Jews. Indeed, Jews were part of the supply of human capital that the expanding demand required. However, over time the occupational concentration of Jews combined with economic contractions resulted in conflict and competition among Jews and between Jews and non-Jews (Weinryb, 1946; and Chapter 9). Indeed, conflict and competition should be viewed as integral to the processes of occupational and economic changes accompanying modernization. It is inadequate to view the changing occupational structure of Jews in terms of their assimilation, or to ignore the conflicts and disruptions generated by these changes among Jews or between Jews and others.

EDUCATIONAL EXPANSION AND THE EAST-WEST GAP
Educational changes were another early manifestation of modernization. In France, the leaders of the consistories used new Jewish schools to integrate large portions of the Jews into French society. They introduced secular materials into the Jewish curriculum in order to spread liberal values and to begin the "regeneration" of their people. By 1821, there were twelve modernized Jewish primary schools. These schools emphasized French language and culture rather than the traditional components of Jewish education. Other Jews attended French government schools (Albert, 1977, pp. 128–36).

By expanding and modernizing the Jewish school system and by increased attendance at government schools, education became a major vehicle in the rapid transformation and integration of French Jewry.

By the 1840's the Jews had adopted many of the French behavioral norms. Observers often cited changes in Jewish behavior, e.g., greater regard for personal cleanliness and appreciation of modern secular education. Jews began to dress in the general style (even in the country-side of the eastern provinces). In Paris an entire generation of the young had been raised in French culture, and only the oldest Jews and the newest arrivals spoke Yiddish or Judeo-Alsatian. [Albert, 1977, pp. 38–39]

As the rabbis lost power to the consistories, they bemoaned the sorry state of religious knowledge and observance among the Jews, especially those living in Paris and in the new communities (Albert, 1977, pp. 300–301).

In Germany, the expansion of educational opportunities occurred largely in government primary schools, gymnasia, and universities. Cologne is a good illustration. Before 1815, this city had a population of nearly 50,000 but no schools of any sort. In 1825, the city council instituted compulsory education. A year later, a royal commission recommended that the Jewish community establish a separate school in order to encourage their social integration. The kehillah's leaders demurred, responding that the Christian schools were perfectly adequate. At that time, sixteen of the sixty Jewish youngsters of school age in Cologne attended the Catholic gymnasium. Over the next several decades, the pattern continued. In 1859, half of the 400 Jewish children attended Christian schools in Cologne (Kober, 1948, pp. 259–63, 328–43).

Cologne reflects general trends in Western Europe. In 1847, nearly half the Jewish students in Prussia attended Jewish schools; the remainder were in Christian and secular schools. As early as 1839, 40 percent of the Jewish youngsters in Berlin studied at Jewish schools; eleven years later the percentage had declined to 29 percent. In 1867, Jews accounted for 15 percent of the students in the Berlin gymnasia, four times their share of the population (Lowenstein, 1976, pp. 43–44; Rurup, 1975a, p. 22; Richarz, 1975, p. 71; Toury, 1977b).

Several instances from the early years of the career of Samson Raphael Hirsch bring additional evidence of changed levels of Jewish education among German Jews. Rabbi Hirsch ended his career as the leader of Neoorthodoxy in Frankfurt, renowned for its blend of secular and Jewish scholarship. Hirsch obtained his first post in Oldenburg, where he excelled with regard to religious piety and knowledge—even though he had completed studies at neither a university nor a rabbinical seminary. The Jewish communities in the small towns and cities of Germany did not have a command of religious texts, knowledge of the Bible, or, in particular, the Talmud. When Hirsch took a position farther East, as Chief Rabbi of Moravia, his mastery of the Talmud paled in comparison to many laymen in the community (Rosenbloom, 1976). They found his discourses simplistic, and Hirsch discontinued the traditional practice by which the Chief Rabbi gave public lectures on *Halacha* (Jewish law). "Much to his chagrin, Moravia was not Oldenburg or East Friesland. . . . Even those who were willing to recognize Hirsch as the titular chief rabbi refused to accede to him in practice, since, in their eyes, he was grossly inferior. His demands for recognition and respect were countered with resentment, lack of cooperation, and, most devastating of all, derision. At times, they tried to embarrass him by posing certain questions that he could not answer or whose humor he could not fathom. . . .[T]hey called him a *siddur lamdan*, a 'prayer book scholar' " (Rosenbloom, 1976, p. 91). In Germany, however, his scholarship, which blended university and traditional piety, placed him at the helm of the Neoorthodox community.

These examples from Hirsch's career point to the growing differences between the Jews of Western Europe and those living in the East. By 1850, France, Germany, and Austria had commenced processes of social change. In Russia, nothing yet challenged the old order. Even efforts to bring Jews into the schools did not hide a desire to convert them. As important, there were still very few schools and students in the Tsarist Empire. In 1836, there were only 2,000 students in all the universities of Russia. Twelve years later, the number had reached 4,500, which was still far below the population of the German universities at the turn of the century. Indeed, as late as 1859, there were not even 5,000 university students (Alston, 1969, pp. 27–45). The old order in Russia maintained itself.

In Eastern Europe, the traditional schools, the *hederim* and *yeshivot*, flourished. At the same time as these schools grew in the East, the yeshiva in Furth closed (Lowenstein, 1976, p. 44; Albert, 1977, p. 242). A description of the yeshiva in Mir, Byelo-Russia, illuminates the strength of the traditional Jewish institutions.

This school which has become famous among the Jews is located in a
rather large though old and dilapidated building not far from the synagogue. This building includes a large hall and a room where the students
congregate for the entire day, from five in the morning until ten in the
evening. Altogether there are about one hundred students, almost all of
them striplings. Almost all are very poor and are maintained by contributions collected for this purpose in numerous Jewish settlements.
[Cited in Greenberg, 1944, 1:58]

The source of this description was the Haskalah educator, Mandelstam, who
visited the yeshiva in 1840, while on his way to attend Moscow University as
the first Jewish student. If there were about 100 students at the Mir yeshiva,
and at least several other yeshivot equally as large and many smaller in size,
there were probably as many Jews in the yeshivot as non-Jews in the
universities of the Tsar's Empire (see Blackwell, 1968, pp. 333–36; Alston,
1969, pp. 27–45).
     A section from an autobiography makes a similar point about the status of
elementary education at roughly the same time:

Educational institutions in the modern sense of the word were conspicuous by their absence in our town. There was no government or public
school of a secular character in Kopyl. The Christian population was
without exception illiterate. The Jewish population, on the other hand,
had an over abundance of schools, though of a special type. [Cited in
Greenberg, 1944, 1:58]

The author then describes the twenty hederim of Kopyl where approximately 200 boys were taught. These schools educated most if not all Jewish
boys at a time when few others received any formal education at all.
     There are other contrasts between the place of education in Jewish and
general society in the Russian Empire. In 1836, there was a total of 15,476
students in the gymnasia in Russia (Alston, 1969, p. 35). Few of them were
Jews. In Shklov, a city of 10,000 Jews, there were twenty-seven pupils in the
government's Jewish school. Vitebsk had thirteen in 1849 and nineteen
eight years later. In 1857, a decade after the first such school opened, slightly
more than 3,000 Jewish youngsters in Russia attended government schools,
and most of them were orphans and public wards. Hundreds of thousands
attended the hederim (Greenberg, 1944, 1:40–41; Baron, 1976a, pp. 34–39).
     These examples point to sharp differences between the Jewish communi-
ties in Eastern Europe—which maintained their traditional cohesion—and
those in the West—which were rapidly being transformed. The general
question of why modernization processes began earlier in the West than in
the East is beyond the scope of our inquiry, and we accept it here as a given.
     There is no evidence that the premodern communities in France and
Germany were any more receptive to change than those in Poland (see

Chapter 2). There is as well no evidence that Western Jews preferred the new order more than did those in the East. After all, when change did come to the lands east of the Oder-Neisse, it affected the Jews in much the same ways as it had earlier in Germany (see Chapters 7 and 8).

Variations in pace and strength characterized European modernization. In France and Germany, the political power and economic cohesion of the Jewish communities responded to the political and economic revolutions. Those revolutions had made few inroads in Eastern Europe before mid-century. In short, the socioeconomic transformation of Jews varied directly with the transformation of their societies. While the Jews in Eastern Europe may have been better educated then their rural, non-Jewish neighbors at mid-century, they had yet to undergo the transformations that characterized their coreligionists in the West.

The same explanation of the East-West gap in modernization accounts for differences within Jewish communities. In the first period of European modernization, some Jews participated earlier than others in the processes of change: wealthier Jews compared to poor Jews, urban Jews compared to Jews in towns and rural areas. Variation, heterogeneity, and polarization in life style, values, and ideologies reflected these structural differences within and among Jewish communities. New sources of conflict and new bonds of Jewish cohesion emerged in this process.

POPULATION GROWTH AND MIGRATION

Waves of population growth and movement joined political modernization, changing occupational structures, and new educational systems to transform the Jewish community. Massive population growth increased the complexity of society and facilitated the growing economic diversity. Population expansion allowed people to deviate from traditional norms by making it more difficult for the community to control individual behavior. As a result, social and cultural diversity increased.

Population growth meant pressure on existing economic resources, educational and job opportunities, housing, and other needs. This pressure resulted in out-migration from local areas to places where new and better opportunities were emerging. For Jews, as for others, migration meant a release from the social constraints of traditional village society. It often facilitated the breakdown of control exercised by the extended family over resources. The geographic separation of family members forged new ties of interdependence, but initially loosened the constraints and control over individual social mobility.

When Jews migrated to places without organized communities, they entered settings without either the institutional support or sanctions of the traditional society. In these new communities, the Jewish polity did not weaken; it never existed. In Western and Central Europe, these migrations pushed and pulled Jews into areas with weak communal institutions, as in the capital cities of Paris, Berlin, and Vienna. In contrast, two patterns of migration characterized Jews in Eastern Europe. Some moved from rural areas and small towns to Vilna, Warsaw, and other established communities. Others went into new areas, such as Odessa, Lodz, and Budapest, and to rural localities in the Hapsburg Empire. These different streams of migration had variable implications for Jewish continuity (see Chapters 7 and 8).

Evidence is available to document the theoretical relationships among population growth, migration, and social transformation (Engelman, 1973, pp. 103–10; Baron, 1976a, pp. 64–67; 1976b; Lestchinsky, 1922, 1928a). An estimated 1,500,000 Jews were in Europe in 1800; twenty-five years later there were more than 2,700,000, and by mid-century the number had grown to more than 4,120,000. In 1880, at the start of mass emigration of European Jews from the continent, there were nearly 6,800,000 Jews there, and at the end of the century the total approached 8,700,000. In 1800, approximately 60 percent of world Jewry lived in Europe; eighty years later nearly 90 percent did. The Jewish population within the Russian Empire grew 250 percent between 1825 (1.6 million) and 1880 (nearly 4 million) and continued to grow to more than 5 million in 1900. This growth occurred despite mass Jewish migrations out of Eastern Europe during the last decades of the nineteenth century (see Chapters 7 and 11). Similar patterns of population growth prevailed throughout Europe. In Galicia, the 270,000 Jews in 1825 became nearly 700,000 by 1880, and the Jewish population of Hungary grew from 200,000 to 638,000 during the same period (Laszlo, 1966, p. 62). Between 1815 and 1860 the number of French Jews doubled from 45,000 to 96,000 (Albert, 1977, p. 317). When German unification was complete in 1871, there were more than 500,000 Jews there; over three times that of 1837 (Pulzer, 1964, p. 9). Only in the West did the rate of population expansion slow appreciably in the last quarter of the nineteenth century. The patterns parallel differences between general population growth in Eastern and Western Europe.

Demographic patterns reflect the differential timing of modernization in Western and Eastern Europe, that is, fertility and mortality declined first in the West. Jewish fertility tended to fall somewhat earlier and more rapidly than non-Jewish fertility, even within urban places (Bachi, 1976; Della Pergola, 1981a; Goldscheider, 1967; A. Goldstein, 1981a, 1981b; Ruppin, 1973; Lowenstein, 1981b; Hyman, 1981; Shofer, 1981). Population growth resulted from natural increase—the excess of births over deaths. In Eastern Europe, this was due to early and universal marriages and declining mortality rates. In Western Europe, Jewish fertility had already declined, especially among those in cities. Moreover, not all Western Europeans married, and those that did married later than Eastern European populations. Jews were not exceptions to this general pattern (see A. Goldstein, 1981b; Knodel, 1974; Shofer, 1981).

Migration enhanced population growth in some areas and mitigated it in others. It provided one of the first indications of major social change. In 1808, there were 50,000 Jews in France, less than 0.2 percent of the country. In thirty-one departments (administrative geographic areas), their ratio was lower than the national average. In seven departments, they ranged from 0.2 percent to 0.9 percent, and in three others from 2 to 3 percent. There were no Jews in the remaining departments, which comprised 46 percent of the country's population. By 1866 there were only four departments with no Jews and they comprised less than 5 percent of the total population (Szaj-kowski, 1970, p. 91). The dispersal of the Jewish population brought many to areas formerly without Jews. Most remained, however, in regions of established Jewish settlement: Alsace-Lorraine and the southwest around Bordeaux and Bayonne. During this time there was a rapid increase in the Jewish population of Paris and in the relative size of that community within French Jewry. In 1808, the 2,700 Parisian Jews comprised approximately 6 percent of the total Jewish population in France. In 1861, there were 25,000 Parisian Jews, more than a quarter of French Jewry (Albert, 1977, p. 322). Although the number of Jews in Alsace and Lorraine grew to 54,300 from 40,000, they were a smaller proportion of French Jewry: 57 percent in 1861 compared to nearly 80 percent at the start of the period (Albert, 1977, p. 324). Many Jews left their homes in the villages of Alsace to move to cities, a pattern which occurred across Western Europe.

Many factors are responsible for these shifts in population in France. Outbursts of anti-Semitism and fear of maltreatment could hardly account for the number who moved into areas where no Jews lived and, indeed, where they had been excluded. The pull of new opportunities, the absence of legal restrictions on residence, the competition engendered by increasing numbers, and the push from limited jobs in areas of origin played more substantial roles than the fear of the mob. Jews fled the penury of their traditional existence and reached for new economic opportunities. Many left their place in the old order to find new ways of working and living.

French Jews were not alone in moving to the capital cities. Berlin, Vienna, and Pest had long kept out all but "tolerated" Jews, those with royal permission to live there. This barrier too fell. In 1816, 3,373 Jews represented 1.7 percent of the total population of Berlin; in 1849, 9,595 Jews were 2.3 percent; and in 1880, 53,949 Jews represented 4.8 percent (Seeli-ger, 1958; Engelman, 1973, p. 234; Shofer, 1979, p. 29; Pulzer, 1964, p. 10; Lestchinsky, 1922). Berlin Jews also accounted for a growing share of German Jewry. In 1816, 1.3 percent of the German Jews lived there; in the 1830s, 5 percent did; nearly 10 percent in 1880; and nearly one-fifth in 1900 (Engelman, 1973, p. 234; Schmelz, 1982; Barkai, 1981; Seeliger, 1958).

Similar patterns characterize Vienna. As late as 1847, only members of the 197 tolerated Jewish families had legal permission to live in the Hapsburg capital; the total Jewish population did not exceed 4,000 (Schmidtbauer, 1980). In 1857, there were 6,217 Jews there, 1.3 percent of the total; in 1869, the number grew to 40,227, 6.1 percent; and in 1890, before the consolidation of many suburbs into the city, there were nearly 100,000 Jews there, 12 percent of the total population (Pulzer, 1964, p. 10; Grunwald, 1936, p. 389; Goldhammer, 1927, p. 9; Rosensaft, 1976, p. 59; Schmidtbauer, 1980). In Pest, which in 1871 joined with Buda and Obuda to form the Hungarian capital, the same pattern prevailed. The first Jews legally settled there in 1786. By 1812, 163 Jewish merchants and their families lived there (Moskovits, 1964, p. 3; see also Laszlo, 1966, p. 63). In 1840, there were 10,000 Jews; in 1860, the number reached 45,000 (Katzburg, 1969, p. 139). As early as 1840, half of the Hungarian Jews who lived in cities were in Pest-Buda, but, as was still true in Germany and France, they were a small proportion of the total Jewish population. More than 90 percent of the Jews of Hungary lived in small towns and villages (Laszlo, 1966, p. 63).

Not all Jews moved to towns or large urban areas. The movement of French Jews to new rural areas finds parallels in Bohemia and Moravia where, following the revolution of 1848, the government lifted restrictions on the residences of Jews. In three years, there were more than 1,200 new Jewish settlements. Contemporaries feared the havoc that would ensue as these new communities sought to build Jewish institutions—schools, synagogues, and associated organizations (Kestenberg-Gladstein, 1968, p. 27). As in France, movement to rural areas and new urban areas changed the established Jewish society and polity.

The Jewish masses in Russia too were pushed and pulled in different directions. Jews were required to live in the Pale of Settlement. Moreover, in 1804, the Tsarist regime prohibited Jews from living and working in areas close to the Western borders of the empire. In the early decades of the century, Jews were on the move, approximately 12,000 to New Russia, where they tried to survive as farmers (Greenberg, 1944, 1:45–47; see also Ruppin, 1973, pp. 159–60; Baron, 1976a, pp. 67–69).

Most of the migrations in the Tsarist Empire, however, led Jews out of tiny rural communities into highly structured centers of Jewish life in the Pale. The 7,000 Jews in Vilna in 1800 grew to 20,000 in 1832 and nearly 40,000 in 1875. In 1816, there were more than 8,000 Jews in Grodno, and by 1859 the number surpassed 10,000. Others expanded even more rapidly. In 1802, Minsk contained 2,700 Jews; in 1847, 13,000; and in 1897, 48,000. In 1800, there were approximately 2,500 Jews in Berdichev; by the mid-1880s the number had increased to 60,000 (Baron, 1976a, pp. 67–69; Mendelsohn, 1970, p. 4; Halevy, 1976, p. 35). In Warsaw, the number of Jews expanded from 8,000 in 1800 to nearly 100,000 in 1876, and 127,000 in 1882, and from 8 percent of the city to one-third of the total (Halevy, 1976, pp. 22–23; Davies, 1982, 2:204; Engelman, 1973, p. 147; Dobrosycki, 1981). Here, urbanization increased Jewish population density and by inference the cohesion of the community.

In other parts of Eastern Europe, Jews moved into areas that did not have established Jewish communities. At the start of the nineteenth century, there were no Jews in either Lodz, the future center of the Polish textile industry, or Odessa, on the Black Sea. In 1910, more than 100,000 Jews lived in Lodz, and in 1897, nearly 140,000 Jews lived in Odessa. (Halevy, 1976, pp. 20–24; Greenberg, 1944, 1:246; Baron, 1976a, p. 67; Lestchinsky, 1922). This type of urbanization had different implications for Jewish cohesion.

ACCELERATIONS IN THE PACE OF CHANGE

The middle of the century witnessed a dramatic surge in the pace of change. In Western Europe, the revolutions of 1848 drew Jews to both sides of the barricades. The successes of the revolutionary movements intensified Jewish hopes of complete political integration. The 1850s also marked a period of rapid industrialization in Germany, which in turn further weakened the power of the guilds, increased the number of journeymen, and led them and their former masters into the industrial proletariat. Rapid industrialization also weakened the burghers' control over the cities, as they became centers of an expanding industrial population. It drew more Jews into the cities as they too joined the growing areas of the German economy, particularly trade and service rather than heavy industries. Full legal equality of the Jews followed the completion of German unification. Soon thereafter the German universities removed limits on entry (McClelland, 1980). Political, social, and economic change intensified their impact on the Jews of Germany.

These transformations began to occur in the Empire of the Tsars (Greenberg, 1944, 1:75–84; Baron, 1976a, pp. 39–42). In 1844, the government removed the political power of the kahals, and thirteen years later they stopped the cantonist system. The 1860s saw rapid change toward a more liberal policy regarding the Jews. "It is permitted" now replaced "It is prohibited," in the Tsar's edicts. Jewish university graduates could now enter the civil service; Jews could now join the merchant guilds and could live permanently in some areas heretofore barred to them, if they had sufficient wealth. Jewish artisans received permission to live outside the Pale of Settlement, and all Jews could now join the army. It seemed not to matter that the Tsar hated the Jews; he forbade, for example, the distinct clothing of the Hasidim. The new government policy attracted Jews into Russian society. Indeed, it now forbade proselytizing among Jewish students in government schools. Alexander II's most revolutionary change, of course, referred not to the Jews but to the peasants, the group that composed most of the Russian population. In 1861, he freed the serfs. Even in Russia the old order was crumbling.

As in the West, many Russian Jews took advantage of the new opportunities. In 1853, there were 179 Jewish students in all the gymnasia and pregymnasia of Russia (1 percent of the total). Ten years later, the number had grown to 552 (3 percent of those enrolled), and in 1873, the 2,362 Jews in those schools accounted for 13 percent of the student population. In that same year, the government closed the special Jewish schools (Nossig, 1887, p. 84; Greenberg, 1944, 1:83; Baron, 1976a, pp. 39–42). The Hebrew poet, Gordon, described the changes in the Jewish community:

I remember that in our city there was one Jewish student in the gymnasium. The youth would walk to school stealthily. He never appeared in the street in the school uniform, but would always leave it with the janitor in the gymnasium. He would come to school attired in his orthodox garb. Once there, however, he would change into his uniform, hide his earlocks behind this ears, and become a completely different person. This was his usual routine. Today, however, there is not a town where Jewish children do not drink the refreshing waters from a strange fountain. And they do it openly, without embarrassment. [Cited in Greenberg, 1944, 1:82]

Between 1870 and 1881, the total number of students in the middle schools and universities increased from 36,000 to 60,000 (65 percent); the growth of the Jewish student population was even higher, In Congress Poland, Jews were 4 percent of the university students in 1862 and 16 percent in 1880. Education was increasing for everyone, especially for the Jews (Nossig, 1887, pp. 85–86).

These changes varied by the institutional strength of the local Jewish communities. The older and more established the Jewish community, the lower the proportion of Jewish students in general schools. In Warsaw in 1879–80, there were 450 hederim and 494 government schools. All but 860 of the Jewish children attended the traditional Jewish schools. The proportion of Jews in government schools was considerably below their proportion of the school-age population (Nossig, 1887, pp. 84–85). In 1881, Jews in Vilna, another example of an established Jewish community, were 27 percent of the gymnasium and pregymnasium students and 40 percent of the city's residents. In contrast, Odessa, with a very new Jewish community, had the same proportion of Jews in the schools as in the population, 35 percent in 1881 (Greenberg, 1944, 1:117–18; Alston, 1969, p. 122). Similarly, in Petersburg, Moscow, Kiev, and Kharkov, all new cities of Jewish immigration, the percentage of Jews in the gymnasia equaled or exceeded their percentage in the population. In Congress Poland, in contrast, Jews were no more likely than non-Jews to attend the university (Nossig, 1887, pp.

85–86). In Hungary, Jews who moved into new areas where there were no Jewish schools sent their children to church or government schools. Those who remained in the rural communities kept their youngsters within the traditional Jewish hederim and yeshivot. In 1858, the total school population of Pest amounted to 18,270, including 1,973 Jewish boys and 493 Jewish girls. Thirty percent of these Jewish youngsters attended schools sponsored by the Jewish community. During the following school year, more than half the students in the Catholic secondary schools were Jews (Moskovits, 1964, p. 42). The pattern persisted even as the Jewish community built more schools. In 1868, there were 4,500 Jewish students in the combined area of Budapest; less than one-fourth attended the schools of the Jewish community. The remaining three-fourths depended entirely on the new type of religious as well as secular education that was prescribed by the government. (Moskovits, 1964, p. 123). Most Hungarian Jews still lived in the rural areas, and there they maintained their attachment to the traditional schools. Their children went to the hederim or nowhere at all. As late as the mid-1880s, 27 percent of the Jewish children in Hungary did not go to any school. Only the Greek Catholics had a higher percentage of nonattendance among their youngsters (Moskovits, 1964, p. 148). The evidence fits the argument that the relative availability of Jewish and secular schools was a crucial determinant of the patterns of school attendance.

Where the institutions of the Jewish community retained their strength, most Jewish children attended Jewish schools. It follows that urbanization by itself did not lead to the secularization of Jewish values and the disintegration of the Jewish comunities. Under some conditions, the move to urban places reinforced Jewish cohesiveness.

Unlike Germany and France, where the initial burst of industrialization resulted in increasing wealth of the Jewish communities, the beginnings of industrialization in Russia added to the poverty and unemployment of Jews. Improvements in transportation adversely affected the traditionally Jewish occupations of coachmen and innkeepers. Freeing the serfs reordered economic conditions in the countryside and affected those who worked for landowners and those who sold to peasants (Greenberg, 1944, 1:160–66; Baron, 1976a, pp. 94–98).

Overall economic development destroyed old and created new jobs (Baron, 1976a, pp. 80–84). I. J. Singer's novel, *The Brothers Ashkenazi*, depicts the tidal wave that threw Jewish artisans into Lodz:

Like a river in thaw, bursting its banks and carrying before it the dams and barriers which had long held it in, the Jewish population of Lodz and the surrounding country swarmed to the weaving trade, overthrowing in the rush of their hunger all the barriers, the special laws, ukases, prohibitions which a hostile government had erected against them. Thousands of country innkeepers, peddlers, and village merchants had been ruined with the ruin of the nobility. In the general movement which ensued—the search for bread—it was Lodz which sucked in the largest part of the unsettled population. In the little towns the Jewish dry-goods stores either were closed or stood empty from morning to night; young sixteen year-old wives, the supports of scholarly husbands who gave all their time to study the Talmud, sat there waiting for customers who came no more. For the nobility was either impoverished or exiled, and the liberated serfs were as poor as ever. Steadily the weaving business spread out of Lodz, and looms were set up in the townlets and villages; but Lodz remained the metropolis and chief center of attraction. . . . they came pouring in, setting up their looms everywere. . . . It was the custom to apprentice the boys for three years. A sum of money, the savings and scrapings of God knew how many seasons, was paid into the hand of the master weaver. They would get their meals and a place to sleep in, and from morning to night they would learn.

They stood in the hundreds at their looms, their skullcaps on their heads, the ritual fringes hanging over their cheap canvas trousers, pieces of colored thread clinging to their curly hair and sprouting beards, while their hands flew swiftly over the looms, weaving before sunrise till long after sunset the pieces which were made into dresses and women's handkerchiefs. As they worked they sang snatches from the synagogue services, trilling with bravura passages like real cantors, pausing with special joy on the sacred words of the high festivals. The master weavers paraded up and down the aisles, keeping an eye on the heaps of merchandise, urging the workers on, infuriated if one of them stopped to wipe the perspiration from his forehead or to roll himself a cigarette. [1959, pp. 24–26]

Swept along by the force of the industrial revolution, the Jewish artisans and journeymen of Russia, like other workmen across the continent, joined the industrial proletariat. Here, the Jews of Russia and Germany differed. In the West, where few Jews had been artisans and most were merchants and tradesmen, very few became workers. In Eastern Europe, where approximately one-third had been artisans, a proletarianization of the Jews accompanied the growth of various sorts of capitalists. Across the continent, some Jews quickly moved into the newly developing school systems, but in Russia some Jews also became increasingly poor and unable to afford education. As a result, the initial stages of the industrial revolution produced a sharper gap between Jews in Germany and in Russia than that caused solely by the timing and tempo of modernization.

THE EXPLANATION OF CHANGE
The movement of Jewish artisans and workers into the industrial proletariat of the Tsarist Empire serves again to emphasize the structural determinants of change, that is, the extent to which the transformation of personal lives and communities occurred not for reasons of preference or volition but as

the result of broader economic conditions and opportunities. Poverty, underemployment, and changing economic demand propelled people to change jobs. What was available combined with acquired skills to determine minimum conditions for occupational change. The location of the job and, for Jews, the relative economic opportunities established access and eligibility. It is not surprising that few Jews became farmers or agricultural workers—hardly anyone was then entering agriculture. No wonder Jewish artisans became industrial workers—so did most others like them. As Landes (1974) has argued, "The flow was not peculiar to the Jews. The nineteenth century was one of heightened geographic and occupational mobility for everyone" (p. 14). Jews moved with the forces that changed the societies in which they lived.

Did the Jews move faster than others? Landes combines motivational and structural factors into an affirmative response:

But the Jews were unquestionably quicker than most to take advantage of these opportunities, for many reasons: the rootlessness imposed on them by their general exclusion from ownership of land and by the precariousness of their residence; the adaptability they had learned in centuries of dodging persecution; the lack of ties to established professions. [Pp. 14–15]

Having begun the industrial revolution with "commercial interests and experience," they were especially well placed to take advantage of the new opportunities. At the same time, Landes adds, the Jews "were most comfortable" in independent economic activities, and they "preferred" commerce (p. 15). To support this position, Landes cites the atypical spread of the Jews into German cities and their prominence in the service industries and the liberal professions as well as in commerce and manufacturing.

Landes's use of motivational factors—"rootlessness," "adaptability," "preference," and "comfort"—to explain the pace of Jewish modernization must be qualified. The proletarianization of many Jews in Russia implies that preference and comfort mattered little where they did not have commercial skills, where they could not afford to go to schools, and where workshops and factories provided the only available jobs. Similarly, variable access to government and communal schools, more than educational values, determined which children entered the public schools. The very high proportion of town dwellers among the Jews made it much easier for them and others in the cities to become educated. Prince Nicholas Volkonsky, a landowner in Riazan province of Russia, bemoaned the fate of the nobles and their children: "Imagine the peculiarity of a government, which so laid out its school system that it serves townspeople preponderantly, while in the western region the majority of the urban population is Jewish, up to 90 percent in some places. Their broad scale education on state funds is at the expense of the basic population" (cited in Alston, 1969, p. 122). The modernization of Jewish communities over time and in different places reflected the particular structural features of the general societies and the Jews within them.

An analysis of the relative speed by which Jews modernized requires appropriate comparisons. All Germans are not the relevant benchmarks. Neither should all those in the Russian Empire be compared with the Jews. Rather, the process of Jewish modernization should be arrayed against those who shared similar conditions of life: Jews and other urban dwellers; all those in the merchant classes; Jews, Poles, Ukrainians, Russians, and Galicians in small villages in Eastern Europe; and similar examples. To compare, as many have done, the rate of Jewish urbanization and that of the German population as a whole is to relate a group that began the industrial revolution living in and around cities with another group consisting almost wholly of peasants. The different premodern conditions of Jews and non-Jews better explain the trajectory and pace of modernization (see Barkai, 1981; Shofer, 1981).

Within the Jewish community, the rate of modernization varied enormously. So much attention has been lavished on change that the millions of Jews who remained in traditional statuses are frequently overlooked. Economic development took longest to reach villages as well as small towns in Bavaria, Baden, Poland, the Ukraine, and Byelo-Russia. Yiddish remained the language of the vast majority of European Jews, and it persisted in strength even in parts of Germany, not only in Eastern Europe (Lowenstein, 1976; Freimark, 1979). Where Jews lived in or moved to rapidly developing areas—Berlin, Vienna, Paris, Lodz, Odessa, to name some of the most familiar—they changed rapidly. In the new areas, the institutions of the Jewish community were weakest and the power of the windstorm strongest. In the old areas, the well-established yeshivot and synagogues, associations and guilds, parnassim, and assorted organizations resisted the powers of change that had not yet reached gale force.

5 · New Religious Ideologies and Institutions: The Judaic Reformation as a Sociopolitical Process

As the ordered society of estates eroded and new social and political institutions emerged, the religion of the Jews changed. New religious ideologies, changes in the forms of public worship, and declines in personal religious observance accompanied the initial phases of modernization. In Western Europe, Judaism became the legal, political, and ideological definition of the Jewish people. Did the new religious ideologies determine changes in the synagogues? Did they lead to declines in the religious practices of the Jewish masses? Did they, on the other hand, halt the slide of the Jews toward assimilation and apostasy (J. Katz, 1972, pp. 84–87; 1974)? How is the modernization of Judaism related to the broader processes of transformation?

Religious ideologies are the work of the intellectual elite. The philosophers and rabbis who organized the Reform movement, the Historical school, and Neoorthodoxy provided new understandings of the place of Jews and Judaism in a modernizing world. They responded to philosophical challenges met in the universities and brought them from there to the Jewish communities. The ideologies developed as their spokesmen competed to control communal institutions, not as the unfolding logic of ideas. New synagogues and changes in the form of public worship emerged in response to conflicts between lay leaders and rabbis. They also derived from changes in government policies toward general issues of modernization and the specific place of Jews and Judaism.

Neither the new ideologies nor the ritual changes was the direct consequence of the demands of the Jewish masses. In Western Europe most Jews opposed or were indifferent to religious reforms. During the period of greatest intellectual innovation, the first half of the nineteenth century, the new religious ideas reached the smallest number of Jews. The era of greatest visible impact on the Jewish masses occurred when the ideologies had lost their intellectual vitality (Meyer, 1971; Rudavsky, 1967; Marcus, 1972; Weiner, 1962; Graupe, 1978).

The new ideologies and synagogues did not restructure the lives of the Jews. Religious decline resulted neither from the inability of old ideas to adapt to new conditions nor from the less demanding nature of some of the new religious ideologies, but from transformations in social conditions. Migrations to towns and cities with weak Jewish institutions, the growth of secular public education, and interaction with non-Jews in jobs and in new neighborhoods had much more to do with declining levels of personal religious observance. Similarly, continuing patterns of occupational and residential cohesion had more to do with the persistence of Jewish communities than the new religious ideologies. Our argument emphasizes the role of structural factors in determining ideological, institutional, and behavioral changes. The evidence we present rejects the assertion that ideological changes led the forces of religious modernization.

THE IDEOLOGY OF REFORM JUDAISM

Reform Judaism was the first of the new religious ideologies that emerged in Germany. It viewed Judaism as the Jews' unique quality. Jews were individuals with distinct religious beliefs but similar in all other ways to their Christian neighbors.

The movement's intellectual leaders persistently reiterated common themes: we have come not to diminish Judaism but to make it more meaningful to each Jew and to reach the increasingly indifferent masses, especially the youth. Sermons in German would uplift the spirit and the moral character, as would a service that is quiet, dignified, and orderly. These themes echoed the calls of reforming Protestant clergy. All these changes would combine to "edify" the Jew, and, thereby, bring him closer to the feelings of his Christian neighbors and the eternal tenets of Judaism (see Weiner, 1962; Plaut, 1963; Petuchowski, 1975; Graupe, 1978; Glatzer, 1978; Altmann, 1978; Sorkin, 1983).

They emphasized the religious feelings of individual Jews and their place in the changing Germany, while deemphasizing the importance of the Jews as a separate people and the distinctive Jewish ceremonies that would isolate Jews from modern society. Efforts to reform the prayer book rested on these principles: "That the people of Israel no longer lives, that Amalek has lost its significance for us, that Hebrew no longer lives, and that no hope is associated with Jerusalem" (Petuchowski, 1975, p. 45). A response to the blood libel in Syria, in 1840, highlights the importance of Jewish entry into German society and rejects a broader conception of Jewish peoplehood: "That the Jews in Prussia may have the chance to become pharmacists or lawyers is much more important to me than the rescue of all the Jews of Asia and Africa, an undertaking with which I sympathize as a human being" (Abraham Geiger, cited in Weiner, 1962, p. 90). The religious and lay leaders who joined the Reform efforts were particularly interested in smoothing the integration of Jews into German society (Rudavsky, 1967; Altmann, 1978).

The Reformers bemoaned the state of Jewry and Judaism. They claimed that the masses were religiously ignorant and performed the commandments by rote. They saw increasing rates of conversion to Christianity accompanying this religious indifference. The Reformers attacked the established rabbis for being unwilling and unable to respond to the exigencies of the times. Changes in religious norms, they argued, would reinvigorate religious practices. Many of their demands focused on the synagogue service and public worship. Decorum, sermons in the German language, clerical robes, choirs and music, they contended, would produce a properly dignified worship. All would result in the edification of the individual Jew, whose conscious acceptance of the commandments became the requisite for proper, religious behavior (Plaut, 1963; Weiner, 1962; Meyer, 1967, 1971; Rudavsky, 1967; Graupe, 1978; Altmann, 1964a; Glatzer, 1978).

These ideas legitimated the most visible religious changes of the era, new synagogues and alterations in the worship service. In 1817, the group establishing the Reform temple in Hamburg proclaimed:

Since public worship has for some time been neglected by so many, because of the ever decreasing knowledge of the language by which alone it has until now been conducted, and also because of many other shortcomings which have crept in at the same time—the undersigned, convinced of the necessity to restore public worship to its deserving dignity and importance, having joined . . . together to arrange . . . a dignified and well-ordered ritual . . . Specifically, there shall be introduced at such services a German sermon and choral singing to the accompaniment of an organ. [Cited in Mendes-Flohr and Reinharz, 1980, p. 145]

Other communal leaders reiterated the same claims.

Those seeking to change the worship service struggled to control the religious institutions. The legal proclamations issued in Cassel, Westphalia, in 1810, at the inauguration of the first of these new synagogues, introduced a set of directives that reappeared over and over again, emphasizing order, decorum, and dignity (Petuchowski, 1968, pp. 106–11; Marcus, 1972). The first paragraph permits services in only one synagogue in Cassel, a political statement of particular importance. The second paragraph establishes the role of the warden as the supervisor of the synagogue, and the next permits the employment of only one cantor-sexton, to be approved by the temple board. Other paragraphs proposed to enforce a dress code, prohibit children younger than four years of age from attending services, and establish the central role of the temple's cantor, and no others, in the worship service. Paragraph 16 sets out the new form of sermon: "Since rabbinical discussions do not belong in the synagogues, no rabbi is to deliver Talmudic or Kabbalis-

tic or mystical discourses. He should speak about the teachings of religion or
ethics only" (Petuchowski, 1968, p. 109). Another paragraph limits the
calling-up to the Torah to those who have taken family names, thereby
fostering integration into the general society. This synagogue opened to a
procession of dignity and pomp in which Jews and Gentiles entered together
to the peal of church bells (Marcus, 1972, pp. 86–88). The goal of the
temples and new services was to establish a Judaism befitting the times and
the equal place of Judaism in the emerging Germany.

THE RESPONSE OF THE ESTABLISHED RABBIS

The Reformers did not enter a Jewish community devoid of alternative
ideologies and rabbis. The various Jewish communities were led by established rabbis, whose power rested on political as well as religious legitimacy.
The established rabbis denied the Reformers' criticisms and plans. Most
fundamentally, they denied the Reformers' right to an ideology. The members of various rabbinical courts responded to the intellectual and religious
challenges as well as to the attacks on established authority (Burak, 1967;
Jung, 1953; Schwab, n.d.; Plaut, 1963, pp. 34–37; A. Guttman, 1977). The
Hamburg Rabbinical Court evoked these themes in 1815 as they responded
to the new temple:

These are the words of the covenant with Jacob, a law unto Israel, an
eternal covenant; the word of God is one forever and forever. [These
words are uttered] in accordance with the Torah and by judgment of the
court of justice of the holy community of Hamburg—may the Lord bless
it well—with the support of the leading men of learning in Germany,
Poland, France, Italy, Bohemia, Moravia and Hungary. All of them join
together . . . to abolish a *new law* [which was fabricated by several
ignorant individuals unversed in the Torah] instituting practices which
are not in keeping with the law of Moses and Israel. [Cited in Mendes-
Flohr and Reinharz, 1980, p. 150]

Their political legitimacy derived, they maintained, from God and the
Torah.

The court then prohibited the "three cardinal sins" of the Reformers:
changes in the prayers, German sermons, and the use of musical instruments
in the synagogues on Sabbaths and festivals. The rabbis based their injunc-
tion on their established authority as a court and not on the religious-legal
sources of the halacha. The Reformers lacked the piety, holiness, and
knowledge, so they argued, to effect religious changes. These were not only
differences of ideological posture and attachment. These were mainly conflicts over authority. They concluded their pronouncement:

Brethren, the children of Israel, it shall not be; Israel has not yet been
abandoned. There are still judges in the land who are zealous for God's

sake and who will rend the arm, crack the skull of him who pursues the sin of the Reformers. To these judges we shall hasten for aid. . . . Accordingly, we have girded our loins and written to the famous learned men of the holy communities of Germany, Poland, Bohemia, Moravia and Italy. We have sent them our legal judgment. [Cited in Mendes-Flohr and Reinharz, 1980, p. 152]

Calling on the police as well as the legal and religious authority of the established communities, these rabbis pronounced their negation of the Reformers' efforts.

Conflict between the established rabbis and the Reformers did not occur uniformly across Germany. Not all areas had movements for religious reform, and in those places the established rabbis did not take part in the conflict (Lowenstein, 1981a). They, therefore, did not develop any ideological response. Only in those areas where Reform emerged, as in Hamburg, was there an immediate reaction. Over time, these ideological disputes were translated into political maneuvering which involved large numbers of rabbis and their institutions.

When the established rabbis deigned to examine the Reformers' intellectual claims, they dismissed them out of hand. Since the commandments were established by God, their habitual performance was not necessarily a problem. Personal edification, in and of itself, was not the point of the prayer service. Legal authority prescribed that public prayer could be conducted in no language but Hebrew:

Our sages of blessed memory said that the world was created in Hebrew. . . . If this is so, then this is the language of the Holy One, Blessed Be He, in which He gave us His Torah and it is inconceivable to speak before Him in our everyday language. Rather, we should speak the special language befitting His holy words. This is the opinion of the men of the Great Assembly who established the texts of the prayers and benedictions in the Holy Tongue. [Moses Sofer, cited in Mendes-Flohr and Reinharz, 1980, p. 155]

Communal prayer is bound by the traditions and legal precedents of the community's courts.

The different styles of language that emerge in these documents reflect profound conceptual differences. In turn, these divergences tie to dissensus and conflict over communal authority. There were few halachic prohibitions on prayer in languages other than Hebrew, and legal precedent abounds in rabbinic literature to permit prayer in local languages. These precedents were not invoked. The issue was not only legal but political as well. The primary concern seems to have been less with theological correctness than with authority structure and political legitimacy.

As much as the established rabbis understood the political challenge of the Reformers, they misjudged their own strength. They could do little to shore up the erosion of their authority. Even a generation earlier, Berlin was not Vilna (see Chapter 2). As political conditions in the general and Jewish communities changed, so did the power of the established and Reform rabbis. Over time, others used new ideas and political techniques to defend the received religion. Conflict between the Neoorthodox and the Reformers also occurred in the language of theology and religion. It derived, however, from efforts to control communal institutions.

IDEOLOGIES AND INSTITUTIONAL CHANGES

The established rabbis erred in another way. Although Reform rabbis called for changes in the rituals and worship services, their pronouncements were neither necessary nor sufficient conditions for these changes. In France, rabbis became preachers and pastors, not judges; they wore clerical robes, gave sermons in French, and introduced choirs into the worship service. More generally, the French rabbinate echoed the role and organizational structure of the Catholic Church (Albert, 1977). No conferences of Reform rabbis met in France, no journals of Reform theology were published, no new historical studies were completed, and yet the same changes that occurred in the religious service in Germany took place in France. Indeed, Reform Judaism, as an ideological movement, did not arrive in France until 1905, when church and state formally disassociated (Marrus, 1971; Hyman, 1979).

These same changes followed the extension of French rule and the establishment of consistories. Reforms in Cassel occurred when Westphalia was ruled by Jerome, Napoleon's brother, who permitted the new temple. When French rule ended in 1815, the consistory and temple collapsed (Schwarzfuchs, 1979; Marrus, 1971). Similar changes occurred farther to the East. Napoleon's short-lived Grand Duchy of Warsaw also witnessed the inaugurati on of a Reform Temple, which dissolved when French rule ended (Hagen, 1980). The comparison of areas under French and German governments makes clear that political change played a direct and central role in effecting change in religious institutions. Hence, an ideology of religious reform was not a necessary condition for the emergence of new synagogues.

What accounts for an ideology espousing religious reform in Germany and not in France? In part, the answer relates to dominant philosophical issues in the German universities as well as the employment patterns in these countries. The rise of a Reform ideology and movement reflected intellectual and employment problems particular to German university students, especially those in the arts and humanities. The giants of German philosophy, first Kant and then Hegel, attacked Judaism and challenged the faith of many Jewish students. At the same time, those who sought to pursue careers in philosophy and teaching were legally barred from employment in the gymnasia and universities. Many accepted positions in the newly created

Jewish communal schools or as rabbis who could give sermons in the German language. The university world in France may have been as harsh on the faith of Jewish students, but it provided them with jobs in French schools. The rise of a new Jewish ideology required both new ideas and a mechanism for their diffusion into the Jewish community.

In the world of German universities at the end of the eighteenth century, no figure challenged Kant's intellectual supremacy. He provided the agenda for scholarly discussion and his answers dominated all others (Altmann, 1964a; Rosenbloom, 1976; Schorsch, 1977; Graupe, 1978; Low, 1979; Rotenstreich, 1963). His challenge to Judaism was direct and overpowering. Accepting Mendelssohn's definition of Judaism as a religion of laws and actions, not beliefs, Kant argued that Judaism was not a religion since it did not require conscious individual choice. The religion of Jewish students was not only the social, economic, and political burden that it had always been but it was now an intellectual embarrassment. "Kant's views on Judaism must have been especially agonizing for the Jewish intellectuals of the period. Not only did Judaism fail to compare favorably with Christianity, it was inferior even to polythesim" (Rosenbloom, 1976, p. 14). Jewish intellectuals could not repel his attack, and "agonizingly acquiesced" (ibid., p. 14; see also Marcus, 1972; Schwarcz, 1971; Graupe, 1978; Ben-David cited in Mendes-Flohr and Reinharz, 1980, p. 94).

Many of the fundamental ideas of the Reformers were responses to Kant. Not being able to refute his philosophical claims, they attacked the accuracy of his understanding of Judaism. Redefining the faith, they reduced the place of the commandments and increased the significance of personal meaning attached to religious action. Prayer and the worship service, they argued, must uplift the individual. It must, therefore, take place in a language that he understands. In Judaism, like all religions that fit Kant's definition, the individual must freely choose to do good. Obedience to external law, like the halacha, stands at the most distant edge of religion. Furthermore, Judaism is a set of principles and beliefs. It is not the religion of a particular nation or ethnic group. It does not require a halacha and a system of political controls to sustain its validity. Hence, it will persist as the religion of those who autonomously choose to live by its tenets, without their being a people and without political autonomy. Only this view, argued the Reformers, permits Judaism to stand as a philosophy of equal value to the other religions of Germany.

A generation later, Hegel provided an alternative to Kant's philosophy and another challenge to Jewish intellectuals (Meyer, 1967; Rotenstreich, 1959, 1963). Hegel's ideas led to a new justification for Jews and Judaism, tying them to the historical link between ideas and people. According to the Hegelians, the idea-structure of Judaism was not necessarily religious and was not controlled by the rabbis. Rather, it emerged out of the life of the people and was best understood by the intellectuals. Reflecting their academic world, they formed the institutions of what would become known as the Historical School, The Society for the Preservation of the Jewish People, and the Society for the Culture and Science of the Jews (*Wissenschaft des Judentums*). They too were embarrassed by Judaism's intellectual weaknesses and adapted the dominant philosophy of their day to support their ideas (Glatzer, 1964, 1976). They attacked the intellectual bases of the established rabbis as well as their political power (Schorsch, 1977, 1980). The intellectuals who formed the Wissenschaft des Judentums offered a new understanding of the place of Jews and Judaism in the rapidly changing world of Germany (Rudavsky, 1967, pp. 188–217; Mendes-Flohr and Reinharz, 1980, pp. 186–214; Glatzer, 1964; Schorsch, 1981).

The members of the Historical School remained a small group of scholars. Few were appointed rabbis or assistant rabbis; few controlled synagogues; at best their influence was felt in the community schools and the new rabbinical seminary in Breslau. They offered an intellectual challenge when only political success led to change in religious institutions. These intellectual issues affected very few Jewish students and, therefore, relatively few Jews. In any year during the first third of the nineteenth century, fewer than 1,000 Jews were among the 10,000–15,000 university students in Germany, and at the very most one-fifth of them studied in the faculties of humanities (Ringer, 1979, p. 291; McClelland, 1980, p. 157). We assume, therefore, that these intellectual challenges affected fewer than 200 Jewish students. Contemporary sources indicate even smaller numbers (Philippson, 1962; Meyer, 1974, 1979). A total of forty-two rabbis attended Reform rabbinical conferences in Germany in the 1840s (Lowenstein, 1981a). Hence, hardly any Jews took part in these intellectual debates.

The problems for these students extended beyond the realm of philosophy. The path to teaching in the gymnasia and universities was blocked to Jews who sought to pursue their philosophical interests. Several career options stood before them: they could forego their intellectual interests for a commercial career; they could leave Germany and pursue their scholarship in France; they could renounce their attachment to Judaism and convert to Christianity, thereby obtaining the "key to entrance into European civilization." If they maintained their attachment to philosophy, Judaism, and their families, they could pursue a career only within the educational and religious institutions of the Jewish community. Although most took careers in commerce, several chose Christianity and others migrated to France (J. Katz, 1972; Philippson, 1962). Most remained in Germany as Jews.

The primary career possibilities in the Jewish community outside the world of commerce were teaching in the new schools, such as the Freischule in Dessau, and serving as rabbis in synagogues seeking clergy fluent in German (Philippson, 1962; Schorsch, 1977; Galliner, 1958; Meyer, 1979,

1980). Hence, the intellectual and career sources of all Reform rabbis and members of the Historical School fit this pattern. The philosophical and occupational pressures on these intellectuals were necessary conditions for the formation and diffusion of these new ideologies.

The same pattern applies to those who became leaders of Neo-orthodoxy, the other religious ideology to form during the middle third of the century. Unlike the established rabbis, the leaders of Neoorthodoxy attended universities and grappled with the same philosophical issues as the Reformers (Weiner, 1962; Rosenbloom, 1976; Schorsch, 1981). Having resigned as Chief Rabbi of Bohemia and Moravia, Hirsch returned to Frankfurt to lead an independent synagogue (see Chapter 4). He installed an ideology and movement distinct from the Reformers and the traditional Orthodox. Hirsch insisted on a quiet, dignified service, and delivered sermons in German. Hirsch battled the Reformers with their own weapons. He wrote religious treatises in the idiom of German philosophy. Using their political tactics, he maneuvered within the Jewish and general communities, established newspapers, journals, separate schools, and synagogues.

The new ideologies—Reform, Neoorthodox, and the Historical School—had little impact on the religious beliefs and practices of the Jewish masses in Germany. Most Jews fit into one of three types (see Ben-David in Mendes-Flohr and Reinharz, 1980, pp. 92–94; Meyer, 1980; Graupe, 1978; Petuchowski, 1964): (1) Those who would change no part of the worship service, retaining the prayers and observances handed to them by their fathers. Even at mid-century, this group probably amounted to a majority. (2) Those like the founders of the temples in Cassel, Hamburg, and Berlin, who sought a service sufficiently dignified and modern to enable them to stand proud in the general community. This group predominated among the commercial elite and the lay leaders of the communities. (3) A third group remained part of the Jewish community but did not follow any of the religious practices and knew little of the beliefs (see Ben-David in Mendes-Flohr and Reinharz, 1980, pp. 92–94; Meyer, 1980). None of these groups contained individuals with profound theological and philosophical concerns. The relative size of the groups varied by locale and over time, but the variations had little to do with the ideology espoused by the local rabbi. Similar patterns characterize French Jewry (Albert, 1977; Szajkowski, 1970).

POLITICS AND CHANGE IN RELIGIOUS INSTITUTIONS

Political factors rather than ideologies or mass demands account for the diffusion of new temples and changes in religious services. In France, relatively high national unity, government centralization, and official ties between the state and the Jewish community through the consistories ensured that religious institutions changed in a generally uniform way across regions. Only resistance from some communities and rabbis in Alsace slowed this process (Albert, 1977, p. 295). There is no evidence to support a claim that in Germany changes in a worship service occurred because the congregants sought a more meaningful form of prayer. Neither did the retention of the established service result from the preferences of the Jewish masses.

Was it economic or political factors which determined religious institutional change? Evidence indicates that there is no correlation between areas of economic expansion and the presence of Reform temples and rabbis. Nor does the size of the Jewish community vary systematically with type of synagogue present. Reform rabbis were as likely to serve rural small towns as large urban congregations. The areas of Western Germany, where most Jews were agricultural middlemen, were those with the largest number of Reform institutions (Lowenstein, 1981a).

Our emphasis on the centrality of political factors in determining the presence of new religious institutions helps clarify what appears puzzling and unexplained by previous research. Three political factors are critical: (1) a state government with a general policy of modernization and a specific policy fostering the use of the German language and the economic integration of Jews, (2) lay leaders who sought to further the integration of Jews by having a more impressive worship service with an emphasis on German sermons, (3) a rabbi who identified with the Reform movement. Where all three came together there were German sermons, clerical garb, choirs, decorum, and the other ritual changes of Reform. The regions of Nassau, Saxe-Weimar, Wurttemberg, and Baden were among the first to exhibit this pattern (Schreiber, 1892; W. Mosse, 1981, 1979; Lowenstein, 1981a; Rudavsky, 1967; Petuchowski, 1968; Weiner, 1962; Strauss, 1966). Where all three opposed change—the government as part of a general reactionary policy, the lay leaders, and the rabbi too—these ritual reforms did not occur. After a start toward political modernization, Bavaria exemplifies this pattern for much of the century.

It is possible to rank these factors in their relative order of importance. The policy of the local government seems to be most important. It served as a necessary condition for religious reform and at times came close to being a sufficient condition as well. One key element was the law that lasted until mid-century that limited each Jewish community to one synagogue. Hence, control of the synagogue determined the nature of the worship service for all members of the community. The first and most obvious example of the effects of this law in Germany occurred in Cassel, Westphalia. Another government policy required rabbis to have university degrees and academic training. Modernizing governments in Baden, Hesse, and Wurttemberg, western areas with predominately rural Jewish populations engaged in cattle dealing, illustrate this pattern. In 1834, the Wurttemberg government dismissed forty-five rabbis who had not passed the state qualifying examination (Schorsch, 1981; Lowenstein, 1981a). Hence, once this political policy is taken into account, it is not at all surprising that the western areas of Germany had relatively large numbers of Reform rabbis. Modernizing civil servants bent on rationalizing governments and economies took as one of their policy goals the education and the reorganization of the local Jews.

Where government policy opposed all forms of change, it precluded the spread of religious reform among the Jews. The case of Berlin clearly illustrates this point. Given the history of the Prussian capital as an early center of the Jewish Enlightenment, and given the presence of a Reform temple there in 1815, it may seem surprising that Berlin did not emerge as a leading center of religious reform. Prussian political reaction, in general, and specific policies that followed Napoleon's defeat in 1815 explain the relative absence of the Reformers until after mid-century. The Prussian Emperor simply forbade religious reform among the Jews. In 1823, a Prussian court decreed that rabbis might not wear clerical robes or preach in German. These being Gentile customs, they must not be brought into the Jewish community. It took seventeen years of appeals for the Reformers to have the decision reversed. The Prussian government served as the court of last appeal in the struggles between the Reform and Orthodox and almost always favored the latter. It ruled, for example, that the Reformers might not enroll all the Jewish children in their schools (Meyer, 1979; Rudavsky, 1967; Strauss, 1966). Thus, in regions of political reaction, government policy blocked all forms of change, including religious reform among the Jews.

Where the government had no policy, the desires of the lay leaders and the rabbi determined the nature of the worship service (see Altmann, 1978). Where they agreed, they prevailed. Resistance by local Jews could be overcome, and indifference certainly provided no barrier. Where the rabbi and local leaders split, then the rabbi's legal power allowed him to block their demands (Carlebach, 1964; Lowenstein, 1981a). The lay leaders required government intervention to overcome their rabbi's resistance. Where the rabbi opposed reform, lay leaders sought government permission to hire an assistant rabbi to preach in German. Where there was a Reform rabbi, the lay leaders turned to the legal authorities to dismiss him. Sometimes, only the establishment of a new synagogue resolved the conflict. This too required government approval (Lowenstein, 1981a; Weiner, 1962; Rosenbloom, 1976). The Neoorthodox success in Frankfurt used interest group politics to obtain from the Prussian government the right to secede from the legally sanctioned Jewish community. Hirsch succeeded in the face of massive opposition from the Jews of the city, whatever their religious ideology. Those who joined his synagogue either worked for him or, as Polish immigrants, had no ties to the local community. Hirsch did not ride the crest of a mass movement. Instead, having obtained legal independence, he used the institutional bases of a separate community, especially the schools and synagogue, to build the movement (Rosenbloom, 1976; Schwab, n.d.). Government policy and political maneuvering within the Jewish community helped to spread Neoorthodoxy as well as Reform.

Over time, and particularly after mid-century, government policies played a smaller role in Jewish communal life. Increasing economic, educational, and linguistic integration of the Jews resulted in declining government intervention in the internal affairs of the Jewish community. Subsequent religious institutional change, therefore, derived less from government policies than from conflict and competition among Jews.

The religious ideologies were elite expressions. Where their spokesmen fought with each other, very few Jews entered the fray. The most well known of these battles occurred in Breslau in the middle of the nineteenth century and involved a vote among 1,500 householders (10 percent of the Jewish population). The Reformers lost (Weiner, 1962, p. 32). Where one group prevailed, there is little evidence that they actually affected the beliefs and practices of their congregants. The schools of the Reform and the Neoorthodox initially reached relatively few Jewish students.

Nahman's windstorm, as we have seen, moved Jews into new homes and places of living, weakened old institutions, and created new ones. As the kehillot declined, adherence to the established religious norms rested on personal choices. The observance of religious commandments had previously rested on the absence of other alternatives and the sanctions of the established community. It is not surprising, therefore, that we find declines in the frequency and intensity of personal religious practices as new alternatives emerged and as traditional social, economic, and political sanctions weakened. As the Jewish population expanded, existing schools and synagogues were overwhelmed. As people moved to new cities, they encountered relatively few institutions of the Jewish community. In Paris, for example, there were four synagogues for the more than 50,000 Jews who lived there at mid-century (Marrus, 1971, p. 56). No more than 15 percent of the male adults could have attended synagogue services together in the French capital. The same pattern applies to other new centers of Jewish population. As long as the prohibition of more than one synagogue in the various German towns and cities held, most German Jews had little or no contact with that most important agency of a Jewish community. Hederim, private teachers, and new schools could not accommodate the growing number of Jewish children. New educational opportunities in general schools provided attractive alternatives. Informal Jewish education did not compensate for these new patterns of schooling. These transformations did not mainly reflect preferences for one type of education but the availability of alternative schools. The structure of opportunities and access, not values, determined educational choices.

Over time, those who studied in established, Neoorthodox, and Reform schools were taught different curricula. More important, they developed allegiances to these branches of Judaism. Many had no formal Jewish education, and their Jewishness was likely to be associated with nonreligious communal institutions. Hence, synagogues and schools provided some bases for cohesion, while generating competition and conflict within the Jewish community. At the same time, the institutions maintained an image of a distinct body of Jews. They did not cause that distinction but helped to sustain it in the minds of Jews and non-Jews alike. The image neither determined nor impeded Jewish continuity. It legitimated and rationalized the broader changes that were unfolding.

The rise of new ideologies, declining personal religious observance, and the formation of new forms of public worship were all responses to political and social modernization. They paralleled similar developments in the broader society (Field, 1980; Lidtke, 1980). Hence, while focusing on the Jews as a case study, our hypotheses derive from a general orientation to modernization and group cohesion. Our key explanatory factors are particular elements of political and educational modernization combined with population growth and urbanization. The new ideologies did not determine changes in religious behavior or institutions. The ideas of Reform, the Historical School, and Neoorthodoxy are what must be explained. It is inadequate, therefore, to view the new religious ideologies and institutions as examples of assimilation. Similarly, those who obtained no Jewish education or rarely attended religious services had other bases for Jewish continuity. Communal organizations, socioeconomic, and residential patterns maintained Jewish cohesion in new forms. Modernization meant the differentiation of religious from other institutions as well as the creation of new supports for the Jewish community.

Part III: The Transformation of European Jewish Communities

Western and Eastern Europe provided distinctive settings for the Jewish communities of that continent. By the decades surrounding World War I, Germany, Austria, and France exemplified various patterns of rapid and thorough modernization and housed relatively small and highly urban Jewish communities. Poland and other parts of the former Russian Pale contained relatively larger proportions and numbers of Jews living in dozens of medium-sized cities. Here the pattern of general occupation change, educational expansion, and political modernization was relatively slow and incomplete. There were, therefore, sharp contrasts between the transformations of the Jewish communities in the two areas. Even in the West, however, the changes led to new bases of ethnic cohesion, not assimilation. In both areas, the advent of revolutionary regimes fundamentally altered the conditions of survival for the Jewish communities. Nazi and Soviet terror destroyed almost all the Jewish communities of Europe.

6 · The Tempo and Intensity of Modernization: Assimilation or Transformation in Western Europe

The pace of modernization intensified across Europe during the decades around the turn of the twentieth century. The processes of social, economic, and political change continued to transform the cities of Western Europe and began to reach towns and villages. Nahman's windstorm was recarving the face of Europe. Accelerated change, diffusion throughout the various economic sectors and social strata within nations, and the extension of these changes throughout Europe became the dominant features of modernization as the new century began.

How did these patterns of intensive modernization affect the Jews and their communities? We shall describe the ways in which the rapid increase and spread of social changes—particularly urbanization, education, and occupation—characterized Jews and extended to encompass larger segments in Western Europe. In particular, we focus on whether the intensification of modernization resulted in the continuous assimilation of Jews and the disintegration of their communities. We begin in Western Europe where modernization was most intense, where there were relatively few Jews, and where the organizations and institutions of the Jewish community were poorly developed compared to the Jews of Eastern Europe.

The way modernization affects a Jewish community reflects three factors: the initial levels of modernity, the strength and pace of change in the broader society, and the particular characteristics of the Jewish community. The degree of urbanization among German Jews in 1900, for example, derived from changes in German urbanization, the prior extent of Jewish urban concentration, and the opportunities for Jews in particular sectors of the economy. Similarly, differences among Jewish communities result from these processes. Prior levels of Jewish urbanization, the general pace of urban change, and differential economic structure and opportunities account for differences in the urbanization of German and Polish Jewries at the turn of the twentieth century.

We draw on general theories of ethnic continuity to analyze the consequences of intense social change (Chapter One). One model posits that the

increased pace of change led to the disintegration of the traditional sources
of cohesiveness in the Jewish community. The breakdown of the old order
began the assimilation of Jews into the new society. Losing their distinctive
place, Jews moved geographically and socially, finding new jobs and becoming more educated. In the more modern, urban sectors of societies, the
workings of the economic market, residential and occupational integration,
and the absence of traditional sources of Jewish social and political control
led to the community's disintegration. National integration and universalism led to ethnic assimilation and discontinuity. In the transition to full
assimilation, some countries, regions, and social groups (for example, Eastern Europe, the rural poor, the least educated, the most "traditional")
participated later. Over time, however, these differences are expected to
disappear and areas, groups, and countries converge. For Jews, the lags and
timing differences in modernization reflect local political and social conditions. Sometimes anti-Semitism, perhaps the strength of Jewish values, and
the resistance of the religious elite slowed the effects of modernization and
its diffusion. But these variations in pace and intensity are viewed as transitory and largely unimportant in the grand sweep of modernization, diffusion, and assimilation. The model argues, in effect, that nothing stands in
the way of the windstorm.

Another model has a different set of predictions and interpretations. It
argues that as the pace of modernization increased and the old order
declined, conflict and competition along ethnic lines developed. While
modernity allowed some to assimilate, most did not. Occupational, residential, and educational changes moved Jews to new locations and jobs and to
greater exposure to non-Jews. But in the new order, Jews continued to
interact with Jews. They concentrated in new occupations and built new
communal institutions. Hence, modernization created new forms of Jewish
cohesion as it destroyed old forms. In particular, the socioeconomic redistribution of Jews continued to distinguish them from non-Jews and create
conditions of ethnic solidarity. The structural bases of Jewish continuity is
central, therefore, to the argument.

Variations within and across nations do not necessarily represent lags or
transitions. Rather, the theory argues, as the pace of modernization intensified, competition and conflict emerged over jobs and opportunities. In
turn, this competition reinforced ethnic group solidarity. Hence, over time,
the process of uneven modernization created gaps within and between
groups, each seeking to preserve its own cohesion and defend its own
interests. Within countries, forms of "internal colonialism" emerged.
Ethnicity did not disappear. In particular, new ethnic organizations and
institutions replaced older institutions to reinforce the new bonds. Diverg-
ence of ethnic groups, reinforced political interests separating communities,
and ideologies legitimating the new order appeared.

These two models guide our interpretation of the evidence. Our own perspective emphasizes the role of community size and institutions, occupational patterns, the structure of opportunities, and the pace of change in the broader society as the main shapers of emergent Jewish communities in modernization. We find little evidence for cultural lag, the centrality of Jewish values, or the role of anti-Semitism as major sources for variations across and within nations or over time. In addition, we argue that the relative size and economic structure of the Jewish community affected the pattern of internal conflict. The larger the community and the greater the occupational diversity, the more likely were Jews to compete with other Jews over jobs, salaries, access to schools, and other valued positions and opportunities. Variations in the pace of general and local modernization and levels of political and social conflict combined with the size of the Jewish communities and the extent of communal organization to determine the pattern of Jewish cohesion.

INTENSIVE MODERNIZATION

Rapid industrialization, urbanization, political mobilization, and national integration were the most conspicuous manifestations of intensified change. An increasing number of people left farm labor and artisan workshops seeking work in the expanding factories of urban places. Mechanization and the use of inanimate sources of energy expanded. Cities grew in size and in density of population. National school systems extended within the burgeoning cities and into towns and villages. Improved means of travel and communication facilitated the spread of the national language and fostered new attachments to the nation and the state. Military conscription, particularly during World War I, was a major step in national political integration.

While reaching all of Europe, the level and pace of change varied. At any point in time, therefore, there were major differences among and within nations in the amount of change that had occurred and the extent of diffusion through the social strata. While patterns of growth and change might have been similar for two nations, their different starting points imply different levels at any point in time. A simple example illustrates the importance of the point. Britain, the country that inaugurated the industrial revolution, had a capacity of steam engines of 620,000 horsepower in 1840. This compared to 90,000 in France, 40,000 in Germany, and 20,000 in Austria and the entire Tsarist Empire. Toward the end of the nineteenth century, the capacity of steam engines had increased to almost 14 million horsepower in Britain, 6 million in France, 8 million in Germany, 2.5 million in Austria, and over 3 million in Tsarist Russia (Milward and Saul, 1977; Minchinton, 1973; for related data see, among others, Berend and Ranki, 1974; Crisp, 1976; Wandycz, 1974; E. Weber, 1976). These and related pieces of evidence on urbanization, industrial expansion, economic infrastructure, productive capacity, and other indicators of industrialization-modernization point clearly to the different starting points, the varied rates of change, and their various levels at any point in time. The data reveal as well the enormous expansion, rapid pace, and diffusion of change throughout the nations of Europe. Thus, while all these countries were increasing their levels of production and consumption, and incorporating new technologies in new places, the levels of development remained different.

The patterns of change in Europe transformed the lives of individuals. For many, the travail of the factory took the place of working the land. Advances in technology and transportation increased agricultural production and brought more and better food to the cities. The prospect of famine disappeared. Thus, the number and proportion of persons whose lives were little more than a struggle for survival declined.

POPULATION GROWTH, URBANIZATION, AND MIGRATIONS

Demographic changes in the Jewish community are one manifestation of intensive modernization. During the last decades of the nineteenth century and the first few of the twentieth century, the number of Jews in Central and Western Europe increased, as did the proportion of Jews living in cities. Between 1880 and 1900, the number of Jews there (excluding Hungary) grew by about 25 percent, reaching 1,318,500 at the turn of the century. In 1925, the population was 1,677,000 and its rate of increase had slowed (Lestchinsky, 1928b; Engelman, 1973, pp. 108–10; Rubinow, 1975, p. 495). More important, Jews became heavily concentrated in large cities. Between 1880 and 1900, the size of the Jewish population in Berlin doubled, reaching nearly 100,000 Jews, and increasing to over 170,000 by 1925 (Pulzer, 1964; Shofer, 1981; Seeliger, 1958; Ruppin, 1904, p. 42; Della Pergola, 1981a; Engelman, 1973, p. 234; Lestchinsky, 1928b). In Vienna, we find a similar pattern: 73,000 in 1880, 175,000 in 1910, 202,000 in 1923, over 10 percent of the population (Pulzer, 1964; Rosensaft, 1976; Goldhammer, 1927).

The rate of Jewish urban growth was significantly higher than the general increase in population and was the result of migration to cities. These patterns translated into a high urban concentration for the Jews of Western Europe (Weinryb, 1946, pp. 16–18). Moreover, urbanization was higher among Jews than non-Jews. In Germany at the turn of the century, nearly half the Jews (compared to 17 percent of the non-Jews) lived in cities with populations greater than 100,000. By 1925, two-thirds of German Jewry were in these cities compared to one-fourth of the non-Jews (Engelman, 1973, p. 202; see also Schmelz, 1982). In 1900, approximately one-fourth of the Jews and 10 percent of the non-Jews of Austria lived in cities with populations greater than 50,000 (Ruppin, 1904, p. 44). In 1934, nearly 93 percent of the Austrian Jews lived in Vienna (Engelman, 1973, p. 203). By 1920, Western European Jewry was fully urbanized.

All these examples highlight several major features of population growth and urbanization of Jews. First, Jewish population size increased in absolute numbers and shifted to new locations and residential concentrations. It was not fortuitous that Jews moved to urban places where social and economic modernization was most intense. It is likely that the Jewish pattern was closer to that of non-Jews within their country than to Jews in other countries. Urban Jews in Western Europe had lower fertility than the non-Jewish population and lower even than other city dwellers. Part of these distinctive Jewish patterns reflected the particular social and economic circumstances of Jews. Some part might have reflected their sociopolitical status and position as a minority group. Nevertheless, there is no evidence to suggest that some universally shared Jewish values or distinctive Jewish family patterns were the primary determinants of the differences between Jews and others. Given the variations across countries and the changes within countries, no universal Jewish value on fertility can be postulated.

A second feature of the evidence is the relative concentration of Jews compared to non-Jews in large cities. This directly resulted from migration, not a high natural increase in cities. Urbanization had greater consequences for the Jewish community since a larger proprotion of Jews lived in cities. Nevertheless, while most Jews were in cities, most city dwellers were not Jewish. City life exposed Jews to expanding economies and new opportunities. Growth in size implied changing forms of authority and control of the Jewish community and the expansion and transformation of institutions. Urban growth brought about new residential patterns and migrations.

Much of the particular expansion in local areas—in cities and urban places—was, thus, the direct result of net migration. As others, Jews were on the move toward the larger urban centers where new industrial jobs and related economic activities awaited them. Much of Posen Jewry went to Berlin (Seeliger, 1958; Hagen, 1980; Ruppin, 1973, p. 63). Significant numbers of Jews from lower Austria and many from Galicia went to Vienna (Tartakower, 1967). From Eastern Europe many moved to Western cities. By the thousands, Jews left small towns and their traditional communities.

For Jews and non-Jews alike, the pull of economic opportunity, the push of population growth, and declining rural opportunities determined migrations. Agricultural changes were less important for Jews since they were less concentrated in those areas and were neither agricultural workers nor farm owners. Hence, the specific combination of factors was different for Jews than for others. Jewish networks and contacts may have facilitated more rapid urban social mobility. At times, restrictions or perceptions of anti-Semitism might have differentially influenced a choice of destination. To be sure, Jews had distinctive jobs, residences, contacts, and education before modernization intensified. These characteristics helped place Jews in positions that, in turn, facilitated the response of Jews to opportunities. It is probable, although the evidence is incomplete, that Jews and non-Jews in similar socioeconomic and residential circumstances migrated to cities at about the same rate.

The economic, political, and social attraction of Western Europe, particularly its urban and industrial centers, was enormous. Few Jews from Central and Western Europe immigrated overseas as the pace of modernization increased, even though there were no quotas to restrict their entry to the United States and previous waves of German Jewish immigrants had established themselves economically and institutionally in America after mid-century. Indeed, the expansion of cities in Central and Western Europe was so great as to retain Jews who moved from towns and smaller urban places within their countries and absorb as well immigrants from countries to the East.

The movement to cities loosened family and friendship ties as well as bonds of economic dependencies. The forms of control that applied in the small communities did not work as well in the metropolises. The Jews who flocked to the cities interacted with many who did not share their economic and political ties. As the individual became more anonymous to his neighbors and community leaders, he became more autonomous as well. As families split and younger people moved away, control over resources and over people shifted from the local community and the extended family to the individual and the nuclear family. All contributed to changes in the established order.

At the same time, new forms of cohesion emerged. The extremely high percentage of Jews living in large cities led to new patterns of interaction and shared life circumstances. Whether Jews lived in the same neighborhoods out of preference for the company of other Jews, out of fear of non-Jews, a need to be near synagogues and suppliers of kosher food, or because they grouped near their jobs, friends, and family members, there is strong evidence of residential clustering.

Each of the major centers of Jewish immigration had clearly defined Jewish neighborhoods, typically centered about the first areas of Jewish settlement. In Berlin where Jews were less than 4 percent of the population in 1925, they were nearly 14 percent in one of the city's seventeen districts, more than 8 percent in two others, and less than 1 percent in nine of them (Hamilton, 1982, p. 85; Zander, 1937, pp. 121–22). In Hamburg, Jews were nearly 2 percent of the population and more than 15 percent in two areas, about 3 percent in one, and none in any of the eighteen other districts (Hamilton, 1982, pp. 104–7). Jews in Vienna were 9 percent of the city's residents in 1930. However, they were more than 23 percent of those who lived in three districts; in one district, the proportion of Jews was more than one-third, and in ten they were below 6 percent (Simon, 1971; Rozenblit, 1983). In Budapest, they were 20 percent of the total population; in 1930 they accounted for more than 40 percent of three districts and less than 7 percent in three other districts (Vago, 1974, p. 39). Similar patterns appear in Paris (Hyman, 1979; Weinberg, 1977). In Prague, Jews moved into particular apartment houses (G. Cohen, 1979). Residential clustering provided one source of frequent interaction and shared life circumstances among Jews, even as they entered the new urban centers (Della Pergola, 1981a; see also Hyman, 1983). The new clustering of Jews in urban places was different than the premodern pattern. It was voluntary, and therefore, some Jews moved to non-Jewish neighborhoods, while most moved to new areas of Jewish concentration. The new Jewish neighborhoods facilitated the integration of migrants into occupations and schools, while reinforcing ethnic ties and visibility.

EDUCATIONAL CHANGES

A key manifestation of intensified change within the Jewish community was the rapid influx of Jews into the secular school systems of their native countries. In turn, this resulted in the relatively higher proportion of Jews in these schools and a general increase in the level of education of the Jewish population. The growing educational levels in non-Jewish schools resulted in exposure to secular beliefs and values; interaction with non-Jews; declining control of the Jewish community over the young—hence, decreasing generational continuity. The changing educational patterns responded to economic expansion: occupations and economic opportunities demanded new skills, and higher levels of family wealth allowed children to remain in school longer. Jews responded to these educational opportunities by flocking to the schools and universities, viewing them as the keys to social mobility and occupational success.

Entrance into the universities is one of the clearest illustrations of the expanding educational opportunities, and Jews entered these institutions more rapidly than others. In Germany in 1875, there were 16,400 university students, a number only slightly greater than that of 1835. The last quarter of the nineteenth century marked a time of rapid and widespread growth in the number of German university students: 21,000 in 1880; 27,100 in 1885 to 40,800 in 1905, and more than 55,000 in 1911, representing 1.5 percent of those aged 20–23, a threefold increase in thirty-six years (Ringer, 1979; McClelland, 1980). The rapid expansion drew many Jews and made places for them. During the autumn semester of the years 1886–90, there were 1,134 Jewish students, 9 percent of those enrolled in Prussian universities. Ten years later, there were 1,200 Jewish students, 8 percent of the total. At that time, Jews accounted for only 1 percent of the general population. Jews accounted for 17 percent (2,700) of the students in Austrian universities in 1896 (and 3–4 percent of the country's population). In 1886, 1,170 Jews composed one-fourth of the students in Hungarian universities, and 5 percent of those living there (Ruppin, 1904, pp. 206–8). At the end of the 1920s, in Germany, they were 3.4 percent of the university population (3.7 times their proportion in the general society); in Czechoslovakia, 14.5 percent (5.6 times); in Vienna, 21.3 percent (twice). Nowhere in Western or Central Europe were they simply at their proportion of the general population (Ruppin, 1973, p. 313). Everywhere, and over time, Jews were disproportionately concentrated in universities relative to their size in the population and relative to the non-Jewish total.

Why were Jews overrepresented in institutions of higher secular learning? We have already documented that Jews were disproportionately located in cities. As a result, Jewish children accounted for especially high proportions of students in lower schools, the pool of those eligible to attend universities. Over time, new occupations and the increasingly middle-class status of Jews provided additional impetuses for Jewish entry into the universities.

Rapid entry into the universities followed from the movement of Jews into the general elementary schools and gymnasia. In 1901, for example, they were 8 percent of Prussian gymnasia students and 15 percent of the Austrian students (Ruppin, 1904, p. 164). These data parallel the proportions of the Jews in the universities. As early as 1867, Jews accounted for 15 percent of the gymnasia students in Berlin. In 1876, Jews were one-fourth of the school children of Budapest's public schools (Moskovits, 1964, p. 103). In 1880, they accounted for 15 percent of the students in Austrian gymnasia (Nossig, 1887, p. 64). Similar patterns occurred in other cities of Western and Central Europe.

Differences between Jews and non-Jews derive less from Jewish cultural peculiarities than from their structural characteristics. Controlling for social class and residence reduces the disproportionate concentration of Jews in Prussian universities. At the turn of the century, Jews were 1 percent of the general population and 9 percent of the university students. Entrepreneurs and traders, the class of most Jews, were also overrepresented: 19 percent of the general population and 34 percent of the students. While accounting for 12 percent of this social class, Jews were 26 percent of the children of traders and entrepreneurs in the universities. Their overrepresentation in universities is reduced from a ratio of 9:1 to a ratio of 2:1 by controlling for but one structural factor. An examination of the place of Jews in the universities of Budapest and Vienna supports these conclusions. For example, in 1910 Jews were 25 percent of the students at the University of Vienna comparable to their proportion among the self-employed professionals and businessmen, those most likely to send their children to the university (Goldhammer, 1927, pp. 50–51). Again, when we control for one other factor, the extent of Jewish distinctiveness changes dramatically, In Budapest, Jews were 26 percent of the university students in 1890, one-fourth of the city's population and half of those in commerce. The unusually high proportion of Jewish university students diminishes, when we compare Jews to others with similar social and economic positions.

As Jewish children entered secular schools, decreasing proportions attended the Jewish communal schools. In 1886, fewer than 40 percent of the Jewish children in Prussia were educated in Jewish schools. In 1931, the proportion had declined to 16 percent. Almost all the remainder attended public schools (Rurup, 1975a, p. 22; Ruppin, 1973, pp. 306–10; Lamberti, 1978). In 1897, 92 percent of the Jewish students in Budapest received all of their religious education in the public schools (Moskovits, 1964, p. 103). In Prague, the vast majority of the Jewish students attended German or Czech language schools. Between 1880 and World War I, about 425 completed their instructions at the Talmud Torah of Prague, while there was a yearly average attendance in the public schools of 3,000 (G. Cohen, 1979, pp. 314–15).

It would be misleading to assume that Jews who entered the public schools were "modern" and assimilating while those who studied in the Jewish schools were "traditional." Those attending public schools continued to live with their Jewish families and to participate in various Jewish activities. Interactions with non-Jews frequently led to conflict and competition, which, in turn, reinforced Jewish identification. Contacts with non-Jews in public schools, therefore, did not necessarily and inevitably lead to intermarriage, assimilation, and universalism. Attendance at the Jewish communal schools did not necessarily isolate Jews from the broader currents of economic, residential, and political change. Jewish schools in 1850 were not the same as in 1890 or 1930. Curricula, teachers, and courses changed. Indeed, had the proportion of students in Jewish schools compared to that in public schools remained the same, it would not have ensured stability. The patterns of modernization affected all institutions, even if differentially, and few could remain outside its influence.

OCCUPATIONAL CHANGES

As modernization intensified, occupational concentration lessened and diversification ensued. The occupational distinctiveness of Jews declined primarily because of the entry of non-Jews into economic sectors dominated by Jews. This implied continuous occupational specialization among Jews, with concomitant high levels of interaction among them. It also introduced competition between Jews and non-Jews operating in the same economic sphere. Moreover, professional opportunities and the entrance of Jews into the universities moved Jews into high-income jobs. Here, too, there was specialization. Jews entered the liberal professions and almost never worked in heavy industry or for the government. Occupational diversification did not mean assimilation.

The occupational changes did not introduce class divisions into the Jewish communities of Central and Western Europe. Relatively few Jews were industrial workers. Relatively few Jews were capitalists employing other Jews. The high proportions of self-employed businessmen and professionals did not control the economic and educational opportunities of other Jews. Hence, conflict within the Jewish community was relatively low in this regard.

There were declines in the distinctive economic positions held by Jews and, hence, growing similarities in the overall occupational structure of Jews and the general community. In 1907, Jews were 1 percent of the Prussian population, and in only two economic spheres were they above that proportion: the clothing and cleaning trade (2.7 percent); and banking, commerce, and insurance (8.9 percent). In five of the ten sectors of industry and agriculture, they were below 0.3 percent of the total (Ruppin, 1973, p. 142). In the 1925 Prussian census, there was an increase in the proportion of Jews employed in almost all areas in which they had been especially low and a decrease in the percentage where they had been especially high. Most significant of all is the finding that at that time Jews accounted for only 5.7 percent of those in banking, commerce, and insurance (Ruppin, 1973, p. 112). In addition, in German cities, 10 percent of both Jews and non-Jews were in the professions, public and private service (Weinryb, 1946, p. 27).

Evidence on the place of Jews within commerce—an area that had been distinctively Jewish—over an even longer period of time shows clear and rapid declines. In Prussia, they were 21 percent of the total in 1861, 9 percent in 1907, and 6 percent in 1925. The same pattern applies when we examine Germany as a whole: 6 percent in 1895, 4 percent in 1907, 3 percent in 1925, and 3 percent in 1933. If we examine the category of salesmen, we again find the same trend. In 1895, Jews accounted for 22 percent of all salesmen and agents, and by 1925 their proportion had declined to 9 percent (Ruppin, 1934, p. 148; Rurup, 1975a, p. 21; Engelman, 1973, p. 93; see also Schmelz, 1982, p. 64).

How much of the converging occupational patterns of Jews and non-Jews derived from urbanization? The answer emerges from an examination of the occupational structure of different cities. Evidence from Prague at the turn of the century highlights parallel occupational structures among the Jewish and non-Jewish members of the German Casino, the elite of Prague social life. Most of the members of both communities came from the professions and wealthy manufacturers, landowners and rentiers (82 percent of the non-Jews and 92 percent of the Jews). Within each group, relatively similar proportions derived from each of the listed categories, except that 47 percent of the Jews were merchants compared to 32 percent of the non-Jews; 19 percent of the Jews were lawyers compared to 11 percent of the non-Jews (G. Cohen, 1979, p. 319). In the middle of the 1920s, Jews and non-Jews of Berlin and Budapest had similar occupational patterns. Indeed, in the combined sphere of government work and the professions they were just about the same (7 percent of each in Berlin and 17 percent of each in Budapest). They differed in that 45 percent of the non-Jewish work force in Berlin worked in industry and handicrafts, and 26 percent were engaged in commerce. This compared to 27 percent and 44 percent of the Jews who worked in these jobs. Similarly, in Budapest, 36.5 percent of the non-Jews worked in industry compared to 26 percent of the Jews; 14 percent of the non-Jews were in commerce, banking, and transportation compared to 34 percent of the Jews (Ruppin, 1973, pp. 145–46, 210; see also Schmelz, 1982, p. 64; on Vienna see Goldhammer, 1927). Here, too, there is evidence of growing parallels between the occupational structure of the Jews and non-Jews.

The occupational categories comparing Jews and non-Jews are too broad and often distort the specific distinctiveness of the Jewish pattern. An examination of the concentration of Jews in self-employment, within occupational categories, clarifies this point. In Vienna in 1923, 30 percent of the Jews in commerce and transportation were working for themselves compared to about 10 percent of the non-Jews. Only 4 percent of the Jews in the liberal professionals were salaried compared to over one-fourth of the non-Jews (Goldhammer, 1927, p. 55). In the large cities of Germany, Jewish self-employment within industrial categories, in 1907 and in 1933, was consistently higher than for non-Jews. Equally important, over time the proportion of non-Jews who were self-employed declined, while the proportion among Jews remained relatively stable (Schmelz, 1982, p. 67). Large proportions of Jews continued as self-employed merchants in the most modern sectors of the most industrialized country of Europe.

The decline of Jews as a proportion of those employed in "Jewish" occupations derived less from changes within the Jewish community than from the entry of non-Jews into those areas. For example, in 1882, there were 13,234 persons in the German banking industry: 2,908 Jews (22 percent) and 10,326 non-Jews. In 1895, the total had grown to 19,108. The number of Jews *increased* (3,045) but less than the number of non-Jews (16,063). Therefore, there was a clear decline in the *proportion* of Jews in banking (down to 15.9 percent) but a slight increase in the *actual number* of Jews engaged in banking. In 1925, the same pattern holds. The total had skyrocketed to 146,235. The actual number of Jews increased significantly (to 5,620), but their share of the industry had slipped dramatically (to 3.8 percent). The same patterns hold when we examine other Jewish occupations (Ruppin, 1973, p. 210; Weinryb, 1946; and for similar patterns in Czechoslovakia, see A. Rabinowicz, 1969, p. 206). In Berlin in 1882 Jews were 55 percent of all self-employed persons; by 1925 they had declined to one-third. This pattern was the result of a 250 percent increase in the absolute number of self-employed Jews, while the increase among non-Jews was an astounding 100-fold (374–34,394) (Lestchinsky, 1932, p. 93). In sum, to analyze the patterns of change within the Jewish community one must examine the social and economic structure of the Jews per se as well as changes in the general population. Changes in the proportion of Jews in an occupational category are affected by changes in the denominator (the general population) as well as by changes in the numerator (the Jews).

Expansion of opportunities in professional and technical areas of the economy attracted Jews. Here, too, there was occupational specialization. In Vienna in the 1920s, Jews were 2 percent of the salaried professional classes but 11 percent of the self-employed professionals (Goldhammer, 1927, p. 55). Jews in Prussia in 1925 were one-tenth of 1 percent of government workers, except for those in health and education. Even among the health workers, Jews were disproportionately self-employed. Among Jewish self-employed professionals, fully 50 percent of the Jews were physicians and dentists, and another 25 percent were lawyers (Lestchinsky, 1932, p. 103–15). In 1925, Jews composed 16 percent of the physicians, 15 percent of the dentists, and one-fourth of the lawyers in Prussia (Lestchinsky, 1932; see also Ruppin, 1973, p. 219). In contrast, Jews were underrepresented among architects and engineers. At the turn of the century, 62 percent of the lawyers in Vienna were Jews, as were half the doctors and dentists, 45 percent of the medical faculty, and one-fourth the total faculty of the city's university (E. Schwarz, 1979, p. 173). These patterns point to the relative wealth of opportunities for mobility and the relative absence of economic bases of conflict within the Jewish communities of Western Europe.

Therefore, the entry of many Jews into the professions did not necessarily lead to declines in contacts among Jews. Frequently, it increased such interactions. Moreover, these contacts had consequences for the formation of Jewish organizations. Jewish lawyers formed and led Jewish defense organizations that served to maintain forms of Jewish cohesion—albeit in new forms. Similarly, the large number of Jewish university students resulted in the formation of Jewish student groups, sustaining high levels of interaction among Jews and separating them from non-Jews. As the intensity and levels of modernization increased, the Jewish community was transformed and new forms of Jewishness, patterns of interaction, and expressions of Jewish communal interests developed.

MARRIAGE AND FRIENDSHIP TIES
Perhaps nothing better illustrates the breakdown of the barriers between Jews and non-Jews than the growth in marriages across ethnic and religious lines. In Germany, at the turn of the century 8 percent of the Jews married non-Jews; a decade later, the proportion reached 12 percent, and in 1930 nearly one-fifth of the Jews were marrying persons of another faith (Ruppin, 1934, p. 108; Della Pergola, 1981a; Schmelz, 1982). These trends hold for

various regions of the country as well. In Berlin during the period 1876–80, nearly 14 percent were out-marrying, and by 1929 the proportion had doubled to 30 percent. Even Bavaria, which had long withstood the forces of modernization, showed similar trends. In 1876–80, less than 2 percent of the Jews were marrying non-Jews, but in 1901–5 the proportion had reached 4 percent, and in 1925–27 it had increased to 13 percent. In Vienna, intermarriage increased from 8 to 19 percent in the forty years from the last decades of the nineteenth century (Della Pergola, 1981a). In 1933, in Bohemia, for every hundred marriages between Jewish partners, twenty-eight occurred between Jews and non-Jews. Of all these cases, the Jews of Trieste had the highest percentage of intermarriage. In 1927, 56.1 percent of the Jews married non-Jews (Engelman, 1973, pp. 190–201; Ruppin, 1973, p. 319; Della Pergola, 1981a). Here, too, we find clear indications of ongoing declines in Jewish distinctiveness and increases in interactions with non-Jews. Although more detailed evidence would make the case more convincing, it appears that intermarriages between Jews and non-Jews were higher where the size of the Jewish community was small, the Jewish communal institutions were relatively new and weak, and Jews were more concentrated among the professional and upper-middle classes.

Does the evidence on increasing rates of intermarriage in Central and Western Europe indicate the erosion of the Jewish community? Are not out-marriages the clearest indication of assimilation? If social and economic modernization resulted in significant rates of Jewish losses through intermarriage, does it not follow that modernization brings about the disappearance of the Jewish community and the end of the Jewish people? Several major challenges qualify the leap from increasing intermarriage rates to assimilation. First, the actual number of intermarriages was small. In Germany when the rate of intermarriage was at its peak in 1933 (one-fourth married non-Jews), this involved 1,200 males and 500 females out of over 6,000 who married (Dinur et al., p. 127). More generally, the Jewish community in the period of intensive modernization in Western Europe had powerful economic, social, and residential ties among Jews as well as few sources of internal conflict. In addition, there were internal social and political organizations and religious institutions which were sources of ethnic and cultural cohesion. While these community patterns were significantly different from premodern, traditional structures, they were far from indicating dissolution and disintegration.

Another caution in the analysis of intermarriage rates is more general. While the rates of intermarriage were increasing over time, it cannot be assumed that such patterns of increase would continue indefinitely. We cannot know the future, but straight-line extrapolations from past trends are often mechanical exercises. Projections of increased out-marriages reveal more about the intense concerns focused on the present situation than on likely future patterns. Indeed, the presence of institutions and elites concerned with intermarriage levels reflect the strength of communal cohesion in the face of the challenges of change.

Neverthless, Western European Jewish communities were characterized by demographic losses through intermarriage. These were likely to have involved Jews who were on the fringes of the community rather than those who exhibited strong Jewish ties. As such, the cohesion of the community was less diminished by their out-marriages. While modernization allowed some to choose both their ethnic identity and out-marriage, it also led to the reformation and strengthening of the Jewish community and the emergence of new forms of cohesion. The Jewish community existed sui generis despite the departure of some of its members. Indeed, even in the 1930s, most Jews in the communities of Western and Central Europe were marrying within the Jewish community.

There is an additional point which is more difficult to document systematically. Despite the greater interactions between Jews and non-Jews associated with the intensive modernization of Western Europe, friendship patterns continued to link Jews together. Gershom Scholem has provided a particularly telling analysis of division and cohesion within the German Jewish community before World War I—a community long considered to epitomize assimilation. He distinguishes three "social psychological" types (1979, pp. 13–16): a small group of "consciously and totally 'Germanized' baptized Jews, living on or beyond the borderline of Jewishness"; a small group of "wealthy Jews" who constituted the social and political elite of the Jewish community; and "numerically by far the strongest group was the broad Jewish liberal middle and small bourgeoisie." This last group provides the major focus of Scholem's analysis.

The real situation within this class is nowadays largely misjudged. This is due to the manifest contradiction . . . between the ideology which professed assimilation or declared it as already achieved, and the actual behavior in important situations of life and the psychological reality. [P. 17]

Scholem then provides four examples of these contradictions from the personal experience of his family: the retention of particular forms of religious observance, in the face of manifest claims in support of nonbelief; ambitions for contacts and careers that precluded baptism as an "entry ticket"; the normative rejection of and low levels of intermarriage; and a social ostracism that clearly limited actual contact between Jews and non-Jews even where they shared occupations and formal membership in social organizations:

One day it dawned upon me that for friendly intercourse our house was exclusively visited by Jews, and that my parents paid visits only to Jews.

There were exceptions: on formal occasions some of my father's colleagues from the typographic profession . . . came to tender their congratulations—practically always unaccompanied by their spouses. . . . Upon my enquiry, my father answered that a social return visit to the families concerned would not be welcome. At that time, my father was a lively, witty and polite man, popular and respected in his profession. This rather far-reaching social ostracism of the Jews, though often denied in family discussions, was especially pronounced in commerce and trade, whereas in the free professions non-Jewish colleagues were socially more accessible. [P. 17]

The social group described by Scholem was the great majority of German Jewry. Their occupational and residential distinctiveness had been transformed. They spoke only German and thought of themselves as Germans. "It was stressed again and again that one belonged to the German people within which one formed a religious group, the same as the others" (pp. 16–17). Yet, Scholem's analysis sets out these Jews as a particular subgroup within Germany, interacting socially mainly with each other.

The forces of modernization, even where intensive and where the Jewish communal structure was weakest, did not destroy the powerful bonds that held Jews together and apart from non-Jews. Jews and their communities were transformed. Their total assimilation was challenged by the new economic, social, cultural, and political bonds which were shaped by the forces of modernization

7 · Modernization in Large and Organized Jewish Communities: Comparing East and West Europe

Differences between the Jewish communities of Eastern and Western Europe are a major issue in the analysis of Jewish society and politics during the processes of modernization. Our general argument maintains that the more intense were the forces of modernization, the greater were the declines of traditional sources of Jewish cohesion. Intense change generated rapid differentiation of the economic, social, political, and religious components of the Jewish community. The rapid pace of change split Jews away from established Jewish communities, forming new bases of cohesion. Equally important, the larger the Jewish community and the longer it had existed, the more likely were the traditional forms of cohesion to remain. In these communities, differentiation was slower and, therefore, the overlap of the social, political, religious, and economic dimensions of the community was greater. Large and long-established Jewish communities were also most likely to contain a complex institutional infrastructure—schools, synagogues, courts, kehillot—which helped to maintain the bonds of the Jewish community. They were also more like total societies, exhibiting various forms of internal conflict. These propositions guide our analysis of the different patterns characterizing the Jewries of Western and Eastern Europe.

Modernization begins from and is conditioned by existing structures. The modern world did not emerge suddenly with new scenery, players, and a new script. We would expect to find, therefore, greater persistence of high levels of interaction, both consensual and conflictual, among Jews in Eastern Europe compared to the Jews in the West, since this had long characterized the former.

At the turn of the twentieth century, more than two-thirds of the 9 million Jews of Europe lived in the Tsarist Empire and Galicia. In the eastern portions of the continent, there were scores of cities, each with a Jewish population in excess of 30,000 and containing well-established communal institutions. Most Jews in the West, in contrast, lived in five or six metropolises, some of which had young and poorly institutionalized Jewish communities. In addition, the forces of modernization came later and were less intense in the eastern portions of Europe. As a result, traditional forms of cohesion persisted there longer than in the West. At the same time, some of the new sources of change that divided and reunited the Jews of Western Europe emerged among the Jews of the East as well. In the East, however, greater sources of internal conflict accompanied modernization.

THE ECONOMIC BASES OF JEWISH COHESION

Economic clustering provides a most important source for the persistence of traditional forms of Jewish cohesion and distinctiveness. Jewish communities in areas where the forces of modernization came latest and were weakest retained the pattern by which ethnic, religious, and occupational ties overlapped. Economic categories continued to define Jews in ways that distinguished them from others. In contrast, where modernization arrived first and was most intense, traditional forms of Jewish economic distinctiveness declined. These did not inevitably lead to economic assimilation but to new occupational concentrations which became bases for Jewish cohesion (see Chapter 6).

The persistence of traditional forms of economic cohesion may be readily observed among the five million Jews of the Tsarist Empire. The census of 1897 provides an important source of information which can be compared to surveys taken at that time by the Jewish Colonization Society (see Bramsohn, 1903) and to censuses taken after World War I. (The major data of the 1897 Russian Census on Jews have been organized by Rubinow, 1975. Unless otherwise indicated, our analysis of these data are based on his collection.) The Russian Jews, with few exceptions, remained confined to the Pale of Settlement, where they were a distinctively urban group in an overwhelmingly rural society. Almost 95 percent of the Jews of Russia lived in the Pale, where they composed nearly 12 percent of the population. Among the Pale's twenty-five administrative provinces, the proportion of Jews varied from nearly 20 percent in Warsaw and Grodno to 5 percent in four localities. Across the Pale, the Jews composed nearly 40 percent of the residents of urban areas, and more than three-fourths of the Jews lived in those areas (Rubinow, 1975, pp. 490–94).

These patterns reflect a situation in which residence overlapped with economic, religious, and ethnic ties, continuing to distinguish Jews and non-Jews. About two-thirds of the Gentiles in the Pale earned their living from the land, while almost no Jews (3 percent) were in agriculture. Conversely, almost no Gentiles were in commerce (1.4 percent), and nearly one-third of the Jews (400,000 of the 1.5 million employed) were in trade and related occupations. Nearly 40 percent of the Jews worked as artisans and laborers in "manufacturing and mechanical pursuits" compared to 11 percent of the non-Jews. Even within this sphere, Jews and non-Jews labored in very different kinds of factories and workplaces. At the turn of the century, as had been the case for decades, Jews held distinctive occupations in the economic structure of Eastern Europe (Rubinow, 1975, pp. 500–502).

The overwhelming and highly visible place of Jews in trade and commerce may be detailed on the basis of the census. In the Pale of Settlement, the Jews provided the bulk (72.5 percent) of those in trade: nearly 90 percent in Lithuania and Byelo-Russia, 76 percent in the southwest sections, 54 percent in the south, and 72 percent in Poland (Rubinow, 1975, p. 556). In some areas, there were no other traders. For example, in Minsk, Pinsk, and Grodno, they accounted for more than 92 percent of all those in commerce (Rubinow, 1975, p. 554; Lestchinsky, 1931, pp. 101–4). Jews monopolized selected areas of trade. In Lithuania and Byelo-Russia, Jews were 97 percent of those who traded in grain. In Poland, 91 percent of the grain traders were Jews (Rubinow, 1975, p. 556). Jews continued to labor as middlemen, linking peasants to markets. Nearly half the Jews in commerce worked in this field (Rubinow, 1975, p. 557); few non-Jews were in this sphere of economic activity. In Galicia, the same patterns are present. In 1910, Jews accounted for 85 percent of those in banking, commerce, and insurance, and 76 percent of the liquor dealers and innkeepers (Ruppin, 1973, p. 142; F. Friedmann, 1929). In Eastern Europe, commercial activity continued to define many Jews at the end of the nineteenth century.

The Jewish communities of Eastern Europe, unlike those of the West, had long contained many artisans and laborers. In the census of 1897, those working in manufacturing and mechanical pursuits were the single largest occupational category, amounting to more than 540,000 Jews, 38 percent of the work force (Rubinow, 1975, p. 501). The distribution of Jewish laborers among categories of work shows how closely tied they were to their traditional pursuits and modes of labor. Most were artisans, working in small shops, often at home. Most worked primarily for the immediate needs of very small markets. Nearly 40 percent of the Jewish artisans worked on clothing and wearing apparel; another 30 percent labored on goods related to agricultural products. Only 20 percent of the Jewish artisans worked for markets outside of their immediate environments (Rubinow, 1975, p. 522).

These data describe Jewish artisans as tailors, shoemakers, carpenters, bakers, and butchers, serving small towns and neighborhoods of cities. In short, there is overwhelming evidence that occupational specialization and segregation resulted in a structural and cultural division of labor.

One marked difference between the Jewish workers in the East and other European laborers living in cities was the massive overcrowding that affected the former. The forced eviction of Jews from the villages of Russia raised the number and proportion of Jewish artisans in the towns and cities to unmanageable levels. This density resulted in three forms of change: Jews moved into the factories, they competed with each other for limited numbers of jobs and economic opportunities, and they emigrated to areas in Western Europe and abroad.

The years that ended the nineteenth century exhibited rapid growth in the number of mills and factories in the areas of heavy Jewish settlement. In 1889, in the Pale (but excluding Poland), there were about 65,000 workers in more than 4,000 factories. By 1897, the number of factories had nearly doubled to 7,120 and the number of workers had surpassed 180,000. There are estimates that factory labor accounted for one-fifth to one-fourth of the Jewish working class (Rubinow, 1975, p. 536; see also Greenberg, 1944; Mendelsohn, 1970; Frankel, 1981; Tobias, 1972; Bramsohn, 1903).

The Jewish movement into the factories was conditioned by their initial skills and experience and by whether a particular workplace was owned by Jews. They rarely worked for non-Jews. In addition, Jews labored in relatively smaller and less mechanized factories than did non-Jews. This flow of industrial labor maintained high levels of interaction among Jews and low levels of interaction between Jews and Gentiles. The processes of industrialization sustained shared circumstances of life for hundreds of thousands of Jews.

Some illustrations convey the skewed distribution of Jews in particular industries. In 1898, Jews accounted for half the factory workers in Lithuania and Byelo-Russia, while accounting for extremely high portions in some specialties: gloves (100 percent), brushes (96.8 percent), matches (95.2 percent), tobacco (92.1 percent), soap (84.7 percent), buttons (84.2 percent), hides and tanning (64.6 percent), candies (62.4 percent), wool spinning (57.7 percent), and flour milling (51.1 percent). At the other extreme, Jews played negligible roles in lumber mills (18.3 percent), cast-iron mills (14.9 percent), and machinery (4.2 percent), spheres in which they had no prior experience or skills and in which the necessary labor could be supplied by former peasants. Similar patterns characterized Jewish workers in Polish factories (Rubinow, 1975, pp. 542–45; see also Bramsohn, 1903, p. 179). There is little evidence that industrialization drew Jewish and non-Jewish workers into the same factories.

The movement of Jews into industrial labor was conditioned by noneconomic factors as well. Almost none worked for non-Jewish capitalists. In Poland, one survey counted less than 3 percent of the Jews working in factories owned by Gentiles. In Bialystock, where Jews were approximately one-third of those in textile factories, almost all worked for Jews (Rubinow, 1975, pp. 543–44). Whereas Gentile bosses did not employ Jews, Jewish capitalists hired both Jewish and non-Jewish workers but rarely in the same workplace. Jews appear to have worked almost exclusively in the relatively nonmechanized and small workshops owned by Jews. Non-Jewish labor prevailed in the mines and large factories. Ethnic and religious segregation prevented the formation of class ties among the industrial workers of Eastern Europe. The pattern reinforced ties among Jewish workers and fostered conflict between Jewish proletarians and capitalists.

POPULATION GROWTH, ECONOMIC COMPETITION, AND MIGRATIONS

Industrialization in the Pale did not increase the standard of living for most Jews as it had in Germany and France. Migrations from rural areas and population growth drew more and more Jews into the cities and towns, adding to the number of artisans and traders competing for a shrinking market. In the Tsarist Empire, there were nearly 4 million Jews in 1880, nearly three times their number in 1825. In 1900, they reached over 5 million, even though 1 million had emigrated between 1881 and 1897. In Galicia, there were 675,000 Jews in 1880, more than three times their number in 1825; and in 1900, there were 825,000, notwithstanding large-scale emigrations there as well. Similarly, there were 200,000 Jews in Hungary in 1825, 638,000 in 1880, and 852,000 in 1900. These growth rates were high relative to those in the West (Engelman, 1973, pp. 108–11; Rubinow, 1975, p. 495; Lestchinsky, 1928b, p. 6; Bachi, 1976). The number of Jews living in cities increased as well. By the end of the century, places that had contained several thousand Jews housed tens of thousands. In 1847, there were 2,000 Jews in Brest-Litovsk; half a century later, there were 25,000 (65 percent of the city's population). The size of the Jewish population of Vilna more than doubled during the period 1847–97, from 23,000 to 63,000 (41 percent of the population). Odessa, which was a small rural area in 1800, had a Jewish population of 17,000 in 1847 and nearly 140,000 in 1897. Warsaw was the largest of all—nearly 250,000 Jews, more than one–third of the total population in 1900 and five times larger than in 1846 (Dobrosycki, 1981). By the end of the century, nearly half of the Jews of Russia lived in cities. More generally, in 1897 there were fifteen cities with more than 30,000 Jews and eighteen more with Jewish populations between 20,000 and 30,000 (Lestchinsky, 1922, pp. 71–77).

The contemporary sources depict sharp rises in the number of artisans, which flowed from population growth and urbanization. It was estimated that there were enough Jewish tailors to supply clothing for half the urban population of the Russian Empire. There were major differences in the number of artisans living in the cities within and outside of the Pale. Mogilev (within the Pale) had seven times as many tailors as did nearby Smolensk (outside the Pale), and Vitebsk (within the Pale) had four times as many as did its neighbor Pskov (Mendelsohn, 1970, pp. 14–15; see also Baron, 1976a, pp. 82–83; and Greenberg, 1944, 1:165–71, 2:72–74). These illustrate a widespread development.

The growing number of artisans and their intense competition over limited resources led directly to poverty among Jews. A contemporary description of an artisan's home in Mogilev is revealing:

The homes of the artisans are small and crowded. But no matter how small and crowded, tenants are often admitted, and there is seldom more than one room for a family. The room serves as kitchen, living and sleeping room, and workshop. And it is not unusual for a tailor to rent the same room for school purposes, so that instruction is served to a small class of private pupils in the same room where the tailor works with his apprentice; the tailor's wife cooks the food and washes the clothes, and the tailor's prolific family mingles its joyful noise with the monotonous chanting of the Hebrew teacher and the scholars. [Cited in Rubinow, 1975, p. 526]

The workday of this tailor and apprentice, and all others like them, was limited solely by their physical endurance. Only at the turn of the century did the number of hours spent at work each day drop to twelve or thirteen. These same poor living conditions could be found as well among the families of factory workers. The Jewish workers in Byelo-Russia and Lithuania were described as living "in the semi-darkness of cellars and similar hovels that had wet walls and floors, and were crammed together in an oppressive, stupefying atmosphere" (cited in Mendelsohn, 1970, p. 131; for similar descriptions of other places see Mendelsohn, 1970, p. 29; Rubinow, 1975, pp. 547–48; Greenberg, 1944, 2:160–70).

The many Jewish traders, middlemen, shopkeepers, and small business-men were affected by similar competitive pressures. They too found them-selves facing a shrinking economic pie as their numbers also increased. They tried to fight back by lowering their prices. One result was the growth in the number of "paper merchants," peddlers, and owners of empty stores, too poor to stock their wares. Another was the proletarianization of many small traders (Rubinow, 1975, p. 561; see also Greenberg, 1944; and Baron, 1976a).

Under these conditions, we find as well migrations to the cities and to other countries (Anderson, 1980). A commission sent by the American government reported on the condition of the Jews of Moscow just after their expulsion in 1891:

Nearly all of (those who remained) are artisans or have been business-men of some kind. . . . All told the same story: the tailor, whose cus-tomers have left; the butcher, whose business has been ruined because of the exodus; old men, women and children importuning the committee (Moscow Jewish Relief Committee) to give heed to their cries and help them get away from their surroundings, any place being better than where they are living in constant terror of persecution. Homes are de-stroyed, businesses ruined, families separated, all claiming that they are not criminals except that they are charged with being Jews; all express-ing a willingness and an anxiety to work, begging for the opportunity to begin life somewhere, where they do not know nor do they care. [Cited in Greenberg, 1944, 2:74]

The influx of Jews into the cities of the Pale exacerbated the already overcrowded working and living conditions. These factors more than any other precipated the massive emigrations that began in the late 1870s and carried through the First World War.

More than three million Jews left the Russian Empire and the Eastern portions of the Austrian Empire during these years. Between 1887 and 1911, 1,246,668 Jews left Russia. Political factors help explain variations in timing and the relative size of the flow. The events of the Revolution of 1905 spurred a large migration. Nearly 250,000 left between 1905 and 1907 (Engelman, 1973, p. 162). Those who traveled abroad and to Western and Central Europe did not leave as seasonal workers or temporary migrants as did many of the Poles and Italians who left their homes. Jews migrated to find new homes for themselves and their families. In doing so, they acted counter to the demands and pleadings of the rabbis and community leaders (Greenberg, 1944, 1:62–64; see Chapter 11). At the same time, many Jews stayed in their residences, and most did not emigrate. While some Jews attempted to preserve the old order of authority and control, the diffusion of modernization penetrated even those who were most insulated and isolated: those on the move to new places and new countries were the most freed from the traditional constraints and, hence, the most receptive to change.

As economic conditions deteriorated, additional members of the family were sent to work as well. There is much evidence of child labor (both boys and girls) as well as female artisans and factory laborers. Women, boys, and girls composed 30 percent of the Jewish artisans at the turn of the century (Rubinow, 1975, p. 524). Women alone made up 15 percent of the Jewish labor force in the Pale. Among factory workers, their proportions were even higher. In the poorest region, the Northwest (Lithuania and Byelo-Russia), women were 27 percent of the Jewish industrial workers, and boys and girls added another 15 percent to the total. In Poland, women and children composed nearly 38 percent of the Jewish factory workers (Rubinow, 1975, pp. 545–46). They were concentrated in textile factories and in some mechanized industries as unskilled labor. Emigration and female and child labor were manifestations of the increasingly distressing and depressed conditions among the Jewish masses. This is not to suggest that absolute poverty determined emigration. Rather, it was the combination of deteriorating economic conditions in the shift toward industrialization, growing density of Jewish settlement, the increasing competition, and the restrictions on Jewish residence rights. The poorest and most traditional did not emigrate. Nevertheless, for significant numbers of Jews, the pushes and pulls resulted in emigration and, in turn, relieved the pressures of growing numbers, limited opportunities, and increasing density (see Chapter 10).

The selective emigrations affected the distribution of income within the Jewish communities of Russia. Jewish capitalists and professionals emerged during industrialization, as did large numbers of poor and unemployed Jewish workers and petty merchants. As a result, the distribution of income became more unequal. In Western Europe, where no native Jewish proletariat emerged, it is likely that the distribution of income was less skewed toward the extremes.

How extensive was the development of professionals among the Jews of Russia? Is there evidence of their assimilation into Russian society? More than 20,000 Jewish lawyers, physicians, and other professionals appear in the census of 1897 (Rubinow, 1975, p. 566). In 1880, Jews were nearly 7 percent of the university students; 7 years later, when the government imposed the *numerus clausus*, they were more than 14 percent of the total. They remained at that level through World War I (Brym, 1978, p. 55; Halevy, 1976, p. 93; Alston, 1969; Rubinow, 1975, p. 490). Here, as in Western Europe, the pattern of change developed new forms of cohesion within the Jewish community. With few exceptions, all Jews in the liberal professions were barred from government service. Jewish intellectuals and teachers could not find employment in public schools, gymnasia, and universities. As had occurred in Germany earlier in the century, Jewish graduates of government schools faced three career options: religious conversion, emigration, or return to work in the Jewish community. As had also occurred in Germany, few converted. Many more opted for emigration. Those who returned to the Jewish community brought with them the ideas of the university. In Russia, in the decades before the turn of the nineteenth century, this meant political not religious philosophies (see Chapter 8). Jewish lawyers could find no government employment. As was also the case in Western Europe, they interacted with each other in the private sphere. Only Jewish physicians, and they only in numbers that did not exceed a legally defined quota, could work in the public sphere (Rubinow, 1975, pp. 568–69). Jews entered the professions, though not as much or as rapidly as in Western Europe.

With the growth of industrialization, the number of Jewish capitalists increased. At the turn of the century, in northwest portions of the Pale, Jews owned about half the factories and employed about the same portion of the industrial workforce. In the southwest of the Pale, they owned about one-third of the factories, employing a somewhat smaller percentage of the laborers (one-fourth). In the south, the proportions controlled by Jews were lower. As would follow from our analysis of the relationship between occupation and ethnic cohesion, Jewish capitalists predominated in the textile and garment industries as well as those associated with animal products and tobacco (they owned more than 75 percent of all factories in these areas), but not in mining, metallurgy, or other heavy industries. Their factories used relatively less steam power and employed relatively fewer workers. They had, therefore, a lower average value of production. Indeed, most controlled what were really little more than large workshops. "The 155 Jewish textile factories employ 12,848 men, or about 83 workingmen per factory, while the 112 non-Jewish factories employ 31,953 men, or about 282 workingmen per factory, and that of the Jewish factories 37 percent have no mechanical power, while of the non-Jewish factories 14, or only 12.5 percent, are without such power" (Rubinow, 1975, p. 541; Bramsohn, 1903, p. 179; on Galicia see F. Friedmann, 1929, pp. 14–15). The same pattern held in Bialystock, which contained even more factories owned by Jews. The processes of industrialization maintained the economic distinctiveness of Jewish capitalists as well as Jewish workers.

The presence of relatively large and growing numbers of Jewish industrial workers in factories owned by Jews exacerbated class divisions within the Jewish community. Jewish capitalists controlled the jobs and salaries of Jewish workers. Population growth and economic declines led to class conflict among Jews. Jewish trade unions and political parties deepened the splits within the Jewish community of Eastern Europe.

The 5 million Jews of the Russian Empire were buffeted by the winds of modernization. New social and economic divisions appeared with the formation of industrial classes. At the same time, ethnic divisions between Jews and non-Jews persisted, and they revolved around occupational and residential concentrations as well as religious differences. Thus, internal conflicts within the Jewish population emerged at the same time as Jewish-non-Jewish divisions were reinforced.

CHANGING AND REINFORCING PATTERNS OF COHESION
In the years between the two world wars, the pace and level of modernization intensified in Eastern Europe. Increasing numbers of Jews spoke the national languages, studied in public schools, and moved to cities. Growing industrialization affected the Jews' occupational structure. Nevertheless, in these areas of large and well-established Jewish communities, the changes maintained the cohesion of the communities. In the Soviet Union, the government controlled the transformation of society. We will examine separately the effects of Communist rule on Jewish communities (see Chapter 9). Interwar Poland illustrates the retention of traditional forms and the emergence of new bases of Jewish cohesion in the face of increased modernization in Eastern Europe.

As had occurred decades earlier in Western Europe, some of the Jews of the East began to use the national languages. In the census of 1897, 200,000 Jews (4 percent) in the Tsarist Empire listed Russian as their mother tongue, and almost half the men and more than one-fourth the women between the ages of ten and forty claimed to be able to read Russian (Rubinow, 1975, pp. 576–79). In 1910, three-fourths of the Hungarian Jews listed Magyar as their native language (Barany, 1974; Braham, 1981; Katzburg, 1981). In the Polish census of 1931, although 80 percent of the Jews listed Yiddish as their language, 7.7 percent noted Hebrew, and the remainder indicated that Polish was their mother tongue, and most if not all of the Yiddish and Hebrew speakers were bilingual, with Polish as their second language (Castellan, 1974, pp. 188–89; Mendelsohn, 1983, pp. 29–32; Heller, 1980, pp. 65–68, 216). There is, therefore, mixed evidence of linguistic assimilation.

These changes were associated with increases in the extent of identification by Jews with their native countries. The patterns emerged earlier in France and Germany and appear in the East by the end of the century. In the Czechoslovak census of 1921, approximately half those who claimed to be Jewish by religion did not list Jewish as their nationality. The pattern in 1930 was about the same (Fleischmann, 1969, p. 267; see also Rothkirchen, 1968, p. 92; Sole, 1969, pp. 136–44). These patterns of Jewish national identity emerge in Hungary even earlier. There is evidence that three-fourths of those who were Jewish by religion, in 1910, claimed Magyar as their nationality. Some of these relatively low levels of Jewish national identification were inspired by the Hungarian and Czechoslovak governments. Nevertheless, for many, their identity as Jews no longer had joint religious and national connotations. As had become clear earlier in the century in France and Germany, for many Jewishness was losing its political dimension and national character. Indeed, the total overlap of Judaism and Jewish peoplehood which characterized the premodern era (see Chapter 2) was breaking down. The separation of religious and national identities is but one illustration of the general process of differentiation associated with modernization.

Changes in language and national identity partially derive from the growing number of Jewish children in national educational systems. As the governments opened public schools, Jews entered them. In Poland, for example, 80 percent of the Jews in primary schools of any kind in 1930 attended public institutions (Minzin, 1928, pp. 242–43; Heller, 1980, p. 223). Four years later, two-thirds of the Jews in all schools were in state-run institutions (Dobrosycki and Kirschenblatt-Gimblett, 1977, p. 261). In addition, new Jewish schools opened. As had occurred decades earlier in France, these institutions taught secular topics, occupational preparation, and vocational trades. Some employed Yiddish as the language of instruction; some used Hebrew; most taught in Polish (Minzin, 1928, pp. 242–43; Mendelsohn, 1981, pp. 186–206; 1983, p. 66). In addition, Jews began to enter the universities in relatively large numbers: at the end of the 1920s, Jews were 10.5 percent of the university students in Hungary (1.8 times their proportion of the national population, notwithstanding formal limits on entrance), they were 19.3 percent in Poland (1.9 times), 15.4 percent in the Soviet Union (5.9 times), 8.7 percent in Latvia (1.8 times), and 9.7 percent in Lithuania (3.2 times) (Ruppin, 1973, p. 313).

Declines in the distinctive economic place of the Jews of Eastern Europe appeared. As had occurred in the West with the advent of intensive modernization, there were decreases in the proportions of merchants and others engaged in commerce and trade who were Jews. In Hungary in 1910, Jews were 47 percent of the merchants; ten years later, they accounted for 41 percent, and in 1935, 35 percent. In Poland, they were 63 percent of the merchants in 1921 and 53 percent in 1931. In Galicia, they were 83 percent in 1910 and 74 percent in 1921; in Lithuania, 86 percent in 1897, 73 percent in 1923, and 55 percent in 1935; in Czechoslovakia, they were 19 percent in 1921 and 12 percent ten years later. Similar patterns may be found in the cities of Eastern Europe. In Warsaw, Jews were 80 percent of the merchants in 1882 and 60 percent in 1921. By the middle of the 1930s, Jewish tradesmen accounted for less than half the total in the city. In Lodz in 1897, Jews were 68 percent of the merchants, and in 1921 they were 62 percent (Ruppin, 1934, pp. 148, 173, 210; Weinryb, 1946, p. 32; Lestchinsky, 1931, pp. 142–46; Mendelsohn, 1983). All over Europe, the distinctive place of Jews as merchants was declining.

At the same time, Jews entered the professional classes in Eastern Europe. In the Hungarian census-of 1920, Jews were more than half the lawyers, 46 percent of the physicians, 39 percent of the engineers and chemists, and one-third of the editors and journalists. There, as in Poland and in Czechoslovakia at that time, Jews accounted for approximately the same proportion of the professionals and officials as they did of the general population (Laszlo, 1966, pp. 146–48; Ruppin, 1973, p. 220).

These changes reflect as well growing urbanization. Between 1897 and 1921, the proportion of Jews living in rural areas of Poland dropped from 14 percent to 7 percent. During those years, the proportion of Jews living in Polish towns with fewer than 10,000 declined from 45 percent to 38 percent. At the same time, the proportion in large cities increased from 20 percent to 27 percent (Weinryb, 1946, p. 28; Engelman, 1973, pp. 202–23; Ruppin, 1934, p. 67).

As in Western Europe, these alterations in the social, economic, and residential patterns of the Jewish communities contained traditional and new bases of cohesion. Modernization brought Jews together in new ways, while building on and modifying old ties. Moreover, given the relatively greater size and institutionalization of the Jewish communities and the relatively weaker forces of modernization in Eastern Europe, we would expect to find more sources of cohesion among the Jews of the East than the West, even as modernization intensified.

Urbanization in the East, unlike the West, continued to reinforce Jewish communities, which were relatively large and well established. In 1925, 31 percent of the Jews of Poland lived in cities containing 100,000 or more residents, 8 percent were in cities between 50,000 and 100,000, 17 percent in cities of 20,000–50,000, 45 percent in smaller communities. This compares to two-thirds of the Jews of Germany who lived in cities of 100,000 or more, 6 percent in cities of 50,000–100,000, 6 percent in cities of 20,000–50,000, and 21 percent in towns with fewer than 20,000 residents. In Poland, there were 34 cities with 10,000 or more Jews: Jews were more than one-third of the population in 70 percent of the town and cities, and in one-third they were more than half the population. In Warsaw, where Jews were 27 percent of the nearly half-million inhabitants, residential clustering is evident. In the 1930s, Jews composed 90 percent of the Nalewki and Muranow sections. Urbanization in Hungary combined aspects present in both Germany and Poland. While half the Jews there lived in Budapest in 1934, the remainder lived in medium-sized towns and cities with long-established Jewish communities. In the West, almost all the Jews lived in metropolises or small towns. In Eastern Europe, most lived in small cities, with densely organized and highly structured communities containing 10,000–30,000 Jews (Koralnik, 1928, pp. 217–19; Schmelz, 1982, p. 40; Heller, 1980, p. 72; Engelman, 1973, p. 203; see also Mendelsohn, 1983).

Furthermore, the distribution of the Jews in Poland more closely resembled the Polish urban population than it did the distribution of the German Jews. In addition, the rate of urbanization between 1897 and 1921 in Poland shows a doubling of the number of Jews and a fourfold increase among non-Jews in cities of 50,000–100,000. Jews declined from 55 percent to one-third of the population of such cities. In the large cities, Lodz and Warsaw, both groups doubled their populations during those decades (Koralnik, 1928, pp. 216–19).

As in Western Europe, declines in the Jewish proportion of the merchant class did not diminish economic ties among Jews in the East. In Poland, and elsewhere in Europe, these proportional declines resulted from increases in the number of non-Jews in commerce and trade, not declines in the number of Jews. Poland and Germany differed in the relative number and location of Jewish and Gentile merchants. In the East, the number of Gentile traders did not overwhelm their Jewish competitors. In Poland, however, where they were relatively equal in number and located in the same markets, the postwar Polish government enabled the Polish merchants to compete successfully with the long-established Jewish traders. It nationalized areas that had long been monopolized by Jews and supported Polish cooperatives and merchants. The level of Polish economic expansion could not absorb all those in commerce. As a result, the number of Jewish traders dropped, as many were forced into bankruptcy and to emigrate (see Chapters 9 and 12).

The hundreds of thousands of Jews who remained in trade and commerce continued to exhibit economic concentrations. In Warsaw, in 1925, two-thirds were self-employed, and more than half the self-employed Jews were in trade and commerce. At the same time, nearly three-fourths of the self-employed businessmen were Jews (Lestchinsky, 1928c).

Similarly, Jewish workers retained their traditional places in local economies. More than one-third of Warsaw's Jews were in industry and crafts, nearly 40 percent of them as independent craftsmen. As had long been the case, half the Jewish workers labored in clothing, and nearly 20 percent were in textiles and food. In addition, Jews continued to work in relatively smaller and less mechanized factories. Hence, relatively few could be found in the machine and metal industries of Warsaw (Lestchinsky, 1928c, 1972; Garncarska-Kadari, 1976). These patterns continued to define the Jewish workers, maintaining ties among them, against Jewish capitalists, and separating them from Polish workers.

As had emerged in Western Europe, Jewish professionals and civil servants found few places in government agencies. In Warsaw, to continue the example, Jews were 13 percent of all the professionals and civil servants, 43 percent of self-employed medical professionals, 12 percent of salaried medical professionals, and 2 percent of the salaried lawyers and government officials. Similarly, almost no Jews (168 out of nearly 26,000) worked in the departments of communications, railroads, gas, water, and electricity. Nearly half the Jewish professionals compared to 15 percent of the non-Jews were self-employed.

The Jewish professionals in Warsaw differed from those in the West. Nearly half were teachers, 22 percent physicians, 8 percent lawyers and officials, and 5 percent rabbis. Even among the self-employed professionals, the same pattern applied. Teachers, self-employed and salaried, predominated among the Jewish professionals of Warsaw. Physicians predominated in Prussian Jewry. (The data on Warsaw are from Lestchinsky, 1928c, 1931, 1932, which also show similar occupational patterns among the Jews of Poland, Rumania, and Hungary; see also Mendelsohn, 1983).

The presence of large numbers of working-class Jews and many Jewish teachers are part of a pattern that produced different levels of secular education among the Jews of Eastern and Western Europe. In Poland, government policy forced ethnic Poles, between the ages of seven and fourteen to attend school, while leaving the children of the ethnic minorities to their own devices (Davies, 1982, 2:418). The high levels of poverty among Polish Jews and the absence of economic opportunities combined with this government policy to limit the number of Jewish youngsters in school. In 1925, half the Jewish youngsters and 90 percent of the non-Jews of school age were in school. In addition, the relative availability of work for Jewish boys further depressed their school attendance. At that time, three-fourths of the Jewish girls and 30 percent of the boys attended school. Furthermore, the Jewish teachers were part of a private Jewish school system, offering studies in schools as varied as traditional hederim and Polish language academies. Jewish boys tended to go to the private schools, while the girls attended the public schools. In 1925, 83 percent of the Jewish children in public schools were girls. There was, too, a tendency for Jews in small- and medium-sized cities to attend schools with Hebrew- or Yiddish-language instruction. In Vilna, for example, nearly half attended such schools. In Warsaw, less than 10 percent did (Minzin, 1928). Unlike Germany, large numbers of Jewish children did not go to the most modern institutions of education in Poland (see also Mendelsohn, 1981, 1983).

Hence, patterns of education among the Jews of Paris, Berlin, Vienna, and Budapest differed dramatically from those of Warsaw, Lodz, Vilna, and the medium-sized cities and towns that housed most of the Jews of Poland, Rumania, and half those of Hungary. The greater the number of working-class Jews and the lower the number of liberal professionals, the lower the proportion of Jews in the public schools. In addition, the greater the presence of Jewish schools, the less likely were Jews to be in public schools. The intensity of modernization combined with the size, structure, and organizational strength of the Jewish community to determine educational patterns among the Jews. There is no evidence that differential Jewish values on education among these communities account for the differences.

Similarly, the greater secularization of Berlin Jews compared to those in Vilna needs to be studied in this framework. The renown of the Lithuanian yeshivot and Torah academies compared to other Eastern European areas (particularly Galicia) or to the West is clearly not a reflection of genetic differences or the accidents of history locating particularly keen Jewish scholars in these places. Rather, a more fruitful avenue of investigation focuses on two important economic facts correlated with high enrollments in Jewish academies in Lithuania: (1) the higher proportion of women (Jewish and non-Jewish) working in the factories of Lithuania, and (2) the high levels of unemployment of men, higher poverty levels, and lack of available economic opportunities. Although causal factors are difficult to isolate, it seems reasonable to argue that the great Jewish learning associated with Lithuanian Jewry was a product of the absence of alternative opportunities in jobs and education for men. Where opportunities for work and education emerged, there was less emphasis on extended study in Talmudic academies. With few jobs and opportunities, the values placed on traditional study for men were reinforced.

Past occupational concentration resulted in the strong crossnational similarities of Jews. Within the industrial sector in Eastern and Western Europe there was a heavy Jewish presence in clothing and textiles. In Russia, in 1897, 47 percent of the Jews worked in clothing and 6.4 percent in textiles; in Austria, in 1910, 41 percent were in clothing and 6 percent in textiles; in

Germany, in 1907, the distribution was 40 percent and 5.5 percent. The pattern holds over time. In Russia, in 1913, 55 percent of the Jews in industry worked in clothing and 6 percent in textiles. In postwar Poland (1921), 47 percent were in clothing and 8 percent in textiles; and in Czechoslovakia in that year the proportions were only slightly different, 32 percent in clothing and 4 percent in textiles (Kuznets, 1960, pp. 1612–13; Lestchinsky, 1928c). Across time and space, strong similarities in the distribution of Jews within industries emerge. We find the persistent place of Jews in distinct spheres of economic activity and circumstances of labor. Jews were more concentrated in these occupations and activities compared to non-Jews.

The pattern can be located even in Prussia, our example of advanced industrialization in Europe. In 1925, 60 percent of the Jews in industry and handicrafts were in the subsectors of food and clothing. In addition, Jewish immigrants from Eastern Europe to Prussia clustered into particular subcategories of the occupational structure. For example, about half the Jews working in the fur, tobacco, and shoemaking industries were immigrants from Eastern Europe, where many had worked in those trades (Ruppin, 1973, pp. 183–84). In other parts of Western Europe, and in the United States, Jewish immigrants also entered occupations in which they already had experience and skills. The extraordinary presence of these immigrants in the garment industry occurred not only in New York but in London, Manchester, Leeds, and Paris as well (Ruppin, 1973, pp. 186–87). The same patterns have been documented in Warsaw and Vienna. They occur as well within the professions. Jewish distinctiveness in various industries persisted even in the face of advanced modernization.

Patterns of occupational specialization may be found in trade and commerce as well. In Prussia, in 1925, 80 percent of the Jews in commerce were in wholesale and retail trade. Nearly two-thirds of these Jews owned their own businesses or worked for their parents or spouses (Ruppin, 1973, pp. 212–13). This parallels the patterns in Poland and Hungary where Jews had retained their places in those areas of trade where they had long worked. In Vienna and other cities we again find the same patterns: Jews in the textile trades and in liquor and wine sales as well as lower but still very high percentages in other spheres of trade (Laszlo, 1969, pp. 146–48; Ruppin, 1934, p. 160; and see Chapter 9).

The crossnational similarities among very diverse Jewish communities derive from preindustrial concentrations in particular economic niches. As economic modernization moved across Europe, Jews entered a much wider range of occupations. Diversification, however, did not mean randomization. The occupational mobility of Jews was tied to past economic experiences. Even when Jews entered new professions, they concentrated in particular specializations. Migration between countries within Europe and across the oceans diffused these patterns of economic specialization. There is no reason to postulate particular Jewish values for clothing rather than metal industries. Nor need we suppose that the desire to work with other Jews was the major determinant of occupational specialization. Both derive from structural features.

EXPLAINING THE PATTERNS OF CONTINUITY AND CHANGE

Many have taken the information that we have surveyed to support the assimilation theory of modernization. Indeed, most of those who have analyzed the Jewish communities of Europe, and who first gathered much of the data that we have presented, accept those arguments. Engelman argued that the urbanization of the late nineteenth and twentieth centuries would lead to the disintegration of the Jews as a people:

> The danger to a population in a very high degree of urbanization is apparent. In the case of the general population, however, this danger is partly neutralized by the influx of people from rural areas and small towns, where the birth rates are higher. . . . In the case of the Jews the migration is not from rural areas to cities but from smaller towns into larger ones. This naturally leads in each country to their very high degree of urbanization with its concomitant processes of sinking birth rates, rising death rates and an ageing population. This triple process, if unchecked, will in the end result in the complete disintegration of the Jewish population. That this is not merely a theoretical speculation is attested by the experience of the Jewish population in Vienna, Budapest, Berlin, Hamburg, Paris, London, Padua, Trieste, and other cities. [1973, p. 205]

Drawing on the general processes of social and economic modernization, Ruppin pointed to very similar conclusions:

> The most important process in the social life of the Jews since the eighteenth century has been the weakening of their ethnic homogeneity and of their sense of unity, and their assimilation to the economic and cultural life of their non-Jewish surroundings. [1973, p. 271]

He singled out five critical factors: declines in religious observance, weakening of the links of common descent and fate, loosening of family ties, economic adaptation to their surroundings, and differentiation. Together, they disintegrate the Jewish community. These arguments parallel the structural-functional theorists and the imagery of the windstorm in predicting that modernization leads to assimilation.

The evidence that we have presented—much of it taken from Engelman's and Ruppin's works—denies their interpretation. Even in the areas of most intense modernization various economic, residential, friendship, and familial factors continued to provide structural bases of Jewish cohesion. Change occurred. Some left the Jewish community; most did not. The Jews remained a distinct subgroup of European societies. Engelman and Ruppin erred in assuming that change on any one dimension meant assimilation on all dimensions.

These analysts erred with regard to another issue. They ignored the significance of new Jewish social and political associations and movements that combined with the religious institutions and legal communities to provide the organizational bases of Jewish cohesion.

THE ORGANIZATIONAL BASES OF JEWISH COHESION

The established organizational bases of Jewish communal life weakened with modernization. Kehillot were disbanded, courts were closed, and the political power of the rabbis and the centrality of the synagogue declined. They did not disappear but were joined by new institutions. Following the processes of differentiation, the new organizations centered around specific aspects of Jewishness—ethnic, occupational and class, political, religious, and social. Few integrated more than one element. The organizations frequently competed with each other, each claiming to be the legitimate inheritor of the past communal institutions, the exclusive voice of the Jewish community, and the best guarantor of Jewish survival in the modern world. Together, the established and new organizations maintained the presence of the Jews as a distinct group—in the eyes of Jews and non-Jews alike—and provided alternative bases for Jewish cohesion.

The most visible manifestations of these new associations were the political movements. In 1893, the *Centralverein* (CV) formed in Germany—a liberal Jewish defense organization. Four years later, Jewish socialists organized the *Bund* in Vilna, and in that same year the first Zionist Congress took place in Basel, Switzerland. Other movements followed soon thereafter. Socialist, religious, and political Zionists formed separate organizations. Ethnic Jewish political parties emerged in Central and Eastern Europe, as did the *Agudah*, a political movement organized by Orthodox rabbis in self-conscious political defense of religious orthodoxy. By the early 1920s, the various Jewish political movements criss-crossed the Jewish communities of Europe.

These groups organized portions of Jewish communities, providing new bases for sustained interaction among Jews. In Eastern Europe, where political organizations predominated, they also drew Jews into conflict with each other. By the 1920s, there is evidence that between one-fifth to one-fourth of the Jews were formally members or identified with these social, economic, and political movements.

An examination of the Centralverein demonstrates growth over time and questions again the assimilation of German Jews into German society. In 1894, the year after its founding, the Centralverein had approximately 1,500 members (Lamberti, 1978, p. 20). Nine years later, the number was 16,000, but then it declined to 12,000 in 1904, representing 100 affiliated local communities. During World War I, the CV had 35,000 members and claimed to represent nearly half the Jews in Germany. In 1920, the number of members was 55,000, and five years later there were approximately 70,000 members (Reinharz, 1975, pp. 52–53). Information on the German Zionist Federation shows a relatively smaller size but a similar pattern of growth: 4,500 members in 1903, 6,200 in 1910, and 9,800 in 1914 (Walk, 1979, p. 370; Poppel, 1976, pp. 175–76; Reinharz, 1975, p. 154). The active members of these organizations also took part in several other Jewish political groups that arose during those years, the fledgling Jewish Peoples Party, the *Verband* that fought anti-Semitism, and the *Hilfsverein*. By World War I, 8–10 percent of the adult Jewish population in Germany were claimed as members of the political movements.

Information on membership in the Bund is much less complete. In 1900, three years afrer the organization formed, there were 5,600 members (Tobias, 1972, p. 98). Five years later, following intense efforts to expand, there were approximately 30,000 Bundists, and there were thirty-five cities with Bund chapters (Rubinow, 1975, pp. 548–53; Brym, 1978, p. 91). They had the same number at the start of World War I in 300 branches across the Pale (Gitelman, 1972, p. 72). The number of Bundists grew rapidly following the effort to expand the organization, between 1895 and 1905, and did not change until after World War I.

Broadening the definition of membership in the Bund to include those who took part in their activities or those which were in line with Bund goals, such as strikes and other union activities, provides another way of examining the political behavior of the Jewish masses. Union activities in the 1890s involved about 1,000 organized workers in twenty-seven crafts in Vilna and a similar number in twenty-one crafts in Minsk (Mendelsohn, 1970, pp. 67–68; Tobias, 1972, p. 37). In these and other cases, approximately one-fourth of the Jewish workers had joined the Bundist unions (Tobias, 1972, p. 98).

A study of strikes during the decade 1895–1904 found approximately 2,300 well-documented strikes of which 1,673 took place between 1900 and 1904 (cited in Mendelsohn, 1970, p. 85). A calculation of the number of Jewish workers on strike during those years found a similar pattern. By including the approximately 2,000 members of the government-sponsored union, it appears that about 30,000–40,000 Jews were actively involved in Jewish unions.

Sources on membership in Zionist organizations provide rough estimates and do not cover all years or locales. In addition, it is difficult to define Zionist activity, since it ranged from emigration to Palestine, joining a local branch of the *Hovevei Zion* (Lovers of Zion), paying the *shekel* dues, and reading Zionist newspapers. During the years of the first Zionist emigration (1881–1904), 20,000–30,000 left Europe for Palestine, approximately 1,000 per year. There were twelve branches of Hovevei Zion in 1882, 138 six years later, and 193 local groups in 1891– 92. In 1898, there were 913 local Zionist associations, of which 373 were in Russia and 250 were in Austria-Hungary. There were approximately 10,000 active members during the decade 1885– 95. Taking the broadest possible definition of membership, there were probably between 30,000 and 100,000 members (Vital, 1976, pp. 155–58; 1982, p. 66).

The years following the Revolution of 1905 saw a marked growth in membership in Zionist organizations. The entry of Zionist Socialist groups rapidly attracted adherents (Tobias, 1972, p. 245; Gitelman, 1972, p. 48; Brym, 1978, p. 29). By World War I, there were as many as 300,000 Zionists in Russia belonging to 12,000 local branches of the various Zionist movements (Gitelman, 1972, p. 71; Baron, 1976a, p. 118). At that time, there were approximately ten times as many Zionists as Bundists in Russia.

With the establishment of communal and governmental elections in various countries after World War I, the Jewish political movements battled each other for the votes of the Jewish masses. In the elections for the Russian Constituent Assembly, held in 1918, the Jewish parties received 500,000 votes, of which nearly 420,000 went to Zionist or religious parties. Other elections in Russia report similar patterns. The Zionist and religious parties consistently outpolled the Jewish Socialists by wide margins (Gitelman, 1972, pp. 78–81). In Poland during the 1920s and 1930s, the Jewish political parties gathered 750,000 votes. In each of the national elections, the Agudah, the Zionists, and the other "bourgeois" parties gathered over 500,000 votes (Vago, 1974, pp. 40–41; see also Mendelsohn, 1981, 1983). Nowhere did the Bund succeed in gathering as much as one-fourth of the Jewish voters. Indeed, we find consistent strength for the autonomist parties, the Zionists, and the Agudah in Rumania as well as Poland, and predominance for the autonomists and Zionists in Czechoslovakia. In Germany, Austria, and Hungary, Jewish voters maintained their ties to the liberal parties, notwithstanding the presence of various Jewish political movements (Vago, 1974; Simon, 1971; Frye, 1976; Rosensaft, 1976). In their defense of Jewish rights, in their discussions, campaigns, rallies, demonstrations, and strikes, these organizations provided new bases for Jewish interaction and identity.

The Zionists and the Bund led the way in establishing networks of schools, sports and youth activities, publishing houses, and trade unions. At the same time, cultural, social, economic, and ethnic associations, with no political ties, developed as well. In Germany, for example, a Jewish Feminist Association was established in 1904. Ten years later, it claimed 35,000 members, and in the late 1920s it had 50,000 members (one-fourth of the eligible Jewish women). The number of affiliated societies grew from seventy-two in 1905, to 215 in 1917, to 430 at the end of the 1920s (Kaplan, 1979, p. 89). Evidence about youth organizations shows similar patterns. In 1887, Jewish university students formed a fraternity, and several years later they established a national association. In 1901, there were nearly 1,300 members of the *Jugendverband*, A year later, the number grew to 7,000; 8,669 in 1911; 14,500 in 1913; and in 1919, there were 41,000 in the movement, making it the largest of all German Jewish organizations at that time (Strauss, 1966, p. 210). This group joined its parent, the *B'nai Brith*, and others like the Blue-White and the Maccabi sports federation, to provide a network of Jewish social and cultural activities across Germany. In Eastern Europe, the pattern of youth organizations was even more dense. Each of the many political and religious organizations formed youth movements, as did several apolitical movements. By the 1920s, all the Jewish communities of Europe had several youth organizations (Mendelsohn, 1981, 1983).

In Eastern Europe, especially Poland, Rumania, and portions of Hungary and Czechoslovakia, the new organizations overlapped and competed with established institutions of the Jewish communities. Large numbers of Jewish schools, for example, predated the establishment of those sponsored by the government or the political movements. The hederim and the yeshivot competed with the new schools. They still produced teachers and rabbis who filled positions in the religious institutions. Various Hasidic groups maintained hundreds of thousands in tightly knit communities. The rise of the Agudah political party helped to organize the traditional religious movements. In the countries of Eastern Europe, a plethora of new Jewish political, economic, and social organizations joined relatively well-established religious associations, each seeking to represent the Jews. Zionists, Bundists, Agudists, and others organized segments of the Jewish community, binding their constituents together in competition with the others.

In the West, where the Jews had long lived in smaller and less-structured communities, the new Jewish organizations reinforced the level of interaction among the Jews, providing new ways and institutions in which people expressed their Jewishness. At the same time, their pronouncements, rallies, court actions, and other activities increased the visibility of the Jews as a distinct group in society, without producing much internal conflict. A close look at Germany, from 1890 to the rise of the Nazis, shows the presence of a large number of diverse organizations, not the absence of Jewish communal activity. There were several political and defense groups: the Centralverein, the Zionists, and the Agudah were only the most visible. There were political and independent youth, feminist, and sports organizations. The locally established communities were alternately divided into Reform, Orthodox, and United congregations. There were professional associations, as the Jewish Teachers Association. In addition, large numbers of parallel

political, social, economic, and religious institutions existed among the
Jewish immigrants from Eastern Europe. Not only were all German Jews
formally members of legally recognized local Jewish communities, but most
were also at least nominal members of a Jewish organization. Some portion,
probably about one-fifth, were active members of different organizations.
The dominance of the CV and the absence of class divisions meant that these
organizations served as bases of cohesion without bringing about much
internal conflict (see Chapter 8).

In France, the consistories had long organized the Jewish communities.
While all Jews were nominal members, most did not take part in its activities. In 1898, only 900 of the 50,000 Jews of Paris contributed to the
community's welfare funds. At that time, there were only a few organizations—three student associations (one for Russian Jews), two burial associations, and a men's club (Marrus, 1971, pp. 71–81). The growth of the Zionist
movement in France, the influx of a large number of immigrants from
Eastern Europe, and the formal separation of church and state changed this
pattern. The Jews from Eastern Europe brought with them religious, social,
cultural, and political organizations. Many political exiles came after the
failed Russian Revolution of 1905, establishing in France the political organizations of Russian Jewry. The separation of church and state in 1905
allowed as well for the establishment of independent religious congregations, many of them composed of the 150,000–200,000 Jews from Eastern
Europe who settled in France between 1906 and 1939. As a result, they
changed the ethnic composition of French Jewry. By the middle of the
1930s, there were political, social, cultural, and economic associations,
landsmanschaften, political parties, and Jewish trade unions (Hyman, 1979,
pp. 77–78). Half the Jews of Paris were members of these organizations
(Weinberg, 1977, p. 22). In France, as in Germany, the period before and
after World War I was less one of general assimilation than one of the rapid
growth of Jewish organizations and new forms of Jewish cohesion, and
relatively few sources of internal conflict.

The new organizations provided alternatives to the centrality of religion
as the sole form of legitimate Jewishness. Numerous, well-respected, and
visible, leaders of most of these organizations pronounced it possible,
indeed necessary, to be Jewish and not religious, except in a formal sense. In
Germany, for example, the leaders of the CV campaigned against separate
Jewish schools (Lamberti, 1978). Bundists and Zionist-Socialists opposed
the rabbis and religious organizations. Most other political activists were at
best indifferent to Judaism. These organizations provided employment
opportunities for Jewish professionals, and as such they competed with the
rabbinate and with the Jewish schools for their services. Just as the CV, the
Bund, the Zionist federations, and the sports and cultural associations
competed with the agencies of the general society for the affiliations of the

Jews, they also battled each other and the older religious institutions. The result of the first competition was to provide new institutions for Jewish survival. The latter competition helped to distinguish different ways of being Jewish, especially to disentangle religious from other forms of Jewish identity and practice.

Hence, the organizations provided new bases of cohesion within the Jewish community. As they competed with each other for members and support, they involved large numbers of Jews. In turn, they bound their adherents together and divided them from other Jews. At the same time, their presence and activity maintained the visibility of Jews in the general society and their distinctiveness. These organizations are part of the social and political patterns which demonstrate that the Jews of Europe were not assimilating during the process of modernization.

Therefore, in large portions of Europe, especially but not exclusively in the East, the transformations of modernization reestablished bases of Jewish cohesion, distinctiveness and religion. Occupational and residential clustering overlapped with ethnicity. Political and social organizations reinforced these ties, as did the bonds of family and friendship. The distinctiveness of the Jews was less evident in Western Europe, where their numbers were smaller, their institutions weaker, and the forces of modernization stronger than in the East. Everywhere in Europe, new forms of Jewish identification and new bases of Jewish cohesion emerged with the processes of modernization.

8 · The Rise and Development of Jewish Political Movements in Europe

The emergence of Jewish political movements was one of the most visible transformations that accompanied the processes of modernization. Jewish political parties, defense organizations, and pressure groups opened offices, ran candidates in communal and general elections, demonstrated, and rallied. They espoused ideologies and offered solutions to questions about Jews and Judaism. As the religious movements before them, they too were elite responses to the Jewish Question. Even though their actual effects did not match their goals, they had important consequences for Jewish communities. They reshaped the ways in which Jews thought about themselves and their place in the world, and interacted with each other, and restructured the ways others related to the Jews.

Jewish political movements did not emerge everywhere. They were not automatically associated with social and economic modernization. We explore three issues about these movements: (*a*) What explains the formation and initial claims of the political groups? (*b*) What accounts for the groups' organizational developments? Why did they organize when they did, and what factors explain their different organizational patterns? (*c*) Why did the different political ideologies unfold as they did? What explains the particular ideology of each and the differences among them?

Our analysis follows the same theoretical approach that we used to study the rise of new religious movements in Germany in an earlier period (see Chapter 6):

1. The political changes within the Jewish community reflected transformations occurring within the general society. Jewish political movements emerged when other political parties, interest groups, and trade unions developed. Jewish political movements are best studied, therefore, by placing them in the context of political movements forming at that time.

2. The new political ideologies were with few exceptions the work of intellectuals, living in and emerging from the universities, reflecting the dominant ideas within that world. As more Jews were exposed to universi-

ties, the new ideologies spread among them and through them to the Jewish masses.

3. Each of the ideologies developed and organizations formed in competitive response to the claims and activities of other political movements. Therefore, where there was little competition among Jewish political movements, there was little ideological development beyond the initial principles and relatively little organizational elaboration. The greater was the competition, the more intense the organizational and ideological growth.

4. The political organizations made the new ideologies visible within the Jewish and general communities. The organizations became the primary objects of loyalty for the activists, while they mobilized relatively few Jews.

5. The political organizations competed with each other and with traditional religious institutions for the loyalties and commitments of Jews. The new bases of Jewish interaction, the growing complexity of organizational life, and the differentiation of religious from political issues are exemplified in this process. Hence, Jewish political movements served as Jewish institutions of modernity, providing a way to be both Jewish and modern at the same time (see Chapter 7).

We begin by specifying the distinct ideologies set forth by the principal political movements. The CV (*Centralverein deutscher Staatsburger juedischen Glaubens*, Central Association of German Citizens of the Jewish Faith) illustrates Jewish liberalism, the Bund (General Union of Jewish Workers in Russia and Poland) exemplifies socialism, and nationalism was articulated by the Zionists. The CV addressed the problem of the integration of Jews into society, the Bund addressed the issue of the role of Jews in the political and economic revolutions, and the Zionists argued that the Jewish Question could be solved only by removing the Jews from Europe. The general claims of our analysis fit other Jewish political movements as well—the ethnic parties, the defense organizations, the Agudah, and others. We focus on these three because they were the most important and visible political movements among Jews during the period 1890 to World War II.

The Political Ideologies

The leaders of the Jewish communal organizations in Western and Central Europe espoused political liberalism. Those who formed the CV proclaimed their commitment to Germany, liberalism, and the Enlightenment. They professed the belief that the growing political success of liberalism would inaugurate an era of Jewish Emancipation. The formation of a separate Jewish organization was justified not as an act of isolation but as an aid to the fulfillment of liberalism for all Germans. Soon after the formation of the CV in 1893, the leaders issued a pamphlet explaining their aims:

[T]o defend the rights of Germans of the Jewish faith against attack and to implant in the Jews themselves the feeling of belonging collectively to the German people, Through word of mouth and publications, through public meetings and lectures, the Centralverein wants to arm the individual Jew with ammunition that will enable him to withstand the daily struggle in the light of truth; it wants to enlighten the public, both friends and enemies, through all available public media, about the nature of Judaism. . . . We invite all citizens to enlist in our endeavours. . . . Through defense of our equality we fight for the highest ideals of humanity, for the holiest interests of our German fatherland. [Cited in Reinharz, 1975, p. 47]

Jews are defined as a religious group with no political and social bonds, a view continuous with earlier religious ideologies (Chapter 5). The claims made by the founders of the CV echo statements issued by the Jewish leaders of France. Only the patria to which they claim filial loyalty differed. Even in the Tsarist Empire, Jewish voices espoused political liberalism (see the statements of Andre Spire and Chief Rabbi Zadok Kahn cited in Marrus, 1971, pp. 264, 223; and the statement signed by 6,000 Jews at the time of the Revolution of 1905, cited in Greenberg, 1944, 2:114.). Especially, but not exclusively in the western portions of Europe, Jews formed political groups that adopted the principles, strategies, and tactics of political liberalism.

The Jews who formed the Bund in 1897 proclaimed their loyalty to the Socialist revolution and commitment to defend the special interests of the Jews:

A general union of all Jewish socialist organizations will have as its goal not only the struggle for general Russian political demands; it will also have the special task of defending the particular interests of the Jewish workers, carrying on the struggle for the civic rights of the Jewish workers and, above all, carrying on the struggle against discriminatory anti-Jewish laws. This is because the Jewish workers suffer not only as workers but also as Jews, and we must not and cannot remain indifferent at such a time. [Cited in Levin, 1977, pp. 258–59]

These activists turned to Jewish workers after more than a decade of struggle within Russian revolutionary circles. Their proclamation joined general and Jewish political demands. Over the next two decades, the Bund increased its Jewish concerns, declaring itself by the Revolution of 1905, the representative of the Jewish masses in the Pale and calling for national political autonomy for the Jews in Russia.

The Zionists rejected the liberals' trust in the prospects of peaceful democratic change and the revolutionaries' dream of total transformation of European societies. There could be no solution for Jewish individuals without a change in the Jewish people. The Jews were neither a particular group within the working class, to take the definition offered by the Bundists, nor only a religious community. The Jews like the Italians, Germans, Poles, and others were a nation with the rights to a homeland. Some sought a haven for the Jewish masses, defining the Jewish Question as the condition of the Jewish people. Some sought a place where idealistic youth could create a new society, defining the Jewish Question as the condition of Judaism. Some sought to merge both considerations by building a model society. Still others saw Zionism as a religious return to Zion. All maintained that only emigration to a national home could solve the Jewish Question.

These political views appear in the earliest Zionist pronouncements. In September, 1881, Pinsker published *Autoemancipation*, in which he maintained:

The essence of the problem, as we see it, lies in the fact that, in the midst of the nations among whom the Jews reside, they form a distinctive element which cannot be assimilated, which cannot be readily digested by any nation. Hence the problem is to find means of so adjusting the relations of this exclusive element to the whole body of the nations that there shall never be any further basis for the Jewish question. [Cited in A. Hertzberg, 1975, p. 182]

Civil and political emancipation would not solve this problem. There were too many poor Jews, and the nations would never fully emancipate the Jews. Rather:

The proper and only remedy would be the creation of a Jewish nationality, of a people living upon its own soil, the auto-emancipation of the Jews, their emancipation as a nation among nations by the acquisition of a home of their own. [Cited in ibid., p. 198]

This view emphasized the need to help the poor Jews of Eastern Europe. It carried no exclusive focus on a particular territory as the place for the new homeland. Any "piece of land (that) might form a small territory in North America, or a sovereign pashalike in Asiatic Turkey . . . " would be appropriate (cited in A. Hertzberg, 1975, p. 197). Others differed, maintaining an absolute attachment to Israel as the only home for the Jewish people. The early Zionists and those who joined the movement after the First Zionist Congress in 1897 agreed that only political action would lead to emigration to a national homeland and the solution of the Jewish question.

THE SOURCES OF POLITICAL IDEOLOGIES

The ideologies of the political movements—liberalism, revolutionism, and nationalism—emerged from the universities and the societies in which they were found. As Jews entered the gymnasia and the universities, they came in contact with the political ideologies. Where political liberalism prevailed—

in France, Germany, and Italy, for example—most Jewish students were political liberals. Where revolutionary groups competed with liberals—in the Tsarist Empire, for example—Jewish students also divided between liberals and revolutionaries. Initially, Jewish students responded to the prevalent political developments without forming separate Jewish movements.

The creation of ideologies that contracted general political beliefs into principles attuned to Jewish concerns is accounted for by three hypotheses. First, the more restricted were the employment opportunities for Jewish intellectuals and university graduates, the more likely they were to move back into the Jewish community, bringing with them the ideologies of the university. Second, the less successful were Jewish political activists among non-Jews, the more likely they were to seek followers within the Jewish community. Neither intellectual commitment to a set of ideas nor an emotional attachment to the Jewish community moved Jewish students from liberal to Jewish liberal organizations or from revolutionary to Jewish revolutionary movements. Their ability to find places within the general liberal or revolutionary worlds were the key factors.

At the same time, it is inadequate to argue that limited employment opportunities and political successes alone led Jewish intellectuals back into the Jewish community. Rather, and this is our third hypothesis, the greater the number of Jewish students in universities, the more likely they were to form political groups like those present in the universities among fellow Jewish students and within the broader Jewish community. In particular, as more Jews entered the universities, conflict and competition with non-Jews ensued, as did the exclusion of Jews from student associations. As more Jews entered the university, the interaction among them grew, providing the social bases for group cohesion. Moreover, as their numbers increased, more came from communities, occupations, and residences characterized by strong Jewish cohesion. This affected the Jewish character of student life. More important, these students conveyed the new ideologies to their communities of origin. In this chapter, we focus primarily on the political factors that account for these developments (social, demographic, and economic analyses were presented in Chapters 6 and 7).

THE IDEOLOGICAL SOURCE OF THE CV

The CV's ideology blended Jewish defense with a belief in the values of German liberalism. These ideas appeared first among Jewish university students in the 1880s who established a separate Jewish fraternity. The formation of this organization and the ideology that sustained it followed from changes within the world of German universities. German student organizations formed, emphasizing the nationalistic and romantic virtues of honor, physical combat, and courage, while questioning liberal principles.

The fraternities excluded Jews, defining them as outside the bounds of the student community. At the same time, large numbers of Jewish students, many from Posen and the eastern reaches of the German Empire, entered the universities. Jews altered their vision of liberalism as the general commitment to liberalism changed and as their numbers grew.

Jewish students responded to the exclusions in two ways. Some reasserted their faith in liberal ideology and called upon the Christian students to do the same. Others formed groups that modified liberalism with the new values asserted by the Germans. This second response permitted Jewish fraternities. In 1886, twelve Jewish students at the University of Breslau formed the *Viadrina*, the first of these groups. In the founding statement, they justified their action:

Meeting with people with the same interests and ideas, joining a community forms the basis of social life and plays an important part in the life of an undergraduate. We are either completely excluded from these communities or offered membership in a form and under conditions unacceptable to most of us. A strict exclusion of Jewish fellow-students is to be found particularly in the sports clubs, which are of such eminent importance above all for students. [This and subsequent quotations are cited in Asch and Philippson, 1958, pp. 123–25]

Their solution was to form an Association of Jewish Students which would "revive the almost extinguished consciousness that we are Jews, that we belong to a great community, important in the history of civilization and justified in its existence. It will show that there is no reason why our opponents should despise us and no reason why we should be ashamed of being Jews." Lest anyone claim that they too were breaking with liberalism, the students argued that they could be "Jews and good Germans at the same time, and we shall prove it by our behaviour. . . . A union of Jews does not in any way mean seclusion. . . . " They denied too the utility of an association of Jews and non-Jews to fight anti-Semitism. "Such an organization would consist mainly of Jews as members, and the same difficulties would arise. . . . " Finally, they argued that the Catholic students had already organized many members "and may be proud of their far-reaching influence." It is striking how many of the arguments used to justify the formation of the CV seven years later were already set forth by these twelve students in Breslau.

The influence of the German student associations leaps forth from the activities and goals of the Viadrina:

Our association is to be, first of all, a place for physical training of every kind: gymnastics, fencing, rowing, swimming. We have to fight with all our energy against the odium of cowardice and weakness which is cast on us. We want to show that every member of our association is equal to every Christian fellow-student in any physical exercise and chivalry. . . . We hope to acquire a firm foundation for this self-respect and self-confidence by studying Jewish history, the deeds and suffering of our ancestors.

The Viadrina's members imported their goals and mode of organization directly from the German students around them. The principles were echoed by other Jewish fraternities formed over the next decade at other universities and in the *Kartell Covenant*, the national association of German Jewish students (Asch and Philippson, 1958, pp. 135–36; Reinharz, 1975, pp. 30–32). The same Jewish students who formed the fraternities founded and worked for the CV.

THE SOURCES OF BUNDIST AND ZIONIST IDEOLOGIES

In Russia, too, Jewish students joined liberal political groups. The weakness of these groups in the Tsarist Empire meant that they attracted and retained relatively few adherents. Several of the earliest Zionist leaders became Jewish nationalists after government policies and the rise of powerful revolutionary movements threatened the survival of political liberalism in Russia. In addition, the political beliefs of Russian student revolutionaries were the ideological source of the Bund and important segments of the Zionist movement. The overwhelming success of the revolutionaries among student activists was mirrored among Jewish students.

The fundamental ideas set forth by the Bund and the Zionists echoed political beliefs present among Russian student revolutionaries in the 1870s. The source of these political movements was the same for each. The break between them came at the end of the decade. The split reflected alterations in the ideologies occasioned by the initial failure of the revolutionaries and subsequent strategic considerations that ensued.

The failure of the *Vai Narod* (Movement to the People) structured all revolutionary movements in Russia in the last quarter of the nineteenth century (Venturi, 1960; Carr, 1966, 1970; Schapiro, 1964). In 1873–74, several thousand students of the Russian universities and gymnasia went out to live among the peasants and workers, both to learn from them and, especially, to educate them on the need for a revolution against the tsar. The students envisaged a new Russia based on collectivist agriculture, modeled on the peasant community—the *obschina*—without nobles and aristocracy and moving rapidly to a socialist society. Jews were among the students who "went to the people"—the Narodniks. At that time, the Jews amounted to approximately 5 percent of the university students, and they were about that proportion of the Narodniks as well. Their political behavior, as well as that of the others, was directly affected by the collapse of the student movement.

The Jewish revolutionaries placed themselves squarely within the general movement. They identified with the Russian—not the Jewish—masses.

Many of these students recounted in their memoirs their reasons for "going to the people" and their views of the Jewish people.

> For us, Jewry, as a national organism did not present a phenomena worthy of support. Jewish nationalism, it seemed to us, had no raison d'etre. . . . For a Jewish Narodnik the motto—"Go to the people"—meant to the Russian people. [Zundelevich, cited in Greenberg, 1944, 1:148]

> We were convinced assimilationists and found salvation for the Jew in the Russian enlightenment. . . . As to the laboring masses of Jews, we believed that the liberation of the Russian people from despotism and the oppression of the ruling classes would liberate all other people in Russia, including the Jews.
> The Russian literature which has imbued us with affection for the Russian peasant, created in our mind a picture of the Jews not as a people, but as a class of parasites. Such opinions . . . prompted us to desert the Jewish people. [Jochelson, cited in Levin, 1977, p. 29; see also Akselrod, cited in ibid., p. 34; Deich, cited in Greenberg, 1944, 1:147–48; Gozhanski, cited in Mendelsohn, 1970, p. 34]

Few of the Jewish revolutionaries took any interest in the condition of the Jews. With but one or two exceptions, all rejected any effort to marry particular Jewish concerns with the revolution.

The failure of the Vai Narod split the revolutionary movement. Those who emphasized direct action turned to terrorist activities that culminated in the assassination of Tsar Alexander II on March 1, 1881. The others maintained the necessity of working among the masses, but they were divided over the issue of who was most likely to lead the revolution. Those who formed the Socialist movement worked among the industrial laborers and adopted Marx's analysis of the bases of revolution. Others retained their ties to the peasantry, by far the largest group in Russian society, and sought a new socialist life based on collectivist agriculture. Until the end of the century, these groups had no formal organizations. Each movement was tightly bound by informal ties of friendship, shared experiences, conspiracy, and revolutionary beliefs.

The Jewish students who worked among the laborers gravitated to Jewish artisans and proletarians, not out of commitment to Jewish issues and interests but because their primary successes were among Jewish workers. Ethnic barriers limited their appeal to non-Jews. Memoirs of early Jewish Socialists leave little doubt that tactics, not ideology, moved them to work among the Jewish proletariat:

> We wanted them to assimilate as quickly as possible; everything that smelled of Jewishness called forth among many of us a feeling of contempt, if not more. . . . We all believed that as soon as Jews began to

speak Russian, they would, just as we had, become "people in general, cosmopolites." [Deutsch, cited in Tobias, 1972, pp. 17–18; see also Kopelson in ibid.]

It is not clear to many why we began to work among the Jewish laborers. Weren't there other workers in Vilna? Certainly, there were artisans . . . among the Poles, Lithuanians, and Belorussians. Why were we shut up in our own world? That comrades is impossible to understand if one fails to recall the nature of the Jewish ghetto. The nationalities were separated by an impenetrable wall; each lived its own life, and had no contact with the other. [Cited in Mendelsohn, 1970, p. 32]

Other sources note how difficult it was for the Jewish Socialists to work among Russian and Polish workers. One picturesque account described experiences in a Christian-owned bindery:

Very often, someone would send along a bottle of "monopolke" (whiskey). They would pour it into tea glasses and drink it down like a glass of water. I had to drink along with them, otherwise I would not have been a "good brother." I had hoped that by becoming their "good brother" I would be able to make them class conscious. In the end neither of us achieved anything. They could not make me a drunkard, and I could not make them class conscious. [Levin, cited in Mendelsohn, 1970, p. 33]

During these early years, work among the Jewish laborers carried neither a Jewish emphasis nor an effort to organize large numbers. They used Yiddish as a tactic to reach Jewish workers, in the face of much ideological opposition within the revolutionary movement. No principles drew them to the Jewish workers. Rather their primary successes occurred among Jewish artisans and industrial laborers.

Jewish student revolutionaries, who retained the belief in the virtues of tilling the soil and of collectivist agriculture, had no peasantry. Their work among the Russian narod had resulted in abject failure. "Are you not a Zhid?" had been the peasants' retort to their efforts. In response, many turned to their people, the Jewish masses. But they had to create *de novo* Jewish peasants. How and where to do that became their central problem. They opted to establish Jewish collective farms, and chose emigration as the means to transform themselves and their people.

Where were they to build their new society? Some opted for America. Some opted for Palestine. The question of distination was tied directly to the availability of adequate land and working conditions for their farms. The choice between Palestine and America was a minor question in a generally agreed-upon agrarian socialist philosophy.

One such collective farm, *Beth Lechem Yahudah* (Bethlehem, Judea), was established in 1881 in the United States (in South Dakota). Its radical, agrarian goals may be seen from a letter written by one of the members and by the preamble to the collective's statutes:

A large number of colonists of Beth Lechem Yahudah live on a genuine communistic basis; others on the lines of the obschina (the old communal farm in the Russian village).

Beth Lechem Yahudah . . . will serve as a living example for the future colonies of Russian Jews in order to influence the Jewish people, to redeem them from the yoke of long national slavery, and to revitalize them to a new period of truth, freedom and peace. The colony will show the enemies of our people, all over the world, that the Jews are capable of doing agricultural work. [Cited in Epstein, 1969, p. 25]

These emigrants sought to lead the transformation of the Jewish people by bringing them to a relatively open land to work the soil.

In Kharkov University, students formed a similar group. The BILU (an acronym of the Biblical words, "House of Israel, let us go up!") began the era of modern politically based emigration to Palestine. Like the students who established colonies in America, they sought to transform their narod, the Jewish people, through collective labor on farms. They would lead; the masses would follow (see Frankel, 1981, p. 96).

The largest of these groups the *Am Haoylam*, founded two communes in America—one on Sicily Island, Louisiana; another near Portland, Oregon. Their members wavered between emigration to America or Palestine, opting for one, then the other, and finally to America.

One of the members of the group wrote in his diary:

Our motto is a return to agriculture, and our aim, the physical and spiritual rehabilitation of our people. In free America, where many peoples live closely in peace and amity, we Jews, too, shall find a place to lay our heads; we shall demonstrate to the world that we are capable of manual labor. [Cited in Menes, 1972, p. 162]

The government-sponsored pogroms of 1881–82 increased their desire to act. They believed that the intelligentsia had to find the proper place to lead its narod. Where they went, therefore, depended on an assessment of where they were most likely to succeed. It also rested on where their friends were going and where the next group to leave was heading (Menes, 1972; Frankel, 1981, pp. 90–93). Their ideology did not distinguish between Palestine and America.

Over time, emigration to establish agricultural collectives in America ended. Did those who went to Palestine have greater ideological commitment? Did the strength of their beliefs determine the persistence of a radical agrarian emigration to Palestine and not to America? There is no evidence that those who opted for Palestine held their ideals more intensely. No weakening in ideology led to a decline in the revolutionaries' emigration to

America. No strengthening of revolutionary ideology kept alive the movement to Palestine. Four factors help to account for subsequent events: (1) The abject social and economic failure of the agricultural colonies in America, None lasted past 1884. The attempt to establish urban cooperatives fared no better (Frankel, 1981; Menes, 1972; Epstein, 1969; Herscher, 1981). In capitalist, industrializing America, it is not surprising that these failed. (2) The survival of some of the colonies in Palestine. Even in Palestine, they did not succeed as collective farms. They did, however, remain visible as symbols of successful settlement. (3) Baron Rothschild's financial support and the use of Arab labor kept the colonies in Palestine alive. (4) The established leaders of Jewish communities in Eastern Europe aided the effort to settle Israel. In sum, the early settlement in Palestine survived relative to the American experiments largely because of the employment of Arab workers and the dependency on outside capital investments. Dependency and colonialism (external and internal) defined the early period of Jewish resettlement in Palestine (see Chapter 12).

This turn of events is ironic. A group that began within the Russian revolutionary movement found success only where it drew on the financial resources of capitalist wealth and on the traditional ties within the established Jewish community to the national homeland. Revolutionary emigration to America drew on neither. It declined as an ideological response to the Jewish Question, not as a popular answer among the masses. The persistence of the Palestine answer among the revolutionary emigrants rested in large part on its acceptance by others within the Jewish community.

The Jewish intellectuals brought the political ideologies into the Jewish community. They did so because they were excluded from the general society and not because the logic of the ideas pointed them in that direction or because of their commitment to the Jews. The Jewish revolutionaries worked among the Jewish masses only after the Vai Narod collapsed and the Russian peasants and workers rejected them. The Jewish liberals became nationalists after the pogroms of 1881–82. The flow of Jewish intellectuals into the Jewish community increased as the number of Jewish university students grew and as limitations were placed on Jewish entry into the professions.

IDEOLOGICAL AND ORGANIZATIONAL DEVELOPMENT
The political movements that developed these ideologies symbolized the political modernization of the European Jewish community. How and why did these clusters of students and others form political organizations? How did the core ideas develop into elaborate ideologies of Bundism, of the various streams of Zionism, and the political liberalism of those who headed the Centralverein?

Jews formed political parties and organizations and elaborated political ideologies in much the same manner that other people did. Jewish political organizations formed to defend previous gains. A challenge to a political group's continued existence or past successes is a necessary condition for organizational formation. The structure of the organization resembles that of the political movement's competitors. The political ideologies were neither unchanging blueprints for action nor logically unfolding arguments. As is usually the case, they developed in competitive response to the claims of others in their political arenas. The more competitors present, the more elaborate is each ideology. The more arenas in which a political group competes, the more elaborate is its ideology. Where competition was intense, as among émigré student groups at European universities, the ideologies flourished and the organizations grew. Where a movement faced weak opposition, as did the CV, no new principles and organizational advances appeared. The development of Jewish political organizations and ideologies parallels the emergence of other European political movements at the turn of the last century.

THE FORMATION OF THE CENTRALVEREIN

Changes in the political constellation of Germany account for the formation of the Centralverein in March, 1893. The CV formed in response to the weakening of liberal parties and the rise of political anti-Semitism. The preceding year witnessed charges of ritual murder, efforts to outlaw kosher slaughter, attacks on Jewish loyalty by intellectuals, the emergence of anti-Semitic political parties, and the adoption by older parties of anti-Jewish campaign appeals (Lamberti, 1978; Ragins, 1980; Reinharz, 1975; Schorsch, 1972; Toury, 1968). At the same time, the liberal parties, traditional allies of the Jewish leadership, lost political ground (Sheehan, 1978; White, 1976; Eley, 1978, 1980). The CV formed as well as part of a process by which the general level of politicization in Germany expanded. The founders of the CV announced the importance of responding to these initiatives:

Living in an age of interest groups, the Jews have discovered how necessary it is to form an interest group of all German Jews. [Fuchs, cited in Lamberti, 1978, p. 15]

The CV's organizational structure and activities echoed the forms of German political liberalism. The left-liberal parties were loosely organized clusters of notables. Unlike the Socialists, Catholics, and Polish parties, they had no trade unions, merchants associations, banks, and cooperatives (see Blackbourn, 1978, 1980; Evans, 1978a; Hagen, 1980). Factors associated with educational, class, ethnic, and religious backgrounds precluded ties to the Conservative and anti-Semitic parties as well as the Catholic Center party and the Polish and Social Democratic parties. Class factors tied

Jews to others who were urban and middle class and, therefore, to the liberal political parties.

The CV used action based on legal rights to exert political pressure. They defended their particular interests by showing how they were but a manifestation of the general good. The propensity of the CV to engage in court action to defend Jewish rights fits the conceptions of liberals and the skills of many CV activists who were lawyers. The Centralverein may best be understood as a group defending their view of Jewish interests from within the world of German liberalism, using the modes of political organization and action that predominated within that world.

For the first decade and a half of the CV's existence, it stood alone within Jewish communal politics in Germany. The Centralverein did not have to compete to influence the Jewish masses. It developed, therefore, neither an elaborate organization nor a series of ideological appeals that could attract their support. It did not move beyond an incessant repetition of the principles set out in the founding of the organization. Its position within the German political arena maintained this organizational and ideological rigidity. Unlike those who sought to lead the workers, the Catholics, the peasants, and the Poles, the CV did not have to face competing appeals and the organizational inroads of other movements. Indeed, the primary electoral task assumed by the CV's leaders was to help prop up the left-liberal parties. Both of these groups retained the style, organization, and ideology of liberalism after it had lost its effectiveness within the German political arena. As a result, the left-liberal parties persistently lost strength in national elections, fading as important electoral contestants by the end of World War I. The CV, however, retained its dominance within the Jewish community, where little competition existed.

The CV adjusted its claims only in response to the attacks of German Zionists in the years just before World War I. They answered the proclamation that membership in the Zionist organization entailed a commitment to include in "one's life program personal emigration to Palestine" (cited in Reinharz, 1975, p. 161) by intensifying their attachment to Germany. They responded to an increase in the number of Zionists by prohibiting what had theretofore been permitted, joint membership in CV-associated groups and the German Zionist Federation (Reinharz, 1975, p. 206). Responding to the Zionist claims, the leader of the CV declared:

Deutschtum and *Judentum* are not basically different and conflicting *Weltanschauungen*. Both are of great worth to humanity and their synthesis within German Jewry can have only positive results. We cannot reverse the trend of history and try artificially to accentuate our uniqueness by going back to Palestine and speaking Hebrew. We do indeed want to adhere to our Jewish tradition, but only here in Germany. [Cited in Reinharz, 1975, p. 194]

The leaders of the CV responded to the Zionists' ideological attacks by reaffirming and strengthening their initial and long-standing ties to political liberalism and Germany. The meaning of "our Jewish tradition" is not clear; the vagueness of the definition may have been important. Indeed, in this context, Jewish tradition may have meant political liberalism! Their continuing dominance within the Jewish community precluded the need to adjust their ideology to Zionist demands.

What accounts for the Zionists' attack on the CV? Why did this not occur in 1897, when the Zionist Federation formed, but in 1910? It is helpful to examine the changes within the world of university students as the source of new political views within the Jewish community. The turn of the century witnessed an increase of nationalist groups within the German universities, which espoused the romantic virtues of the people of nature and which decried the rationalism of liberalism (Mosse, 1970). These changes affected Jewish students as well (Gross, 1959; Walk, 1979). Moreover, by the turn of the century, approximately 25 percent of all Jewish students in the German universities were immigrants from Eastern Europe (Ruppin, 1904). They brought with them ties of Jewish ethnicity and nationalism, which frequently translated into Zionism. A combination of basic change within the general world of the university and the entry of large numbers of Jewish students increased the number espousing Zionism and led to conflict within the Jewish community (Reinharz, 1975; Poppel, 1976). The liberals prevailed by controlling the political arena within the Jewish community. They were the legitimate spokesmen, since they were the heads of formal Jewish organizations and were German by birth. They could respond to the Zionists, therefore, by reaffirming their attachment to Germany, not by reasserting their Jewishness. Firm in their power within the Jewish community, recognized by the non-Jewish community, they reassured the general society that the Zionists did not speak for German Jews.

THE FORMATION OF THE BUND

What accounts for the formation of the Bund in 1897, nearly two decades after the first Jewish Socialists began to succeed among the Jewish proletariat? Until the middle of the 1890s, the Jewish Socialists had continued on their same course. They sought to construct, through the medium of small educational circles, a workers' elite who would join other such workers in leading a Socialist revolution in Russia. They remained a small and tightly bound cluster of friends and colleagues, working among the masses. They denied the existence of a separate Jewish ideology and did not establish a separate Jewish organization.

The Bund organized in competitive response to the actions of competing political groups. In 1897, Jewish Socialists in Lithuania and Poland were threatened by the planned establishment of the Russian Social Democratic

Workers Party (RSDWP). At the same time, the Polish Socialist Party (PPS) was making major inroads among Jewish workers in Warsaw. These threats, not ideological dictates and not a desire to respond to the Jewish masses, determined the formation of the Bund and the structure of its organization (Frankel, 1981, pp. 206–8; see also Tobias, 1972, pp. 52–54; Mendelsohn, 1970, p. 47; Wandycz, 1974).

At about the same time, the first Zionist Congress was convened. And, in turn, the Zionist movement affected the Jewish Socialist movement. A contemporary Bundist source makes this point:

Before Herzl came out with his *Judenstaat,* the Zionist . . . movement had no roots in Jewish life in Russia and Poland.

This movement remained absolutely dead among the Jewish *workers.* It is significant that at all three previous congresses of the Bund the question of Zionism did not appear on the agenda.

After *Judenstaat* appeared and the idea of a Jewish state in Palestine began to spread gradually . . . it became clear that the Bund could no longer ignore the new movement. If not today, then tomorrow Zionism would appear among the Jewish petit bourgeoisie. [Cited in Tobias, 1972, p. 108]

The spectre of Zionism, while not yet a direct challenge to the Jewish Socialists, again raised the need to protect their movement.

Finally, the Bundists found justification for a separate Jewish organization from other Socialists. Karl Kautsky, the leading theoretician of European socialism, had just supported the formation of autonomous national states within a revolutionary Austria-Hungary (Tobias, 1972, p. 108; Frankel, 1981, p. 217). Other national Socialist parties had formed, not only in Poland but in Lithuania and the Ukraine within the Russian Empire. The strategic and defensive needs of the Jewish Socialists were legitimated by Socialist theory as well.

Factors related to the competitive position of the Bund affected the subsequent development of the movement's ideology. The Bund's political position was especially complex. It competed within several arenas: the Russian revolutionary movement, the Marxist groups of Europe, local Polish Socialist groups, and the Jewish political world. The development of Bundist ideology responded to the pressures of the groups in these arenas. When Bundists interacted with Jewish nationalists, their ethnic claims increased; when they competed with socialists and revolutionaries, their nationalist claim faded from view. Bundist ideology combined the different claims of internal groups, each responding to its particular political arena.

The years after the formation of the Bund witnessed a marked growth in the Jewish nationalist content of their ideology. From the claim that the Bund was the exclusive representative of the Jewish proletariat, the Bund proclaimed the necessity, first of Jewish civil rights (Third Congress, 1899), then recognized the Jews as a nationality, and then insisted on Jewish national rights (Fourth Congress, 1901). They moved from a grudging acceptance of Yiddish as a tactical necessity to a proclaimed ideological attachment to the language itself. At the Sixth Congress (October, 1905), after the outbreak of revolutionary activities in Russia, the leaders proclaimed their attachment to Jewish national autonomy (see Frankel, 1981, p. 247). The Jewish Socialists moved from finding it tactically useful to work among Jewish laborers to asserting their leadership over the Jews as a nation.

The pattern of gradual increase in national demands appears to support the claim that the Bund's leaders were responding to the demands of the Jewish masses. It also fits the argument that Bundist ideology unfolded logically from a set of initial premises. Neither of these positions explains the development of the ideology. The Bund issued its most nationalistic statements only after leaving the Russian Social Democratic Workers Party and before returning to the party, during the period 1902–6. Until they struck out on their own, they called only for civic rights for Jews. When they returned to the Russian party in 1906, they turned away from nationalist claims (Frankel, 1981).

Until 1905, the Bund stood almost alone among Jewish political groups in Russia. The Zionists did not enter the fray until a few years earlier (Gitelman, 1972, pp. 46–47). As a result, until the Fourth Congress (1901) the Bund permitted its members to belong to Zionist associations as well. After the Kishinev pogrom (1903) and with the beginnings of Zionist political acitvity, the Bund responded competitively to Jewish political groups by increasing the Jewish nationalist content of its claims. With the Revolution of 1905, the number of these groups multiplied rapidly, including for the first time Zionist-Socialist groups. This further increased the competitive pressure on Bund leaders. The pronouncement of 1905 grew out of this new and strong competition within the Jewish community. It responded to the unanimous attack of all the others that the Bund was not sufficiently interested in Jewish questions.

The aftermath of the 1905 Revolution produced severe problems for the Bund. While many Bundist leaders fled abroad, the general Russian Socialist movement regrouped into a unified organization. At the same time, the Zionists began to engage in political work in the Jewish communities and several Zionist-Socialist movements formed as well. A deeply divided and weakened Bund returned to the Russian Social Democratic Workers Party. Policy and ideological changes responded to political pressures (Frankel, 1981, p. 251; Tobias, 1972, pp. 176–78).

Bund congresses were far from scenes of ideological and political unanimity. In earlier years, the Workers Opposition had fought efforts to engage in mass agitation, preferring to retain the emphasis on educational circles (Mendelsohn, 1970; Frankel, 1981; Tobias, 1972). Other groups fought over whether to organize, the proper place of Yiddish, and the Bund's position on the Jewish Question. Policy and ideological decisions taken at congresses frequently passed by very close votes. Ideological change was not a collective change of mind. It was the victory of a particular group's point of view, while the others acceded out of loyalty to the organization and general commitment to the revolution.

Those within the Bund most disposed toward a nationalist ideology competed with other Jewish political movements. The colonies of student émigrés that clustered around universities in Western and Central Europe were the centers for these conflicts:

The national question was brought to the Bund more from abroad than from within the country. The Bundist intelligentsia which was studying in Germany, Switzerland, and Austria, where at that time all possible questions were discussed in the Russian "colonies," was particularly interested in the national question which was debated more than any other in their clashes with the Zionists or simply with the nationalists. It was the Bundist intelligentsia abroad which placed the national question on the agenda of the Bund. [Zivion, in Frankel, 1981, p. 182]

As the Jewish Socialists sought to expand among the Jewish intelligentsia, they encountered students committed to nationalist positions (Weizmann, 1966, p. 50; see also Tobias, 1972, pp. 158–59). To reach them, the Bundists increased their nationalistic claims.

The student colonies turned intellectual debates into political arenas. The confrontation required each of the sides—Zionist, nationalist, Bundist, and Marxist—to respond to the claims of the others. They could not repeat their positions to an already committed body of followers. They had to compete for the loyalties of students without hardened political attachments. The currency of the contests was neither patronage positions nor policy promises, the usual coins of political contestants in the world around them. They had no common political foe. They only had each other, the coffeehouses, the beer halls, and plenty of time to fight with words. The structure of their political arena did not lead to coalitions but to increasingly passionate conflict over ideas and the development of elaborate political ideologies.

The Jewish Socialists had to grapple with Jewish issues or leave the world of the Jewish students and join forces with the Russians. Conversely, the Zionists had to respond to problems existing not in Palestine but in the countries of Europe. They could not insistently repeat the call for emigration as the only solution to the Jewish Question lest they be mocked by the Socialists and ignored by others. Bundist and Zionist ideologies developed in large part in response to the debates in this political arena.

Therefore, those Bundists who competed with Jewish groups emphasized the importance of Jewish national demands. Those that remained in close contact with the Russian revolutionaries insisted on their loyalty to the general movement and persistently focused on organizational issues of how to reach the Jewish masses. The latter were not likely to elaborate their initial ideological position. The development of the movement's ideology is a tale of several factors: the relative size and political importance of those Bundists engaged in competition with Jewish groups, and the persistent attachment of Bundists to the revolution and to the organization itself.

THE FORMATION OF THE ZIONIST MOVEMENT

The fundamental Zionist answer to the condition of the Jews in Europe was emigration to a national homeland. What accounts for the turn to political work in the Diaspora that was not directly related to emigration? How do we account for the formation of organizations that competed within the Jewish communities and developed political parties, schools, social and athletic associations? As with the case of the Bund, why were there activists and devotees without a formal organization for almost two decades? Why did they decide to organize a congress in 1897 and not earlier? Once formed, why did there develop a plethora of Zionist subgroups?

Until the end of the 1890s the Zionists rarely debated or competed with the other poltical movements. The Hovevei Zion groups were poorly organized, involved in meetings and discussions, and supported small groups of emigrants. They were not involved in political contests (Vital, 1976, p. 184). Efforts to form a united Hovevei Zion association in Russia had dissipated by the end of the 1880s. No one challenged their leaders and nothing threatened continuity. As a result, the Russian Zionists remained clusters of local associations with no ties among them.

Herzl's "political solution" to the Jewish Question necessitated efforts to change the policies of various governments. He sought and obtained direct contacts with government officials and the support of Jewish communal leaders in Western Europe. Both tactics followed the competitive logic of the politics of notables: arrangements among gentlemen solve political problems. This was consistent with Herzl's class, educational, and cultural milieu and those of the leaders of the associated liberal parties. Herzl sought to convince political leaders that Jews could be gentlemen. His political Zionism assumed that the politics of liberal notables was the appropriate strategy.

Herzl's approach did not succeed either with heads of state and government officials or with Jewish notables. On the verge of absolute failure, Herzl established the Zionist Congress in order to draw on new political resources—the Jewish masses—and to expand the conflict beyond any individual's sphere of influence (see Lowenthal, 1962, pp. 183–88). It was a logically compelling strategy, which followed and paralleled the development of other mass political movements across Europe.

Herzl and his supporters controlled the first Zionist Congress, the Executive Committee, and the various Zionist offices across Europe. Thus, the other Zionist groups faced the choice of accepting his complete dominance or organizing to compete for control. Student liberals and revolutionaries from Eastern Europe quickly organized the Democratic Fraction, which later split into liberal and various Socialist Zionist groups. Religious Zionists formed the Mizrachi (Frankel, 1981; Vital, 1976, 1982; Schiff, 1977; Don-Yehiya, 1981; Mendelsohn, 1981). The growth of the Zionist organization led to organized factions within the movement.

The Zionist groups competed with each other and with non-Zionist political movements as well. In Western Europe, Herzl and his followers vied with the CV and other liberal groups for the control of the Jewish communities. The members of the Democratic Fraction and the Socialist Zionists competed with the other Zionist groups and revolutionaries, especially Bundists. Religious Zionists battled the Democratic Fraction as well as the established rabbis, who formed the Agudah in opposition to the Zionists. The number of interlocking competitive arenas grew.

Interactions among the various contests affected the organization and ideology of each of the Zionist subgroups. The dominance of the political Zionists in the general organization and their competition with liberal political movements meant that they did not move beyond their initial organization of notables leading loosely organized masses. Like the liberals, the political Zionists maintained that government action was the key to success. They supported the Democratic Fraction's call to "conquer the communities," because mass agitation brought pressure to bear on the CV and other liberal leaders and on the governments. Given the political weakness of the rabbis in Western Europe, Herzl and his followers sought no confrontation with them and worked with the religious Zionists as well.

The Democratic Fraction and the Zionist Socialists competed with the political Zionists as well as the Bund, Marxist revolutionaries, the *Mizrachi*, and the established rabbis of Eastern Europe. Competing in a world of university students and intellectual debates and in communities in which most Jews attended schools controlled by the established rabbis, they maintained the need to revitalize the Jewish people through new forms of education. Hence, they attacked the political Zionists' indifference to cultural issues. They confronted as well the established rabbis of the Jewish communities of Eastern Europe (Vital, 1982). This contest involved more than theological differences. It was a fight for control over the Jewish masses. The student Zionists demanded "freedom of action," access to synagogue podiums, and a share of communal authority. The rabbis responded by denying their right to an ideology and to communal power, and by demanding control over the educational decisions of the Zionist movement. Increased conflict, not compromise, ensued.

The competition between the student Zionists and the Bund and other Socialists increased their revolutionary pronouncements and influenced the structure of their organizations. The more direct these confrontations, the more the Zionists emphasized organizing the Jewish masses, transforming their economic positions, and working for revolution, and the less they emphasized emigration to Palestine. All these groups had tightly knit conspiratorial organizations. The failure of the Russian Revolution of 1905 directly affected this competition. As the Bundists returned to the general Socialist movement, the Zionist Socialists reasserted their call for emigration to Palestine (Frankel, 1981).

These diverse sources met at the Zionist Congresses, but could not be welded into a united ideological body. Zionist ideology is best viewed as several ideologies, agreeing only on the conception of the Jews as a national group, and the centrality of emigration to a national homeland as the solution to the Jewish Question. The different views developed in competitive response to each other. The movement and the frequently called congresses served less to dampen conflict than to provide an arena where ideological differences were debated.

These same processes determined the pattern of political conflict within the various Jewish communities. The greater the number of competing political movements present, the more elaborate the particular organizations and ideologies present and the greater the communal conflict. Thus, conflict in Germany and France differed considerably from competition with the Jewish communities of Poland and Russia. Over time, these movements and competitive arenas structured the politics of Jewish communities in Europe (see Mendelsohn, 1981, 1983).

Offered as total solutions to the Jewish Question, as blueprints for the transformation of Jewish society and politics, the political movements that espoused these ideologies had a very different impact on the Jews. Relatively few took up the Zionists' call for emigration to Israel or took part in the Bund's activities. Even the more limited goals of the Centralverein met with failure at the hands of the Nazis. The new political movements did not transform the face of European Jewry. The CV, the various Zionist groups, and the Bund, however, did have an enormous impact upon Jewish social and political life. They established organizations, held meetings, built schools, published newspapers, and founded youth and sports clubs. They provided new ways of being Jewish. They increased the number and kind of social institutions in which Jews interacted with other Jews. At the same time, their public visibility in the form of rallies, press releases, newspapers, and political campaigns provided new bases for Jewish cohesion. They helped, as well, to maintain the visible presence of Jews as a separate sector in the general society.

9 · European Political Development and Jewish Continuity: Political Anti-Semitism, the Holocaust, and Soviet Policy

Government policies concerning Jewish political rights and institutions represent a major theme in the modernization of the Jewish community. One fundamental question emerged at the start of political modernization: What was the proper place, if any, for religious and ethnic minorities? Liberal governments assumed that the processes of change would erase differences of race, caste, ethnicity, and religion. Authoritarian governments acted to minimize all forms of conflict. However, ethnic conflict did not decline with the extension of political rights. As Jews and non-Jews interacted, competition occurred. As commercialization and industrialization proceeded, the redistribution of wealth, income, and economic opportunities altered the bases of political conflict. Political anti-Semitism emerged out of these changes. Where Jews maintained economic strength and where they were seen as especially benefiting from the new economic structures, their competitors used political forces to change the balance of power. Some insisted on the legal exclusion of Jews from the new polities. Others conceded the Jews' formal rights but sought to limit their access to valued places in educational institutions, government positions, and economic opportunities; others encouraged Jewish emigration. The Nazis solved the question by exterminating Jews. Increasing levels of general politicization led to various efforts to resolve the place of the Jews through governmental action.

The Holocaust and Political Anti-Semitism
The enormity of the Holocaust dominates the effort to understand the place of the Jews in European political development. From the start of World War II, if not earlier, Nazi policy was a concerted effort to kill the Jews (see especially Dawidowicz, 1975). Ruling over the lands between the Atlantic and the outskirts of Moscow and between Norway and the Mediterranean, the German government and its allies massacred two-thirds of the 9 million Jews that were in Europe in 1939. It is not difficult, therefore, to suppose that much of European politics that preceded Nazi rule led to the extermina-

tions. It is also not difficult to view the Jewish Question, to which Hitler prepared his Final Solution, as the central issue of European political development. Does not the magnitude of the Holocaust—as a theoretical, empirical, and normative issue—reflect the central place of the Jews in Europe during the century and a half before the killings began?

In contrast, theories of European political modernization do not revolve about the place of the Jews. Questions of nation building, revolution, elections, and class conflict dominate studies of national politics, as the topics of war and peace charactertize scholarly work on international affairs. The Jewish Question stands as a minor theme emong these issues. Similarly, the destruction of European Jewry is one of many topics of the Second World War. Conflict over the place of the Jews is one issue, and hardly the most important, in theories of European political development.

How can the Jewish Question be only a minor theme when the resolution of the issue engulfed Europe in flames for six years and led to the death of tens of millions, the destructions of societies, economies, and polities (Arendt, 1958; S. Friedlander, 1981)? And yet, how can it be a major issue, when there is little evidence that its political importance outweighed those of the battles between classes, nation builders and reactionaries, Communists and Fascists? Most scholars have accepted the power of the contradiction and opted for one or the other of the perspectives.

The contradiction rests on broader theoretical propositions. On the one hand, Nazi policy on the Jews typified the actions taken by all governments and the political claims made by all other anti-Semitic political movements. On the other, the Holocaust was an aberration. It neither typified Nazi policy nor any of the other political actions taken on the Jewish Question. Only by accepting the first of these claims can one justify substituting the analysis of other forms of political anti-Semitism for the Holocaust (as did Arendt, 1958, with the Dreyfus case), or claim that all previous manifestations of political anti-Semitism led to the Nazis (see for example Ettinger, 1982; Pulzer, 1964; and G. Mosse, 1964, 1970, 1978). Only the second position allows the dismissal of the Holocaust's importance (as do Marxist historians).

The competing analytic positions pose a false dilemma. Nazi policy was neither typical of all government actions nor an aberration irrelevant to European political development. Conflict about the place of the Jews before the rise of the Nazis was generally a minor theme in European politics; yet, the destruction of European Jewry was the major theme of Nazi policy and the Second World War. Moreover, the importance of the Holocaust does not depend on its relationship with conflicts over the Jewish Question during the pre-Holocaust period.

The manifestations of political anti-Semitism varied during the processes of modernization. Hence, the analysis may assume neither its constant

importance nor unimportance but must examine it as a phenomenon that
rises and falls over time and across political systems. From this perspective,
the Holocaust appears as an extraordinary form of political anti-Semitism,
so different from other examples as to require a separate analysis.

How did the political importance of the Jewish Question vary over time
and in the different countries of Europe? Where there were no Jews present,
they were not a political issue. Where there were Jews, political movements
disagreed on regulating Jewish access to universities, business opportunities, and government positions. They differed as well in the importance
attached to the Jewish Question. Most of the Socialist left and liberal center
downplayed the issue in their electoral appeals and programmatic statements. Others proclaimed the Jews as enemies and sought to restrict their
political and economic rights. These views were not the simple derivations
of attitudes toward Jews or political philosophies. The exigencies of political
conflict during the 1920s and 1930s induced Socialist parties across Europe
to champion Jewish rights. They did so as part of their opposition to the
Fascists, not out of a commitment to the Jews per se (see for example Simon,
1971). Positions taken on the Jewish Question varied across time and place.
They reflect differences in the size of competing political groups, in their
political interests, and other general factors.

The policies of governments varied with regard to the Jewish Question.
Imperial Germany differed radically from Nazi Germany (Eley, 1978, 1980;
Blackbourn, 1978, 1980; Farr, 1978; Evans 1978a, 1978b). Polish and
Hungarian policies to limit the place of the Jews in universities and in the
economy differed between the 1920s and the end of the 1930s (Braham,
1981; Katzburg, 1981; Wynot, 1974; Polonsky, 1972; H. Rabinowicz, 1965;
Davies, 1982, vol. 2; Segal, 1938; Trunk, 1974). Soviet policy began with an
effort to sustain a separate Jewish national culture, but then limited the
educational and professional opportunities of Jews (Gitelman, 1972; Baron,
1976a). Other countries varied in their policies toward Jews as well (Mendelsohn, 1983).

The political movements and governments had different effects on the
structure of the Jewish communities. The anti-Semitic political movements
that emerged at the end of the nineteenth century did not control governments. Their activities did not affect the high levels of interaction among
Jews, the complex and varied Jewish institutions, and the other structures
that maintained the cohesion of the Jewish community (see Baron, 1976b;
and Chapters 7 and 8). The Nazis and the Soviets overwhelmed the Jewish
communities. The processes of European political modernization abound in
different forms of political action taken on the Jewish Question.

THE RISE OF POLITICAL ANTI-SEMITISM
Political anti-Semitism is the attempt to use government power to limit the
place of Jews in the polity, economy, and society. It is exemplified by

proposals made in electoral campaigns, by legislation suggested, and government policies taken and implemented. Statements made against Jews, whether by members of the intellectual elite or by others not engaged in political action, fall outside the concept of political anti-Semitism. Before the advent of the Nazis and the Soviets, it emerged most clearly in the campaign appeals of parties of the political right; in the demonstrations and pronouncements of students seeking to limit the number of Jews in universities; and in the actions of governments, most notably those of the Tsarist Empire, independent Poland, and Hungary.

The movements espousing political anti-Semitism opposed the Jews as one element in a strategy defending various social and political groups. They did not focus exclusively upon the Jewish Question. The growing extension of government power necessarily increased the politicization of social and economic competitions (Gellner, 1980). In multiethnic societies, majority groups used political power to defend and extend their political dominance. The claims against the Jews may have been legitimated on traditional and religious grounds, but they derived from other sources. In an era of secularization in Western and Central Europe, it is unlikely that Christian anti-Semitism determined changes in political behavior (Freimark, 1979). Similarly, those who supported these movements did so less out of hatred of Jews than defense of their own interests. Jews were simply not the overwhelming concern of most non-Jews. Little political mileage could have been obtained from an exclusive focus on Jews. Political anti-Semitism was not simply an offensive against the Jews of Europe.

Several factors account for the political attacks on Jewish legal rights and economic positions. Declining rural economies raised the vulnerability of those in direct economic competition with Jews, especially the traders and merchants in small towns and cities. Those not in direct competition, like peasants, viewed the mobility and prosperity of Jews as the cause of their own economic deprivation. In addition, the number of political parties and the pattern of electoral competition, especially in Germany and Austria, increased the number, intensity, and visibility of political claims against Jews.

As economic development redistributed wealth and opportunities, the extension of suffrage rights and the proliferation of political parties carved new political divisions. By the 1880s, four political blocs were present in Germany. The National Liberals, Progressives, and other liberal parties, who were closely associated with the newly forming national economy and polity, competed to represent the urban middle class (including most of the Jews). A second bloc was the Social Democratic Party, developing a powerful organization around the urban working and salaried classes. Catholic political groups formed the Centre Party in response to the Socialist's organizations and activities, governmental discrimination against Catholics, and the political inroads of the right-wing. A fourth cluster of political

parties—among them the Conservative party as well as the more vitupera-
tive Anti-Semitic People's Party, the German Social Alliance, the German
Social Party, the German Reform Party, the German Social Reform party—
fought to defend the interests of Protestant landowners, peasants, and
small-town burghers and artisans (Pulzer, 1964; R. Levy, 1975; Eley, 1978,
1980; Blackbourn, 1978, 1980; Bieber, 1979; Sheehan, 1978; Hagen, 1980;
Evans, 1978a; White, 1976). Similar political blocs formed in France and
Austria, where the Catholic movement overlapped directly with those defending the traditional economy and polity (Byrnes, 1950; Marrus, 1971;
Wilson, 1978; Hyman, 1979; Pulzer, 1964; Schwarz, 1979; Whiteside, 1975).

Catholic and right-wing political parties competed to defend peasants,
artisans, and village traders against the encroachment of the national government and economy. In the declining economies of the small towns and
rural agricultural areas, local merchants suffered in competition with
businessmen with national and international connections, many of them
Jews. The apparent economic success of Jews and their visibility associated
them with the threats engendered by the expanding national market and
polity. Political parties seeking the support of these newly vulnerable groups
attacked the Jews in campaigns and pronouncements against modernization
(see the sources cited in Pulzer, 1964, pp. 38, 339–40; R. Levy, 1975;
Whiteside, 1975).

Competitive interaction among the political parties of the right also
fostered the growth of political anti-Semitism. The initial electoral successes
of the Anti-Semitic People's Party induced its competitors to include attacks
on Jews in the political repertoire. As these parties expanded, political
anti-Semitism spread along the political spectrum, entering the campaign
appeals of the Conservative and Centre Parties in the early 1890s and
inducing the Socialists to maintain an ambiguous position on the Jews
(Levin, 1977). When the parties of the radical right declined, so too did the
number and intensity of political attacks on Jews by all parties. By the
middle of the 1890s, political anti-Semitism had nearly vanished in Germany
(R. Levy, 1975; Pulzer, 1980; Whiteside, 1975). The rapid rise and fall of
these parties indicate that political anti-Semitism did not develop as the
logical unfolding of a set of ideological principles, Christian theology, or in
response to mass political attitudes.

How did the parties' positions on the Jews affect their political fortunes?
The parties of the radical right gained and lost votes based on the state of the
rural economy, their leadership, and organizational strength. As the economy improved and their competitors added organizational weapons, the
anti-Semitic parties declined. It is difficult to maintain, therefore, that
attitudes toward the Jews determined the rise and fall of the anti-Semitic
political parties in Imperial Germany (R. Levy, 1975; Eley, 1978, 1980;
Farr, 1978; Evans, 1978a; Blackbourn, 1978, 1980; Rurup, 1975a; Bieber,
1979).

Variations in the importance of general economic and political factors account for differences in the presence of anti-Semitic political movements in other countries of Europe before the First World War as well. In Poland, the National Democratic Party formed in 1897, the same year as the Bund, the Russian Marxist Party, and the first Zionist Congress. It appealed for the support of the peasants and the burghers and artisans of small towns and medium-size cities. The party grew with the development of the Polish middle classes, and declines in the economy exacerbated conflict between Polish and Jewish merchants (Wandycz, 1974; Polonsky, 1972; Roos, 1966; Davies, 1982, vol. 2). In Hungary, the almost complete absence of a Magyar commercial class mitigated the economic sources of conflict. In addition, before World War I, Magyar nationalists encouraged Jewish political inclusion as a means of ensuring a Hungarian speaking majority in their country (Braham, 1981; Katzburg, 1981; McCagg, 1972; Barany, 1974; Seton-Watson, 1974; and Chapter 7). Furthermore, in neither Poland nor Hungary were there competing parties outbidding each other in anti-Semitic political rhetoric. There is little evidence associating levels of traditional and political anti-Semitism. In Poland and Hungary, the interrelationship between new political and economic forces associated with modernization determined the manifestations of political anti-Semitism.

These same factors help to account for discriminatory policies. The rapid entry of Jews into the universities increased and not infrequently led to competition and conflict between them and non-Jews. There is a positive correlation between the percentage of Jews in the universities and incidences of anti-Semitism on the campuses. In particular, where Jews were a relatively large and increasing proportion of the students, the number, intensity, and violence of anti-Semitic acts increased.

Efforts to restrict the entry of Jews into the universities were tied to the number of available openings for students. Where there was an adequate supply, like in Germany, Austria, and Hungary before World War I, there were no limits on the number of students (McClelland, 1980; Ringer, 1979; Ruppin, 1973). In Russia, the numerus clausus of 1887 was instituted precisely to limit the number of Jews and others in the urban middle class in order to make room for members of social strata closely tied to the regime (Wolf, 1912; Alston, 1969; Baron, 1976a; Halevy, 1976; Pennar et al., 1971). The continued availability of places in the universities of Germany and the reduction in the Jewish portion of the student body after World War I was accompanied by relatively few manifestations of anti-Semitism. There was, as well, no effort to limit Jewish entry. Indeed, there was a student organization of Jews and non-Jews which supported Jewish rights. The numerus clausus in Hungary in 1920 followed declines in the number of available universities and increases in the number of Magyar students occasioned by the contraction of Hungary's borders and the immigration of many Hungarians from areas no longer part of the country. These factors increased the level of competition for entrance into the universities and increased the political pressure on the new government to restrict the entrance of Jews (Braham, 1981, p. 30; Katzburg, 1981, p. 214). In Poland in the 1920s, Jews grew from 10–12 percent of the university students to a quarter of the total. Competition with Polish students ensued. In response, the government imposed a numerus clausus (Trunk, 1974; H. Rabinowicz, 1965; Heller, 1980).

The same general factors account for other manifestations of political anti-Semitism in the interwar years as well. In Poland, government policies to benefit Poles hurt all minority groups. In the Southeast, the government acted against Ukrainians; in the West, it limited the power of Germans. Its economic policy favored the Polish middle classes in their competition with Jewish merchants. The government nationalized sectors of the economy long controlled by Jews—tobacco, export-imports, alcohol, and matches (see Chapter 7). At the same time, it encouraged Polish tradesmen and shopkeepers. Subsequent declines in the economic position of Jewish merchants, in the mid-1920s, led many to emigrate (see Chapter 13). The overlap between ethnic and economic conflict structured government policies (Polonsky, 1972; Roos, 1966; Trunk, 1974; H. Rabinowicz, 1965; Davies, 1982, vol. 2).

In 1936, the Polish government's actions against Jews entered a new stage. It countenanced a rise in anti-Semitic demonstrations in the universities and announced plans for the forced emigration of the Jews to Palestine. The increasing pauperization of the Jews that followed earlier policies, especially the declines in the number of Jewish shopkeepers and tradesmen in the small towns, make it unlikely that economic conflict between Jews and Poles spurred the new policies (Lifschutz, 1974; Trunk, 1974; H. Rabinowicz, 1965; Segal, 1938). There is as well no evidence that the government was responding to sudden increases in the levels of mass anti-Semitism. Rather, pressure from the German government and competition within the Polish elite engendered the policy change. Political instability followed Pilsudski's death. The right-wing parties, including the National Democrats, were aided by the Nazis and scored political victories. Both factors led the government to increase its anti-Jewish statements and actions (Melzer, 1977; Wynot, 1974; Polonsky, 1972; Roos, 1966; Davies, 1982, vol. 2).

In Hungary, no effort to limit the place of the Jews in the economy accompanied the numerus clausus on entrance into the schools. Indeed, there is evidence that these restrictions were ignored in practice as well. Until 1937, there were no additional manifestations of government policy against the Jews. What accounts for the new anti-Jewish laws enacted during the subsequent five years? Again, there is no evidence of popular anti-Semitism causing the new policies. Rather, domestic and international political factors provided the major impetus for policy change. The alliance with Germany and Nazi support for Hungary's radical right were the major new factors in the equation (Braham, 1981; Katzburg, 1981; Vago, 1981).

In addition, economic conflict between Jewish and non-Jewish members of the middle class began to emerge in Hungary at the end of the 1930s. Until then, the relatively small commercial and industrial middle class contained too few Magyars and too many Jews for competition to occur. Contemporary sources document the predominance of Jews in these economic spheres. Jews owned nearly half of the industrial enterprises employing more than twenty workers. In the twenty largest industrial enterprises of Hungary, 235 board members out of 336 were Jews, and only one of these enterprises did not have a majority of Jewish directors. Jews owned three-fourths of the privately owned, medium-sized enterprises, including the entire asphalt and tar industry. (Cited in Katzburg, 1981, pp. 254–55; see also McCagg, 1972). In 1939, the head of the Hungarian government resisted Nazi pressure to act against the Jews, on the grounds that it would be counter to Hungarian national interest. The German ambassador's report of his meeting notes:

[He] himself is a convinced anti-Semite; nevertheless it is clear to him that it is very dangerous in Hungary to take measures against the Jews too hastily and too radically. They occupy an extraordinarily mighty position in Hungarian economic life, and in many fields they cannot yet be replaced by Hungarians. We cannot kill the cow that we want to milk. [Cited in Katzburg, 1981, pp. 126–27]

The Jewish predominance in the commercial and industrial classes of Hungary precluded anti-Jewish policies until the more powerful political forces of Nazi Germany intervened.

The proportions of Jews among the German middle classes and university students in the interwar period kept declining. Unlike Hungary and Poland, these reductions did not result from government policies but were part of broader changes in Jewish and German societies. In addition, the contraction of the German borders after the war reduced the importance of minority issues in German politics. Furthermore, the political left and center dominated the government during the 1920s. As a result, the Weimar government passed no laws restricting the political rights and the educational and economic opportunities of Jews.

What accounts for the coming-to-power of the most radical and successful anti-Semitic political movement, the National Socialist Workers Party? Does not their rise mean that other sources of anti-Semitism were still present? Does our analysis rest too heavily on the economic and political determinants of political anti-Semitism? There is little evidence that Nazi racism alone attracted significant political support. Rather, political factors, such as the party's organizational superiority over competitors on the German right, and rapid declines in the economy, especially among Protestant peasants and small-town burghers, and generally among city dwellers not part of the Socialist movement, as well as Hitler's charisma, determined the political successes of the Nazis (Hamilton, 1982; see also Lipset, 1963). Several regional studies deny claims that Hitler's and the party's avowed anti-Semitism attracted votes and show that the Nazis downplayed this issue in electoral campaigns (Allen, 1965; Heberle, 1970; Pridham, 1973). The Nazis did not ride to power upon a wave of Jew hatred.

Even among Nazi activists, anti-Semitism was only one of many issues that attracted them to the movement. A study of nearly 600 of the first to join the Nazi party showed that one-third gave no evidence of anti-Semitic attitudes. Among an additional 14 percent, statements against Jews appeared to be "mild verbal projections and party duties." No more than 13 percent were preoccupied with the "Jewish conspiracy." Jews alone or in combination with Marxists and Communists were the "chief object of hatred" for less than 15 percent of these early Nazis compared to well over half who chiefly hated Marxists in general and Communists (Merkl, 1975, pp. 449–522). Even before the Nazis reached power, when careerism provided another basis of party membership, there is little reason to contend that hatred of the Jews was the primary reason for joining the movement. It follows as well that anti-Semitism alone cannot account for the extent to which those in the SS and other Nazi organizations obeyed orders to kill the Jews. Factors in addition to personal animosity toward Jews and traditional anti-Semitism determined the rise of the Nazis and the implementation of Hitler's solution to the Jewish Question.

Political anti-Semitism reflected a range of political and economic factors that varied during European political modernization. It had little impact on the diverse organizations, the overlap of ethnic and occupational patterns, and the social ties that maintained the cohesion of the Jewish communities of Europe. In contrast, the revolutionary regimes of Nazi Germany and the Soviet Union destroyed the institutional bases of the Jewish communities: the Soviets replaced them with other structures, the Nazis killed as many Jews as they could. Both thus decimated the Jewish communities of Europe. The advent of Nazi rule in Germany and later in other countries and Soviet power in Russia marked a turning point in political anti-Semitism.

THE HOLOCAUST

Nazi Germany's policies and actions concerning the Jews were an extraordinary form of political anti-Semitism. The government's ability to reach those it ruled expanded dramatically, as the revolutionary regime sought to transform totally the societies it controlled. Within the regime, opposition to state policy was sporadic, ineffective, and eliminated. For various

reasons—careerism, fear, charismatic obedience, and ideological acceptance—few within the party, SS, and government disobeyed orders. Hitler's
commands obtained acceptance. The destruction of Jewry lay at the heart of
those demands, providing the foundation stone for government policy. In
Germany, a revolutionary regime replaced Weimar democracy and spread
its terror across Europe by conquering neighboring states. Its successes
overwhelmed the Jews of Europe.

In the mid-1930s, approximately 9 million Jews lived in European lands
between the Atlantic and the Urals. There were fewer than 3 million by the
end of World War II. Between 1933 and 1939, about two-thirds of the Jews
of Germany and Austria, amounting to several hundred thousand persons,
left Europe. With the start of the war, emigration became nearly impossible.
Except for those who reached the eastern portions of the Russian Republic,
who passed as non-Jews, or who survived the concentration camps, the rest
died: between 2 and 3 million in the concentration camps; nearly a million by
the hand of the *Einsatzgruppen*, as these mobile killing units swept through
eastern Poland and the western portions of the Soviet Union; disease,
starvation, gassings in vans, and random brutality took the rest. These are
the bare outlines of the destruction of European Jewry.

The Holocaust's devastation is unimaginable. Its ultimate meaning
beyond the ken of humans. We seek, therefore, not to explain why the
Holocaust occurred but to outline its general patterns and assess its effects
on the Jewish communities.

The Holocaust's death toll varied across the continent. Approximately 90
percent of the Jews of Poland, Lithuania, Estonia, Germany, Austria, and
the Protectorate (with a total 1941 population of more than 3.8 million)
died; as did 80 percent of the Jews of Slovakia and Greece (total prewar
Jewish population 160,000); three-fourths of the 140,000 Dutch Jews; 70
percent of the 650,000 Hungarian Jews; 65 percent of the 375,000 Jews of
Byelo-Russia; 60 percent of the Jews in the Ukraine, Belgium, and Yugosla-
via (with a prewar total of Jews of more than 2 million); half the Jews of
France, Rumania, and Bulgaria (totaling 1 million Jews in 1941); one-fifth
the Jews of Italy and Luxembourg (which had a prewar total of approximately 45,000 Jews); and 11 percent of the nearly 1 million Jews of the
Russian Republic. Only the small Jewish communities of Denmark and
Finland suffered relatively few deaths (Dawidowicz, 1975, p. 403; Fein,
1979, pp. 52–53). As the Nazis moved eastward, they encountered most of
the Jews of Europe and intensified and systematized their killing procedures.

What accounts for these extraordinary death totals? What explains the
variation in the proportions killed? Two factors are most important: the
mode of Nazi rule, and the strength of political anti-Semitism in the country.
Where the SS ruled directly and there had been a successful prewar anti-

Semitic political movement, almost all the Jews died. "Thus, one finds that two causes alone—prewar anti-semitism and SS control in 1941—account for virtually all (86%) of the variation in Jewish victimization" (Fein, 1979, pp. 52–53, 82). Indeed, in all areas of direct SS rule, the death rate was over 80 percent. In Hungary, variations in the death rate followed changes in the mode of rule. When the country was a German ally, relatively few Jews were murdered. When, in the spring of 1944, the SS took control of Hungary, they immediately began to deport Jews to the death camps. During the spring and summer of 1944, nearly all the Hungarian Jews killed by the Nazis were sent to Auschwitz (Braham, 1981; Dawidowicz, 1975; Fein, 1979; Hilberg, 1967). At the same time, the Nazis did not work alone. The Slovakian and Rumanian governments organized their own massacres, and Lithuanians, Ukrainians, Poles, and others in Eastern Europe formed auxiliary units that aided the SS. In other areas, like Denmark and Belgium, local opposition slowed the killing process and reduced the death rates. Variations in the power of the Nazis and their allies determined the variations in the death rates of the Jews.

It follows that Jewish responses to Nazi destructions had little effect on the death toll. The difference between survival and death of communities and individuals rested with the Nazis, not the Jews.

Jews responded to the efforts to destroy them in diverse ways: some fled, some hid, some prayed, some attacked their hunters, some smuggled contraband, some served in the ghettoes as policemen, some worked, some went to school. Most combined one or more of these and other activities. It is impossible to specify the proportions that responded in different ways. It is clear, however, that relatively few—no more than 20 percent, and most of them from Western Europe—escaped before the Nazis caught them. An even smaller proportion—5–7 percent—engaged in political or military action against the Nazis. No widespread fear produced a uniform response (Fein, 1979; Dawidowicz, 1975; Trunk, 1972).

Jews responded to the Nazis much as other people have reacted to political terror. Indeed, their behavior conforms as well to responses to natural disasters, like hurricanes, earthquakes, and windstorms. Few panic, few radically alter their existing ways of living, most continue their normal routines as best they can (Solzhenitsyn, 1973; Medvedev, 1971; A. Zuckerman, 1984). Most people respond to political terror conditioned by the social structures around them and the need to make decisions in extraordinarily new and incomprehensible political circumstances. Most people, calculating to survive, choose to remain where they are. Jewish responses to Nazi terror conformed to these general patterns.

Some fled and escaped the Nazis. Indeed, flight appears to have been the response most likely to lead to survival (Fein, 1979). What accounts for the decision to leave? What accounts for the variations in emigration rates?

Why did most of the prewar Jewish populations of Germany and Austria escape? Why did relatively few emigrate from Eastern Europe?

In Germany and Austria, a relatively long period of time between the advent of the Nazis and the beginning of the killing process correlates with high levels of emigration. Between 1933 and 1941, 70 percent of the German Jews left the country. The same proportion of Austrian Jews emigrated between Ocober, 1938, and October, 1941 (Dawidowicz, 1975, p. 189; Hilberg, 1967; pp. 715–17; Fein, 1979, p. 205). There is no evidence, however, that those who left "knew what was coming" and behaved accordingly. Rather, the relatively long warning time provided a necessary but not sufficient condition for emigration. Where there was relatively no warning time, almost none emigrated and almost all died (Fein, 1979, p. 57). In Poland, a month after the Home Army fell, the Jews were marked. A year later, they were locked behind the ghetto walls (Katsch,1973; Hilberg, 1967, pp. 144–56). In the Soviet Union, there was no time at all. The Nazis simply moved in and began systematically to massacre the Jews at the rate of 100,000 per month (Hilberg, 1967, pp. 177–256).

Where there was a relatively long warning period, several factors determined how people responded. Individuals opted to emigrate when they had the means and opportunity to leave. More concretely, emigration entailed transit and destination visas, tickets for travel, and a reason to believe that their destination would be safer than their current locale. Emigration was heaviest from Germany and Austria partially because these Jews had the easiest time obtaining visas. The American quotas on immigration favored people from Western Europe and allowed the entry of nearly 100,000 of these Jews (Wasserstein, 1979; Hilberg, 1967). In addition, the geographical routes available to German and Austrian Jews and the fact that most left during peacetime facilitated their departures. Neither cultural factors peculiar to Jews of Western Europe nor psychological responses to victimization determined their relatively high rates of emigration. In addition, those who left were no more attuned to political events than those who stayed behind in Germany and Austria. Rather, the flight of these Jews—like most people faced with natural and political disasters—is clearly associated with age and the obligations of family ties (A. Zuckerman, 1984). Between 1933 and 1939, more than 80 percent of the German Jews younger than age forty emigrated. In 1939, three-fourths of those who remained were older than age forty and less than 13 percent were younger than twenty-four (Dawidowicz, 1975, p. 191). The relative availability of visas also mitigated the need to divide families in order to emigrate from Germany and Austria. As *Night* (Wiesel, 1969) and other memoirs indicate, the calculation that family cohesion implied safety frequently meant the rejection of visas, when all family members could not obtain the requisite travel documents. In circumstances of relatively long warning time, in which the means of emigration were available to families, large portions of the Jewish community escaped.

In Eastern Europe, not only was warning time almost absent but there were relatively few visas available. Jews there were almost completely denied entry into the United States. British policy restricted their admission into the United Kingdom and reduced the number of immigrants to Palestine to a trickle. Between April, 1939, and the end of 1942, fewer than 40,000 were allowed into Palestine (Wasserstein, 1979, p. 52; see also Chapter 12). As their options to emigrate declined, fewer Jews left Poland. During the years 1931–35, approximately 17,000 departed annually, most of them to Palestine. In 1937–38, 9,000 left each year (H. Rabinowicz, 1965, p. 187; Mendelsohn, 1983, p. 39). Between September, 1939, when the Nazis invaded Poland, and October, 1940, when the Jews were herded into ghettoes, the Soviet Union was the only place to which Polish Jews could run. Several hundred thousand went there (Wasserstein, 1979, pp. 40–41). The general absence of visas for the Jews of Eastern Europe as well as the near impossibility of travel during the war effectively ended evacuation as a response for most Jews.

The responses of religious Jews—especially Hasidim—were affected by additional social and personal constraints. Their attire, the men's beards and sidecurls, and the women's short-cropped hair, marked them as Jews. To change their appearance meant that they denied their religion. In the context of the Holocaust, this was seen as denying God when they most needed Him. The tightly knit Hasidic communities limited freedom of individual action (see especially Zimmels, 1977; Schindler, 1972).

Political responses to the Nazis were also usually extensions of routine behavior, not radical alterations to meet the new circumstances. Almost all who represented the Jewish communities in negotiations with various governments and most who served on the *Judenrate* (Nazi-controlled Jewish councils) had been leaders of prewar Jewish political organizations and kehillot (Trunk, 1972; Dawidowicz, 1975; Fein, 1979; Braham, 1981; Vago, 1981; Gutman and Hanft, 1979). Almost all who engaged in armed resistance in the ghettoes had been members of the youth wings of the Jewish political parties (see Kohn, 1971; Borzykowski, 1972; Gutman and Rothkirchen, 1976; Kermish, 1976; Halperin, 1976; Y. Zuckerman, 1976). Indeed, many who fought the Nazis in Poland had been part of Jewish self-defense units during the 1930s (Rowe, 1974). Since relatively few Jews had been involved in prewar political activities, relatively few responded to the Nazis with political action.

Similarly, Jewish political movements reacted to the Nazis in the ways in which they had always responded to government pressure and political anti-Semitism. The leaders of the Centralverein and the heads of the Hungarian Jewish community attempted to persuade by lobbying the governments. Bundist and Zionist leaders in Eastern Europe sought to rally the Jewish masses. At the same time, the political organizations joined with the social and cultural associations to sustain Jewish communal life. Those forced out of jobs and schools found new places in Jewish institutions. Enrollment in Jewish schools expanded, as did Jewish hospitals, orchestras, and institutions of higher education. The Jewish organizations continued to provide the institutional bases of the Jewish community. In circumstances of pre-Nazi political anti-Semitism, for example in Rumania and before the Nazis took over the government in Hungary, the communal leaders success-fully defended the Jewish communities. Where the Nazis ruled, the Jewish organizations tried various strategies and tactics. None affected the Nazis' ability to massacre Jews (see especially Dawidowicz, 1975; Trunk, 1972).

The Jews sought to cope in conditions of extreme uncertainty. A report of the Jewish Fighting Organization in Warsaw underscores this point:

Common sense could not admit even the possibility of such a fact as the extermination of tens and hundreds of thousands of Jews. . . . Unjustified optimism went along with complete ignorance. People were cut off from the outside world and they were apt to resort to their pre-vious experience. [Cited in Friedman, 1954, p. 6]

Given the uncertainties, predictions of doom were as nonrational as unbri-dled optimism. The report cites a professor of history who "tried to per-suade us that we were gripped by a psychosis of pessimism which distorted our sense of reality. He tried to refute all our objections by . . . citing innumerable examples . . . where people had likewise been the victims of a collective psychosis of fear before a danger which had likewise not actually existed. . . . " (Ibid. p. 143). In case after case, few understood and antici-pated the stages of the killing process. Even when they did, they could do nothing to stop it.

The uncertainty of events, the limited options on flight, and the strong constraints of family ties mitigated against radical alterations in the behavior of most people. Conversely, where options for escape were great, many people fled. As killings and deportations divided families, the number who attacked the Nazis and who ran away increased as well. Calculations to survive in highly constrained circumstances led most people to continue their established lives as best as they could. As a result, they were in place when the Nazis reached them.

Soviet Policies
Marxism offered an alternative solution to the Jewish Question: after the Socialist revolution, the overlapping class and ethnic ties that held Jews together would disappear, as would the Jews, and the Jewish Question would be resolved. The Bolshevik seizure of power in the fall of 1917 began

a process by which political control directed the forces of social and economic change. Subsequent government and Communist party policies affected the more than 2 million Jews in the Soviet Union, as they reshaped the lives of tens of millions of others.

What accounts for Soviet policy toward the Jews? To what extent was it based on the Marxist solution to the Jewish Question? To what extent was it a continuation of prerevolutionary policies and attitudes concerning the Jews? Marxists—among them many Jews—had long grappled with the question of the Jews in the Revolution and Socialist society. In Russia, Bundists and Zionist Socialists fought with each other and with the Mensheviks and Bolsheviks (see for example Sawyer, 1979; Halevy, 1976; Baron, 1976a; and the works of the relevant Russian political leaders; as well as Chapter 8). Tsarist policy had long maintained limits on Jewish access to schools, residential areas, and sectors of the economy. On balance, however, Soviet Jewish policy was more affected by changes in political phenomena than ideological debates over the definition of nationalities and the specific place of the Jews. In addition, there is little evidence that the policies resulted from changes in the attitudes of party leaders or the Soviet masses toward the Jews.

During most of the 1920s, Soviet policy on the Jews was a manifestation of the New Economic Policy (NEP), specifically the destruction of political opposition and the religious, and educational institutions of prerevolutionary Russia. The party replaced them with new institutions designed to educate—not force—the masses into the Revolution's new Socialist world. The end of formal limitations of Jewish residency and educational rights as well as the destruction of the hederim and yeshivot grew from these policies. Between 1921 and 1924, the government closed several thousand of the traditional religious schools and placed scores of their teachers on trial. By 1929, no more than 12,000 (less than 5 percent of the Jewish children in school) attended the now clandestine hederim (Halevy, 1976; Baron, 1976a, p. 227; Gitelman, 1972, p. 337). The party established new Yiddish language schools and general public schools to take their place. Both school systems educated Jewish children in the values of the party and revolution. Between 1922 and the mid-1930s, the number in these Yiddish schools tripled and equaled the number attending the general public schools (Gitelman, 1972, pp. 336–37; Baron, 1976a, p. 227; Halevy, 1976, pp. 168–70).

NEP also ended the Jewish political movements. At the start of the decade, the Jewish Sections of the Communist Party dismantled the remnants of the traditional kehillot and closed the Jewish political parties. Members of the Bund were forced to choose between their organization and the Revolution. The former entailed emigration, while the latter meant joining the Communist Party. Most Bundist leaders entered the Soviet party (Gitelman, 1972, pp. 210–13). At the same time, new Jewish political institutions were established. In many areas of Byelo-Russia and the Ukraine, local courts and councils used Yiddish as the official language. A "semi-autonomous" area was set aside for Jews in Biro-Bidzhan. The activists in the party's Jewish Sections roamed the areas closing synagogues, establishing new schools and institutions in which Marxism replaced traditional religious culture (see especially Gitelman, 1972; Baron, 1976a; Abramsky, 1970).

Policies promoting social and economic modernization affected indirectly the Jewish communities. Jewish industrial workers benefited from preferential access awarded to proletarians in schools, while Jewish artisans and merchants were heavily taxed and encouraged to change their occupations. The growth in educational opportunities drew increasing numbers of Jews into the public schools and universities. The intensification of urbanization attracted hundreds of thousands of Jews to Moscow, Leningrad, and Kiev. In the three years 1923–26, more than 70,000 Jews moved to Moscow and Leningrad. At the end of the decade, Moscow became one of the largest urban centers of Jewish population in Europe (Baron, 1976a, pp. 206–14; Nove and Newth, 1970; Lewis et al., 1966; Pennar et al., 1971). As the Communist party eliminated the traditional institutions of the Jewish community, social and economic modernization attracted large numbers of Jews into new areas, without the organizational bases of Jewish community life.

The changes that emerged during the era of the New Economic Policy did not eliminate the Jewish communities of the Soviet Union. In the census of 1926, nearly three-fourths of the Jews reported that Yiddish was still their language of daily use (Baron, 1976a, p. 192). Jewish residential concentration in areas of established settlement continued. In the Ukraine, there were twenty-six communities with 10,000 or more Jews, in Byelo-Russia there were six, and in Russia four (Zander, 1937, pp. 67–70). While the Soviet Yiddish schools sought to transmit new values, they maintained the centrality of Yiddish in the lives of Jews and brought Jews together in sustained interactions. The large number of books published in Yiddish—texts, magazines, journals, newspapers, and novels—and the theater and other cultural events fostered this as well. These Soviet sponsored institutions maintained Jewish ties and reinforced the distinctiveness of Jews. Similarly, patterns of occupational concentration remained. In the census of 1926, Jews were still disproportionately unlikely to be peasants, notwithstanding government efforts to attract Jews to agricultural collectives. At the same time, Jews were especially likely to be in the salaried, trade, and working class occupations of cities (Gitelman, 1972, pp. 379–88). In the Ukraine, more than half the Jews worked in the clothing industry, where they accounted for between two-thirds and three-fourths of all those working in that sector of the economy (Baron, 1976a, p. 214; see also Nove and Newth, 1970). It is likely as well that residential, friendship, and family ties also reinforced the cohesion of the Jewish community. NEP policies destroyed the formal political and religious bases of the Jewish community, but they did not obliterate all the sources of Jewish communal cohesion.

In 1928, the Soviet Union entered a period of extraordinary transformations. Government policy forced rapid industrialization and collectivization of agriculture. In the subsequent decade, the occupational, residential, and institutional structure of the Soviet Union was overturned. Millions of private farms became collectives and state farms. Thousands of factories were built. Tens of millions left the countryside to work in cities. Millions of members of the Communist Party were arrested and killed. Millions of others died of starvation, disease, and government repression (Medvedev, 1971; Solzhenitsyn, 1973; Tucker, 1977). Chaos swept the Soviet Union.

These general patterns contained particular effects for the Jews. The government dismantled the newly established Jewish institutions. Yiddish schools, publishing houses, and other cultural institutions were closed. The Jewish Sections of the Communist Party were eliminated and their members purged. The formal bases of Jewish cohesion that had emerged with the Revolution disappeared (Halevy, 1976; Baron, 1976a; Gitelman, 1972).

The Nazi invasion of the Soviet Union continued the attack on the Jewish community. The Einsatzgruppen followed the German army, massacring 600,000 Jews between July, 1941, and January, 1942 (Hilberg, 1967). They wrecked particular havoc among the Jewish communities in Eastern Poland, Lithuania, Byelo-Russia, and the Ukraine, the old Pale of Settlement. At the end of the war, more than half of the 1.6 million Jews who remained in the Soviet Union were living in the Russian Republic. The combination of Stalinist terror and the Holocaust devastated the Jewish communities of the Soviet Union.

What remained of the Jews of the Soviet Union after the ashes of the war had settled? There were approximately 3.5 million fewer Jews than in 1917. There were a handful of synagogues; no kehillot; no political organizations; no philanthropic societies; no Jewish schools, yeshivot, or other educational institutions. In addition, efforts to resurrect Jewish cultural institutions in the years after the war were quickly stopped and their leaders arrested and killed (Gilboa, 1971; Schapiro, 1974). Indeed, by the end of the decade, Stalin had concocted the "Doctor's Plot," apparently as the first step in an effort to remove the remaining Jews to Siberia (Solzhenitsyn, 1973). At the same time, there is some evidence of persisting social and economic bases of cohesion, albeit in much reduced form. Residential concentration persisted in the old cities of the former Pale and in large urban centers like Moscow, Leningrad, Kiev, and Odessa. Concentration in technical occupations and in universities was still present, even as government quotas limited Jewish access to these sectors (Pennar et al., 1971; Baron, 1976a; Nove and Newth, 1970). Ties of family and friendship were also present. Furthermore, government actions against Jews have had the indirect consequence of reinforc-ing their ethnic ties to each other and maintaining their visibility and distinctiveness in the society at large.

These limited sources of Jewish ethnicity gained strength after the 1967 war between Israel and the Arabs and the concomitant anti-Israel policy of the Soviet government. Israel's victory rekindled the ethnic identity of many Soviet Jews. As a result, many initially emigrated to Israel. Over time, many others went to the United States. The institutions aiding both emigrations—the Hebrew Immigrant Aid Society, the Jewish Agency, and local Jewish communities in Israel and the United States—have further strengthened the sources of ethnic continuity of Soviet Jews (Gitelman, 1982; Freedman, 1978). The interdependence among these Jewish communities has been a determinant of the growth of Jewish ethnicity in the Soviet Union.

Political modernization in Europe had variable consequences for Jewish communities. Anti-Semitic political movements rose and fell with altera-tions in the relative size and economic conditions of Jewish and other groups. In most cases, even where political anti-Semitism flourished, the cohesion of Jewish communities had more to do with the characteristics of the Jews and the economic structure of the society than with the actions of those who opposed the Jews.

The Nazi and Soviet regimes were radically different than other anti-Semitic political movements. The revolutionary polities fundamentally altered the place of the Jews. No longer one of many variably cohesive ethnic or religious groups, Jews became the objects of government policies. As a community and as individuals, Jews under Nazi and Soviet rule could not affect their fate. In Nazi Germany, government policy meant the de-struction of the Jews and their communities. In the Soviet Union, a general process of total transformation killed hundreds of thousands of Jews, re-moved the institutional bases of the Jewish community but did not eliminate all the structural sources of Jewish cohesion. The revolutionary regimes ended the predominance of the Jewish communities of Europe within world Jewry.

IV: Jewish Cohesion in America

American society provides two distinct cases for the analysis of the cohesion of Jewish communities. The first is the immigrant society in which relatively large numbers of Jews come in contact with rapid and widespread patterns of modernization. Here, the Jewish community was characterized by economic, residential, and linguistic overlaps but few communal and religious institutions. The second case presents contemporary America, in which high levels of modernization continue and new economic and social concentrations appear as well as a plethora of ethnic and religious organizations.

10 · The Formation of the American Jewish Community

American society has long been characterized by the arrival of immigrant groups from diverse countries of origin. It has provided opportunities for ethnic isolation, integration, acculturation, and assimilation. The power and scope of American modernization have transformed immigrants. American society has had none of the rigidities of the old order. Neither caste nor class has defined the character of society for whites. American ideology has supported the integration of immigrants, the preservation of religious diversity, and political rights.

The place of Jews in the American policy has reflected this fluidity. An expanding economy and a relatively small national Jewish population have made political anti-Semitism insignificant. In places where there were relatively few Jews, they were not a political issue. Where Jews were concentrated, so were other ethnic groups. Their presence in areas with expanding economies made attacks on Jews ineffective political strategies. Appeals for Jewish votes, not denunciations of Jews, have characterized most elections in which Jewish issues have appeared. These factors and open, socially diverse political parties limited the formation of Jewish political movements to defense organizations protecting Jewish rights with the tactics of political liberalism. Only during the era of massive Jewish immigration, when Jewish trade unions and socialists organized Jewish workers against Jewish capitalists, did other political patterns appear. The politics of American Jews differed from those in Europe.

Jews responded in diverse ways to the process of becoming Americans. They were socially and geographically mobile, became educated, entered the middle classes, and reformed their religion. These changes have had consequences for Jewish continuity and cohesion in America. To what extent has American modernization led to the disaffection of Jews from their Jewishness and the disintegration of the Jewish community? To what extent do the patterns of Jewish cohesion found in European modernization appear in America as well? America is the major test for Jewish survival during modernization. The Jewish community had relatively few institutions to absorb the masses of immigrants during its formative years. Jews from traditional European communities faced a relatively free and open, pluralistic society, characterized by a sustained high level of social and economic modernization.

IMMIGRATION AND THE JEWISH COMMUNITY: THE EARLY WAVE

Many have argued that Jews were the only group which arrived as a minority from countries where they also had been a minority. While Italians, Irish, Germans, Poles, and Russians became minority groups in the United States, Jews moved to a new type of minority status. As a result of their previous minority experiences, Jews were better prepared to adjust to the new society (Sklare, 1971). It must be noted, however, that few of the other immigrant groups considered themselves as having come from a country where they were part of a dominant majority. Sicilians, for example, did not think of themselves as Italians. Poles knew that they were an oppressed minority under Russian rule. The continuous minority status of the Jews is not what determined their adaptation to America.

What role did Jewish values play in the integration of American Jews? Did the poor, impoverished Jewish immigrants carry middle-class values? Did their religious traditions and culture result in their early successes in school and economic mobility? Those who have argued for the centrality of Jewish values as the explanation of rapid Jewish integration in America minimize the importance of social class and residential differences between Jewish and non-Jewish immigrants. The superficial similarity of mass immigration from diverse countries and the initial depths of urban poverty common to all immigrants obscure critical differences in the occupational and urban background of Jews and others. Comparisons between Jewish immigrants and those who remained behind reveal the particular characteristics and selectivity of the migrants. Comparisons between Jewish and non-Jewish immigrants indicate the specific advantages Jews had upon arrival in America, their settlement patterns, and subsequent rapid mobility. We emphasize the structural factors which distinguish Jews from others and the expanding educational and economic opportunities which they confronted in their initial adjustments to American society.

The formation of the American Jewish community was conditioned by the timing and rate of population growth. Starting with 1,200 Jews in 1790, the Jewish population increased to about 50,000 in 1848 and to slightly less than a quarter of a million before the mass immigrations from Eastern Europe. Reflecting high rates of net immigration and natural increase, the Jewish population in the United States increased to over 1 million by the turn of the twentieth century and to over 4 million by the mid-1920s. Jewish population growth during this period was greater than that of the American population as a whole. Hence, the proportion that Jews composed of the total U.S.

population increased from one-tenth of 1 percent in 1840 to 3.6 percent in 1927. The American Jewish population explosion ended in the mid-1930s, as the level of Jewish immigration from Eastern Europe declined substantially, following the quota restrictions a decade earlier, and as fertility levels of second-generation Jews plummeted to replacement levels during the economic depression (Goldscheider, 1982; S. Goldstein, 1981).

What were the effects of entry into the rapidly changing world of America? How did the changing levels of American modernization shape the waves of Jewish immigration? How different were the responses of the relatively small number of Jewish immigrants from Germany and the millions from Eastern Europe? How did their different occupational, political, and religious backgrounds affect their integration into American society?

Between 1820 and 1870 an estimated 50,000 German Jews immigrated to America, and the Jewish population increased from about 6,000 to over 200,000. (For different estimates see Linfield, 1927; Hersch, 1949; Lestchinsky, 1960; *The American Jewish Yearbook*, 1977). Most came from the commercial classes, although artisans from Posen could be found as well (Lestschinsky, 1960; and Chapter 4). Many came from villages and small towns, where formal religious education was weak but structural sources of Jewish cohesion were strong. Economic reasons were the primary motivation for emigrating to America. Religious and political issues determined the timing, not the decision, to leave Germany or to emigrate to America. Most were young adults without families, with previous training and education suited for mercantile-related occupations (Mostov, 1978, 1981). Some had been squeezed by repressive legislation, burdened by taxes and restrictions on marriage, residence, and jobs (Goren, 1980, p. 576; Toury, 1971). Their socioeconomic background, social mobility, geographic dispersion, and their prior exposure to secularization resulted in rapid integration into American society. German Jews in America moved from traditional to Reform Judaism. They did not establish Jewish educational networks, and significant proportions were intermarrying. Many have interpreted these changes as indications of assimilation. They have argued that were it not for the subsequent mass immigration of Eastern European Jews who were more traditional and less modern, German Jews would have vanished (see for example Glazer, 1957).

This argument is incomplete. It omits the social structural bases that were emerging to underpin Jewish continuity in America. First, German Jews were residentially concentrated in several states and in the largest urban places. In 1877, almost two-thirds of American Jews lived in five states (New York, California, Pennsylvania, Ohio, and Illinois); an estimated 65 percent lived in the ten largest cities compared to only 10 percent of all Americans (Linfield, 1927; Mostov, 1981). Within these cities, there was considerable Jewish residential segregation as well (Mostov, 1978; S. Hertzberg, 1978;

Raphael, 1975). As in Europe, American Jews were an overwhelmingly urban group within a predominantly rural society.

The geographic distribution of German Jews and their distinctive residential clustering reflected commercial opportunities within America and the shipping routes from German port cities (Mostov, 1978). Their residential concentration was associated with occupational patterns. In mid-nineteenth century Boston, 70 percent of all employed Jews were in six occupational categories compared to one-fourth of the city's total labor force. Peddlers, tailors, and clothing or dry goods merchants accounted for over one-half of the Jewish employed. In contrast, one-third of Boston's entire labor force worked in menial, semiskilled, and service jobs compared to only 2 percent of the Jews. About half of the German Jews and all German immigrants in Boston were artisans. Jewish artisans, however, were almost exclusively tailors, opticians and watchmakers, cigarmakers, and furriers; non-Jewish artisans were bakers, shoemakers, and smiths (Mostov, 1978).

The Jewish occupational pattern in Boston paralleled those prevalent in Germany (see Chapter 4) and was strikingly similar in widely scattered American cities. A comparison of Jewish occupations in Boston; New York; Detroit; Columbus, Ohio; and San Francisco in 1850–70 shows the very high concentration of peddlers, merchants, and artisans (about 80 percent). In eastern cities there was a larger proportion of artisans among Jews, reflecting the presence of manufacturing (Mostov, 1978). Unskilled and manual labor, as well as professional or semiprofessional jobs, were occupational categories containing few German Jews in America. German Jews dominated selected urban industries, particularly dry goods, clothing, and cigar making. The rapid growth of cities on the eastern coast provided expanding economic opportunities for tradesmen and small merchants. Between 1825 and 1860, the population of New York City almost tripled to 805,000; its Jewish population rose from 500 to 40,000. A merchant's guide to the city in 1859 listed 141 wholesale firms in the garment industry whose owners had Jewish names. German Jews controlled the entire clothing industry by 1870. In New York, Jews owned 80 percent of retail and 90 percent of wholesale clothing firms. In the rest of the country, the figure was only slightly lower (Goren, 1980, pp. 576–79).

The very heavy occupational and industrial concentration of Jews led to an extensive network of contacts among Jews. In turn, such concentration facilitated and was reinforced by an internal system of credit. A German-Jewish economic network emerged in America in the 1860s and 1870s in which Jewish manufacturers and wholesalers in the East provided credit to Jewish wholesalers in the West, who in turn supplied credit to Jewish retailers and peddlers (Mostov, 1981; Goren, 1980). The system of internal credit supply was a product of necessity more than preference. The reliance on private capital and family connections and the emphasis on personal reputation as a sufficient basis for collateral had a major impact on the social mobility patterns of Jews. Credit networks combined with occupational-industrial concentration to reinforce the structural and cultural bonds in the emerging Jewish community in late nineteenth century America.

Furthermore, despite the reform in religious services and the changing levels of traditional observances and ritual practices among German Jews, most Jews had ties to synagogues and temples (Glazer, 1957). Local community records detail the synagogues, burial societies, welfare and social institutions, fund raising, and Jewish educational activities among German Jews in late nineteenth-century America. New institutions and organizations were developing in America to meet the needs of the increasing Jewish population. The religious reforms were adaptations to the American scene rather than simply carryovers from Germany (Jick, 1976). They clearly represented a major break from traditional Judaism and Jewish practice but not from Reform Judaism in Germany. German Jewish immigrants had already been exposed to religious changes in their country of origin. Jews in America were defined along religious lines, not ethnic or social class. Hence, German Jews in America were developing religious institutions and religious ideologies that were consistent with their place in America and legitimated their continuity. Only from the perspective of traditional Judaism was religious reform the symbol of total assimilation.

National organizations, communal institutions, and changing modes of religious expression were therefore not signs of a vanishing, chaotic group. Indeed, despite patterns of change and transformation, most Jewish economic and social activities involved only other Jews and took place within the confines of Jewish neighborhoods and business activities. These patterns were quite similar to Jewish communities in Western Europe, where new forms of ethnic-religious cohesion were emerging (see Chapter 6).

In this regard, a comprehensive analysis of the center of Reform Jewry in America—Cincinnati between 1840 and 1875—concludes:

Cincinnati's Jews remained a distinct subcommunity. What made the Jews different from other subcommunities was the degree of their distinctiveness in an economic in addition to a social, ethnic, and religious sense. To be a Jew in Cincinnati meant not only that one might pray in a different place than non-Jews, or belong to a separate set of organizations. Rather, one's Jewishness was also an important factor in how one happened to have settled in Cincinnati and how long one remained, of where one resided and worked within the city, and how one made a living. [Mostov, 1981, p. 238]

These patterns—documented for the largest, most influential, and prosperous community of the Midwest—apply to Jews in other American cities as well. From the mid-to-late nineteenth century, Jews were linked to each other economically, but their communities were local rather than national. Residential, occupational, and cultural distinctiveness defined the cohesiveness of German Jewish immigrants and their children in America. Few bases of internal conflict were present. The secularization of Judaism and the opportunities to integrate transformed the content of Jewishness in America without assimilating German Jews.

MASS IMMIGRATION FROM EASTERN EUROPE: SELECTIVITY
We shall never know what would have happened to German Jews in America in the third or subsequent generations, since a new immigration transformed American Jewry. Between 1881 and 1924 approximately 2.5 million Jews from Eastern Europe entered the United States. In the first decade alone, the number of Jewish immigrants more than doubled the American Jewish population. Natural increase and further immigration enlarged the American Jewish population from less than a quarter of a million in 1880 to over 4 million in the mid-1920s. Although mass immigration did not begin until 1881, estimates suggest that approximately 100,000 Eastern European Jews immigrated to the United States before then—70,000 in the decade 1871–80, and 30,000 between 1820 and 1870 (Lestchinsky, 1960; Joseph, 1914).

This mass immigration converted American Jews from a string of local communities into a national subcommunity (Goldstein and Goldscheider, 1968). While German Jewry and their descendants continued for a while to control the economic institutions and communal organizations, Eastern European immigrants and their children defined the character of American Jewish life.

The overwhelming majority of Eastern European Jewish immigrants remained permanently in the United States. Sex-ratio data, the proportion of children, and evidence on family migration point in this direction. Direct data on return migration show that of the more than 1 million Jewish immigrants in 1908–25, only 52,000 emigrated—about 5 percent. This compares to 40 percent of the Poles and 50 percent of the Russians who returned to their countries of origin and to 56 percent of the Italian immigrants who returned to Italy. Even one-sixth of the French and English immigrants returned—three times as high as Jewish return migration (Joseph, 1914; Lestchinsky, 1960; Kessner, 1977). Jewish immigrants were exceptional in their permanent settlement in America relative to other immigrants. Factors particular to the immigration of these East European Jews led to their relatively permanent settlement in America.

Who were the Jewish immigrants from Eastern Europe? Why did they come to America? Did they reflect a cross-section of Eastern European Jews? How were they affected by the rapid industrialization and urbanization in America?

Immigration to America from Tsarist Russia and Poland was the result of a complex combination of pushes and pulls. Political oppression, restrictive legislation depriving Jews of jobs and places of residence were important determinants of out-migration. The constraints on economic and educational opportunity and political status had fluctuated over time but remained uncertain in the upheavals of Eastern Europe. Even when equal opportunities were open for the Jewish masses, government policies continued to be restrictive. Relocations to towns and cities were occasions for socioeconomic mobility for Jews as well as for new competition and confrontation with non-Jews. The push factors were powerful incentives for immigration.

Nevertheless, this is not the whole story. All Jews did not come to America, even when there were no restrictions on immigration from Eastern Europe. Most Jews remained in Eastern Europe. Indeed, despite the large, mass immigration, Jewish population size continued to increase in Eastern Europe. Thus, from the point of view of Eastern European Jewry, immigration to America was selective. And while it may be viewed as "mass" immigration from the perspective of absolute numbers and from the point of view of the American Jewish community, it was not "mass" from the point of view of Eastern European Jewish communities.

The rapid increase in the number of Jews in Eastern Europe found an outlet in emigration. It was not the source of change within Eastern Europe nor did it empty out the Jewish communities there. While the migration of such large numbers affected families and communities left behind, the structure of the communities was not disrupted. Indeed, these communities and their organizations continued to survive and thrive. Internal changes and emigration were alternative responses of different sectors of the Jewish population to the social, economic, and political upheavals in Europe.

As in other migrations, the young were more likely to move than the old. Only 5 percent of Jewish immigrants in the first decade of the twentieth century were age forty-five and over, similar to the non-Jewish pattern (Joseph, 1914, p. 180).

The impulse to emigrate was stimulated by the lack of opportunity and by persecution but it had its deeper source in the restless energy of young people discontented with their lot. [Dawidowicz, 1982, p. 11]

Moreover, the migration was selective on socioeconomic grounds. Property owners and those with good jobs were least likely to migrate. Most professionals stayed in Europe. They accounted for 6 percent of the Jewish workforce in the Russian census of 1897 and 1 percent of the Jewish immigrants between 1899 and 1910. As among other people, the poorest and least educated were least likely to move. There was a much higher proportion of skilled laborers and a much lower proportion of unskilled workers and servants among the immigrants than among the Jewish work

force in the Tsarist Empire. In addition, merchants and dealers were unlikely to emigrate during the first decades of mass emigration. They
accounted for one-third of the gainfully occupied Jews in Russia and 6
percent of the immigrants in 1899–1910 (Rubinow, 1975, pp. 500–501;
Kuznets, 1960; Kessner, 1977). These data suggest that pressure for emigration was greatest in urban areas, where Jews were squeezed by industrialization. They also indicate that emigration occurred especially among artisans
whose skills could most easily be transferred abroad. As in other migrations,
those most receptive to change were already somewhat freed from the
constraints of family and tradition and already socially and economically
mobile.

Most of the religious elite and their closest followers remained in Eastern
Europe. They labeled America the *trayfa medina*, the impure and unholy
land. Religious leaders saw that American society transformed Jews, secu-
larized them, provided alternative avenues of Jewish expression outside the
closed community of religious authority, and challenged their role as the
sole source of Jewish identification (Helmreich, 1982; Sklare, 1971). The
rabbinical leaders assumed that the decline of traditional Judaism led to
assimilation. They did not perceive the emergence of new forms of Jewishness as acceptable substitutes for the end of the old order. Between 1899 and
1910, .06 percent of the Jewish immigrants (305) had been rabbis in Europe;
in 1897, Jewish clergy were twice that proportion of the Jews in Russia
(6,030) (Kessner, 1977, p. 33; Rubinow, 1975, p. 498). As a result, there
were relatively few rabbis to lead the newly forming synagogues in America
and to establish Jewish school systems. In 1900, there was only one Orthodox rabbinical seminary in the United States and no Jewish day schools. It
took a generation for the educational infrastructure of the Orthodox religious community to develop (Elazar, 1976; A. Liebman, 1979).

In the early years of mass immigration, there was a disproportionate
number of Socialists and secularists responding to the political and economic opportunities in America and the restrictions on Jewish university
graduates in Eastern Europe. They saw America as the "golden land," the
"new world," and the "promised land." They brought with them the cultural societies, unions, and political parties of Eastern European Jewry
(Howe, 1976; A. Liebman, 1979; see Chapter 8).

RESIDENTIAL SETTLEMENT AND ECONOMIC CONCENTRATION
Jewish immigrants to the United States were different from Jews remaining
in Eastern Europe. How different were they from other immigrants? Did
they transfer their unique socioeconomic and demographic characteristics in
Eastern Europe to their new country? At the most general level, most
immigrants were poor and most settled in the largest cities which were
expanding in the late nineteenth and early twentieth centuries. Most of the

immigrants came in response to the economic opportunities American industrial growth offered. Yet, a careful examination of the evidence suggests some key differences between Jews and other immigrants.

A much higher proportion of Jewish women immigrated compared to other immigrants. Thirty percent of the total immigrants to America in 1899–1910 were women compared to 43 percent among Jews. Most of the immigrants were in the prime working ages, but Jews were distinguished by an exceptional proportion of children accompanying parents. Most immigrants indicated that they intended to settle in the North Atlantic states which were the industrial and commercial centers of America in the first decade of the twentieth century. Yet, that was the choice of 86 percent of the Jews compared to 67 percent of the total immigrants (Joseph, 1914, pp. 176–78, 196). Hence, family migration to the largest commercial and manufacturing centers was more characteristic of Jews than of other immigrants at the turn of the century.

Indeed, the pattern of Jewish immigration and settlement resulted in a very high Jewish population concentration in the Northeast. In 1918, almost half of the Jews in the United States lived in New York and almost two-thirds lived in but three states (New York, Pennsylvania, and Massachusetts). In 1927, almost 85 percent of America's Jews were concentrated in cities of 100,000 or more population compared to less than 30 percent of the total population. Less than 3 percent of the Jewish population lived in rural places compared to 46 percent of the total. Crude estimates show that over two-thirds of all Jews in the United States were in the ten largest cities. Between 1877 and 1927, the proportion of Jews living in regions other than the South and West increased from 76 percent to over 90 percent; at the same time, the proportion of the total American population in those areas declined from 70 percent to 61 percent (Linfield, 1927, pp. 13–14, 28, 68).

In 1880, 10 percent of New York City's population was Jewish; by 1915 the number of Jews increased from 80,000 to 1,400,000 and represented almost one-third of the total. Three-fourths of all Jews who immigrated in 1881–1911 immediately or soon after settled in New York City. By 1927, over 40 percent of all American Jews were living in New York City (Schappes, 1950; A. Liebman, 1979, p. 137; Linfield, 1927, p. 28). Even within New York City, Jews were highly concentrated. An area of twenty-five square blocks (Lower East Side) contained three-fourths of the city's Jews in 1892 and about half in 1903. The decline was in proportion, not in absolute numbers; the move away did not mean random dispersal (Rischin, 1962; A. Liebman, 1979; Kessner, 1977). A study of the fifty-six neighborhoods of New York City in 1930 showed that in thirty-four Jews accounted for less than 21 percent of the total, in four they were more than 60 percent, and in nine they were about half of the residents (Moore, 1981, pp. 19–33).

Patterns of residential concentration were linked to the economic opportunities available and the skills of Jewish immigrants. Their occupational patterns distinguished them not only from those who remained in Eastern Europe but from other immigrants as well. The rapid economic mobility of Jews reflected the fit between their occupational skills and the expanding American economy. The occupational concentration that characterized them in their places of origins continued in their country of destination.

Given the occupational origins of Jews in Germany and Eastern Europe, it is not surprising that the occupations of Eastern European Jews were significantly different than the earlier wave of German-Jewish immigrants. In 1889, American Jews from German-speaking countries and their descendants were heavily concentrated in trade. Bankers, brokers, wholesalers, retail dealers, collectors, and agents accounted for 62 percent of their occupations. In addition, 17 percent were professionals. Thus, almost 85 percent of these Jews were white-collar workers (Billings, cited by Goldberg, 1945–46; see also Kuznets, 1960). In sharp contrast, a study of a quarter of a million gainfully employed Jews in three New York City Jewish districts in 1890 showed that 60 percent worked in the needle trades, 15 percent were other industrial workers, and 11 percent were peddlers. There was a sharp contrast between the two groups: Germans in trade and at middle occupational levels, and Eastern Europeans in clothing and in skilled and semiskilled labor (Kuznets, 1960). These class divisions and the frequent overlap between class and ethnicity produced conflict within the Jewish community.

These differences reflect the background skills and experiences of the two migration streams and the different economic conditions in their places of origin (see Chapters 4 and 7). In addition, economic and industrial changes in America between the middle and end of the nineteenth century as well as the greater length of time that German Jews were exposed to American society affected the differences between the two groups of Jewish immigrants.

The proportion of Jews who declared upon entry to the United States that they were laborers, farmers, or servants averaged less than 25 percent in 1900–1902 compared to 80–90 percent of the other immigrant groups. In 1910 and 1914, for example, about 90 percent of Croatians, Slovenians, Finns, Greeks, Hungarians, Poles, Russians, and Italians compared to 20 percent of the Jews were laborers, farmers, or servants (Lieberson, 1980). Other data show that most Jewish immigrants worked in industry. Between 1899 and 1914, fully two-thirds of the Jews entering the United States had been engaged in manufacturing and mechanical pursuits in Europe, more than three-fourths as skilled workers (Kuznets, 1960; Joseph, 1914; Kessner, 1977).

The overwhelming concentration of Jewish immigrants in skilled labor represents a significant difference from Jews in Russia in 1897 and in Austria in 1900 (see Kuznets, 1960). The selectivity of Jewish immigration fit into the particular labor demands and occupational opportunities in America and provided Jews an enormous structural advantage over other immigrants in the pursuit of occupational integration and social mobility (Steinberg, 1981; Kessner, 1977).

At the same time, Jews entered particular segments of the economy, establishing, thereby, an overlap between ethnicity, religion, and occupation, similar to what existed in nineteenth-century Europe. Data on the Russian-born in the United States census of 1900 (most of whom were Jews) indicate high levels of occupational concentration among these immigrants (Goldberg, 1945–46; Kuznets, 1960; Kessner, 1977; Lieberson, 1980). Over 60 percent were in manufacturing, half of them as tailors. An additional 30 percent were in trade and transportation. The pattern holds for women as well—72 percent of the Russian-born women working in the United States in 1900 were in manufacturing, and 55 percent were in the needle trades and related positions (Kuznets, 1960).

There is dramatic evidence of the specific occupational concentration of Jews. An examination of working males outside the South in 1900 indicates that Jews were heavily concentrated in particular jobs. Fully 43 percent of all hucksters and peddlers were Russian Jews; as were 42 percent of the hat and cap makers; 49 percent of all shirt, collar, and cuff makers; one-third of all tailors; 16 percent of all newspaper carriers and newsboys; 17 percent of all paperhangers; and 13 percent of all tobacco and cigar factory operatives. These levels of concentration are impressive, since Jews represented less than 3 percent of the total population (Lieberson, 1980).

EDUCATION AND NEW BASES OF COHESION

Educational attainment of American Jews relates to these occupational patterns as well as to other distinctive features of the Jewish immigrants. Jews did not simply enter schools and universities because they valued education. Their social and economic background, residence, and family characteristics allowed them to take advantage of the expanding educational opportunities.

Jews came to America as families, with a disproportionate number of children. Fully one-fourth of the Jewish immigrants in the decade 1899–1909 were below age fourteen compared to about 10 percent of non-Jewish immigrants (Joseph, 1914, p. 180). It is therefore not surprising that Jews were overrepresented numerically in the urban school systems where they resided.

About one-fourth of the Jewish immigrants in 1899–1910 were illiterate—20 percent of the men and 37 percent of the women. Overall, the level of illiteracy among Jewish immigrants was about the same as other immigrants.

Comparisons that examine literacy levels separately for men and women and for specific countries of Eastern Europe reveal that here Jews were somewhat advantaged (Joseph, 1914, pp. 192–94; Lieberson, 1980; Kessner, 1977).

While levels of illiteracy did not sharply distinguish Jews from other immigrants, the rate at which Jews learned English in America was higher than that of all immigrants from non-English speaking countries. Within five years from immigration, two-thirds of the Jewish industrial workers spoke English compared to 29 percent of all other immigrants (Steinberg, 1974, p. 85). This too reflects the greater permanence of Jewish immigration and the importance of language for those who were going to reestablish their families and communities in America.

The occupational links to education were more important. Working in more skilled and stable occupations, Jews earned more money than did other immigrant groups. Their relative income and occupational security made it easier for Jews to invest in the schooling of their children. This combined with the permanency of their immigration, urban residence, and the availability and access to public school education. Together these structural features explain why Jewish children were in school longer than other immigrant groups and why Jews accounted for relatively high percentages of those who attended schools and universities in the large cities of the Northeast. As in Western Europe, occupation, residence, and access account for educational attainment levels.

While the initial links were from occupation to education, over time educational attainment became a major avenue of occupational mobility. It was not the only avenue nor did it characterize all Jewish children. Continuity in self-employment and in family businesses were other paths to mobility. In addition, educational changes did not appear for most Jews overnight. Immigrant Jews did not all flock to high schools and colleges. Most were caught in the immediate struggle for economic survival.

Exposure to high schools and universities brought Jews together in new institutions. Patterns of interaction occurred among the large number of Jews in educational settings. Student organizations were formed which contained large numbers of Jews.

By 1920 both City College and Hunter College had become 80–90 percent Jewish. Before Columbia University instituted restrictive quotas after World War I, 40 percent of its enrollment was Jewish. Similar patterns of Jewish concentration in institutions of higher learning characterized other schools on the East Coast where Jews were residentially clustered. In comparison to most other immigrant groups, as well as to native-born Americans, Jewish children were more likely to reach and finish high school and more likely to enroll in college preparatory courses (Steinberg, 1974, pp. 9–11). The timing of their immigration, the expansion of educational opportunities, their location in the urban centers of the East close to public colleges and universities were critical advantages. They were "in the right place at the right time. No other ethnic group in America has found itself in such fortuitous circumstances when it was prepared for its breakthrough into higher education" (Steinberg, 1974, p. 31). Most important, Jews found in these institutions of higher learning the key to occupational mobility and economic integration, careers founded on skills and universalistic criteria. At the same time, Jews found new ties to each other outside of the traditional bonds of family, neighborhood, and culture. The commonalities of background and life-style reinforced bonds of kinship and culture. Similar phenomena were developing in the academies and universities of Europe (see Chapters 6 and 8). These patterns of social mobility depressed class divisions and led over time to the end of class conflict within the Jewish community of America.

As Jewish families became more secure economically, a large proportion of their children applied to the relatively prestigious colleges and universities. Initially, there was little resistance. As competition for the limited number of places emerged, however, formal and informal restrictions on the entry of Jews appeared. These quotas were legitimated by the prevailing ideologies of racial and cultural differences; the fundamental underpinning was competition for a limited number of openings, not anti-Semitism per se (Steinberg, 1974). Again, the parallels to developments in Europe are striking (see Chapter 9).

The structural supports for educational attainment were strong. Opportunities were present and a relatively greater proportion of the Jews than other immigrant groups had the means to take advantage of them. Jewish values stressing study and education supported their ability to attend school in relatively large numbers (see Steinberg, 1974).

The permanence of immigration and the distance between Eastern Europe and America did not imply that as Jews became Americans they severed all ties to their families in Europe. Kinship and friendship ties were the bases of further immigration of relatives and friends from communities of origin. Chain migration, not return movement, was a dominant feature of Eastern European Jewish immigration to America as it had been for others (see Goldscheider, 1971, chapter 7). But here again, Jews were exceptional. Of all European groups, Jews were the most likely to report that relatives had paid their travel costs to America: fully 58 percent of the Jews compared to 26 percent of the Southern Italians and 30 percent for immigrants as a whole. This and other evidence points to the greater social and economic interdependence and wealth among Jews, as earlier settlers helped to bring over to America family and fellow townspeople (Steinberg, 1974, p. 76).

The ties to countries and communities of origin were reinforced by settlement and organizational patterns in America. Immigrants from the same community or region, speaking the same dialect of Yiddish, together built synagogues, and formed charity and aid societies. They conveyed to their American-born children the sense of community and culture of places of origin including the depths of their Jewish identification. Thousands of separate independent associations, landsmanschaften, existed by the first and second decades of the twentieth century (Goren, 1980; Howe, 1976).

Even a casual perusal of the organizations listed in the first several issues of *The American Jewish Yearbook* reveals the enormous institutional developments which characterized American Jewry at the beginning of the twentieth century (Adler, 1899). Local and national organizations emerged; religious and secular institutions were established alongside communal, welfare, economic, and fraternal organizations. In 1888, for example, the United Hebrew Trades was formed; by 1914 there were 111 affiliated unions, and by 1920 over a quarter of a million Jews were members of these unions. Most of these were in needle trades (see A. Liebman, 1979, p. 212). In 1914, there were 12,000 registered Zionists in America; four years later there were 145,000 (A. Liebman, 1979, p. 263; Shapiro, 1976). The Workmen's Circle had 872 members in 1900; 18 years later there were 60,000 members. Social class was the primary source of conflict within the Jewish community.

At work, in neighborhoods, in schools as well as in religious activities, and in social clubs Jews were interacting with other Jews. Yiddish and socialist schools and newspapers competed with public and religious schools, and afternoon synagogue schools. Credit associations, landsmanschaften, local fraternal and defense organizations, and communal institutions appeared and kept expanding. As the number of Jews increased and as they moved to new areas, new institutions developed. While learning English, Yiddish remained the language of business and social life among immigrants. Even when their children rejected Yiddish as their language, it was still the cultural environment of their upbringing. Most Jews in America of the pre–World War II period interacted with other Jews in the community. Some fought with other Jews; most did not. The number of bases of Jewish cohesion was very large indeed. The overlap of occupation, residence, and ethnicity was as high as anywhere in urban Europe. While change was evident for both the first and second generations, there was no question that Jews were a distinct subcommunity within American society.

The Jewish immigrants did not transfer the world of their origins. America was different and so were the immigrants. They left the Old World behind—not all of it to be sure—to become part of the new society. Their Jewishness was conspicuous by their background, culture, and social structure. What would be the source of their children's Jewishness was not clear. How they would convey their traditions was set aside as they struggled to survive in America.

The transition to an Americanized second-, third-, and fourth-generation ethnic group has been the master theme in the sociology and demography of American Jews. Indeed, generational status is a key axis along which vary the range of demographic and social processes of American Jews and the character of American Jewish communities. There have been generational changes in residential location, family structure and size, intermarriage, social class (education, occupation, and income), religious identification, and measures of Jewish religiosity and commitment.

The bases of American Jewish cohesion were many and varied for the immigrants and their children. Structure and cultural commonalities were linked institutionally and organizationally. Communities were formally established; Jews developed informal but powerful social and economic links. Conflict between German and Eastern European Jews and between social classes diminished over time. Traditional forms of cohesion were changing and new classes were emerging. The critical questions are: What would be the forms of Jewish survival among their children and grandchildren? How would the third and fourth generations in America be affected by continued modernization and by greater distance from their traditional, Eastern European roots?

11 · Modernization and American Jews: Issues of Quantity and Quality

In the century subsequent to mass Jewish immigration from Eastern Europe, America's Jews have been transformed. As other white Americans, their political status is defined in terms of individual rights, legal equalities, freedom to practice their religion, to live, work, and study where they chose. The transformation of the Jewish group illustrates the power of achievement, the success of meritocracy, and the value of individual liberty in American society.

In a relatively short period of time following immigration, Jews were integrated into American communities. They shed their particular language and foreign dress, moved to new neighborhoods and cities, attended public schools, colleges, and universities in unprecedented numbers and proportions. Jews interacted with and married non-Jews. Moving away from occupations as skilled workers in particular industries, many became professionals and managers—doctors, lawyers, teachers, social workers, accountants, and computer specialists, to name the most conspicuous. In the process, the level of self-employment declined as Jews went to work for larger, often non-Jewish, companies in diverse industries. In their social mobility they have become affluent. Poverty and unskilled labor are largely uncharacteristic of Jews in America, except selectively among the older generation.

These occupational, educational, and residential changes have been accompanied by shifts in the relative importance of families and religion. Jews in modern America, as most others in their social situation, have moved from family- and child- centered to individual-centered daily lives. They have become less traditional in religious practice than earlier generations.

In short, industrialization, urbanization, and secularization transformed the Jews of America. Indeed, Jews may be viewed as an ideal typical minority group in terms of rapid integration. In almost every way, Jews are America's best success story. Every indicator reveals how Jews have become modern and American in the 1980s. Rapid and high levels of modernization, large concentrations of Jews in a context of ethnic and religious pluralism distant from immigrant status, raise the question of how these structural changes impinge on their continuity as a group. Does change imply the assimilation of Jews and the demise of the Jewish community? Are there new forms emerging that extend, replace, and redefine Jewishness? Along with the dramatic changes and transformations, are there emerging patterns which are the bases of new forms of Jewish cohesion?

Jews have the opportunity of associating with the formal organizations and institutions of the community. They continue to have common traits, values, and life-styles. They have, indeed, organized themselves into hundreds of local and national institutions—religious, philanthropic, educational, political, and social (see for example Elazar, 1976; and the extensive community organizations listed in *The American Jewish Yearbook*). But how important is Jewish survival to Jews? Have Jews emerged in the late twentieth century as a viable, cohesive, and dynamic ethnic, religious group in America? Does being modern in America, where most Jews outside of Israel reside, imply the beginning of the end of Jewish people in the Diaspora? Is American Jewish survival possible? It is clear from the total range of evidence that processes of both transformation and continuity have been occurring in America over the last several decades. American Jews have not disappeared; the Jewish community in the United States also is not identical with other Jewish communities in the past. Theories predicting the demise of Jews and their communities in the process of modernization need to be revised. Theories expecting Jewish continuities without change need to be modified as well.

An analysis of two interrelated themes facilitates an assessment of patterns of American Jewish survival. First, we shall examine changes in the demographic basis of Jewish continuity: population size, growth, family and marriage patterns. Since Jews live in a variety of communities in the United States, we shall investigate the patterns of migration and the issue of Jewish density. A second theme focuses on life-style, socioeconomic status, religious forms, and other bases of Jewish cohesion. The quantitative and qualitative assessments are interrelated. Both point to the variety of bases for Jewish cohesion in America.

QUANTITATIVE ISSUES
By the middle of the twentieth century the American Jewish population was estimated at 5 million—a 100-fold increase in a century. It had survived the immigration quotas and below-replacement fertility of the economic depression of the 1930s. It is likely that the Jewish population of the United States has not yet attained the 6-million mark. Estimates of the size of the Jewish population in 1980 are around 5,775,000, with a margin of error of almost a quarter of a million on either side (see Lazerwitz, 1978;

S. Goldstein, 1981; Goldscheider, 1982). The rate of growth over the last several decades has been slow and, taking into account the entire range of demographic processes affecting growth (mortality, fertility, immigration, emigration, conversions to Judaism, and net losses due to outmarriages), the Jewish community hovers at zero population growth or perhaps slightly below. Because Jewish population increase has been slower than that characterizing American society, the proportion of Jews in America has declined to less than 2.7 percent, the lowest proportion since the first decade of the twentieth century (Goldscheider, 1982).

The decline in the percentage of Jews in America and the attainment of zero population growth or population decline leads to concerns about the vanishing of American Jewry, the political significance of declining numbers, and organizational weakness of the Jewish community. The issue of Jewish demographic vitality has called into question broader issues of Jewish survival in modern society. While the connections between demographic processes and the quality of American Jewish life are strong, much of the concern seems misplaced. Jews have never constituted a numerically large segment of the American population, nor has their political or economic power been functions of population size. America is the world Jewish demographic center. It is not likely that it will be overtaken by any other Jewish community in the world—including Israel—for the rest of this century (see Schmelz and Della Pergola, 1982, 1983; Bachi, 1982).

To analyze the quantitative issue, we need to disentangle the various components of population change. We start with the contributions of immigration to population growth. While legislation ended mass immigration from Eastern Europe in the mid-1920s (see Chapter 10), Jewish immigration did not cease entirely. Between 1925 and World War II almost a quarter of a million Jews arrived, many refugees from Central and Eastern Europe. Furthermore, between 1944 and 1959 about 192,000 Jewish immigrants entered the United States, and an additional 129,000 immigrated between 1959 and 1975. Altogether, from World War II to 1975 over 320,000 Jews immigrated to the United States. These immigrants confronted a well-established Jewish community that had already numbered over 4 million by the mid-1920s, with well-developed communal organizations and social institutions (Goldscheider, 1982).

It is not clear what proportion of those who came after 1925 have followed the generational model of change characteristic of earlier immigrants. Some were no doubt affected by the structures shaped by the children and grandchildren of earlier immigrants. Others have remained outside these patterns. Hasidim and other Orthodox Jews, who rejected modernization in Europe, brought their institutions, communities, and patterns of residential segregation to America after World War II. As a result, they selectively integrated into American life and have affected the religious heterogeneity and polarization of the Jewish community (Kranzler, 1961; Poll, 1969).

Tens of thousands of former Israeli residents have settled in the United States in recent decades. There has also been a significant increase in Russian Jewish immigration to America. In 1973, for example, only 1,449 Soviet Jews immigrated to America (about 15 percent of the estimated total Jewish immigration to the United States). In 1974 and 1975, the number of Russian Jewish immigrants increased to about 9,000, almost 30 percent of estimated Jewish immigration to America (Edelman, 1977; Jacobs and Paul, 1981). The numbers have varied as those leaving Russia increased and as the proportion who immigrated to Israel decreased. In 1979, over 50,000 Jews departed the Soviet Union; over two-thirds came to the United States.

Russian and Israeli immigrants represent new ethnic groups for American Jews and their communities. Much attention and funds have been directed to the integration of Russians into the community. Israeli-Americans have been largely ignored by the organized Jewish community and have set up their own ethnic enclaves (Kass and Lipset, 1982; Jacobs and Paul, 1981). It is likely that most Russians and Israelis will remain in America. But for the latter, powerful norms held by American Jews and Israelis see Israel as the land of immigration, not emigration.

The immigration of Jews to the United States since the 1960s has changed the balance of demographic processes in the Jewish community. An assessment of the demographic importance of immigration reveals that it probably has more than balanced the negative growth resulting from the excess of deaths over births. Whether net Jewish immigration also compensates for losses due to out-marriages is difficult to assess with the available data (Goldscheider, 1982).

Most important, the new immigrations to America in the postwar period—Hasidim, Russians, and Israelis—represent new sources of Jewish cohesion. In part, this is because these immigrants have developed their own communal institutions and organizations; in part, the established Jewish community has attempted, as in the past, to assist their integration. The new immigrants also serve as important links between American Jewry and other Jewish communities (for example, Russia and Israel). The effects of the postwar immigration are clearly not limited to demographic issues.

Similarly, the emigration of Jews from the United States to Israel reinforces bonds of interaction and cohesion among American Jews. American Jewish immigration to Israel has always been small, around 200 per year for the period 1919–48, and 400 annually for 1948–60. Beginning in the 1960s and increasing between 1967 and 1973, several thousand Jews from the United States immigrated to Israel annually (Goldscheider, 1974; Avruch, 1981). Estimates indicate that, after about three years, 30–40 percent return to the United States. In 1971, the number of American immigrants was at a peak (1,049 immigrants and 6,315 potential immigrants); a decade later annual levels had declined to 341 immigrants and 2,043 potential immigrants (*Israel Statistical Abstracts*, 1982, p. 137).

American *aliya* relative to the population size of American Jewry has been miniscule. Barring unforeseen circumstances, no mass aliya of Jewish Americans can be expected to occur in the near future. In large part, this is because the nearly universal American-Jewish concern for Israel coexists with their almost total economic, cultural, social, and political integration in America (see S. Cohen, 1983; Sklare, 1971).

American immigrants to Israel are younger than the American Jewish population as a whole, are more likely to have had extensive Jewish education, and are more committed Jews, religiously, educationally, and organizationally (Goldscheider, 1974; Avruch, 1981). This selectivity, however, does not affect the structure of Jewish communities. Overall, American aliya strengthens the links between the American Jewish community and Israeli society, and the cohesion of American Jews. It reinforces bonds among Jews as part of a broader range of exchanges. These include economic assistance, visits, and educational and cultural projects. The emigration of Americans to Israel and Israelis to America are sources of interdependence between the major centers of Jewish life.

AMERICAN JEWISH FAMILIES

The family has been a primary source of Jewish socialization and group continuity. Young Jews obtain their first lessons in how to be Jews in their homes, and thereby reinforce the Jewish commitments of their parents. At the same time, children link couples and families to the organized Jewish community through Jewish schools and youth groups (see Sklare and Greenblum, 1967). In America, the strength of the Jewish family has been central to the cohesion of the Jewish community.

American Jews have maintained patterns of family stability and cohesion. Despite social and geographic mobility, they have retained almost universal marriage patterns, low divorce rates, and nuclear family structure (Goldstein and Goldscheider, 1968; Goldberg, 1968; Cherlin and Celebuski, 1983; Waxman, 1982; S. Cohen, 1982; Schmelz and Della Pergola, 1983). While there have been indications of delayed marriage, nonmarriage, and increases in divorce (Goldscheider, forthcoming), the Jewish family patterns remain exceptional relative to non-Jews, with a continuing emphasis on marriage and family centrality. Indeed, data from a medium-sized Jewish community in the mid-1970s point to relatively early marriage with some delayed childbearing within marriage for Jewish women compared to others of their social class and educational background. The only data indicating nonmarriage relate to those still in college or graduate school. Whether they will remain unmarried or will delay marriage is unclear from the evidence available. On the other hand, those living alone or with other nonfamily members have important ties to many others within the Jewish community (see ibid.). The increasing proportions of young nonmarried Jews adds to the growing number of divorced and separated Jewish men and women. Together, they represent new groups in American Jewish life and challenge the institutional, organizational, and community structures that have in the past focused almost exclusively on the family (S. Cohen, 1982).

No matter how important the family has been to American Jews, they have long had relatively few children. Indeed, there is consistent evidence that American Jewish fertility has been low in absolute levels as well as relative to other religious and ethnic groups in the United States since the early twentieth century (Goldscheider, 1967, 1982; S. Goldstein, 1981; Della Pergola, 1980). Since the mid-1920s fluctuations around replacement level fertility have characterized Jews marrying. As did others, Jews participated in the baby boom of the post–World War II period; they have also been part of the fertility decline of the 1960s and 1970s.

The patterns of family size among American Jews are consistent with their high educational, occupational, and urban-metropolitan concentration. Nevertheless, fertility differences between Jews and non-Jews appear even within socioeconomic and residential categories; lower Jewish fertility characterized earlier generations before their rapid upward mobility. Some have argued that Jews had a middle-class "mentality" and values, including that of small family size (Rosenthal, 1961). Others relate low fertility to the changing role and status of Jewish women and their changing self-conceptions (Sklare, 1971). Others have attempted to relate low fertility to broader patterns, emphasizing the changing minority status of Jews and the particular position of Jews in the social structure (see Goldscheider, 1971, 1982).

Recent evidence points to the continued low fertility among married Jews—an expected family size of about two children (see Goldscheider, forthcoming). Whether this will characterize all women or compensate for the unknown proportion of Jewish women who will not marry is open to question. The demographic issue of Jewish American continuity is thus specific to the fertility of those currently unmarried and their eventual marriage and fertility patterns.

Are there any subgroups within the American Jewish population that have larger families? Few major differences in the fertility of contemporary American Jews appear. All segments of the Jewish community with but minor exceptions have small families. The traditional variables associated with higher fertility in America—rural residence, poverty, contraceptive ignorance, low education, farm and blue-collar occupations—are virtually nonexistent among Jewish men and women in the childbearing years.

Three important variations in family size need to be underscored. First, Jewish women with the highest levels of education (postgraduate) expect the largest families (2.5 children), a pattern which does not characterize non-Jews. Second, labor force participation of Jewish women does not lower their fertility, suggesting no incompatibility of work and childbearing roles. Again, this pattern does not apply to Protestants and Catholics. There is no empirical support, therefore, for the argument that the work patterns of young, educated, career-oriented Jewish women pose a demographic threat to Jewish continuity (see Goldscheider, forthcoming).

In addition, some variation in the size of families correlates with types of religiosity. Traditional Judaism has emphasized norms favoring large families. Judged by the overall low levels of fertility, these traditional norms have been largely ignored. Scattered evidence indicates that most American Jews are not aware of these norms or prohibitions. Neither Reform nor Conservative Judaism has an explicit ideology of fertility. It is, therefore, not surprising that religiousness has little direct relationship to Jewish fertility. However, impressionistic evidence suggests that among the self-segregated religious Jews in selected metropolitan areas of the United States, higher fertility prevails. These Jewish subcommunities have rejected the path of integration followed by the vast majority of American Jews. Their highly structured neighborhoods, economic ties, and congregations provide the means of retaining traditional roles for women, family and spiritual centrality, and general resistance to acculturation as well as large families. These groups have probably contributed a disproportionate share of the children to the American Jewish community. Average family-size levels of three or four children (or more) among these subcommunities represent a significant shift for American Jewry.

More than fertility levels or changes in family formation, intermarriage between Jews and non-Jews calls into question the quantitative survival of Jews in an open society. No other issue symbolizes more clearly the conflict between universalism and particularism, between the American melting pot and pluralism, between assimilation and ethnic continuity in American society. Marriage between Jews and non-Jews indicates high levels of interaction between these communities. The unresolved dilemma for American Jewry revolves around Jewish continuity reinforced through in-marriages and family-generational cohesion, on the one hand, and the consistency between out-marriages and the structural-cultural features of American Jewish life, on the other.

Until the 1960s Jews in America were the classic illustration of voluntary group endogamy. Social scientists had little reason to question Jewish group continuity when intermarriage rates were low and the family strong. Survival issues were rarely raised when intermarriage was a marginal feature of

American Jewish life, even when Jewish family size fluctuated around two children.

In the 1970s and 1980s, concerns about numerical losses through Jewish intermarriage were heightened, since American Jewish population size was relatively small, geographic dispersion increasing, and growth through im-migration low. High intermarriage rates pose a particular demographic threat to a small minority reproducing at replacement levels. Clearly the concern about population reduction through intermarriage was not directed to macrodemographic issues that have rarely been understood fully or well documented statistically. Rather Jewish intermarriage symbolized signifi-cant shifts in Jewish family life and group cohesion.

Jewish intermarriage in American society does not appear to be the result of a specific desire to assimilate or a consequence of particular intermarriage norms. It is the direct result of the structure of American Jewish life, reinforced by general values shared by American Jews. Growth in residen-tial integration, occupational dispersal, increased social interaction between Jews and non-Jews, and public school and college attendance are the major factors in the higher intermarriage rates among American Jews. Reinforcing these structural features are the belief in the equality of all persons, an emphasis on liberalism, the faith in minority group integration, the rejection of ethnocentrism, and the commitment to unversalism (Sklare, 1971; Gold-scheider, forthcoming).

Intermarriage can no longer be treated as unimportant when it is the result of a deep-rooted sociopolitical ideology and value structure and a function of life-style, residential pattern, educational and occupational structure. It cannot be ignored within the Jewish community when few Jewish families have not experienced intermarriage directly or through friends and neighbors. Indeed, the issue of intermarriage has become cen-tral to the internal struggles of American Jewry. For those who view inter-marriage as a threat to Jewish continuity in America, the ultimate choice appears to be between changing the overall social structure and value orientations of the American Jewish community or accommodation and acceptance of the intermarried. There are no indications that the first alternative has been or will be selected by the majority of American Jews. And there is clear evidence of the growing acceptance of the intermarried (Goldscheider, forthcoming).

What are the rates of American Jewish intermarriages? Have they in-creased? Who intermarries? What are the consequences of intermarriage for Jews and their communities? Overall, Jewish endogamy is high and intermarriage rates are low relative to large American ethnic-religious groupings. An examination of intermarriage rates by age and generation as well as over time, however, reveals an unmistakable pattern of increase in the volume of Jewish intermarriage. Some scattered evidence and impressions suggest that disproportionate shifts in the rate of intermarriage occurred in the 1970s among young Jews (Goldscheider, 1982).

The systematic evaluation of the quantitative significance of changing intermarriage trends is incomplete, since the level of conversions to Judaism is not well documented. Nor do we know the eventual Jewish commitments of the children of intermarried couples. The general impression from studies of American Jewish communities is that the level of conversion to Judaism has increased, and some significant proportion of the children of intermarried couples are being raised as Jews. There is no question, however, that current rates of Jewish intermarriage affect the size of the American Jewish population and have longer term implications for the size of generations yet unborn. It is also clear that Jewish intermarriages do not necessarily imply losses to the Jewish community. To the contrary, substantial evidence shows that the Jewish community gains rather than loses members through intermarriage, conversion, and the Jewish socialization of the children of intermarried couples. Moreover, some data show a tendency among those who intermarry and remain within the Jewish community to be more religious and more Jewishly committed when compared to Jews not intermarried (see Goldscheider, 1982). Nor are the intermarried removed totally from the ongoing activities of the Jewish community. While Jews in intermarried households are less associated with Jewishness and Judaism than those in nonintermarried households, these differences are smaller among younger couples. Overall, there are strong communal and other Jewish ties among the intermarried. It is difficult to argue that young intermarried households are disassociated from Jewish communal life and Jewish community networks when 60 percent say most of their friends are Jewish; about half say most of their neighbors are Jews and define themselves as Orthodox, Conservative, or Reform; and almost two-thirds observe religious family rituals (Goldscheider, forthcoming).

The rate of intermarriage among local Jewish communities varies with the size of the Jewish population, generational and socioeconomic characteristics, as well as the extent of Jewish communal organizations and traditional institutions. This also was the case in European communities (see Chapter 6). The size of the Jewish community and the implied density of Jewish residential patterns and institutions are especially important factors in intermarriage rates.

Intermarried Jews and those married to other Jews have similar class and educational characteristics. In addition, the backgrounds of the Jewish and non-Jewish partners to the intermarriages tend to be quite similar. Both patterns distinguish recent intermarried couples from those of previous generations.

Two social characteristics relate more or less consistently to the probability of intermarriage: Jewish residential segregation, and Jewish education.

Jews living in areas of greater Jewish concentration are more likely to be endogamous than Jews living in areas of low Jewish population densities. This reflects the fact that the more extensive the interactions between Jews and non-Jews in schools, neighborhoods, organizations, social and business activities, the greater the likelihood of intermarriage. It is, however, not clear whether residence in areas of low Jewish population density is a determinant of high intermarriage rates or a consequence of selective migration patterns of intermarried couples. Extensive and intensive Jewish education are generally correlated with Jewish endogamy. This also reflects the importance of interaction among Jews and the connection between Jewish education and other bases of Jewish cohesion.

While there is a relationship between intermarriage and Jewish discontinuity, it is weak and appears to be growing weaker. Intermarriage is not necessarily the final step toward total assimilation. Powerful forces within the Jewish community have resulted in the continued Jewishness of the intermarried. The strong Jewish ties of some of those on the fringes of assimilation forces us to revise the accepted theories of intermarriage.

A final point requires reemphasis: it is not the level of Jewish intermarriages per se that challenges the quantitative survival of Jews in America. Rather the specific demographic context within which intermarriage occurs is significant. The combination of low marital fertility, geographic dispersion, minimum potential sources of population renewal through immigration, changes in family cohesion, *and* relatively high intermarriage rates have resulted in questions about the demographic vitality of Jewish Americans. When the losses *and* gains due to intermarriages and conversions are estimated and these added into population estimates based on projected trends of fertility, mortality, and immigration, the conclusion seems to be that the American Jewish community is at, or just below, zero population growth (see Goldscheider, 1982; different conclusions have been reached by Schmelz, 1981; Schmelz and Della Pergola, 1983).

Population projections that do not take into account the range of demographic factors that influence growth and are based on naive straight-line extrapolations from the past to the future lead to serious miscalculations and absurd conclusions. Dire predictions about the virtual extinction of the American Jewish population over the next 100 years (and general speculations about the vanishing American Jew)—a projection of an American Jewish population size of 10,420 by the year 2076—are seriously misleading and demographic nonsense (see Bergman, 1977; Lieberman and Weinfeld, 1978).

TRANSFORMATION AND NEW SOURCES OF COHESION

Patterns of regional and residential concentration have changed among Jews in the process of Americanization. Between 1930 and 1980 the proportion of Jews living in the Northeast and North Central regions of the United

States declined, while those in the West and South increased sharply (S. Goldstein, 1982; Goldscheider, 1982). A detailed analysis of counties reveals growing dispersal of Jews outside of traditional areas of Jewish population concentration. Between 1952 and 1971, for example, Jews were located in seventy-seven new counties. In part, this reflects suburbanization within metropolitan areas. The overwhelming pattern, however, remains persistent concentration. In 1971, Jews were located in 504 of the more than 3,000 counties; Jewish communities above 10,000 are even more concentrated (Newman and Halvorson, 1979). The Jewish population continues to be far more concentrated than the total white population; they are far less dispersed than Protestant denominations, some of much smaller size than Jews.

In addition to the continuing urban, metropolitan, and regional concentration of American Jews, there are continuing patterns of Jewish residential-neighborhood concentration. Since American society is heterogeneous, and the Jewish population is large and dispersed, it is difficult to generalize. Nevertheless, several findings are important for our analysis (see Goldstein and Goldscheider, 1968; Goldscheider, forthcoming). Jewish residential patterns within metropolitan areas show both concentration and integration. While there have been important changes away from segregation, dispersal has not been random. Housing availability, costs, transportation, schooling, life-style, and social class factors are the major determinants of neighborhood choices, not desires for assimilation. New areas of Jewish concentration have emerged among third- and fourth-generation American Jews that are not the legacy of past immigration patterns of more than a half century ago. At least within the larger areas of Jewish metropolitan concentration, low Jewish density is not associated with alienation from the Jewish community. Even in these areas, new social ties and networks among Jews have emerged.

The geographic redistribution of Jews and the dynamics of neighborhood changes are tied to patterns cf migration. Do migrations move Jews to areas of low Jewish density and uproot them from family and ethnic networks? Clearly many Jewish communities and neighborhoods have lost population through out-migration; at the same time, other areas have gained Jews. The increasing levels of migration among Jews, particularly among younger adults, raises the question of the effects of detachments and uprootedness on Jewish continuity. The conclusions of empirical research are mixed (see S. Goldstein, 1982; Jarret, 1978; Goldscheider, forthcoming). Evidence from Boston in 1975 shows that migration tends to be highest at certain points in the life cycle. In those ages where community attachments are of greatest importance (families with children), migration rates are lowest. Moreover, migration moves Jews to areas of high to medium Jewish density as well as to areas of low density. Most important, the evidence systematically shows that migration does not uproot Jews from Jewish ties, except in the short term. The disruption of networks generated by moving is followed by the formation of new networks, bonds, and ties among Jews and to the Jewish community. Whether this pattern extends to smaller or to newer communities needs more research.

There is therefore no simple association of migration and alienation from Judaism, Jewishness, and Jewish ties in America. Movement does not threaten Jewish continuity or destroy the bases of Jewish cohesion. Often migration links Jews with existing Jewish networks, thereby strengthening them, or brings Jews into contact with other Jews to develop new bases of cohesion. Although the major centers of Jewish residential concentration are likely to remain and new centers of Jewish density will emerge, it is also likely that significant proportions of fourth-generation American Jews will be living in areas of low Jewish concentration. These diverse patterns suggest the beginnings of polarization, if the strength of Jewish cohesion is related to Jewish density.

The social mobility of American Jews has been well documented, both nationally and in local community studies. Jews have attained high levels of education, are concentrated in white-collar occupations, and earn high incomes. The pace of socioeconomic change and the levels attained are exceptional features of Jews compared to non-Jews (see S. Goldstein, 1969; Goldstein and Goldscheider, 1968; Goldscheider, forthcoming; Kuznets, 1972). Occupational mobility and diversification have not, however, resulted in occupational convergences between Jews and non-Jews. The movement away from working in particular industrial jobs has resulted in the reconcentration of Jews in particular, new white-collar positions. While the initial changes between the immigrant and the second-generation Jew were away from occupational homogeneity, recent shifts have been toward new forms of occupational concentration.

In 1957, national data show the very heavy concentration of Jews in white-collar jobs (over three-fourths) twice the level of the overall white population (Kuznets, 1972; S. Goldstein, 1969). Two decades later the patterns have crystalized even further. In Boston, in 1975, fully 60 percent of the Jewish males aged thirty to thirty-nine were professionals, and about 25 percent of them were physicians. Patterns of self-employment in particular occupations have also continued to characterize the Jewish labor force (Goldscheider and Kobrin, 1980; Goldscheider, forthcoming; and compare to similar patterns in parts of Europe in Chapter 6).

These occupational patterns are related to levels of education. Not only have Jewish men and women increased their years of schooling but they have become concentrated among the college educated. While differences between the educational levels attained by Jews and non-Jews have widened, differences among Jews have narrowed. Hence, the sharp distinctions between the more and less educated of the second generation have all but disappeared among the generation of the 1980s.

Neither the occupational shifts nor the educational attainment of Jewish men and women necessarily lead to assimilation. The reconcentration in high-status occupations and the small range of educational variation at upper levels imply shared life-styles, work patterns, types of neighborhoods, and family patterns. In turn, these have become new bases of interaction, networks, and contacts (compare Chapters 6 and 7). The continuing Jewish exceptionalism in socioeconomic status remains one fundamental basis of ethnic cohesion.

Moreover, parents and families facilitate educational attainment so that it does not represent a break with family and kin. Ethnic clusters among students continue to appear. While Jews interact with non-Jews in university settings, various campus institutions, and organizations facilitate interaction among Jews. Since most Jews have college experience and a very high proportion graduate from college, high proportions of both the parental and children generations have common bonds of education. Few if any non-Jewish groups are so characterized.

The American Jewish community has moved rapidly and thoroughly from large proportions with low levels of education and blue-collar employment to college education and professional and managerial positions. This transformation implies internal cohesion. Conflicts between Jews of different social classes, countries of origin, and immigrant status have disappeared. The disappearance of Jewish unions and Socialist organizations mark this development. At the same time, Jews share similar social and economic positions in the general society, thereby maintaining high levels of interaction. Structural factors tie most Jews to other Jews.

In the process of modernization in America, there have been declines in the traditional forms of religious expression. For most Jews in America, however, Judaism is central to their Jewishness, and is linked to social, communal, and other ethnic forms of Jewishness. Hence, declining Orthodoxy, dietary observance, and religious piety for most American Jews must be understood in the context of high levels of ethnic-Israel concerns, Jewish communal activities, and an overall commitment to Jewish survival.

About three-fourths of American Jewry identify with one of the three religious denominations (Orthodox, Conservative, or Reform). The nondenominational are not however without alternative ties. Most Jews celebrate Jewish holidays with family and friends, express Jewish values, identify with the Jewish community, and interact mainly with other Jews (Goldscheider, forthcoming). Most have a wide range of ties to Jewishness and other Jews—through jobs, education, neighborhoods, and social, religious, and ethnic concerns. Organizational reinforcement, the growing use of the media for Jewish socialization, and the continuing issues of Israel are major sources of American Jewish cohesion. The increased conspicuousness and expansion of Orthodox activities, in part reflecting the postwar immigration of religious Jews from tightly knit communities of Eastern Europe, has added a new dimension to the spectrum of Jewishness in America (Helmreich, 1982). These sources reinforce the structural bases of Jewish cohesion in America.

TWO PERSPECTIVES ON JEWISH QUALITY

It is clear that there is no linear relationship between modernization and ethnic assimilation in America. At the same time, it remains unclear how to interpret the array of forces that weaken and strengthen the cohesion of the American Jewish community. Two alternative interpretations highlight this issue. One suggests that the concern about the assimilation of American Jewry is exaggerated and alarmist. At best, it is rhetorical and artificially created, to be rejected with the obvious retorts about the strength of Jewish life. One does not have to go beyond a regular reading of the press to know that Jews are conspicuously present in a wide range of political and social activities. Hardly a week passes without a report of a Jewish organization's attempt to influence American policies in the Middle East; reacting to the subtlest shift in politics about Israel, Zionism, Jews, or Arabs; or reacting to issues of Jews in other countries. Similarly, national American politics has always raised the visibility of American Jewry. Jews have been viewed as supporters of particular candidates and an important interest group. Their geographic concentrations and socioeconomic position—education, occupation, and income—reinforce their political influence and underpin their cohesion.

These and related macropolitical indicators point to the conclusion that the third religious subgroup in America after Protestants and Catholics is vibrant and visible. Surely a vanishing breed is rarely a source of such conspicuous sociopolitical power and influence. Indeed, it has been suggested often that the Jewish group in America epitomizes the fact that power is not necessarily a function of size; larger and more are not synonymous with better and powerful.

Jewish vitality in America is reflected not only in secular political indicators. Since the mid-1960s there has been an enormous growth in Jewish activities, and new forms of Jewish identity and new sources of Jewish cohesion have emerged. These have been particularly concentrated among teenagers, college students, and young adults. The impressive growth of Habad houses, Jewish consciousness among students, kosher facilities, Jewish studies, and Israel–Zionism–Soviet Jewry activities, among others, have been revolutionary forces in American Jewish life.

American Jewry thirty to forty years ago was relatively "silent" about the Holocaust and Israel; institutional heterogeneity and organizational dis-

array characterized the American Jewish community structure in the immediate postwar era. The religiously committed Jews of the 1940s and 1950s
were either older, foreign-born persons, or marginal within the Jewish
community. In contrast, being "noisy" about Jewishness has become the
norm among contemporary Jews. Jews and Jewish institutions have become
vocal about Israel, the Palestine Liberation Organization, Soviet Jewry,
Jewish life in America, Jewish women and Jewish students, and, to a lesser
extent, the Jewish aged and poor.

Indeed, the separation of religion from ethnic elements in Jewish life
implies not only the possibility of being Jewish without being religious but
also that new forms of Jewishness emerge (as do new forms of religious
expression).

These patterns also characterize the development of competing Jewish
institutions. The proliferation, extension, and development of a wide complex of political, social, service, and religious-cultural institutions characterize Jewish communities around the United States. Part of the function of
these institutions (sometimes latent) is to reinforce Jewish consciousness
and continuity. As such they become another form of Jewish cohesion. How
can Jews be vanishing when a plethora of institutions constantly remind
them of how they are vanishing, thereby raising their consciousness as
Jewish survivors?

In many ways, the issue has become how "unvanishing" American Jewry
is. The questions that are raised tend to be addressed to the sources of
Jewish American ethnicity: Is ethnic pride among Jews only an imitation of
black, Chicano, and other ethnic movements in America? Are there inner
sociocultural strengths to American Jewry beyond the external issues of
Zionism, Israel, and oppressed Jewries around the world? Certainly, there
appears to be little basis for the question of whether Jewish life will survive
in America in the foreseeable future and no grounds for positing an end to
the American Jewish community in the ethnic-conscious United States of
the 1980s. An examination of institutional, residential, occupational, educational, and related networks of interaction argue for the continuity of the
Jewish community, even if some individuals leave.

An alternative view argues that the structural and cultural underpinnings
of Jewishness in America are weak and superficial bases of continuity. The
signs of renewal and searching are marginal and transitory, reflecting the
failure of Jewish organizations and the dismay and frustration of Jewish
youth. From this perspective, Jewish commitments lack depth and substantive content. Ineffective, inadequate, and unsuccessful Jewish education
(measured in continuation rates and eventual adult commitments and
knowledge) combined with pervasive ignorance among the middle-aged and
older segments of the community about things Jewish and Israeli are emphasized. The decline in temple and synagogue participation, empty synagogue

schools, and unused community facilities fit this general image of erosion and irrelevance. The increasing growth of secularism among Jews, the emphasis on and acceptance of minimum Jewish commitments, and the mobilization of energies for fund raising devoid of Jewish content as a goal in itself represent substitutes for creative Jewish commitments and have become the major forms of Jewish activities in organizational and community life.

This interpretation stresses rates of intermarriage among Jewish youth and the attraction of a variety of exotic non-Jewish spiritual alternatives among high school and college students. Without a crisis in Israel, a problem of Soviet Jewry, or new forms of ethnic discrimination and insecurity in America, there is insufficient depth and internal commitment for American Jewish cultural or social survival. The pockets of renewal and vibrance are located in specific areas where Jewish population concentration is high; they can be dismissed as a vocal minority. To the many critics of American Jewish life, secularism, universalism, and an open opportunity structure directly challenge the future survival of American Jewry.

Are these alternative views simply reflections of optimistic and pessimistic perceptions of the same phenomena? Are we only dealing with the question as to whether the glass is half full or half empty?

There are elements of accuracy to both points of view. It is clear, however, that American Jewry is not about to vanish either demographically or sociologically. The many structural bases of cohesion present make that certain. The ideological unity of American Jewish life revolves around secular politics—national and international—rather than any cultural or religious consensus. Differences in beliefs have little affect on the structural sources of cohesion. The issue of Jewish continuity in the process of modernization is not primarily related to shared values, communal consensus, or to the desire of Jews to survive as a community. Nor can it be attributed to the will (or lack thereof) of the broader American community to accept or integrate the Jew. Of primary importance are the patterns of residential clustering, strong occupations and education concentrations, extensive institutional networks, and the absence of internal conflicts. In turn, almost all Jews believe in the survival of the Jewish people, which reinforces the structural bases of cohesion.

The question of Jewish continuity in America relates to the quality of Jewish life and to the specification of which segments are likely to remain within the community. Quality refers to cultural content and is clearly associated with the presence of Jewish institutions of welfare, education, and learning. In America, as in Europe, these structures appear where there are enough Jews with sufficient time and economic resources to establish schools, museums, theaters, old-age homes, nurseries, and other such institutions. In turn, these derive from the structural bases of a community.

From the evidence that we have examined, it is clear that where Jews have sufficient resources they build cultural institutions. Where there are too few Jews to finance, work in, and enjoy the welfare and cultural institutions, they do not appear whether or not they are desired. Similarly, the survival of particular segments of the American Jewish community, whether geographic or ideological, relates directly to their size, the number of structural bases present with high levels of Jewish interaction, and the overlap of those bases. The continuity of a subcommunity relates directly to these factors. Its particular characteristics reflect the pattern of educational, residential, occupational, religious, welfare, and political structures present.

The American Jewish community represents one strategy of Jewish survival. It is embedded in a relatively liberal, open society with a wide range of opportunities not restricted by ethnic or religious considerations and provides for its inhabitants an enormous range of options. While individuals can exercise these opportunities in the direction of particularism or universalism, as Jews or Americans, the community as a whole exists sui generis. Will American Jews survive as Americans? Will they continue to survive as Jews? They have, and selected segments will in the future. But American Jews will change as America changes and as their place within it responds to other groups, new opportunities, different organizations and institutions. They will be transformed further as new international conditions change for America and for Jews. New forms of ethnic and religious expression will emerge. New residential and occupational concentrations will result in different ethnic networks reinforcing these new ethnic and religious expressions.

Part V: The Jewish Society of Israel

In Israel, the Jewish community is a total society. The structural bases of cohesion are maximal. Jews interact almost exclusively with other Jews. No job opportunities, educational institutions, or marriage partners draw them out of the community. At the same time, sources of internal conflict are also maximal. Class, ethnic, religious, and political divisions separate Jews from non-Jews and are the basis of competition and conflict.

12 · Immigration and the Emergence of Israeli Society

Jews responded in different ways to issues of nationalism associated with the modernization of Europe. Some denied the nationalistic component of Jewishness and defined themselves solely as a religious group. Some rejected their religious uniqueness to focus on Jewish peoplehood. Others blended religious and nationalistic themes. The initial ambiguities and ambivalences over Jewish nationalism were struggles among elites who battled each other in the arena of ideas. Most Jews who were swept by the windstorm of modernization were either oblivious or indifferent to the issues. Most continued to live in subcommunities within the nations of Europe and America.

For a small segment of the Jewish population, the nationalist idea was of more than ideological interest. It required action—mobilization, organization, political activities, for themselves and for others. The return to Zion, the national homeland, became a political imperative. For some, and over time, for increasing numbers, modernization and Jewish nationalism became synonymous. Nevertheless, most Zionists did not immigrate to the national homeland; many who immigrated to Palestine did not do so for Zionist reasons.

Those who settled in Palestine[1] did not represent a cross-section of their original Jewish communities. Among the tens of thousands who immigrated there, relatively few were motivated by secular nationalist ideologies. Even among the waves of immigration which were more characterized by national ideological sources (for example, the Second Aliya), many were motivated by traditional religious values.

Those who immigrated did not come equally from all communities outside of Palestine. The selectivity of immigrants by country of origin linked Jews who settled in Palestine with those in Europe. The geographic sources

---

1. It is difficult to describe the national homeland without generating political images. "Palestine," "The Land of Israel," even "national homeland" indicate ideological positions. Although our biases are clear, we do not wish to convey a political or ideological statement.

of immigration affected the socioeconomic, political, and cultural composition of the Jewish settlement in Palestine and its subsequent development. Too few came to Palestine to affect the composition of the European communities.

Thus, one consequence of modernization was the formation of a national Jewish polity. First the *Yishuv* (the Jewish community in Palestine) and subsequently the state defined the setting of Jewish cohesion. Here, unlike Europe and America, modernization did not threaten Jewish continuity. Like premodern Jewish communities, there is a total overlap of the bases of Jewish cohesion in their national polity. In Palestine and in Israel, interaction takes place primarily among Jews rather than between Jews and others. Residential, occupational, religious, political, social and cultural ties bind Jews to each other and separate them from non-Jews. Divisions and conflicts within the Jewish community of Israel do not alter the sharp boundaries between Jews and others. The uniqueness of the national polity is the combination of modernization, size, political control, and the accoutrements of a total society. However, the internal conflicts within the Palestine and Israel Jewish communities are sharper than in Diaspora communities. Competition based on class, religiosity, ethnicity among Jews diminishes cohesiveness.

Jews arrived in their national homeland from all over the world. They brought their unique socioeconomic and cultural baggage, at different times. The determinants of who arrived and their transformations are keys to understanding the emergence of Israeli society. The "ingathering of exiles" is more than Zionist sloganeering or a description of sources of immigration. It symbolizes as well the extensive interdependence of Palestine-Israel with the overwhelming majority of Jews who live as a minority subcommunity within other societies.

IMMIGRATION AS THE SOURCE OF DEVELOPMENT
Immigration provided the basis for mass Jewish settlement in Palestine and the subsequent creation of Israel. In the seventy-five years between 1875 and 1950, over a million Jews made their way to their homeland. Those who arrived first established the foundations upon which future immigrants built new lives. The analysis of the sources associated with these population movements necessarily precedes the effort to understand the Jewish society formed in Palestine and Israel.

Three factors structured the international movement of Jews to Palestine. Zionist organizations in the Diaspora established mechanisms and issued calls for immigration. Turkish, and then British, immigration policy in Palestine affected the flow of immigrants. The social, economic, and political conditions of Jews in their various countries of residence were "push" factors that affected decisions to emigrate. Most studies have emphasized the first two factors as the primary explanations of variations in Jewish immigration to Palestine. Our approach reverses this theoretical ordering. Push factors played a much more central role in this process than are generally recognized. Commitment to Zionism and the policy of colonial governments played relatively small parts in the ebb and flow of Jews from various countries at different times to Palestine.

What is the basis for this claim? Is it not obvious that the return of hundreds of thousands of Jews to their national homeland is the embodiment of nationalist ideology? Most people do not decide to transform totally their daily routines and lives—which is what immigration is all about—because of a commitment to a set of beliefs. There is little general evidence of individuals engaging in such wrenching behavior without a clear vision of direct, economic benefits to them, or a powerful tie to a charismatic leader. Ideological commitments move relatively few. No more than 10 percent of the hundreds of thousands of immigrants to Palestine came because of an ideological imperative to settle in a national homeland.

The analytic task, therefore, is to isolate the factors which explain variations in Jewish immigration to Palestine and to place ideology in its social and political context. We need as well to separate factors associated with the decision to move from those associated with the choice of destination. Often the pushes in countries of origin are the primary determinants of emigration; the relative pulls of alternative destinations are the key to understanding the direction of those who are on the move. The complexity of the factors involved and the changing combinations of pushes and pulls over time challenge the oversimplified and superficial association of immigration with nationalist ideology.

Zionist Ideologies of Immigration

To argue for the primacy of Zionist ideology in the explanation of immigration is to assume consensus among Zionists on aliya (immigration to Israel). Zionism, however, provided no clear set of behavioral clues for immigration. Zionist ideology developed around a core of widely accepted beliefs and the accretions and specifications proposed by the different branches of the movement (Chapter 8). These were "to direct Jewish migration to Palestine and establish a community there which would be free from the social and cultural problems that attended the Jewish status as a dispersed minority people in the Diaspora; and to carry out all the transformations in social and economic distribution, create the appropriate social institutions, and foster the cultural changes necessary for such a program" (Halpern, 1969, p. 21). Different factions displayed a considerable range of emphasis in goals, strategies, and tactics. They argued over the following issues: (1) Should there be a mass immigration of Jews during one compressed time period or should it be regulated, planned, and spread over time? (2) Should a cross-section of the Jewish population move to a national homeland, or primarily workers, or a cultural-intellectual elite? (3) Should international political recognition precede immigration or would the facts of settlement bring political legitimacy? (4) Should the goal of Jewish settlement be the immigration of all of world Jewry, the majority, or an optimum number to develop a viable new Jewish society or Jewish cultural center? (See Horowitz and Lissak, 1978; Shapiro, 1976; Vital, 1976, 1982; Avineri, 1981; A. Hertzberg, 1975; Friedlander and Goldscheider, 1979).

The proposed answers may be best understood in the context of differing political and economic conditions for the Jews in the Diaspora and Palestine. Before World War I, "practical" and Socialist Zionists sought immigrants who would work the land in Palestine, establish independent Jewish agricultural colonies, and organize Jewish workers in opposition to local landlords and capitalists. They encouraged a select migration of dedicated revolutionary immigrants. Herzl and other "political" Zionists supported immigration only when it had the blessing of powerful members of the international political community. "Cultural" Zionists adamantly opposed mass immigration. Arguing that the land could not support the Jews of Europe and that most Jews would not emigrate in any event, they sought to establish a modern spiritual center, where an elite could build the foundations of a new Jewish culture. In all these views, immigration to Palestine was only one element of a general strategy of Jewish survival that on theoretical and practical grounds was less important than other activities. These diverse ideologies could not and did not elicit a uniform immigration response among Jews.

After World War I, the British Mandate, and its implied promise of political independence for the Jews in Palestine, the concurrent end of open immigration to America, and increasingly severe economic conditions in Europe helped to reformulate the importance of immigration in Zionist thought. Many Western Zionists began to view Palestine as the sole haven for the aggrieved Jewish masses of Eastern Europe. Competition among the Jewish political factions in Palestine and the influx of a large number of middle-class Jews to Palestine in the 1920s caused the Zionist revolutionaries to expand their appeals beyond the working class to represent all the new settlers (Shapiro, 1976; Horowitz and Lissak, 1977, 1978). They established a political and economic structure in Palestine that enabled them to build a new Jewish Socialist society. The destruction of European Jewry in the Holocaust and the hundreds of thousands of postwar refugees completed the process by which Palestine came to be viewed as the only safe home for Jewish refugees. Over time, aliyah became the centerpiece of Zionist ideology.

The increasing ideological emphasis on mass immigration to Palestine— like the actual movement of Jews—was a response to events. It did not develop logically out of the assumptions of the various factions of the nationalist movement. Each initially viewed immigration to Palestine as part of a complex set of issues, and not necessarily the most important one. New opportunities and needs raised the actual and ideological importance of bringing the Jewish masses to the homeland.

Commitment to Zionist ideology—especially among the practical, Socialist, and religious factions—attracted some Jews to Palestine. Beginning in the late 1870s, small dedicated groups immigrated, and others who shared their beliefs and organizational memberships followed them. Almost all of these immigrants came from Eastern Europe. They provided the political elite that established the insitutional bases of the new society (see Shapiro, 1976; Frankel, 1981; Horowitz and Lissak, 1978; and Chapter 8). Ideological dedication, therefore, explains the movement of a select handful to Palestine. It does not account for the volume and flow of the Jewish masses as a whole.

In Western Europe and North America, intellectuals came to Zionism, "not as potential emigrants but in search of inner dignity and secure personal roots in their people and their history" (A. Hertzberg, 1975, p. 84). They rejected the idea of immigration for themselves; they emphasized its importance for other Jews. Zionism was less a call for action than a way of understanding their individual and group place in the world. In the first pamphlet published by the American Zionist Federation (1898), there was an explicit rejection of the connection between Zionism and immigration to Palestine. Rather, Zionism "wishes to give back to the Jew that nobleness of spirit, that confidence in himself, that belief in his own powers which only perfect freedom can give. . . . He will feel that he belongs somewhere and not everywhere." (Cited in A. Hertzberg, 1975, p. 499). In the West, Zionist ideology entailed little that encouraged aliyah.

An analysis of Jewish immigration to Palestine must examine the conditions in the countries of origin from which the Jews came and the availability of alternative destinations. It must also analyze the efforts of the Zionist organizations to bring Jewish settlers and the actions by the colonial administrations to control the entrance of Jews. Together, these factors determined the rate and volume at which the Jews immigrated. They affected as well which Jews entered and when they entered. This array of factors, not a growing acceptance of Zionist ideology, is the key to understanding the formation of the Yishuv.

JEWISH IMMIGRATION TO PALESTINE

Toward the end of the nineteenth century, there was a dramatic shift in the volume and composition of immigration to Palestine. Organized groups of Jewish revolutionary emigrants appeared (see Chapter 8). In the decades before 1880, Jewish immigration and settlement consisted of small groups, families, and individuals who moved to the Holy Land, mainly for religious reasons. Most concentrated in Jerusalem, Hebron, Tiberias, and Safed—the four "Holy" cities—which were in turn divided into subcommunities and landsmanschaften according to country of origin. These settlers were generally sustained by moneys collected from Jewish communities abroad. They interacted infrequently with the Moslem and Christian populations, did not diversify occupationally or economically, tended to be isolated politically and culturally, and in large part represented transplants of cultures and social institutions from countries of origin. They were not the foundation for socioeconomic and political modernization.

In sharp contrast, the new immigrants to Palestine were secular nationalists. They were not responding to the "pull" of religious values, economic opportunity, or political environment. Social, economic, and political conditions in Palestine at the time were clearly not conducive to immigration. They were a select, small group among the hundred of thousands of Jews who left Europe at the turn of the last century. Relatively well-educated, secular, urban residents, they entered a different cultural milieu with the goal of developing barren wastelands, working in agriculture, to create the basis for a new Jewish society.

In 1880, fewer than 25,000 Jews resided in Palestine, owning less than twenty-five square kilometers of land. Between 1882 and 1903, the period of the first aliya, an estimated 25,000 immigrants arrived—an enormous volume in relation to the small size of the local Jewish population and to the economic opportunities available. They represented an insignificant proportion of world Jewry, and of Eastern European Jews who were emigrating. Their size indicates that Zionism influenced a minority of migrants. Nor were all those who arrived secular Zionists. Religious ideology continued to attract groups of Hasidim and other Jews to Palestine. The pull of secular and religious ideologies, however, caused relatively few Jews to immigrate. (For detailed documentation of these patterns and a more elaborate treatment of the population issues in Palestine, see Friedlander and Goldscheider, 1979.)

During these years, the revolutionary immigrants lacked funds and had little or no agricultural skills. They faced the hostility of the religious Jewish settlements in urban areas, who viewed them as religious offenders and potential competitors for the limited charity moneys available. The real enemies of the pioneers, however, were their naiveté and lack of agricultural experience and the extremely harsh ecological and economic environment. They were rescued economically by outside capital—particularly from Jewish foreign investors (see Chapter 8). Over time, they hired Arab laborers and many of the Jewish immigrants became administrators. Paternalism and inefficiency, along with disillusionment and emigration, became dominant features of the first aliya period. On the surface, the pattern appears similar to colonial European settlement, which exploited cheap native labor for the benefit of the colonialists and the "Mother" country. In this case, however, there was no "Mother" country. Nevertheless, some of the consequences of a colonial relationship emerged during this early period of settlement and subsequently.

Jointly with their sponsors in Europe, the surviving settlers of the first aliya initiated a more modern agricultural settlement in Palestine, overcame ecological hardships, and laid the foundations for further immigration. By the turn of the twentieth century, almost 100,000 acres of land had been purchased and new villages were settled that were agriculturally productive and self-supporting. The Jewish settlement in Palestine despite emigration and high mortality doubled to 50,000 in twenty years (see Friedlander and Goldscheider, 1979). Notwithstanding this development, the Yishuv continued to be dependent economically and demographically on European Jewish communities.

A second wave of immigrants built upon these demographic and economic foundations. During the decade beginning in 1904, an estimated 40,000–55,000 Jews immigrated to Palestine from Eastern Europe. Many, perhaps most, of the immigrants of the second aliya were part of the organized Zionist movement. They responded to the political upheavals in Russia, as did millions of other Jews, but they reacted in political, not individualistic and economic terms. They combined revolutionary Socialist and Zionist themes and rejected the possibility of improving the condition of the Jews in Russia or settling in America. The failure of the Revolution of 1905 made many of them political outlaws. In Palestine, they sought to shape a new social order based on socialist principles and a Jewish nationalist ideology (Shapiro, 1976; Frankel, 1981).

The immigrants of the second aliya expanded existing farms and developed new communally based agricultural enterprises. In addition, they founded new urban and industrial communities. They were educated, politically articulate, and organizationally skillful. They transferred their political parties and thereby laid the foundations for the labor movement, kibbutzim, and secular Jewish cultural activities. The activities and principles of the second aliya were at the heart of the social, political, and economic structure of the Jewish settlement in Palestine and subsequently of the state. By the outbreak of World War I, 85,000 Jewish settlers lived in Palestine. About half belonged to the religious communities.

The Zionist organizations recruited, organized, and financed the secular immigrants. The various movements provided funds to purchase and develop the land. Given the economic conditions of Palestine, the availability of alternative, more attractive, destinations and overall hardships associated with pioneering, these Zionist activities were succcessful. Against the background of either Jewish population size in Eastern Europe or the total number of Jewish migrants, however, the number of Jews selecting Palestine was exceptionally small. Zionist organizational activities facilitated the immigration and settlement of a small number of ideologically committed Jews.

Turkish opposition had relatively little effect on Jewish immigration (see Mandel, 1974–75; Friedlander and Goldscheider, 1979, p. 56). The reasons behind Ottoman policy are complex and not germane to our main argument. Two important points, however, need emphasis: First, Turkish restrictions on Jewish immigration did not derive from specific anti-Jewish attitudes. Rather they related to the political and administrative structure of the Turkish Empire (the system of Capitulations) and to their negative attitudes toward Europeans, especially Russians. The claims of the Zionist movement about their long-term national objectives and the exaggerated number of potential Jewish immigrants added to the apprehension of Turkish leaders.

In addition, there is no evidence that Ottoman restrictions had a direct effect on the volume or pace of immigration. Turkish policies on immigration were not accepted by the European governments whose citizens were potential immigrants (an essential condition because of the system of Capitulations). Moreover, Jewish immigrants could enter Palestine under a variety of categories (for example, as pilgrims and businessmen) which were not restricted, and they could remain in Palestine without being deported. In short, to be effective, formal restrictive immigration policies required a well-organized system of local control, regulation, and enforcement. The machinery for implementing Turkish policy was too defective to have an impact on immigration patterns.

Thus, the early emergence of the Yishuv at the turn of the twentieth century did not follow an established pattern of European modernization. Immigration rather than natural population increase, heavy reliance on imported capital, dependency on economic and political support from Europe, shifts of urban workers to agricultural activities, the lack of expansive economic opportunities as sources of immigration were exceptional features of the early period of Jewish settlement and development in Palestine. These and related processes had major implications for the subsequent emergence of social and political institutions in Palestine and Israel. They also became important links between Jewish settlers in Palestine and the larger Jewish communities of Europe and America.

The Yishuv under British Rule
World War I altered the power distributions in the Middle East. Turkish control over Palestine was replaced first by the British army and subsequently by the British Mandate of 1922. The emerging Yishuv depended on

continuous Jewish immigration to Palestine. Indeed, the interplay among British colonial policy, Arab nationalism, and Jewish Zionism focused on immigration as the master symbol of conflict. Consequently, it is necessary to clarify the intricate politics associated with immigration.

From the beginning of the British military occupation until 1936, colonial policy attempted to regulate types of Jewish immigration. The number of Zionist-sponsored immigrants was adjusted to the country's "economic absorptive capacity." Immigration that was not subsidized was generally not regulated. Overall, during this period of British control, 150,000 subsidized Jewish immigrants and an equal number of nonsubsidized immigrants entered Palestine. Nothing in the policy prevented wide annual fluctuations in the volume of migration (see Friedlander and Goldscheider, 1979). Nothing in British colonial policy or in Zionist ideology accounts for the changes in immigration volume or composition.

Conflict emerged over how to define economic absorptive capacity, who defined it, and who controlled the allocation of entry permits. The vagueness of the immigration regulations and the lack of control over total immigration left a wide latitude for maneuvering. Initially, colonial officials set up quotas. In 1920, for example, a quota of 16,500 heads of families was assigned to the Zionist organization. Hampered by a lack of funds and inadequate administrative coordination, the Zionists could not meet that number. Subsequently, subsidized migrants were defined in terms of those who had a "definite prospect of employment in Palestine" known as the "labor schedule" (ESCO, 1947, pp. 315–19). The Palestine Executive Committee in conjunction with the Jewish Agency estimated the number of workers that could be absorbed, and the British High Commissioner decided on the number of certificates granted. The Palestine Zionist Executive distributed the permits. In turn, the various Jewish political parties battled over the allocations, each striving to bring immigrants of its political persuasion (see Horowitz and Lissak, 1978; Shapiro, 1976). As a result, Jews without party affiliation, those not sharing a particular ideology, non-Eastern Europeans, and those who were more traditionally religious found it relatively difficult to enter Palestine as subsidized immigrants. Therefore, political battles influenced choices among Zionists in Europe, and their outcomes rejected large numbers of potential immigrants from Asian and African countries (on Yemen, see for example Nini, 1981). The regulation of immigration subsidized by the Zionist organization was in effect control over total immigration, because few Jews were willing or able to come to Palestine voluntarily as nonsubsidized immigrants.

The Arabs totally rejected the idea of the national Jewish homeland embodied in the Balfour Declaration and the British commitment to Jewish immigration. Arab pressures to stop Jewish immigration and Jewish pressures for its continuation became the conspicuous issue around which British policies in Palestine revolved for three decades. These political arguments had little impact on rates and sources of Jewish immigration.

The policy of economic absorptive capacity was vaguely formulated and designed only to control subsidized immigrants; therefore, its effectiveness was limited. The first immigration wave during the British period, known as the third aliyah, covered the years 1919 through 1923. In 1919, the Zionist Organization opened immigration offices, and the British military authorities permitted 1,000 artisans to enter. In the four years to 1923, over 8,000 Jewish immigrants entered annually, totaling over 35,000, a significant contribution to the base Jewish population of around 60,000 in 1919. Most of these immigrants were young, single males from Russia and Poland. Most had gone through agricultural training programs organized by the Zionist organizations in Europe (Shapiro, 1976; Gorni, 1975; Mendelsohn, 1981). Some growth of rural settlements, agricultural and small industrial expansion, and general socioeconomic and organizational development characterized this immigration.

Three changes occurring outside of Palestine brought new types of immigrants. Beginning in the 1920s the American government enacted entry quotas that reduced substantially the flow from Eastern Europe to the United States, thereby closing the primary destination of Jewish emigration from Eastern Europe (Wasserstein, 1929; see Chapter 10). At the same time, changes in the politico-economic structure of Poland hurt Jewish shopkeepers, businessmen, and merchants, the bulk of Polish Jewry (see Chapters 7 and 9; and Mendelsohn, 1981). The economic depression that hit Europe at the end of the 1920s provided an additional push to Jewish emigration. Combined, these factors, not Zionist ideology or colonial policy, set into motion the potential for increased immigration to Palestine.

For the three years beginning in 1924, Jewish immigration to Palestine increased: from almost 14,000 in 1924, 34,000 in 1925, and 14,000 in 1926. With a total Jewish population estimated at 92,000 at the end of 1923, the fourth aliya increased the number of Jews by 67 percent. As a result, the ratio of Jewish to total population rose from 11 percent in 1922 to over 16 percent at the end of 1926. In contrast to the earlier waves of immigration, half of the fourth aliya was from Poland, and many were urban middle-class families (see also Mendelsohn, 1981). In contrast to earlier periods, Palestine was the destination of about one-third of all Jewish international migrants. Few came for ideological reasons or as part of a Zionist program. For most, Palestine was the only place that would take them.

The relatively large volume of immigration of 1924–26 did not continue. The economic foundations of the Yishuv were not firm, were concentrated in agriculture, and could not absorb large numbers of urban-oriented migrants. Local economic setbacks, severe unemployment, and several natural disasters aggravated the situation (Giladi, 1975). The worldwide economic depression began to be keenly felt in Palestine, slowing down the inflow and resulting in a relatively large counterstream migration out of Palestine. While almost 82,000 immigrants arrived during 1924–31, 23,000 Jews left. The census of 1931 counted 175,000 Jews and 859,000 Arabs in Palestine (Friedlander and Goldscheider, 1979).

The Arab population reacted to the growing number of Jews. Widespread economic difficulties, particularly unemployment caused by the entry of many Jews, and a downturn in the local economy occasioned Arab protests. Although the Arab reaction (as the Jewish) was couched in political and ideological language, economic competition and political control determined the conflict. Jewish immigration precipitated economic changes and threatened the Arab's population dominance.

Beginning in 1932, the volume of immigration increased again. The number entering Palestine was four times higher than in 1931; it tripled again to 37,000 in 1933, increasing to 45,000 in 1934, and to over 66,000 in 1935. This was a record high, unprecedented since the beginning of modern Jewish immigration to Palestine. The thrust of immigration continued until 1936 when an additional 30,000 immigrants arrived (see also Mendelsohn, 1983). Between 1931 and 1935 about 60 percent of all Jewish immigrants came to Palestine, the only period in the century beginning in 1840 when more than one-third of the Jews on the move selected the national homeland (Lestchinsky, 1960, pp. 1554–56).

The forces generating this immigration were clearly not the better economic opportunities in Palestine nor any change in immigration policy among British or Jewish agencies. It is also clear that most of the immigrants were not motivated by Zionism. Rather, the deteriorating political situation of European Jewry, the rise of Hitler and Nazism in the 1930s, and its spread to Central Europe were the major push factors. The influx of almost 200,000 Jewish immigrants between 1932 and 1936 more than doubled the Jewish population of Palestine to 355,000 and increased the ratio of Jewish to total population from less than 17 percent in 1931 to almost 30 percent in 1936.

In addition, 15 percent of these immigrants came from Germany, representing a significant increase from previous levels. Before 1933, only several hundred German and Austrian Jews were in Palestine. Between 1933 and 1936 over 30,000 arrived; between 1935 and 1938 they accounted for one-fourth of the immigrants. Nevertheless, the beginning of the fifth aliya, labeled a "German" immigration, was still dominated numerically by Polish Jews. The most noticeable decline was in Jewish immigration from the USSR, which dwindled considerably during the 1930s, mostly as a result of the restrictions placed on Jewish emigration. Central European Jews brought with them urban and organizational skills, middle-class backgrounds, and capital for investment. As a result, there was a decline in the

proportion of immigrants arriving on the labor schedule controlled by the
Zionist organization and regulated by the British.

As was characteristic of the earlier period, increases in the volume of
Jewish immigration generated negative reactions among the Arabs and led
to demonstrations, strikes, and attacks. These gained momentum in 1936.
Clearly, the regulatory mechanisms of immigration based on economic
absorptive capacity did not limit the total number of immigrants. Indeed,
the government tried unsuccessfully to control total immigration by severely
restricting the allocation of labor certificates for subsidized migrants. Nevertheless, tens of thousands of Jewish immigrants were in nonregulated categories. The Zionist organizations assisted those who were defined as nonsubsidized immigrants.

Jews pressured for continued immigration, and Arabs counterpressured
to stop it. The British were caught with vague commitments to both
nationalisms and imprecise, unenforceable immigration policies. Their colonial position had become untenable: How could they fulfill the conditions
of the Mandate which charged them with the responsibility to set up the
"political, administrative, and economic conditions as will secure the establishment of the Jewish national home" while "ensuring that the rights and
position of other sections of the population are not prejudiced"? They were
also mandated to "facilitate Jewish immigration under suitable conditions"
(cited in ESCO, 1947, pp. 87–89). Both the meaning of "facilitate" and the
definition of "suitable" were ambiguous.

Acceding to Arab pressure, British policy after 1937 restricted total
Jewish immigration. Despite the imposition of numerical quotas, a large
number of Jewish immigrants entered Palestine, most of them legally.
British policies prevented an even larger number, mainly refugees from
Europe and subsequently the survivors of the European Holocaust, from
entering. Only during these years did British policy affect the timing and
volume of immigration.

Numerous commissions, White Papers, and arguments surrounded
clashes of politics, ideology, and external events in Europe and the Middle
East. British policy attempted to make the Jews a permanent demographic
minority in Palestine. More important, the policy sought to limit Zionist
control over the organization of an autonomous Jewish society. The British
fixed a "political high level" of immigration, that is, an upper limit that
would not be exceeded. It sought to maintain the relative proportion between Jewish and Arab populations (3:10). Subsequent policies went further, formally granting Arab control over Jewish immigration, relinquishing
British control over Palestine to the Arab majority, and ending British
commitments to the idea of a Jewish national homeland. These proposals
were not acceptable to the Jews in Palestine and elsewhere. Conflict among

the British, Arabs, and Jews intensified (Wasserstein, 1979; Gilbert, 1978; Friedlander and Goldscheider, 1979).

Between 1937 and 1944 over 100,000 Jewish immigrants entered Palestine; from 1945 to mid-1948 almost 75,000 immigrants arrived, most of them illegally. Before 1937 there was no need for illegal immigration, since British policy was sufficiently flexible to allow in large numbers of Jews. Once political quotas on total immigration were established, illegal channels became the most important organized Jewish response. Initially, the numbers of these immigrants were small but their symbolic importance was enormous. Illegal immigration became a rallying point for Jewish political activities in Europe, America, and Palestine and was the most dramatic political weapon for the establishment of the State. Deporting illegal immigrants back to Europe or imprisoning them in Cyprus added tension and tragedy to an already volatile conflict and exerted enormous political pressure on the British. Immigration to Palestine dominated all other political issues in the period preceding the establishment of Israel.

As the postwar pressure for the immigration of Jewish refugees in Europe mounted, and as the British were packing their colonial bags, the Arab armies prepared to invade Palestine, and the Jews gathered their military forces. Within two years after the last commission struggled with the triangle of British political control, Arab nationalism, and Zionism in the aftermath of the Holocaust, the State of Israel was declared in May 1948. When the dust of battle had settled. the new country covered part of Mandate Palestine and included about 650,000 Jews and 150,000 Arabs.

The socioeconomic structure of the new Jewish State in 1948 reflected the previous patterns of immigration and selectivity. Almost 65 percent of the Jewish population was from Eastern Europe and the Balkans, and an additional 20 percent originated in Central Europe. Only 15 percent were from Asian and African countries, mostly from Yemen, Aden, Turkey, and Iraq. Despite the enormous growth of rural Jewish settlements (the number had increased from forty-seven to 326 from 1914 to 1948, and its population had multiplied from 12,000 to 110,000), Israeli Jews were predominately urbanites. About three-fourths of the Jewish population was urban in 1948—one of the highest urban concentrations in the world. The kibbutzim represented about half of the rural settlements; only 54,000 Jews lived there in 1948 (Bachi, 1977, pp. 43–44). The State of Israel was established on the basis of an urban, industrial, and European population.

In the period immediately after statehood, immigration patterns altered the size and composition of the Jewish population (see Friedlander and Goldscheider, 1979). There was an extraordinarily high volume of immigrants between 1948 and 1951 and a radical change in their ethnic composition. Nearly a million refugees and immigrants from Europe and the Arab countries came to Israel. World War II and the Holocaust left hundreds of thousands of Jewish refugees scattered throughout Europe. Limited opportunities for immigration to America or for remaining in Europe, coupled with international political pressures, made these refugees the first group of immigrants to arrive in Israel. Jews from Arab countries became part of the flow of 170,000 immigrants in the first seven months following independence and the additional 520,000 who arrived in the following two-and-a-half years. In a short period of three years, 700,000 Jews arrived, doubling the Jewish population. The refugees from Europe and the immigrants from Asian and African countries were not pulled to Israel by secular nationalism. Again, the primary determinants were political and economic with some mix of religious messianism among the Jews from the traditional communities of Asia and North Africa.

At the time of the establishment of the State, Israeli Jews represented 5.7 percent of world Jewry; by 1951 the proportion doubled. Yet, in the first quarter of a century after the establishment of the State and almost a full century after the beginning of the new Yishuv in Palestine, the Israeli Jewish population remained at about 20 percent of the world Jewish total.

In contrast, Zionist attempts to stimulate and encourage immigration from the West generally have occurred when immigration from other countries declined. Measured by rates of immigration, these policies, however, have not succeeded. Indeed, only when socioeconomic and political conditions in Israel were improving (particularly between the Six Day War of 1967 and the Yom Kippur War of 1973) did Western immigration increase. For most Jews outside of Israel the pulls of Israel and Zionist ideology do not generate migration.

Immigration to Israel, as to Palestine in an earlier period, has responded in remarkably similar ways to socioeconomic pushes and pulls that have determined the processes of immigration to countries around the world. Despite the unique forces of nationalism, Zionist ideology and policy, relatively few have immigrated to Israel for ideological reasons.

These immigrations, socioeconomic developments, and political legitimacy created the basis for a viable, stable, Jewish society in its homeland. As Jews from diverse countries formed a new political community in Israel, their social, economic, political, religious, and cultural characteristics were transformed. At the same time, new forms of competition and conflict emerged within the Jewish State. The Jewish national polity was formed as one response to the threats of assimilation and holocaust. Jewish survival in Israel does not depend on the bases of cohesion but on the outcomes of the continuous wars with Arabs, external economic and military dependencies, and on the politics of international interests.

13 · Modernization, Conflict, and Israeli Society

The Jewish community of Israel is a total society. As such it is markedly different from Jewish communities that are parts of other societies. Threats of ethnic assimilation have no meaning with regard to the Jews of Israel. By the very definition of a Jewish total society, the size and structure of Israel ensure that Jews will interact almost exclusively with other Jews. At the same time, a Jewish total society implies that the social class, and ethnic, religious, and political conflicts that Nahman's windstorm brought to other societies may also be found in Israel. Conflict as well as cohesion mark Israeli society.

In 1880, there were fewer than 8 million Jews in the world, almost nine out of ten were in Europe; only 25,000 Jews were in Palestine, three-tenths of 1 percent of the world's Jews. A century later, almost 3.5 million Jews live in Israel, 22 percent of the total world Jewish population of 13 million. The demographic transformation of world Jewry in these 100 years and the emergence of Israeli society are interrelated. They are both tied to industrialization, urbanization, ideological and political revolutions, mass immigrations, world wars, destruction and Holocaust, refugee movements and displacements of the last century. The formation and changes in Israeli society reflect what happened in Europe and America, in Yemen, Iraq, Morocco, Russia, Poland, Rumania, Germany, as well as what happened and happens in its own land and region.

Out of the uprootedness and social upheavals of nineteenth-century European society, Zionism emerged. Out of the turbulence and devastations of World War II, Israel emerged. The change and heterogeneity characteristic of Israeli society reflect the centuries of Diaspora experience and decades of renewed settlement in a national home. The nature of the Diaspora and the original character of the Yishuv are sources of change and conflict inherent in contemporary Israeli society.

The political story begins in antiquity; the modern version starts with the Balfour Declaration of 1917.

His Majesty's government view with favour the establishment in Palestine of a national home for the Jewish people and will facilitate the
achievement of that object, it being clearly understood that nothing shall
be done which may prejudice the civil and religious rights of the existing
non-Jewish communities in Palestine, or the rights and political status
enjoyed by Jews in any other country.

The complex balance and conflict among these provisions—a Jewish
home, Arab rights, and external dependencies on Jews and governments—
not only characterized the British Mandate period but have been fundamental issues in Israeli society. Some things have changed. The proportion of Jews in the total population of Palestine was a basic question during
the British Mandate. The proportion of Israel's population which will be
Arab is a question that has been raised since the establishment of the State in
1948 and most often since the Six Day War of 1967 (Friedlander and
Goldscheider, 1979).

The political parties that competed for power during the Yishuv reflected
the political formations established in the various countries of Europe and
the battles within the Zionist movement. Thus, the emerging polity of Israel
in 1948 had several Socialist, religious, and liberal, middle-class parties and
a right-wing nationalist party. The largest Socialist party, *Mapai*, formed in
1930 by the merger of *Ahdut Ha' Avodah* (Labor Unity) and *Hapoel Hatzair*
(the Young Worker), dominated the political system. Its power stemmed
from the early arrival in Israel of its leaders (after the Russian Revolution of
1905), their political acumen and organizational skills. They built and controlled the *Histadrut* (General Workers Union), and even established their
own army (the *Haganah*), school system, businesses, collective farms, insurance companies, athletic associations, and all the other accoutrements of a
typical Socialist movement. They controlled the Jewish polity during the
Yishuv, the Israeli polity as it formed in 1948, and the political system until
1977 (Medding, 1972; Shapiro, 1976, 1980b; Horowitz and Lissak, 1978).
The structure they established legitimated differences of class and religious
observance among the Jews (the accepted social cleavages of European
socialist politics). Ethnic divisions had no place in this vision. They sought to
unite the nation behind the Socialist movement.

Two Perspectives on Israeli Jews

An analysis of contemporary Israeli society conjures up two somewhat
contradictory images (Smooha, 1978; Bernstein and Swirski, 1981). These
images fit the broader theoretical models guiding our general analysis of
Jewish social structure over the last centuries.

The first model sees Israel as one of a group of new nations in Asia and
Africa emerging in the post–World War II era. Like these polities, Israel has

undergone and continues to undergo changes associated with social, political, and economic development. Israeli society has increased in population size, expanded economically, developed a national culture, and has become an internationally recognized, integrated national polity. Indeed, Israel is an exemplary modernizing country, overcoming a host of problems of building new institutions and expanding older institutions. Israel has been transformed in a short period from a small ideological community to a total society. It has become a microcosm of nation-building processes. Indeed, the deserts have bloomed, the cities have mushroomed, industry has expanded, new suburban areas and development towns have been built.

This framework emphasizes as well the cultural renaissance of Hebrew language and culture—theater, arts, and literature—and religious secularization. Israeli culture has emerged in the context of the new Israeli polity. Israel is a viable democracy, with the cultural, economic, and political integration of the groups that make up the population. Modernization implies increasing levels of Jewish cohesion in Israel.

Israeli society also has some unique features. The uniqueness does not rest primarily on the kibbutz and *moshav* experiments—however interesting and ideologically salient—but with several situational-historical facts: (1) The Labor Movement dominated the political structure from the beginning of the British Mandate in 1920 until the elections of 1977. Its control was central to the process of nation building in Israel. (2) The sources and pace of the demographic expansion of Israel have been primarily a product of mass immigration from diverse countries of origin rather than by the natural increase of its native population. (3) Economic growth has occurred as a result of large external capital investments not only by governments and multinational corporations but by Jewish organizations and communities outside of Israel. (4) The Jewishness of Israeli life is tied directly to the sources of population expansion and economic growth. There has emerged a complex interrelationship between religion (Judaism) and nationalism (Zionism) and between Israeli Jews and Jewish communities in other countries. (5) The Arab population in Israel became a minority group as a result of the establishment of the State. Arabs have important political, economic, and family connections to Arab countries.

Immigration has placed strains on the expected fluid economic growth and sociocultural integration. The strains of nation building, therefore, are viewed primarily in terms of the triangular complex of ethnic heterogeneity brought about through immigration, rapid socioeconomic growth, and the external threats to Israel's survival. They are overshadowed, however, by the thrust of the modernization of Israel's social institutions and ethnic communities, the secularization of Jewish culture, and national political unity. In particular, the model directs attention to social mobility, assimilation, disintegration of the older Diaspora culture (traditional society), and the absorption of the immigrants into the modern, Western orientations of Israeli society.

Israel has thus become a new melting pot, where Jews from Iraq, Iran, Yemen, Morocco, Algeria, and Tunisia are exposed to westernization and modernity. But Israel is not simply European culture transferred, since Jews were only segments of those societies and were themselves transformed upon coming to Palestine-Israel. Over time a new Israeli develops—different from the variety of countries of origin or Jewish communities outside of Israel.

In this regard Israel represents a major transformation for all groups: European Jews have changed from a minority to a majority group in social-political-economic terms; Jews from Asian and African countries have been transformed from traditional to modern settings; and the Arab population has been transformed from a majority to a minority, demographically as well as in every other way.

This theory emphasizes that ethnic differences are temporary and over time will converge toward a new Israeli form. To the extent that at any point in time ethnic variations exist among Jews, they reflect cultural traits of the past or continuing socioeconomic differences, and some residual psychological prejudices of Europeans against Orientals. These, in turn, are tied to the timing of immigration, the sociocultural background of immigrants, and their relative stages of social development. For all groups, the model hypothesizes that time is the great healer of conflict. The strains of development, immigration, and nation building will be less conspicuous in the next generation and will be of little significance in the generation after that. Educational and military institutions are the major mechanisms of socialization of the new generation into Israeli norms. Most important, these institutions are the major equalizers among the diverse ethnic-immigrant groups.

An alternative model, consistent within a conflict emphasis, analyzes social heterogeneity in Israel from a very different perspective (Smooha, 1978; Zureik, 1979; Bernstein and Swirski, 1981). Colonized by white European settlers who exploited land and Arab laborers, the European Jews rejected Middle-Eastern culture. Over time, this colonialism through migration and settlement became internal colonialism. This characterizes relationships between Jews and Arabs as well as among Jews themselves. In place of the absorption of Jewish ethnics from a wide range of countries, the argument points to the exercise of power over the Asian-African immigrants and local Arabs in an expanding capitalist economy. The dominance of European Ashkenazim over economic and political resources is associated with the incomplete and blocked access of Orientals (Asian and African Jews) and Arabs to those resources. In this theory, ethnic political domination replaces immigrant absorption.

The conflict model sees power and interests as integral features of Israeli society. In this context, economic dependencies—externally on the United States and internally on the dominant European groups—make Israel not a symbol of an independent nation-state but a client state of the capitalist West serving the needs of her middle-class constituency (that is, Western Jews).

The conflict theory stresses the connections between social class and ethnic group membership rather than national industrial growth; geographic segregation and social isolation of peripheral towns rather than development areas for the integration of immigrants; the disadvantage of ethnic origin and its reinforcement through educational and community institutions rather than the emergence of the new Israeli. Time exacerbates conflict rather than heals strains. Hebrew culture and Jewish religion are devices to exclude Arabs and neutralize the rich cultural legacy of Jews from non-European countries; hence, these do not symbolize cultural renaissance.

The emphasis of this model is on conflict, inequalities, and internal colonialism. As an inevitable outgrowth of Zionism, immigration, and settlement, a three-layered stratification system emerged—Ashkenazi European on the top followed by Jews from Arab countries, and Palestinian Arabs on the bottom. Assimilation is therefore the adjustment of Oriental Jewish culture to the dominance of Europeans, not a melting pot or the emergence of a new Israeli, and does not apply at all to Jewish-Arab relations. Israeli Arabs are not to be understood as a psychological minority, relatively deprived, alienated from the Jewish nationalism of Israel, yet participants in the processes of modernization. Rather, they are exploited economically, politically oppressed, and the source of Jewish cohesion (Smooha, 1978; Zureik, 1979).

These two models, respectively, are the accepted wisdom and the radical critique of Israeli society. They appear, but are not, mutually exclusive. Both models contain elements that reflect accurately on reality. Clearly, national integration and Jewish cohesion are features of Israeli modernization. Conflict, pluralism, and differential access to power and control over resources are also basic aspects of Israeli life. Israel is both an independent political entity and dependent politically and economically on the American government and world Jewry. We use these models as maps and guidelines to interpret Israeli society. Together they imply that the Jewish community in Israel is characterized by maximum sources of Jewish cohesion and maximum sources of Jewish division.

IMMIGRATION, POPULATION GROWTH, AND ETHNIC GROUP FORMATION
In the three decades following statehood, about 1.5 million Jews immigrated to Israel. This immigration varied over time, and in ethnic composition. In the period of mass immigration (1948–51), when the Jewish population of

Israel more than doubled, about half came from Asian and African countries. Their proportion of the newcomers increased dramatically over the
four-year period—from 14 percent in 1948 to 71 percent in 1951. This
contrasts sharply with immigration between 1914 and 1948, when 90 percent
of the 450,000 Jewish immigrants came from Europe.

The volume and ethnic composition of the immigration streams to Israel
point to three important empirical conclusions: First, there was an enormous number of immigrants during this period—in absolute number as well
as compared to the population in Israel and to available housing and jobs.
Since the non-Europeans arrived later, the Europeans had initial access to
these resources. Third, among the non-Europeans, those from Asian countries—particularly from Yemen and Iraq—arrived earlier than immigrants
from Africa—particularly Morocco, Tunisia, and Algeria.

The timing of immigration affected the initial adjustment to the new
society in terms of the critical dimensions of housing, economic opportunity,
and settlement. Nevertheless, contemporary differences between Europeans and Asian-Africans are not primarily a function of the timing of
immigration. Nor do they reflect solely the wide cultural differences among
the Jewish communities of origin. The most important set of factors that
differentiates European from non-European Jews in Israel relates to the
differential socioeconomic background of these populations and their ethnic
ties within Israel.

Occupational skills, educational backgrounds, family and ethnic ties of
the European immigrants facilitated their relatively successful entrance into
Israeli society and their access to power and opportunity. Europeans took
advantage of the limitied economic opportunities because of their connections to the Yishuv's European-dominated society and economy. Furthermore, Asian-African Jews came from societies that had less modern occupational and educational systems. Hence, they were less able over time to
compete successfully with the Europeans. The timing of immigration and
the cultural differences among Jewish ethnic groups reinforced these
structural factors and community links which divided Israeli Jews.

The structural characteristics of Israel have produced two ethnic groups—
"Asian-African" and "European-American" Jews; within these groups
there are differences in culture and in the timing and volume of immigration.
Nevertheless, social class and political power overlap with the division
between the two major ethnic groups. Rather than eliminating and obscur-
ing ethnic differences, modernization in Israel has created new ethnic
formations and bases for division among Jews (see for other countries
Yancey et. al., 1976; Kobrin and Goldscheider, 1978; Glazer and Moynihan, 1975; Gellner, 1980; A. Zuckerman, 1982).

Over the several decades since the establishment of the state, the Asian-
Africans have become demographically dominant. In 1948, for example,

about two-thirds of the Jewish population was foreign-born, and less than 15 percent were from Asian-African countries. Three decades later, about half the Jewish population was foreign-born, and almost 45 percent was born in Asian and African countries. In 1961, over half the Israeli-born were of European origins; by 1977 over six out of ten Israeli-born Jews were of Asian-African origins (Goldscheider, 1983).

The demographic dominance of Asian-Africans is not matched by equivalent political power. Their socioeconomic characteristics, residential dispersal, and the actions of the Europeans in preserving their position of status and power prevent an easy conversion of demographic size into political power and economic control. Indeed, the tension between demographic change and the overlap of social stratification and ethnicity generates ethnic conflict in Israel (Smooha, 1978; Curtis and Chertoff, 1973).

FAMILY STRUCTURE AND ETHNICITY: CHANGE AND CONTINUITY
Is there evidence of time erasing ethnic differences among Jews in Israel? If modernization results in national integration, differences characteristic of immigrants should disappear by the second and third generations. An analysis of family structure in Israel illustrates the pattern of convergences among ethnic groups in Israel in response to structural changes. Variations in family life which remain reflect structural and cultural factors (Goldscheider, 1983).

In Israel, ethnic or social class variations are not related to the extent of marriage. By ages thirty to thirty-five, well over 95 percent have been married at least once. While it is problematic to infer norms from behavior, the pattern seems to reflect the enormous value placed on marriage; the emphasis on family within Israeli-Jewish culture; and the social, economic, and cultural centrality of the family. This pattern is consistent with the historical pattern universal of marriages among Jews in Asian and African countries as well as in Eastern Europe. The major change in the proportion married is for Western European Jews, who have increased their propensity to marry subsequent to immigration to Israel.

At what point in the life cycle do Israeli Jews marry? Age at marriage for those marrying in Israel increased for Asian-Africans (brides and grooms) and decreased for European-American grooms, remaining relatively stable for brides. Hence, by 1975, the average age at marriage of Asian-African was about the same as for European-Americans (age twenty-five for men and twenty-two for women). This contrasts to a decade and a half earlier when European-American brides and grooms married on an average two years later than Asian-African brides and grooms. It corresponds exactly to the average age at marriage in American Jewish communities (Goldscheider, forthcoming).

This and related evidence (see Goldscheider, 1983) suggest that convergence in the timing of marriage has occurred for the two major Jewish ethnic groups. This does not reflect changes in one group toward the other or toward some native-born Israeli model but is the product of changes in both ethnic groups toward a new model. The paths toward ethnic similarity have been very different. The emerging pattern is different from both the European or the Asian-African communities of origin. It reflects the social and economic conditions of Israel.

The rate of interethnic marriages among Israeli Jews reflects changing ethnic cleavages. Do they indicate assimilation or continued ethnic divisions? Marriage records in Israel show a slow but steady increase in ethnic out-marriages. These increases reflect the loosening of some ethnic constraints and the weakening of some ethnic boundaries. They also derive from the tensions between very strong marriage norms and the limitations of small marriage markets. For some Israelis, the choice is betwen marriages within the relatively limited market of their ethnic group, delayed or non-marriage, or marriage out of their ethnic group. The increase of ethnic intermarriages in Israel, therefore, may be interpreted not only as an indicator of assimilation but also as a traditional response to the pressures of marriage and family (see Matras, 1973b; Peres and Katz, 1981; Goldscheider, 1983). Interethnic marriage is legitimated by the ideology of assimilation. It is not the direct consequence of that ideology.

Despite the increase, the levels of ethnic homogamy are very high for all groups; 75–80 percent of Asian-Africans and European-Americans marry within their own ethnic group. There is greater variation when specific countries of origin are examined and differences between men and women complicate the pattern. These variations derive from factors associated with the size of the marriage market, length of time in the country, size of the ethnic group, and residential-geographic distribution, rather than cultural or ideological factors.

Fertility levels and variations in Israel have been studied extensively and reinforce some of the major family patterns described here. Overall, there are relatively high levels of Jewish fertility in Israel relative to Jews elsewhere and to industrialized nations. These fertility patterns are related to family structure and familism. There have been major ethnic convergences in fertility levels and norms. In particular, fertility reductions among Asian-Africans have been dramatic over the last several decades, and the fertility gap between Asian-Africans and European-Americans has narrowed considerably (see Friedlander and Goldscheider, 1979; Friedlander et al., 1980; Goldscheider and Friedlander, 1981, 1983).

One aspect of this dramatic fertility reduction relates to the transformation of family structure among Asian-African immigrants. The decline in Asian-African fertility preceded major socioeconomic mobility. Changes in family structure followed immigration, especially the breakdown of the family economic connection. The exposure to an opportunity structure outside the control of the extended family and the increased status of women resulted in the sharp decline in family size among Asian-African immigrants.

Continuing ethnic variation in the norms and size of families reflects socioeconomic, educational, and residential differences among ethnic groups. Despite the major convergence over time in ethnic differences in fertility, the paths to this convergence have been significantly different. European families have increased in size, while those of the Asian-Africans have decreased. Jews in Israel have moved toward a model of small families, larger than the traditional Western type, and significantly smaller than the Asian-African level.

Divorce rates have been remarkably stable and low. The pattern contradicts the oversimplified expectation of increased levels of divorce in the process of modernization. Infrequent divorces are consistent with the high marriage rates and have been described in terms of the "stability and centrality" of the nuclear family in Israel (Peres and Katz, 1981). Evidence from the late 1970s suggests there has been some increase in divorce levels. These patterns characterize both Asian-African and European-American ethnic groups. Some evidence suggests that European-Americans have somewhat higher divorce rates than Asian-Africans (Goldscheider, 1983).

This overview of Jewish family patterns in Israel suggests several basic conclusions. Where initial differences have been large, there have been major ethnic convergences. The convergence is not to a European pattern nor to some Jewish family pattern (that is largely nonexistent and certainly not universal). Rather, the overall emerging pattern reflects the social and economic conditions in Israel. Ethnic differences are also related to socioeconomic status, educational attainment, and place of residence. These structural features differentiate ethnic groups in significant ways. Thus, these structural variations are of overwhelming importance for family variation in Israel.

Family convergences do not suggest the absence of ethnic continuity. There is indeed no contradiction between ethnic convergence and ethnic continuity. The convergences in family processes reflect structural pressures toward similar but new patterns. Ethnic continuity is manifest most clearly in the broader realm of ethnic inequalities. These differences are embedded in the society and do not simply reflect cultural legacies or vestigial identities. Emergent ethnic communities are marked by differential advantage and access to resources, reinforced by discrimination and culture, often united nationally by externals, and in turn related to the presence of non-Jewish ethnics.

THE PERSISTENCE OF THE ETHNIC FACTOR

At the same time that ethnic convergences have appeared, structural features of Israel maintain ethnic divisions. Residence, occupational and social mobility, religious, and political divisions are closely associated with ethnicity. These are the bases of social and political conflict within Israel. Those features that provide sources of cohesion for Jews where they are a minority group divide Jews where they are a total society.

The Israeli Jewish population as a whole and the ethnic subpopulations within it are remarkably concentrated in urban areas. For the last two decades, over 90 percent have lived in urban settlements. This pattern continues the high level of urban concentration of Jews. It is remarkable only in the context of Zionism's emphasis on rural settlements (see E. Cohen, 1977; Matras, 1973a). There are no significant ethnic variations in the proportions living in urban areas. The critical ethnic distinctions emerge in areas settled before 1948 (veteran settlements). A much lower proportion of Asians and Africans are located here than are Europeans. This characterizes both first and second generations and holds within periods of immigrant arrival in Israel. Ethnic differences are more pronounced in rural settlements. Among the foreign-born, 62 percent of Europeans compared to 17 percent of the Asian-Africans are located in veteran rural settlements. The same difference characterizes the second generation and holds within periods of immigrant arrival in Israel (Goldscheider, 1983).

Residential segregation reinforces ethnic community institutions and distinctive ethnic consciousness and behavior. It maintains the visibility of ethnic identification for the ethnic group as well as for others. Most important, residence in areas of relatively high ethnic density has a major impact on ethnic socialization, interaction, marriage, and mobility patterns. Indeed, ethnic residential concentration is one of the major mechanisms for the continuity and survival of ethnic communities.

Direct evidence suggests further that ethnic groups are residentially segregated within cities and are likely to remain so at least for the next generation (Klaff, 1973, 1977; Berler, 1970). Annual rates of intercommunity migration support this conclusion. In 1977, for example, internal migration rates were significantly higher for European-Americans than Asian-Africans even within life cycle (age) and period of immigration (Goldscheider, 1983). To the extent that Asian-Africans are located in new towns and nonmetropolitan urban areas, such lower migration rates imply continued ethnic segregation.

This pattern has important implications for political conflict and dissensus and for continuing differential access to schools and jobs. The continuing segregation within urban areas combined with regional ethnic concentration has often resulted in political activities and pressures to demand greater shares and more equal distribution of economic and social resources.

The ethnic factor connects most conspicuously to social inequality. There is a strong persistent relationship between country of birth, generation in Israel, and a wide range of measures of socioeconomic status and social mobility (see Curtis and Chertoff, 1973; Matras and Weintraub, 1976). The differences in educational attainment and occupational achievement of Asian-Africans and European-Americans are a function of two complex processes: (1) the differential social origins, that is, the educational-occupational distributions of their parents; (2) differential changes experienced in Israel. Ethnicity impinges, therefore, on initial stratification differentials as well as on subsequent behavior.

Intergenerational mobility has not closed the educational or occupational gap between ethnic groups. While every group has been characterized by social mobility, the gap between ethnic groups has not diminished. Thus, even when there is rapid development and growth, the opening up of new opportunities within a relatively open stratification system, the salience of the ethnic factor has persisted. The ethnicity-stratification connection appears to be reinforced when additional residential and ecological considerations are taken into account (see Matras and Weintraub, 1976; Spilerman and Habib, 1976; Matras, 1973a).

The continuing residential segregation by ethnicity, marital patterns, and the persistence of the ethnic stratification connection suggest that ethnicity in Israel will continue to be salient at least for the next generation. These structural dimensions imply ethnic tensions, which have sporadically turned into violent protests and demonstrations. The ways in which such tensions and conflicts are managed in Israel will have major implications for the emerging ethnic mosaic in Israeli society.

RELIGIOSITY AND NATIONALISM

Religion and religiosity provide additional sources of national cohesion and division. Judaism and Zionism have been intimately connected, yet many religious organizations and leaders have been anti-Zionist or at least skeptical about Zionism as secular nationalism. Many, if not most, of the Zionist leaders have been secularists and substituted nationalism for religion or at least rejected the traditional dominance of religion.

While the modernization of Jews, particularly in Israel, allows for the separation of religious from national identities, it also generates new forms of interdependence and conflict. New religious expressions emerge in celebration of national occasions and secular events; nationalistic interpretation is applied to traditional religious symbols. The sanctification of the national-secular and the nationalization of the holy-religious are clear expressions of the reintegration of religion and nationalism in new ways in the transformed Israeli society. The relationships between religious and political institutions and, in particular, the role of religious political parties highlight the sources of division generated by the modernization of Judaism in Israel. Issues of synagogue-state relations, legal-political definitions of who is a Jew, religious conflict over autopsies, public transportation on the Sabbath, the control of marriage and divorce by the religious courts are among the issues that divide Israeli Jews. At times, these differences have erupted into violent conflict betwen religious and secular Jews and between the former and the police (Zucker, 1973; Abramov, 1976; M. Friedmann, 1975).

Modernization in Israel creates options for both secularization and new religious expression. These options have been selectively exercised in the direction of both more religious and more secular. The politicization of religion in Israel sharpens this conflict within the Jewish community there and between the Jews in Israel and other countries. These point to religion as the "potentially . . . sharpest dividing line in the society" (E. Katz, 1973).

Modernization has transformed Judaism in Israel. Secularization has occurred and is not specific to a particular ethnic group or social class or to selected dimensions of religiosity. It has not resulted in the total and uniform abandonment of all forms of religiosity. It implies the transformation of traditional religious observances, not assimilation nor loss of Jewish identification.

There has been a dramatic decline in religiosity among the Asian-Africans and continuing secularization among European-Americans. Ethnic differences in the religious behavior of those born in Israel have narrowed considerably (Goldscheider and Friedlander, 1983).

The ethnic convergence in religiosity must be appreciated against the traditional religious background of most of the immigrants from Asian and African countries. Exposure to Israeli society has eroded religious identification and observance. The foreign-born, least exposed to Israel, are the most traditionally religious, followed by those more directly involved in Israeli society and by the Israeli-born. The low level of religious identification and observance characteristic of Jews from European origins tends to be the model toward which the society as a whole is moving. Paradoxically, even in the total Jewish society of Israel, modernization leads to secularization.

At the same time, significant proportions of Israeli Jewish society maintain high levels of religiosity. Schools, neighborhoods, political parties, youth movements, and other institutions are sources of religious cohesion. Hence, there is no clear relationship between level of education and religiosity patterns. While the least educated have the highest levels of religiosity, systematic declines in religiosity with higher levels of education have not been observed. Thus, polarization between the religious and secular segments relates to this pattern. Over the last several decades, the proportion of religious has declined and the proportion of secular has increased. The evidence shows that among recently married Israeli-born, and among the more educated, there is a greater concentration at the extremes of religiosity.

The evidence suggests further that the ethnic factor in religiosity will diminish in the future. At the same time, religious-secular divisions will become sharper. Political conflicts over settlements in areas captured in the Six Day War exemplify the overlap of political and religious conflict. We can expect social and political issues associated with religiosity to become more pronounced and divisive.

Mass Politics

Ethnic, religious, and class divisions characterize mass politics in Israel. No one social division provides the dominant political cleavage. The Labor movement's self-image as the leader of the working class and nation did not produce a class-based politics. The presence of religious parties and secular parties has not tilted the axis of political cleavage along religious lines. Major parties have not politicized the ethnic divisions. Neither class, nor religious observance, nor ethnicity has carved out widespread and persistent political divisions within the Jewish population. At the same time, no pattern of reinforcing cleavages, whereby religious observance and class or ethnicity and class come together, or some other combination, has emerged. The social heterogeneity finds its reflection in a kaleidoscope of political division (Seliktar, 1978; see also Elazar, 1979).

The recurring patterns in Israeli political divisions have not become hardened formations. Large portions of the most religiously observant vote for the religious parties. Older and veteran immigrants from Europe vote heavily for the Labor party. Children of immigrants from Asia and Africa favor the *Likud*. However, nearly twice as many Israelis are religiously observant than vote for the religious parties. The children of veteran Ashkenazi immigrants are not as loyal to Labor as are their parents. Many from Asia-Africa have retained their ties to the Labor party and the National Religious party that helped them in the settlement process. Broad outlines of political cleavages are present, but so are much electoral change by individuals and groups of voters (Arian, 1973, 1977, 1979, 1981; Seliktar, 1978; Etzioni-Halevy, 1977).

The themes of social and political heterogeneity emerge when we examine the political fortunes of the Labor and Likud parties. Labor's dominance was based neither on one social group, whether working class, secular, or European, nor a combination of these groups. Rather, their electoral support came from across the social divisions. The rise of the Likud from the mid-1960s has been closely tied to its strength among Asian-Africans and their relative growth within the population (Akzin, 1979; Lissak, 1972; Arian, 1977, 1979, 1981). As they expanded in the electorate, so did the vote for the Likud. Labor's fall from power in 1977 resulted only partially from the shifting sizes of different ethnic cleavages. The growth in the Likud vote was not substantial enough to force Labor out of power. What was crucial was the presence of the Democratic Movement for Change, which drew votes from Labor voters.

The dominance and decline of Labor had much to do with purely political factors (Shapiro, 1980a, 1980b; Aronoff, 1979). The inability to expand the top levels of party leaders was a key determinant. Similarly, political factors help account for the Likud's successes. The entry into the governing coalition during and after the Six Day War legitimized the party's right to govern. The merger of several parties into the Likud funneled votes together, adding political strength to the combined electoral size. The Labor Party, whose dominance rested on a powerful political machine, fell through organizational decay and the erosions of changing social formations. Ethnic, religious, and demographic factors alone or in combination do not account for the political changes.

The political parties structure the conflicts present within Israeli society. They have not cast their electoral and organizational appeals to particular ethnic or social class divisions. Hence, these social cleavages have not formed political cleavages, and political conflict within Israel is not at maximum levels. At the same time, they have fostered and deepened divisions within the Jewish communities. Party loyalties and ideological beliefs have carved new crevices. Riots, strikes, demonstrations, and protests as well as different voting choices have emerged out of the political and social divisions of Israel.

Emerging in Israel in the 1980s are social patterns and processes that are similar to other developing small countries dependent on large, powerful nations for socioeconomic resources and political support. Yet, there are other patterns that reflect the Jewish condition in recent history and relationships between Israeli and non-Israeli Jews. And still other patterns in Israel can be understood only in the light of Israel's particular history and evolution as a society—internal conditions related to its own development and to its role in Middle East politics.

Undoubtedly we can expect continued modernization, technological innovation, and westernization in Israel. We can also expect conflict, uneven development, greater international dependency, and internal turmoil. The normal society, secular Zionism's dream, is emerging. In its reality Israel confronts a complex set of problems that have few solutions but enormous ramifications and consequences.

The basis of Jewish cohesion remains strong in the continuing boundaries between Jews and Arabs and the connections between Israeli Jews and Jews in the Diaspora. The political, economic, cultural, and social control exercised by Jews over other Jews refocuses issues of Jewish continuity along new dimensions. These revolve around international politics and economic dependencies; they relate in a fundamental way to the internal Jewish conflicts along ethnic, religious, and social class lines. The bases of Jewish cohesion are manifold; so too are the bases of conflict within the Jewish community of Israel.

Part VI: Conclusion

We have followed a primarily inductive mode of analysis. Rather than specifying theoretically derived hypotheses at the outset and then testing them, we posed questions and set out a general approach to the analysis of the cohesion of Jewish communities during modernization. Our descriptions have been closely tied to theoretical issues. Hence, this conclusion serves to elaborate our general findings.

14 · The Bases of Ethnic Cohesion: Jewish Societies in Modernity

Nahman's windstorm transformed the configuration of world Jewry. It uprooted and destroyed. Yet, in its wake, communities grew in new places, often stronger and more cohesive than those they replaced. Standing in the center of the windstorm, many lamented the end of the old, fearing the coming of the new. As new communities emerged and expanded, it became clear that new sources of Jewish continuity were developing.

To understand this transformation, we have disentangled the elements of modernization, historically and comparatively. The growth, economic expansion, and social development of American Jewry and Israeli society, as well as the modernization and destruction of European Jewish communities, were not simple outcomes of random events. A focus on particular Jewish values, ideologies, or anti-Semitism does not provide an adequate framework for understanding the cataclysmic events of the last centuries. We have argued for the systematic analysis of the structural dimensions of modernization—economic mobility, occupational concentration, residential clustering, urbanization, population, and political changes. These patterns shaped the responses of Jews and non-Jews to each other and to the broader society. Changes in the tempo and timing of modernization and their effects on the Jews in different places over time reflected as well the size of the Jewish community, the strength of its institutions, and the political constraints imposed from outside.

We have found no support for those theories that associate modernization and ethnic assimilation. The Holocaust and Soviet terror, not educational opportunities, social mobility, urbanization, and secularization erased the Jewish communities of Europe. Neither political devastation nor assimilation awaits Diaspora Jews. Jewish communities changed but did not dissolve during modernization.

The primary theoretical question of our analysis examines variations in the cohesion of Jewish communities. Cohesion refers not to a state of mind but to the tendency for members of a group to interact peacefully with each other. We have found a pattern of variable but generally high levels of cohesion among Jewish communities during the last two centuries. The relative speed and thoroughness of changes in the elements of moderniza-tion join with the size and institutional resources of a community to affect its cohesion. At the same time, because patterns of change are powerfully affected by existing structures, levels of communal cohesion are closely tied to previous levels. More complete data will enable scholars to make more precise numerical calculations of cohesion. Until then, we must be content with general comparisons, knowing that the theoretical path has been cleared.

THE TWO MODEL JEWISH COMMUNITIES IN THE CONTEMPORARY WORLD: ISRAEL AND AMERICAN JEWRY

There are two paradigmatic Jewish communities, since the destruction of European Jewry: in Israel, and in America. Both are large and have many bases of cohesion. Levels of population growth are higher in Israel. Jews are a political and demographic majority there, with essentially no marriages with non-Jews. In contrast, intermarriage rates are relatively high in the United States, challenging the demographic continuity of American Jews. The effects of economic development have been thorough and intense in the United States. Social class homogeneity—educational, occupational, and life-style similarities—among American Jews represent an important source of cohesion. Class, ethnic, and political conflicts are absent. In contrast, these cleavages divide the Jews of Israel. In America, sources of cohesion coexist with those that pull Jews out of the community. The total society of Jews in Israel has maximum sources of Jewish interaction and maximum sources of internal conflict as well. They are model Jewish communities because they contain most of world Jewry and, more important, because they exemplify alternative patterns of Jewish transformation in moderniza-tion.

The contemporary American Jewish community is characterized by high levels of modernity and very large size. There are no political restraints or ideological imperatives preventing total assimilation. Yet, there are clear indications of Jewish cohesion in America. Residential clustering and family cohesion remain high among Jews in cities and metropolitan areas. The high rates of migration among young and older Jews do not necessarily obliterate ties to communities of origin or destination. New communities have sprouted and older ones have been invigorated by these migrations. The occupational and educational concentrations of Jews have crystallized and have become their most conspicuous feature. As specific jobs and educa-tional levels of Jews have altered over time, processes of occupational and educational reconcentration have taken place.

High educational levels and white-collar occupations, for Jewish men and women, imply more than "integration." Similar jobs, self-employment, and life-styles implied by social class homogeneity bond Jews to each other, linking at least two generations. They are powerful and fundamental bases of American Jewish cohesion. Family ties and generational bonds strengthen these links of Jewish life in an open, pluralistic society.

The large community of American Jews has maintained its demographic and social continuity in the face of relatively high levels of intermarriage. Many intermarried Jews take part in Jewish communal life. Many, if not most, have Jewish friends and family connections. Most retain residential, occupational, and educational bonds with other Jews. Many non-Jews married to Jews develop bases of communal contacts and are part of the Jewish community. Intermarriage, therefore, is not equivalent to assimilation nor does it automatically lead to communal dissolution. On both quantitative and qualitative grounds, the intermarriage patterns of American Jews cannot be linked with the end of the American Jewish community. Those who leave the community through intermarriage are the most marginal to it. As such, community cohesion is weakly affected by their out-marriages.

The religious behavior of American Jews has changed, and specific ritual observances have declined. Nevertheless, new religious institutions have been established, new rituals have been emphasized, and new ways of expressing Jewishness have emerged. The institutional framework of the organized community has expanded in breadth and depth, offering an enormous range of options for Jewish interaction with other Jews. It is difficult to assess the quality of these expressions of religious and secular Jewish activities. Nonetheless, it should be emphasized that these activities are important bases of cohesion within the community. To refer to Reform Jewish identification, some synagogue attendance, selected ritual observances, some Jewish education, cultural, ethnic, and institutional ties as assimilation is to miss the complexities of Jewish life in an open, pluralistic society.

Most important, to focus exclusively on religious issues ignores other bases of communal cohesion. Most Jews who are not formally involved in religious organizations engage in other Jewish activities that tie them to other Jews. Even for Jews who do not actively seek to be Jews, their ties, networks, and connections to other Jews through family, friends, neighbors, jobs, schools, and leisure activities are important sources of Jewish communal strength. The absence of formal synagogue membership and organizational participation at various points in the life cycle are not necessarily indicators of the weakening of Jewish cohesion. Similarly, external rejection and exclusion are not the main sources of Jewish continuity. Anti-Semitism in America does not make Jews Jewish any more than Arab anti-Zionism is the source of cohesion among Israeli Jews. The structure of American Jewry maintains a relatively high level of communal cohesion.

The bases of cohesion among American Jews are not only internal. There are ties to Jews in other countries as the influx of immigration to the United States continues. Bonds of political association, kinship, and identification characterize the complex interchanges between Israel and American Jews. Israeli Jews in America and American Jews in Israel reinforce other links— economic, political, social, and cultural—between these communities.

The relatively high levels of cohesion in the contemporary American Jewish community derive in part from the cohesive immigrant community of an earlier generation. Mass immigration from Eastern Europe brought large numbers of Jews to the United States at the end of the nineteenth century. They did not represent a cross-section of their communities of origin but were selective on economic and religious characteristics. Their class background, occupational skills, family status, educational level, and permanent immigration gave them particular advantages over non-Jewish immigrants. Jews were economically and geographically mobile. Nevertheless, for the first two generations there were clear residential, economic, occupational, and linguistic bases of Jewish cohesion. Despite signs of occupational dispersal, linguistic and residential changes, and increasing educational levels, powerful sources of communal cohesion remained.

Very high levels of occupational concentration and increases in educational attainment were interrelated. Accessibility of public schools in urban areas, permanence of migration, nonavailability of Jewish educational institutions, and the high proportion and number of children among immigrants made for high levels of educational enrollment. Even in schools, Jews interacted with other Jews. New neighborhoods, jobs, and social networks developed among Jews. As new organizations—religious, fraternal, unions, defense—spread, new forms of Jewish cohesion emerged. In the American Jewish community of the early twentieth century, there was an overlap of residential, occupational, and ethnic status as high as anywhere in urban Europe. The free and open political structure, diversified economy, and liberal pluralist ideology changed but did not eliminate the multiple bases of Jewish cohesion.

Contemporary Israeli society is characterized by maximum sources of Jewish cohesion. There is a thorough overlap among the various statuses Jews occupy; Jewish interaction with other Jews is dominant, and the boundaries between Jews and non-Jews are clearly defined and difficult to cross.

At the same time, there are a variety of bases of conflict among Jews. Political, social class, ethnic origin, and religiosity levels are the primary cleavages within the Jewish society of Israel. These divisions do not appear to be temporary or simple outcomes of the timing of immigration and the background characteristics of immigrants. While there have been major changes in Israeli society over the last several decades and some convergences among groups from very dissimilar origins, the class-ethnic overlap remains. Over time, ethnic divisions have been reinforced by residence, education, and occupational patterns. As competition over jobs, housing, education, and other resources in the society emerged, ethnic networks have sharpened.

There is no clear overlap among ethnic, class, and political divisions in Israel. Hence, Israel has been spared this most divisive form of political cleavage. Rather, variously crisscrossing and overlapping differences over domestic and foreign policies, party loyalty, and views of government leaders interact with economic, religious, and ethnic divisions.

There has been a decline in levels of religiosity among Israeli Jews, similar to what has occurred among American Jewry. In both cases, these trends are best interpreted as results of the growth of new and competing institutions and declines in the ability of religious institutions to enforce conformity with the halacha. Religious polarization has been sharper in Israel, since it is linked directly to political and economic interests. Political parties compete to defend their visions of Judaism and press their demands on each other and on nonreligious Jews through government policy. Religious organizations compete to control government resources, further sharpening religious divisions in Israel. Levels of personal religiosity are indirectly tied to religious cleavages within Israeli Jewry.

The same internal structures that unite Diaspora Jewish communities divide the Jews of Israel. In Israel, there is no doubt that Jews interact almost exclusively with each other. At the same time, patterns of occupational concentration, residential clustering, educational divisions, political differences, and religious polarization provide bases of internal conflict. External ties to Jewries in the Diaspora strengthen cohesion within Israel as they do other Jewries. Unlike the latter, however, Israel's survival as a Jewish community depends on the outcome of relations with non-Jews. Military threats make Israel depend on the political, economic, and military support of the American government. The survival of American Jewry does not rest so much on policies of particular American administrations.

TYPES OF JEWISH COMMUNITIES

The two contrasting models of Jewish communities in the contemporary period partially derive from and may be compared with the Jewish communities of Europe. How different are these contemporary models of Jewish communities in American and Israel from the premodern ones? Are the multiple bases of cohesion in contemporary Israel similar to the overlapping statuses of the shtetl? Do American Jews resemble their European forebearers? How similar were pre-Nazi German Jewry and German Jews in America at the end of the nineteenth century? Are patterns of assimilation among Western European Jews comparable to Jews in contemporary America? More generally, how do we account for differences and similarities in the social, economic, political, and cultural patterns of Jewish communities?

The Premodern Jewish Community

The premodern world of European Jewry was heterogeneous, reflecting the variety of places and conditions under which Jews lived. Yet within this diversity commonalities may be located. Hence, our analysis has been directed to identifying the set of conditions which resulted in high levels of Jewish cohesion and clarifying the sources of subsequent modernization.

The primacy of religious norms is the most conspicuous feature of premodern Jewish society. These norms, however, were outcomes as well as sources of cohesion. The religious structure legitimated the existing social patterns. The primary sources of cohesion rested elsewhere.

The keys to community cohesion are the patterns and intensity of interaction. In turn, these depended on the social, political, religious, educational, and occupational contacts among Jews and between Jews and non-Jews. The outstanding feature of premodern Jewish society was the overlap of statuses—residence, class, family, ethnic, and political—into a web of interrelationships which linked Jews to each other. These structural bonds were reinforced by the smallness of the community and political constraints.

Where the size of the Jewish community was small, there were direct pressures on conformity and controls over behavior. The larger was the community, the greater was the space for deviance. Jewish cohesion in the premodern world tended to be curvilinear with size. Ideological constraints operated through the formal and informal control exercised by the kehillah. Hence, they worked best in communities large enough to provide a plethora of Jewish services and small enough to preclude Jews obtaining economic and other resources outside their community.

Voluntary consensus and harmony were neither necessary nor sufficient to ensure the cohesion of premodern Jewish communities. The political status of Jews provided for few if any options outside their politically defined kehillah. Moreover, the economic opportunities for individuals and groups were linked to the community's political status: the more powerful the local authorities, the greater the occupational restrictions on Jews, and the more powerful the extralocal authorities, the greater the economic opportunities for Jews. Where the organized kehillah was strong, economic competition among Jews was further regulated. Hence, variation in occupational concentrations among Jewish communities was not the consequence of the strength of Jewish values or the degree of internal consensus.

The nostalgic image of premodern Jewish life in small, supportive communities must be balanced by recognizing the extent and depths of poverty, economic inequalities between a small Jewish elite and most everyone else in the community, and the political controls exercised by non-Jews and powerful Jews over the behavior of community members. Social pressure, the outcome of overlapping statuses and size, and political constraints, external and internal, were the major sources of communal consensus.

In most communities only the economic elite, and only small numbers of persons, could deviate from the norms of communal life. They alone had powerful ties to non-Jews and controlled the distribution of rewards within the Jewish community. As the link between the Jewish masses and the political authorities, they held powerful positions within the Jewish and often the non-Jewish communties as well. To generalize from these elites to the community as a whole is to emphasize the exceptional and the deviant.

Religious behavior and political status were the conspicuous differences between premodern Jewish and non-Jewish communities. Residential, occupational, and communal patterns structured these differences and their changes during modernization. These, rather than the Jews' "modern values," "capitalistic mentality," or ideological commitments account for their responses to modernization.

In a fundamental sense, premodern Jewry and contemporary Israeli society are similar. In both, the bases of Jewish cohesion are many, the overlap among statuses is considerable, and the probability of Jewish continuity very high. The politically imposed economic dependency characteristic of premodern Jewries parallels the economic and political dependencies of Israel on Western nations, particularly the United States. The threat to continuity comes from the outside. The political units differ; the processes are analogous.

Yet, the conspicuous differences are equally significant. First, the political status of Jews in premodern Europe was externally determined. Jews were a minority group with little power and no control. In Israel, Jews are a political majority, with power and control to regulate their society. Second, there are institutionalized divisions within the Jewish community of Israel which foster conflict along class, ethnic, and religious lines. The internal structure of the premodern community was more homogeneous. Indeed, internal divisions emerged as a result of modernization processes. Third, economic development has led to increasingly higher levels of living in Israel and has generated diverse economic opportunities. The depths of poverty of the premodern world, with large numbers of people living on the precipice of sickness and death, have been eliminated in Israel.

There are few similarities between the American and premodern Jewish communities. The extraordinary differences in their political, social, and economic worlds as well as their internal structures overwhelm the parallels of continued ethnic minority status. In part, this argues that the location of differences in level of communal cohesion does not imply a linear path to the assimilation of American Jewry. Circumstances differ as do the structural bases of cohesion. As a result, the premodern and American Jewish communities have different levels of cohesion.

THE EFFECTS OF ECONOMIC TRANSFORMATIONS ON JEWISH COMMUNITIES IN EUROPE

The growth of European capitalist industrial society changed the economic and political status of Jews, while altering the total overlap of statuses which defined the premodern order. Jews moved from being artisans and small businessmen to skilled workers in small industries and managers and to white-collar professionals. The long-term outcome fits the argument that Jews valued occupational achievement, social mobility, and economic independence. It is, therefore, frequently postulated that the "Jewish Ethic" produced capitalism, if not for everyone then at least for the Jews themselves. Systematic comparisons between Jews and non-Jews and variations among Jews in different countries and in various communities specify the direction of the causal connection between ideological factors and economic modernization.

The determinants of the economic transformation of the Jews were structural and locational, with their social class and occupational background and the general patterns of economic development of particular importance. Where economic opportunities expanded in sectors of the economy containing many Jews, they were occupationally mobile. Overall economic growth did not in and of itself determine the pattern of Jewish economic expansion. The growth of heavy industry, for example, did not directly affect the Jews. The increased demand for manufactured goods, particularly textiles, had a major impact. Similarly, when economic growth occurred in areas where Jews resided or where they could migrate, occupational mobility was rapid. As the old political order and the kehillah dissolved, Jews moved to new places. Patterns of economic dispersal and geographic movement were, therefore, not random. Over time, they resulted in new economic and residential concentrations. To place these changes solely in the context of occupational assimilation is clearly inadequate.

In Western Europe, the first stages of industrial development resulted in great economic expansion. No government policies restricted Jewish mobility. Indeed, the major conflict generated by economic expansion was within the Jewish community. Social class as well as generational and family gaps developed as a result of economic and residential changes. Similarly, economic and political differences between Jews in the West and East Europe were sharpened, since modernization occurred first in the West. However, these differences were not simply a product of the earlier timing of economic expansion in the West. The pace of economic growth and the place of Jews within the economic structure of the different societies were of paramount importance. In Western Europe, modernization resulted in the rapid social mobility of Jews and their increasing wealth. In contrast, in the initial stages of modernization in Russia, poverty and underemployment appeared.

The slow pace and low level of economic expansion coupled with a large and growing Jewish population created a set of economic-demographic conditions in Eastern Europe different from the West. Few economic opportunties emerged and competition between Jews and non-Jews and among Jews intensified. Many Jews sought opportunities elsewhere, and millions migrated westward—mainly overseas. The great migrations of East European Jews reflected the combination of general economic conditions, population pressures, and the location of Jews within local societies, as well as the pull of American industrial development. Political factors (pogroms, political anti-Semitism, and specific revolutionary activities) account for fluctuations in the timing and pace, not the origins or determinants, of the migration. Most Jews in Eastern Europe stayed in their country of origin, moving at times to new cities where more economic opportunities could be found.

Differences between East and West European Jewry reflect, therefore, a complex set of structural conditions—demographic, economic, and residential. Jewish values and preferences play a minor rule in explaining the differences. Initial levels of economic modernization, the intensity of change, and the structural characteristics of Jews account for most of the differences.

In Western Europe, economic expansion occurred in large cities, absorbing Jewish population growth and internal migration. As a result, few Jews moved overseas, and those that did came from particular regions. In the later stages of economic growth in the West, Jewish occupational patterns resembled those of other city dwellers. Most of the declining economic exceptionalism of Jews reflected the entry of large numbers of non-Jews into spheres theretofore containing many Jews, not declines in the number of Jews in those areas. The broad occupational convergences mask concentrations. Self-employment, especially among Jewish professionals, merchants, and businessmen in Western Europe remained high. Even where the number of Jews was relatively small and economic growth rapid and intense, Jews were occupationally concentrated. No class conflicts emerged in the communities populated mostly by professionals and businessmen. Hence, economic expansion led to the reconcentration of Jews in particular spheres of work and business and promoted high levels of peaceful interaction among them.

In the well-established and large Jewish communities of Eastern Europe, where the overlap of residence, economic activity, education, and religion was great, economic exceptionalism and concentration remained. Here, Jewish economic patterns differed in both class level and in specific jobs from non-Jews. Part of these patterns reflected the urban residential patterns of Jews and the large number of farmers among non-Jews. When only city dwellers are examined, class differences between Jews and non-Jews even in the East narrow considerably.

The range in Jewish community size among places in Eastern Europe, the uneven development over regions, the presence of Jewish workers and capitalists, the differential opportunity structure, and the slow pace of economic growth resulted in great inequalities among Jewish communities in the East when compared to the West.

THE EFFECTS OF RESIDENTIAL AND EDUCATIONAL TRANSFORMATIONS ON JEWISH COMMUNITIES IN EUROPE

Urbanization and educational advancement accompanied the economic transformations. Differences in the pace and level of these elements of modernization appeared across Europe, in ways that were closely associated with the variations in patterns of economic expansion. In turn, forms of urbanization and educational advancement affected the cohesion of Jewish communities.

In Western Europe, most Jews moved to the largest metropolitan centers. The urban level among Jews was higher than among non-Jews, but closer to non-Jews in their society of residence than to Jews in Eastern Europe. The flow of population movement drew large numbers of Jews into new urban communities, where only small numbers of Jews had lived previously and where Jewish institutions had to be built. There they developed new communal and religious organizations, carved out Jewish neighborhoods, providing new bases of Jewish cohesion. At the same time, communal and family control declined in these cities and Jews interacted more frequently with non-Jews. Urbanization per se did not result in the assimilation of the Jews of Western Europe.

In the East, as in the West, the picture of Jewish urbanization resembled the general form among city dwellers of the particular countries. The urban pattern of Jews in Poland paralleled that of non-Jewish Poland more than the urban distribution of German Jews. In Eastern Europe, Jews frequently moved to cities with relatively large and well-institutionalized communities as well as new cities and metropolises. Variations in communal cohesion followed these flows. The larger and the newer was the community, the lower was the strength of communal and family control and the greater was the likelihood that interaction with non-Jews was high. Even in the largest cities of Eastern Europe, new forms of concentration appeared. Links of language, residence, religion, occupation, and schooling were present. Transformation, not assimilation, occurred.

There are striking parallels in the processes and effects of urbanization on the Jewish communities of Europe. Relatively young and extraordinarily large centers of concentration like Berlin, Vienna, Budapest, and Odessa resembled each other, as did village Jews across the continent, and the Jews of medium-sized cities of ancient vintage like Vilna, Brody, Minsk, and Pinsk. The analytic factors of size and strength of communal institutions, not geographic location or cultural area, determined the differences across the continent.

The migration of Jews out of small cohesive Jewish communities to cities where there were few and poorly established institutions is frequently viewed as evidence of the modernization-assimilation connection. Such an interpretation is superficial. It is a static view of processes of urbanization and transformation. Jews, as others, moved in well-defined streams with family, friends, and neighbors helping them move out and assisting the integration in the new area. Chain migration characterized Jewish urbanization patterns as it does other people. Over time, these networks generated further migration from specific places of origin to particular locations within places of destination. They also enhanced the development of new communal institutions in the new areas. As the size, stability, wealth, and needs of the new Jewish communities increased so did their institutions. In turn, these developed new bonds of kinship and ethnicity and reinforced older networks. Hence, instead of simply eroding institutional strength, modernization processes have reshaped and strengthened levels of Jewish cohesion.

The educational transformation of Jews was no less impressive than the occupational changes. Indeed, the two processes were intertwined. Steady, good jobs resulted in improvement in economic levels and the income necessary to afford the costs of schooling. There developed less need for the income of children to sustain the household, and there were occupational payoffs to educational attainment. Getting an education often became a necessary condition for obtaining a better job.

In the initial stages of modernization, educational changes widened the gap between Jews and non-Jews and among Jews. As with occupation, the West-East European educational gap increased in relation to the time, pace, and level of educational attainment.

In Western Europe, high levels of education characterized Jews when compared to non-Jews even within social class and urban categories. Yet, most of the educational gap can be accounted for by class and residential concentrations and does not simply reflect a cultural emphasis on "learning" among Jews.

Changes in educational attainment did not imply the assimilation of Western European Jews. Jews concentrated within particular schools. In some cases in the West, there was a concomitant decrease of Jews in Jewish schools; in others, Jewish schools attempted to integrate Jews into the broader society. Whether Jews attended "modern" Jewish schools or public schools, they interacted with each other more than with non-Jews. As a result, new bases of cohesion formed as educational levels increased. In older and more established Jewish communities there were smaller numbers of Jewish children in non-Jewish schools, while in newer areas of Jewish concentration Jews attended non-Jewish schools. Hence, variation in the presence of Jews in non-Jewish schools also reflected broader community features associated with the strength of Jewish communal institutions. They were not determined by preferences per se. On the other hand, attending public schools provided a basis of Jewish cohesion as Jews clustered there as well. In the West, high levels of educational attainment provided new loci for intense and nonconflictual interaction among Jewish students and long-term similarities in occupation and residence among most members of the community.

In Eastern Europe the greater proportion of poor and working-class Jews combined with the greater availability of new and traditional Jewish schools to provide a rather different pattern of educational attainment. Nowhere were Jews more likely than other city dwellers to be in gymnasia and universities. In places with well-established institutions and a large Jewish working class, they were less likely than others to be in public schools and institutions of higher learning. Where there were few occupational incentives to obtain a secular education, the proportion of Jews in school was low.

Cross-national variations in the educational levels of Jews relate, therefore, to two major factors: the social class structure of the community, and the availability of schools. Differences in the value placed on education do not account for the variation. Nor did the increase in the level of education, when it occurred, necessarily imply assimilation.

Sources of Religious Transformation in European Jewish Communities

Declines in levels of personal religiosity and the emergence of new religious ideologies, synagogues, and modes of worship appeared during the modernization of the Jewish communities. These should not be subsumed under the general process of secularization. Rather, declines in observance of the halacha reflected the extent to which religious conformity had previously rested on the tight-knit nature of premodern institutions. Declines were most evident in new and poorly organized Jewish communities in metropolises. They were least evident in small cities with long-established Jewish communities. As new fraternal, economic, and political organizations appeared, they competed with the religious institutions for the time and loyalties of Jews. Most proclaimed the impossibility of being religious and modern at the same time, thereby legitimating religious declines, while strengthening communal loyalties. In the absence of direct benefits of halachic observance and direct costs of religious violations, conformity with religious norms requires the kind of intense commitment that few have. In the United States and Israel today, most of those who live by the precepts of the halacha are surrounded by others who do so as well and who raise the benefits of observance and the costs of violation. Variations in level of observance reflect community size, levels and types of institutions, and the availability of Jewish and other organizations. Structural factors condition choices of personal life-style.

Hence, changes in religious services, when they first appeared in Europe, did not derive from the demands of Jewish masses seeking new ways of praying. They were products of government policies and lay leaders fostering linguistic and cultural integration and the wishes of a small number of rabbis. Government action provided the necessary key to these changes. In France, the policy was national and, hence, uniformly applied. In Germany, state governments fostered and hindered religious reform. Where they led the forces of general modernization, they encouraged German sermons, choirs, orderly services, and uniform clerical garb. To effect these changes, they had only to find Jews able to preach in German. Where the state government opposed change, religious reform did not occur. Where governments had no policies, the determination of whether a Jewish community became Reform rested with the lay leaders and the local rabbi. Political maneuvering and government policy led the forces that transformed the mode of worship.

In time, the government played a smaller role; institutional religious change derived from conflict and competition among Jews. The conflicts were couched in the language of ideology, but the issue was who controlled the Jewish community. One consequence of this competition was ideological development.

The new religious ideologies were first shaped in the German universities. In France, Jews studying in universities could pursue academic careers in institutions of higher education. For German Jewish intellectuals the choices were to enter commercial careers (that is, give up intellectual pursuits), emigrate (that is, pursue scholarly activities in other countries), convert to Christianity and thereby be eligible to teach in the universities, or work in the institutions of the Jewish community. The last meant retaining family ties, Judaism, and philosophical commitments. No other choice allowed all three. Many German Jewish intellectuals returned to the Jewish community, teaching in schools and in religious institutions. They emphasized the use of German, especially where language assimilation was a high priority. In turn, they fostered the development of new Jewish institutions more in harmony with their intellectual and political orientations. In France, the Jewish intellectuals remained in the world of lycées and universities. Hence, ideological change appeared in the Jewish community of Germany and not in France.

There was but a weak connection between the new ideologies and the
religious beliefs and practices of most Jews. Religious ideologies are elite
responses. They are not guides to the behavior of the masses. There is also
no correlation between economic expansion and the growth of Reform
temples or the presence of a Reform rabbi. Nor did the type of synagogue
vary with the size of Jewish communities. Political factors drove the forces of
religious transformation.

It is paradoxical that, as personal religious observances declined, religious
institutions expanded and ideologies developed to address the changed level
of religiosity. The image of a distinct community of Jews is sustained, not
created, by religious institutions and ideologies. The new belief systems,
changed personal observances, and new forms of Jewish public worship
were all responses to political and social modernization. Eventually they
became one of a series of alternative forms of being Jewish and of interaction within the Jewish community.

Changes in Patterns of Friendship and Marriage in European Jewish Communities

Bonds of family, marriage, and friendship underpin ethnic communities.
They link members of the community together in emotionally positive and
not conflictual associations. There is much evidence that Jews have usually
chosen marriage partners and friends from among the Jewish community.
Recent increases in out-marriages in the United States and other Diaspora
communities, however, have served to question this finding. In turn, they
have led some to suppose that intermarriage leads to ethnic assimilation.

In enclosed Jewish communities, like the shtetl and Israel, very low rates
of intermarriage between Jews and non-Jews prevail. Contacts between
communities in these settings are asymmetrical. As such, there is little
incentive to marry out and great pressure to remain within the community.
Marriages from without such communities that occur between Jews and
others do not threaten the cohesiveness of the enclosed Jewish community.

What affects intermarriage rates in open Jewish communities, where
contacts between Jews and non-Jews are relatively symmetrical? Before
World War II, only in Western Europe was the level of intermarriages
relatively high. But even these intermarriage rates did not imply the erosion
of the Jewish community. Increases in intermarriage occurred in Western
Europe, particularly where Jewish communities were small. In Germany,
for example, around 20–25 percent of Jews married non-Jews, and smaller
numbers of Jews were involved in the decade prior to 1933, when new
restrictive laws on marriage were enacted. Other forms of cohesion among
Jews included residential, social class, friendship, and institutional sources.
Hence, it is an error to view these marriage patterns as indicators of a
necessary linear pattern tied to total assimilation and the self-destruction of

the community. Those that intermarried were on the margins of the community, and many did assimilate. Nevertheless, the community remained as a community, with most Jews marrying other Jews.

In the post-Holocaust Jewish communities of Europe and America, intermarriage rates have increased. Where Jewish communities are small and institutions weak, contacts between Jews and non-Jews are high. Many of the intermarried have been swallowed up in the larger society. There are theoretical and empirical grounds for arguing as we have earlier that intermarriage does not necessarily equal assimilation. In the larger Jewish metropolitan areas of the United States, the level of intermarriage is only weakly associated with demographic decline. While it is clear that some Jews have weak ties and are lost to the community, the community itself is not weakened directly by intermarriage. The relationship between modernization and intermarriage is therefore much more complex than simple extrapolations from intermarriage to assimilation.

THE EFFECTS OF POLITICAL COMPETITION AND CONFLICT ON THE JEWISH COMMUNITIES OF EUROPE

What role did anti-Semitism play in blocking or shaping economic and educational opportunities? We have examined political anti-Semitism, the claims of organized political movements and government policies against Jews. Mass attitudes towards Jews, per se, did not play a direct role in the rise and fall of anti-Semitic political movements and of government policy toward the Jews. The extent of economic growth and competition between Jews and non-Jews was a major key to political anti-Semitism. No government policy blocked Jewish economic or educational opportunities in periods of rapid economic expansion and where there were many places in universities. Where economies declined and where Jews and non-Jews competed in the same sphere, the relatively small numbers of Jews tempted politicians to appeal for the support of their competitors.

Political parties used anti-Jewish appeals to attract those in vulnerable economic positions in direct competition with Jews. Traders, merchants, and peasants in small towns were prime targets for these appeals. The more parties that competed for votes, the more elaborate were the political claims against the Jews. Competitive interaction among political parties extended political anti-Semitism across the political spectrum. On the other hand, declines in both competition and organizational response to political parties attacking Jews resulted in the decline of political anti-Semitism.

Our comparative analysis of variation and change in political anti-Semitism reveals the centrality of Jewish–non-Jewish competition. As Polish Jews competed with Poles for limited economic opportunities, political anti-Semitism increased. In Hungary before World War I, when there were few economic competitors to Jews and the Magyars needed Jewish political support, no political anti-Semitism emerged. As the Jews and non-Jews competed over limited numbers of places in universities, educational discrimination appeared. Restrictions placed on the number of Jewish university students in Hungary, Russia, Germany, Poland, and selected universities in the United States at various times can be understood in this context. Anti-Semitic attitudes alone cannot account for variations and changes.

In the 1930s, there was a marked change in political anti-Semitism within Europe. Economic conflict was not the main source; political factors loomed larger. German pressure in Poland and Hungary resulted in greater political anti-Semitism there. In the 1920s none of this occurred in Germany. There were no anti-Semitic laws, no limits on economic activities, no direct competition between Jews and non-Jews. What then accounts for the rise of the Nazi party? It was not anti-Semitism per se but political factors, especially the Nazis' organizational abilities, economic declines, and Hitler's charisma. Even among Nazi activists there were political, not specifically anti-Jewish, motivations. Most did not join the Nazi party because they hated the Jews.

Increasing levels of politicization may also be seen in the formation of Jewish political movements. Jews as well as non-Jews struggled to control government authority, in order to resolve communal problems and to regulate their relations with other groups. The strategies used—the organizations formed and the ideologies espoused—reflected the political arenas in which they participated. Where liberal political movements predominated, Jewish groupings adopted the style and goal of political liberalism. Where revolutionaries grew, we find Jewish revolutionaries. Competitive pressures directly affected the Jewish political movements. Where it was intense—with many competing groups—organizations sprouted and ideologies unfolded. Where there was little competition, there was almost no ideological and organizational elaboration. Since Jewish groups did not directly compete with non-Jewish political movements, they developed no strategy against them but against other Jewish political movements. The formation and development of these political groups—the German Centralverein, the Bund, the various Zionist factions, as well as the others—conform closely to the ways other political movements formed across Europe.

The Jewish political organizations provided additional bases for Jewish interaction. As they competed with each other, they increased the cooperation of Jews within the movements and increased conflict within the Jewish community as a whole. Hence, in Eastern Europe, the plethora of Jewish political movements joined with class divisions to produce high levels of internal conflict. In Western Europe, the relative strength of the liberal movements and the relative weakness of class divisions produced almost no internal conflict.

In the liberal and authoritarian regimes of Europe, but not in the revolutionary regimes of Nazi Germany and the Stalinist Soviet Union, political movements were sharply constrained by social and economic structures. Nowhere did the anti-Semitic political movements fundamentally affect the cohesion and inner workings of the Jewish communities. None of the Jewish political movements successfully transformed their communities in line with their visions. Both maintained the visibility of Jews.

THE EFFECTS OF TOTALITARIAN REGIMES ON EUROPEAN JEWRY

Revolutionary regimes emerged during the processes of European modernization, not only pluralist democracies and authoritarian states. Nazi Germany and the Stalinist Soviet Union overwhelmed Europe. As they did so, they devastated the Jewish communities there. Not secularization, not assimilation, but political terror completed Nahman's windstorm.

We have not explained the rise of the Nazis and the Bolsheviks. Neither have we sought to explain their policies of devastation. Rather, we have examined the effects of their policies on the Jewish communities they ruled and the manner in which they destroyed European Jewry.

During the Holocaust, variations in the extent of Jewish death rates relate to the mode of Nazi rule and the strength of political anti-Semitism. The reactions of Jews did not affect the death rate of a community, even if it saved individual Jews. In general, the Jewish response to the Holocaust paralleled the behavior of most people to terror and natural disasters: few panicked, few radically altered their routines, most continued as they were. About 20 percent of the Jews emigrated and thereby escaped the Nazi terror; 5–7 percent took political or military actions in Jewish organizations. Variations in emigration reflected the extent of time available, the economic means, and the cohesiveness of the family and community. The longer was the warning time and the greater were the economic resources for escape, the higher were the rates of emigration. Family and community ties tended to reduce emigration; young persons without ties were most likely to escape. The Nazis controlled the life and death of the Jews.

Soviet anti-Jewish policies do not derive simply from Marxist ideology. Government policies have fluctuated in the Soviet Union. Two broad phases may be identified. Until 1928, Soviet government policy destroyed older Jewish institutions, replacing the traditional hederim and yeshivot with Marxist-Yiddish secular schools. Thus, along with the persistence of ethnic-occupational overlaps, government policies built new bases for Jewish cohesion. Under Stalin, all Jewish institutional bases were destroyed. The structural underpinnings of Jewish cohesion weakened as part of the broader social, economic, and political policies. Nevertheless, Jewish residential concentration and occupational exceptionalism persisted, even as they weakened.

The Holocaust destroyed many areas of the Soviet Union where Jewish populations were concentrated. Contemporary Soviet policy singles out Jews as a minority group, and there continues to be some overlap between occupational-residential-ethnic status. But there are very weak institutional bases of Jewish cohesion. Hence, despite the size of the contemporary Jewish population in Russia, the bases of cohesion are small in number and weak institutionally.

STRUCTURE AND VALUES AS SOURCES OF JEWISH TRANSFORMATION
Our analysis points directly to the power of structural factors over values, ideologies, and preferences as explanations of the patterns of communal change and levels of cohesion among Jewish communities. The prominence that ideas and values acquire from static descriptions fade when patterns are traced over time. The visibility of the writings of intellectuals hides their unimportance as determinants of most people's behavior. Our study is replete with examples that lead to this conclusion. Religious changes did not arise from alterations in mass beliefs, and they did not spread because of the popularity of the new ideas. The popularity of Zionism among the Jews of Eastern Europe led relatively few to immigrate to Israel. The opposition of religious and political leaders to immigration to America did not stem the flood of Jewish immigrants. The pushes and pulls of economic opportunity and government regulations are keys to the patterns of migration. Similarly, variations in the proportions of Jews in gymnasia, universities, hederim, and yeshivot may coincide with variations in levels of religiosity, but both are explained by variations in the class structure and the relative availability of different schools and religious and other institutions.

There is no doubt, however, that variations in the political and religious beliefs appear during modernization. Our evidence does not lead to the conclusion that Jews have no values or preferences, just as it does not suggest that they share a single set of principles and beliefs. Zionists and Bundists differed. Religious Zionists fought Socialist Zionists, as have liberals and Agudists, Reformers and Orthodox, Hasidim and Mitnagdim and a multitude of distinct ideological groupings. Our conclusions are more precise and powerful. For most Jews, most of the time, ideologies and beliefs justified decisions reached on other grounds. They did not determine individual decisions to migrate or remain, change or retain jobs, enter particular schools, organizations, or synagogues. Rather, occupational decisions were usually made with regard to skills and opportunities. One sends one's child to school when his or her income is not needed and when education is likely to benefit or at least not harm employment opportunities. Most Jews attended the closest synagogue or the one of their friends, workmates, or family. As the direct personal costs of religious laxity declined, so did levels of personal observance. These same factors operate at the community level as well. Hence, while ideological differences have been present, they have not been especially important determinants of individual behavior and community characteristics.

For most Jews most of the time, the constraints of economic position and opportunity, place of residence, educational skills, political limitations and rights, and tugs of family and friends have outweighed personal convictions. At a different level of analysis, these same factors structure the Jewish communities. Hence, many Jews who prefer not to be Jews may be bound tightly by occupational, residential, and other structural ties to the community. Conversely, many who want to be Jews may not do so in the absence of those ties. Where Jews share similar residences, schools, occupations, organizations, and friends their community has the highest level of cohesion, whether the individual Jews value or desire this interaction, whether they think each other apostates or reactionaries.

ETHNICITY AND MODERNIZATION

The comparative-historical analysis of the Jews provides insight into the relationships between modernization and Jewish transformations. The approach of social science has guided our analysis of Jews. In turn, the transformation of Jews teaches us about the general relationships between modernization and ethnic continuity.

Jews are an ideal-typical community for studying these processes. They are models, not exceptions; they and their communities are more appropriate units of analysis than nations or regions. Most important, Jews were located in a wide range of places within Europe. These experienced the initial thrusts and later developments associated with modernization. Within these societies, Jews were located in a variety of urban places and small towns and in a range of social class and political statuses. Over time, Jews established an independent nation state, one of many in the post–Second World War period. Their communities were also part of the industrial development of the first new nation—the United States. Jewish communities in Europe were destroyed and millions of Jews murdered during World War II. Indeed, the most exceptional feature of Jews has been their variable locations within places exposed to the process of modernization. Therefore, generalizations derived from the analysis of Jewish communities draw on a wide-ranging sample of conditions.

There would be no point in returning to our study to isolate hypotheses for the general analysis of ethnic cohesion during modernization. They are there, even if specifically phrased to focus on Jews. Our theoretical approach and method of analysis has not been devised to study only Jews. Indeed, the opposite is true. We have employed generally useful methods to analyze Jews. Hence, what we have isolated as accounting for Jewish continuity and cohesion should apply elsewhere as well.

Our analysis sets out the structural factors that underpin ethnic cohesion. We reject the view of ethnicity as solely a primordial or emotional loyalty. We see it as more than a derivative of social class ties and political interests. Indeed, ethnic groups are one form of social collectivity similar to those based on social class, religion, and politics. In all these cases, there must be enough members to maintain generational continuity. More important, the more spheres of activity in which the members interact peacefully, the stronger is group cohesion. The greater the conflicts over economic, educational, and residential resources, the lower is the level of cohesion. Ethnic ties may unite and split social class groupings, political movements, and religious institutions, just as the others affect the cohesion of ethnic groups. From this perspective, the social scientific analysis of Jews directs one to general processes.

References

Abramov, S. Zalman. 1976. *Perpetual Dilemma: Jewish Religion in the Jewish State*. Rutherford, N.J.: Farleigh Dickinson University Press.

Abramsky, C. 1970. "The Biro-Bidzhan Project, 1927–1959." In Kochan (ed.), pp. 62–75.

Adler, Cyrus (ed.). 1899. *American Jewish Yearbook: 5660*. Philadelphia: Jewish Publication Society.

Akzin, Benjamin. 1979. "The Likud." In Penniman (ed.), *Israel at the Polls*, pp. 91–114.

Albert, Phyllis Cohen. 1977. *The Modernization of French Jewry*. Hanover, N.H.: Brandeis University Press.

Allen, William Sheridan. 1965. *The Nazi Seizure of Power: The Experience of a Single German Town, 1930–1935*. Chicago: Quadrangle Books.

Alston, Patrick L. 1969. *Education and the State in Tsarist Russia*. Stanford: Stanford University Press.

Altmann, Alexander (ed.). 1964a. *Studies in Nineteenth-Century Jewish Intellectual History*. Cambridge: Harvard University Press.

———. 1964b. "The New Style of Preaching in Nineteenth Century German Jewry." In Altmann (ed.), *Studies*, pp. 65–116.

———. 1978. *Moses Mendelssohn: A Biographical Study*. University, Ala.: University of Alabama Press.

Altshuler, M. 1972. "The Attitude of the Communist Party of Russia to Jewish National Survival, 1918–1930." In Fishman (ed.), *Studies*, pp. 134–54.

American Jewish Yearbook. Various years.

Anderson, Barbara A. 1980. *Internal Migration during Modernization in Late Nineteenth Century Russia*. Princeton: Princeton University Press.

Angress, Werner T. 1977. " 'Between Baden and Luxemburg'—Jewish Socialists on the Eve of World War I." *Leo Baeck Institute Yearbook*, 22:3–34.

Arendt, Hannah. 1958. *The Origins of Totalitarianism*. New York: Meridian Books.

Arian, Alan (ed.). 1972 *The Elections in Israel: 1969*. Jerusalem: Jerusalem Academic Press.

———. 1973. *The Choosing People: Voting Behavior in Israel*. Cleveland: Press of Case-Western Reserve.

———. (ed.). 1975. *The Elections in Israel: 1973*. Jerusalem: Jerusalem Academic Press.

———. 1977. "Israel's Elections: A Mechanism of Change." *Jerusalem Quarterly* 3 (Spring): 17–27.

———. 1979. "The Electorate: Israel 1977." In Penniman (ed.), *Israel at the Polls, pp. 59–90*.

———— (ed.). 1980. *Israel—a Developing Society*. Assen, Netherlands: Van Gorcum.

————. 1981. "Elections 1981: Competitiveness and Polarization." *The Jerusalem Quarterly* 21 (Fall): 3–27.

Armengand, Andre. 1973. "Population in Europe 1700–1914." In Cipolla (ed.), *The Emergence of Industrial Societies*, pp. 22–76.

Aronoff, Myron J. 1977. *Power and Ritual in the Israel Labor Party: A Study in Political Anthropology*. Amsterdam and Assen, Netherlands: Van Gorcum.

————. 1979. "The Decline of the Israeli Labor Party: Causes and Significance." In Penniman (ed.), *Israel at the Polls*, pp. 115–46.

Asch, Adolph, and Johanna Philippson. 1958. "Self-Defence in the Second Half of the 19th Century: The Emergence of the K.C." *Leo Baeck Institute Yearbook*, 3:122–39.

Avineri, Shlomo. 1981. *The Making of Modern Zionism*. New York: Basic Books.

Avruch, Kevin. 1981. *American Immigrants in Israel*. Chicago: University of Chicago Press.

Bachi, Roberto. 1966. *Population Trends of World Jewry*. Jerusalem: Hebrew University, Institute of Contemporary Jewry.

————. 1976. *Population Trends of World Jewry*. Jerusalem: Hebrew University, Institute of Contemporary Jewry.

————. 1977. *The Population of Israel*. Jerusalem: Hebrew University, Institute of Contemporary Jewry.

————. 1982. *World Jewish Population*. Jerusalem: Hebrew University, Institute of Contemporary Jewry.

Bamberger, M. L. 1953. "Seligmann Baer Bamberger." In Jung (ed.), *Jewish Leaders*, pp. 194–217.

Barany, George. 1974. " 'Magyar Jew or Jewish Magyar?' Reflections on the Jewish Question." In Vago and Mosse (eds.), *Jews and Non-Jews*, pp. 51–98.

Barkai, Avraham. 1981. "The German Jews at the Start of Industrialization: Structural Changes and Mobility, 1835–1860." In Mosse et al., *Revolution and Evolution*, pp. 123–49.

Baron, Salo. 1937. *A Social and Religious History of the Jews. Vol. 2*. New York: Columbia University Press.

————. 1976a. *The Russian Jew under Tsars and Soviets*. New York: Macmillan.

————. 1976b. "European Jewry before and after Hitler." In Yisrael Gutman and Livia Rothkirchen (eds.), *The Catastrophe*, pp. 175–242.

Barth, Frederik (ed.). 1969. *Ethnic Groups and Boundaries: The Social Organization of Culture Differences*. Boston: Little, Brown.

Bartys, Julian. 1972. "Grand Duchy of Poznan under Prussian Rule: Changes in the Economic Position of the Jewish Population, 1815–1848." *Leo Baeck Institute Yearbook*, 17:191–204.

Bauer, Yehuda. 1978. *The Holocaust in Historical Perspective*. Seattle: University of Washington Press.

Bauer, Yehuda, and Nathan Rotenstreich (eds.). 1981. *The Holocaust as Historical Experience*. New York: Holmes and Meier.

Bein, Alex. 1970. *Theodore Herzl: A Biography of the Founder of Modern Zionism*. New York: Atheneum.

————. 1976. "The Jewish Question in Modern Anti-Semitic Literature: Prelude to the 'Final Solution.' " In Gutman and Rothkirchen (eds.), *The Catastrophe*, pp. 40–89.

Bell, Daniel. 1975. "Ethnicity and Social Change." In Glazer and Moynihan (eds.), *Ethnicity*.

Ben-Sasson, H. H. (ed.). 1976. *A History of the Jewish People*. Cambridge: Harvard University Press.

Ben-Sasson, H. H., and S. Ettinger (eds.). 1973. *Jewish Society through the Ages*. New York: Schocken.

Bentwich, Norman, 1967. "The Destruction of the Jewish Community in Austria 1938–1942." In Fraenkel (ed.), *The Jews of Austria*, pp. 467–78.

Berend, Ivan T., and Gyorgy Ranki. 1974. *Economic Development in East-Central Europe in the 19th and 20th Centuries*. New York: Columbia Univeristy Press.

Bergman, Elihu. 1977. "The American Jewish Population Erosion." *Midstream* (October).

Berkovitz, Eliezer. 1973. *Faith after the Holocaust*. New York: Ktav.

Berler, A. 1970. *New Towns in Israel*. Jerusalem: Israel Universities Press.

Bernstein, D., and S. Swirski. 1981. "The Rapid Economic Development of Israel and the Emergence of the Ethnic Division of Labour." *British Journal of Sociology* 33 (March): 64–85.

Bettelheim, Bruno. 1961. *The Informed Heart*. Glencoe, Ill.: Free Press.

Bieber, Hans-Joachim. 1979. "Anti-Semitism as a Reflection of Social, Economic and Political Tension in Germany: 1880–1933." In Bronsen (ed.), *Jews and Germans*, pp. 33–77.

Billings, John S. 1890. "Vital Statistics of the Jews in the United States." *Census Bulletin*, no. 19 (December 30).

Birnbaum, Max P. 1980. "On the Jewish Struggle for Religious Equality in Prussia 1897–1914." *Leo Baeck Institute Yearbook*, 25:163–75.

Black, C. E. 1966. *The Dynamics of Modernization*. New York: Harper and Row.

Blackbourn, David. 1978. "The Problem of Democratisation: German Politics and the Role of the Centre Party." In Evans (ed.), *Society and Politics in Wilhelmine Germany*, pp. 160–85.

———. 1980. *Class, Religion and Local Politics in Wilhelmine Germany: The Centre Party in Wurttemberg before 1914*. New Haven: Yale University Press.

Blackwell, William L. 1968. *The Beginnings of Russian Industrialization*. Princeton: Princeton University Press.

Bloom, Herbert. 1937. *The Economic Activities of the Jews of Amsterdam in the Seventeenth and Eighteenth Centuries*. Williamsport, Pa.: Bayard Press.

Blum, Jerome. 1978. *The End of the Old Order in Rural Europe*. Princeton: Princeton University Press.

Bogucka, Maria. 1982. "Polish Towns between the Sixteenth and Eighteenth Centuries." In Federowicz (ed.), *A Republic of Nobles*, pp. 138–52.

Bolkolsky, Sidney M. 1975. *The Distorted Image: German Jewish Perceptions of Germans and Germany, 1918–1935*. New York: Elsevier.

Bonacich, Edna. 1973. "A Theory of Middleman Minorities." *American Sociological Review* 38 (October): 583–94.

Borzykowski, Tuvia. 1972. *Between Tumbling Walls*. Tel Aviv: Hakibbutz Hameuchad.

Bottomore, T. B., and Maximilien Rubel (eds.). 1964. *Karl Marx: Selected Writings in Sociology and Social Philosophy*. New York: McGraw-Hill.

Braham, Randolph L. (ed.). 1966. *Hungarian-Jewish Studies*. Vol. 1. New York: World Federation of Hungarian Jews.

——— (ed.). 1969. *Hungarian-Jewish Studies*. Vol. 2. New York: World Federation of Hungarian Jews.

———. 1974. "The Rightists, Horthy, and the Germans: Factors Underlying the Destruction of Hungarian Jewry." In Vago and Mosse (eds.), *Jews and Non-Jews*, pp. 137–56.

———. 1981. *The Politics of Genocide: The Holocaust in Hungary*. Vol. 1. New York: Columbia University Press.

Bramsohn, Leo. 1903. "Statistische Untersuchungen uber die Lage der Juden in Russland." In Nossig (ed.), *Judische Statistik*, pp. 169–87.

Brass, Paul. 1980. "Ethnic Groups and Nationalities." In Sugar (ed.), *Ethnic Diversity and Conflict*, pp. 1–68.

Braudel, Fernand. 1975. *Captialism and Material Life*. New York: Harper and Row.

Brenner, Reeve Robert. 1980. *The Faith and Doubt of Holocaust Survivors*. New York: Macmillan.

Bronsen, David (ed.). 1979. *Jews and Germans from 1860 to 1933: The Problematic Symbiosis*. Heidelberg: Carl Winter.

Brym, Robert J. 1978. *The Jewish Intelligentsia and Russian Marxism*. New York: Schocken.

Burak, Moses J. 1967. *The Hatam Sofer: His Life and Times*. Toronto: Beth Jacob Congregation.

Byrnes, Robert F. 1950. *Antisemitism in France*. Vol. 1. Princeton: Princeton University Press.

Cahnman, Werner. 1974. "Village and Small Town Jews in Germany: A Typological Study." *Leo Baeck Institute Yearbook*, 19:107–30.

Carlebach, Alexander. 1964. *Adas Yeshurun of Cologne: The Life and Death of a Kehilla*. Belfast: Mullan.

Carpi, Daniel. 1976. "The Origins and Development of Fascist Anti-Semitism in Italy." In Gutman and Rothkirchen (eds.), *The Catastrophe*, pp. 283–98.

Carpi, Daniel, and Gedalia Yugev (eds.). 1975. *Zionism: Studies in the History of the Zionist Movement and of the Jewish Community in Palestine*. Tel Aviv: Massada.

Carr, E. H. 1966. *The Bolshevik Revolution 1917–1923*. Vols. 1–3. Baltimore: Penguin.

———. 1970. *Socialism in One Country 1924–1926*. Vols. 1–2. Baltimore: Penguin.

Castellan, Georges. 1974. "Remarks on the Social Structure of the Jewish Community in Poland between the Two World Wars." In Vago and Mosse (eds.), *Jews and Non-Jews*, pp. 187–202.

Chazan, Robert, and Marc Lee Raphael (eds.). 1974. *Modern Jewish History: A Source Reader*. New York: Schocken.

Cherlin, Andrew, and Carlin Celebuski. 1983. "Are Jewish Families Different? Some Evidence from the General Social Survey." *Journal of Marriage and the Family* 45 (November): 903–11.

Cipolla, Carlo (ed.). 1973. *The Emergence of Industrial Societies: Part One*. London: Collins/Fontana.

Cohen, Arthur A. (ed.). 1970. *Arguments and Doctrines: A reader in Jewish Thinking in the Aftermath of the Holocaust*. Philadelphia: Jewish Publication Society.

Cohen, Elie. 1953. *Human Behavior in the Concentration Camp*. New York: Grosset and Dunlap.

Cohen, Erik. 1977. "The City in Zionist Ideology." *Jerusalem Quarterly* 4 (Summer): 126–44.

Cohen, Gary B. 1979. "Jews in German Society: Prague, 1860–1914." In Bronsen (ed.), *Jews and Germans*, pp. 306–37.

Cohen, Israel. 1943. *History of the Jews in Vilna*. Philadelphia: Jewish Publication Society of America.

Cohen, Steven M. 1982. "The American Jewish Family Today." *American Jewish Yearbook*, pp. 136–54.

———. 1983. *American Modernity and Jewish Identity*. New York: Methuen/Tavistock.

Crisp, Olga. 1976. *Studies in the Russian Economy before 1914*. New York: Barnes and Noble.

Curtis, Michael, and M. Chertoff (eds.). 1973. *Israel: Social Structure and Change*. New Brunswick, N.J.: Transaction Books.

Davies, Norman. 1982. *God's Playground: A History of Poland in Two Volumes*. New York: Columbia University Press.

Dawidowicz, Lucy. 1975. *The War Against the Jews*. New York: Holt, Rinehart and Winston.

————. 1981. *The Holocaust and the Historians*. Cambridge: Harvard University Press.

————. 1982. "A Century of Jewish History, 1881–1981: The View from America." *American Jewish Yearbook*, 82: 3–98.

Della Pergola, Sergio. 1980. "Patterns of American Jewish Fertility." *Demography* 17 (August): 261–73.

————. 1981a. "Jewish Fertility, 1830–1980: Similarities and Dissimilarities." Paper presented at a symposium on Demography of the Jews: Historical and Comparative Perspectives, Jerusalem, Institute of Contemporary Jewry.

————. 1981b. "Toward a Typology of Jewish Population Distribution in European Cities." Paper presented at a Study Group on Urban Ecology of the Jews, Jerusalem, Institute of Contemporary Jewry.

De Ruggiero, Guido. 1959. *The History of European Liberalism*. Boston: Beacon.

Deshen, Shlomo A. 1970. *Immigrant Voters in Israel*. Manchester: Manchester University Press.

Des Pres, Terrence. 1976. *The Survivor*. New York: Oxford University Press.

Dinur, Ben-Zion, et al. 1954. *The Community of Israel: Chapters in the Sociology of the Jewish People* (Hebrew). Jerusalem: Mossad Bialik.

Dobrosycki, Lucjan. 1981. "The Fertility of Modern Polish Jewry." In Ritterband (ed.), *Modern Jewish Fertility*, pp. 64–71.

Dobrosycki, Lucjan, and Barbara Kirshenblatt-Gimblett. 1977. *Image before My Eyes: A Photographic History of Jewish Life in Poland*. New York: Schocken.

Don-Yehiya, Eliezer. 1981. "Origins and Development of the *Agudah* and *Mafdal* Parties." *Jerusalem Quarterly* 20 (Summer): 49–64.

Dubnow, S. M. 1916. *History of the Jews in Russia and Poland*. Vols. 1–3. Philadelphia: Jewish Publication Society of America.

Dubnow, W. 1928. "On the Economic Activity of Russian Jews" (Yiddish). In Lestchinsky, *Essays*, pp. 92–97.

Duggan, Paul R. 1972. "German Jewish Relations in the Wilhelmine Period." *Leo Baeck Institute Yearbook*, 17:43–54.

Duker, Abraham G., and Meir Ben-Horin (eds.). 1974. *Emancipation and Counter-Emancipation*. New York: Ktav.

Dutter, Lee E., and Ofira Seliktar. 1978. "Political Stability and Ethnic Diversity: The Case of Israel." Haifa University, Department of Political Science. Mimeo.

Edelman, Joseph. 1977. "Soviet Jews in the United States: A Profile." *American Jewish Yearbook*, pp. 157–81.

Eisenstadt, S. N. 1977a. "Portrait of the Yishuv." *Jerusalem Quarterly* 1 (Fall):28–35.

————. 1977b. "Change and Continuity in Israeli Society." *Jerusalem Quarterly* 2 (Winter): 3–11.

Eisenstadt, S. N., Rivka Bar-Yosef, and Chaim Adler (eds.). 1970. *Integration and Development in Israel*. Jerusalem: Jerusalem Academic Press.

Eizenstat, Stuart. 1981. "State of World Jewry." Address at the 92d Street Young Men's and Young Women's Hebrew Association, New York.

Elazar, Daniel J. 1976. *Community and Polity*. Philadelphia: Jewish Publication Society.

————. 1979. "Israel's Compound Polity." In Penniman (ed.), *Israel at the Polls*, pp. 1–38.

Eley, Geoff. 1978. "The Wilhelmine Right: How It Changed." In Evans (ed.), *Society and Politics in Wilhelmine Germany*, pp. 112–35.

————. 1980. *Reshaping the German Right: Radical Nationalism and Political Change after Bismarck*. New Haven: Yale University Press.

Endelman, Todd M. 1979. *The Jews of Georgian England: Tradition and Change in a Liberal Society*. Philadelphia: Jewish Publication Society.

Engelman, Uriah Zevi. 1973. *The Rise of the Jew in the Western World*. New York: Arno Press.

Epstein, Melech. 1969. *Jewish Labor in U.S.A.: An Industrial, Political and Cultural History of the Jewish Labor Movement*. New York: Ktav.

ESCO Foundation. 1947. *Palestine: A Study of Jewish, Arab and British Policies*. New Haven: Yale University Press.

Ettinger, Shmuel. 1970. "The Jews in Russia at the Outbreak of the Revolution." In Kochan (ed.), *The Jews in Soviet Russia*, pp. 14–18.

————. 1974. "Jews and Non-Jews in Eastern and Central Europe between the Wars: An Outline." In Vago and Mosse (eds.), *Jews and Non-Jews*, pp. 1–20.

————. 1976a. "The Modern Period." In Ben-Sasson (ed.), *A History of the Jewish People*, pp. 727–1097.

————. 1976b. "The Origins of Modern Anti-Semitism." In Gutman and Rothkirchen (eds.), *The Catastrophe*, pp. 3–39.

————. 1982. "Anti-Semitism in Our Time." *Jerusalem Quarterly* 23 (Spring): 95–113.

Etzioni-Halevy, Eva, with Rina Shapiro, 1977. *Political Culture in Israel: Cleavage and Integration among Israeli Jews*. New York: Praeger.

Evans, Richard J. 1978a. "Introduction: Wilhelm II's Germany and the Historians." In Evans (ed.), *Society and Politics in Wilhelmine Germany*, pp. 11–39.

————. (ed.). 1978b. *Society and Politics in Wilhelmine Germany*. New York: Barnes and Noble.

Fackenheim, Emil. 1968. *Quest for Past and Future*. Boston: Beacon Press.

Farr, Ian. 1978. "Populism in the Countryside: The Peasant Leagues in Bavaria in the 1880's." In Evans (ed.), *Society and Politics in Wilhelmine Germany*, pp. 136–59.

Faunce, W., and W. Form (eds.). 1969. *Comparative Perspectives on Industrial Society*. Boston: Little, Brown.

Federowicz, J. K. (tr. and ed.), and Maria Bogucka and Henryk Samsonowicz (co-eds.). 1982. *A Republic of Nobles: Studies in Polish History to 1864*. Cambridge: Cambridge University Press.

Fein, Helen. 1979. *Accounting for Genocide*. New York: Free Press.

Field, Geoffrey M. 1980. "Religion in the German Volksschule, 1890–1928." *Leo Baeck Institute Yearbook*, 25:41–71.

Finkelstein, Louis (ed.). 1960. *The Jews: Their History, Culture and Religion*. Vol. 2. New York: Harper and Brothers.

————(ed.). 1970. *The Jews: Their History*. 4th ed. New York: Schocken.

Fischer-Galati, Stephen. 1974. "Fascism, Communism, and the Jewish Question in Romania." In Vago and Mosse (eds.), *Jews and Non-Jews*, pp. 157–76.

Fishman, Joshua A. (ed.). 1972. *Studies in Modern Jewish Social History*. New York: Ktav.

———— (ed.). 1974a. *Studies on Polish Jewry 1919–1939: The Interplay of Social, Economic and Political Factors in the Struggle of a Minority for Its Existence* (Yiddish). New York: YIVO Institute of Jewish Research.

————. 1974b. "Minority Resistance: Some Comparisons between Interwar Poland and Postwar U.S.A." In Fishman (ed.), *Studies on Polish Jewry* (Yiddish), pp. 3–11.

Fleischmann, Gustav. 1969. "The Religious Congregation, 1918–1938." In *The Jews of Czechoslovakia*, 1:267–329.

Fraenkel, Joseph (ed.). 1967. *The Jews of Austria*. London: Valentine, Mitchell.

Fraenkel, Peter. 1979. "The Memoirs of B. L. Monasch of Krotoschin." *Leo Baeck Institute Yearbook*, 24:195–224.

Frankel, Jonathan. 1981. *Prophecy and Politics: Socialism, Nationalism and the Russian Jews, 1862–1917*. Cambridge: Cambridge University Press.

Frankl, Victor. 1963. *Man's Search for Meaning*. New York: Washington Square Press.

Freedman, Robert O. 1978. *Soviet Policy toward the Middle East since 1970*. New York: Praeger.

Freimann, A., and F. Kracauer. 1919. *History of the Jews in Frankfort*. Philadelphia: Jewish Publication Society of America.

Freimark, Peter. 1979. "Language Behavior and Assimilation—the Situation of the Jews in Northern Germany in the First Half of the Nineteenth Century." *Leo Baeck Institute Yearbook*, 24:157–78.

Fried, Jacob (ed.). 1962. *Jews in the Modern World*. Vol. 2. New York: Twayne Publishing.

———— (ed.). 1968. *Jews and Divorce*. New York: Ktav Publishing.

Friedlander, Albert (ed.). 1968. *Out of the Whirlwind*. New York: Doubleday.

Friedlander, Dov, Zvi Eisenbach, and Calvin Goldscheider. 1980. "Family Size Limitation and Birth Spacing: The Fertility Transformation of African and Asian Immigrants in Israel." *Population and Development Review* 6 (December): 581–94.

Friedlander, Dov, and Calvin Goldscheider. 1979. *The Population of Israel*. Columbia University Press.

Friedlander, Henry, and Sybil Morton (eds.). 1980. *The Holocaust: Ideology, Bureaucracy, and Genocide*. Millwood, N.Y.: Kraus International.

Friedlander, Saul. 1981. "On the Possibility of the Holocaust: An Approach to a Historical Synthesis." In Bauer and Rotenstreich (eds.), *The Holocaust*, pp. 1–22.

Friedman, Philip G. 1954. *Martyrs and Fighters: The Epic of the Warsaw Ghetto*. New York: Praeger.

————. 1980. *Roads to Extinction: Essays on the Holocaust*. New York: Jewish Publication Society.

Friedmann, Filip. 1929. *Die Galizischen Juden in Kampfe um Ihre Gleichberechtigung (1848–1868)*. Frankfurt: Kauffmann Verlag.

Friedmann, Menachem. 1975. "The First Confrontation between the Zionist Movement and Jerusalem Orthodoxy after the British Occupation (1918)." In Carpi and Yugev (eds.), *Zionism*, pp. 103–26.

Frye, Bruce B. 1976. "The German Democratic Party and the 'Jewish Problem' in the Weimar Republic." *Leo Baeck Institute Yearbook*, 21:143–72.

Galliner, Arthur. 1958. "The Philanthropin in Frankfurt: Its Educational and Cultural Significance for German Jewry." *Leo Baeck Institute Yearbook*, 3:169–86.

Garncarska-Kadari, Bina. 1976. "The Jewish Working Strata in Poland between the Two World Wars (A Statistical Analysis)" (Hebrew). In Mishkinsky (ed.), *Gal-Ed*, pp. 155–67.

Gelber, N. M. 1928. "Statistics on Polish Jewry at the End of the Eighteenth Century" (Yiddish). In Lestchinsky, *Essays*, pp. 185–88.

Gellner, Ernest. 1980. "Ethnicity between Culture, Class and Power." In Sugar (ed.), *Ethnic Diversity and Conflict*, pp. 237–78.

Giladi, Dan. 1975. "The Economic Crisis during the Fourth Aliya (1926–1927)." In Carpi and Yugev (eds.), *Zionism*, pp. 157–92.

Gilbert, Martin. 1978. *Exile and Return: The Struggle for a Jewish Homeland*. Philadelphia: Lippincott.

Gilboa, Yehoshua A. 1971. *The Black Years of Soviet Jewry, 1939–1953*. Boston: Little, Brown.

Ginzburg, Eugenia Semyouna. 1967. *Journey into the Whirlwind*. New York: Harcourt Brace Jovanovich.

Gitelman, Zvi, 1972. *Jewish Nationality and Soviet Politics: The Jewish Sections of the CPSU, 1917–1930*. Princeton: Princeton University Press.

———. 1982. *Becoming Israelis: Political Resocialization of Soviet and American Immigrants*. New York: Praeger.

Glatzer, Nahum. 1964. "The Beginnings of Modern Jewish Studies." In Altmann (ed.), *Studies*, pp. 27–45.

———. 1976. "On an Unpublished Letter of Isaak Markus Jost." *Leo Baeck Institute Yearbook*, 21:27–45.

———. 1978. *Essays in Jewish Thought*. University, Ala.: University of Alabama Press.

Glazer, Nathan. 1957. *American Judaism*. Chicago: University of Chicago Press.

Glazer, N., and P. Moynihan (eds.). 1975. *Ethnicity: Theory and Experience*. Cambridge: Harvard University Press.

Gluckel. 1963. *The Life of Gluckel of Hameln 1646–1724*. Written by herself. Trans. Ben-Zion Abrahams. New York: Thomas Yoseloff.

Goldberg, Nathan. 1945–46. "Occupational Patterns of American Jews," *Jewish Review*, vol. 3.

———. 1962. "Demographic Characteristics of American Jews." In Fried (ed.), *Jews in the Modern World*.

———. 1968. "The Jewish Attitudes toward Divorce." In Fried (ed.), *Jews and Divorce*.

Goldhammer, Leo. 1927. *Die Juden Wiens: Eine Statistiche Studie*. Vienna: Lowit Verlag.

Goldscheider, Calvin. 1967. "Fertility of the Jews." *Demography* 4 (May):196–209.

———. 1971. *Population, Modernization and Social Structure*. Boston: Little, Brown.

———. 1974. "American Aliya: Sociological and Demographic Perspectives." In Sklare (ed.), *The Jew in American Society*, pp. 335–84.

———. 1982. "Demography of Jewish Americans: Research Findings, Issues, and Challenges." In Sklare (ed.), *Understanding American Jewry*, pp. 1–55.

———. 1983. "The Demography of Asian and African Jews in Israel." In J. Maier and C. Waxman (eds.) *Ethnicity, Identity and History*. New Brunswick, N.J.: Transaction Books.

———. Forthcoming. *Social Change and Jewish Continuity: Family, Population, and Stratification*. Waltham, Mass.: Brandeis University.

Goldscheider, Calvin, and Dov Friedlander. 1981. "Patterns of Jewish Fertility." In Ritterband (ed.), *Modern Jewish Fertility*.

———. 1983. "Religiosity Patterns in Israel." *American Jewish Yearbook*, 83:3–40.

Goldscheider, Calvin, and F. Kobrin. 1980. "Ethnic Continuity and the Process of Self-Employment." *Ethnicity* 7:256–78.

Goldstein, Alice. 1981a. "The Urbanization of Jews in Baden, Germany, 1825–1925." Brown University. Mimeo.

———. 1981b. "Some Demographic Characteristics of Village Jews in Germany: Nonnenweier, 1800–1931." In Ritterband (ed.), *Modern Jewish Fertility*, pp. 112–43.

Goldstein, Sidney. 1969. "Socioeconomic Differentials among Religious Groups in the United States." *American Journal of Sociology* (May): 612–31.

———. 1981. "The Jews in the United States: Perspectives from Demography." *American Jewish Yearbook*, 81:3–59.

———. 1982. "Population Movement and Redistribution among American Jews." *Jewish Journal of Sociology* 24 (June): 5–23.

Goldstein, Sidney, and Calvin Goldscheider. 1968. *Jewish Americans*. Englewood Cliffs, N.J.: Prentice-Hall.

Gordon, Milton. 1964. *Assimilation in American Life*. Oxford: Oxford University Press.

Goren, A. 1980 "Jews." In S. Thernstrom et al., *Harvard Encyclopedia of Ethnic Groups*. Cambridge: Harvard University Press.

Gorni, Yosef. 1975. "Changes in the Social and Political Structure of the Second Aliya between 1904 and 1940." In Daniel Carpi and Gedalia Yugev (eds.), *Zionism*, pp. 49–102.

Graupe, Heinz Moshe. 1978. *The Rise of Modern Judaism: An Intellectual History of German Jewry, 1650–1942*. Huntington, N.Y.: Krieger.

Green, Arthur. 1981. *Tormented Master: A Life of Rabbi Nahman of Bratslav*. New York: Schocken.

Greenbaum, Alfred Abraham. 1974. "Soviet Nationality Policy and the Problem of 'Fluid' Nationalities." In Vago and Mosse (eds.), *Jews and Non-Jews*, pp. 257–70.

Greenberg, Louis. 1944. *The Jews in Russia*. Vols. 1–2. New Haven: Yale University Press.

Grieve, Hermann. 1975. "On Jewish Self-Identification: Religion and Political Orientation." *Leo Baeck Institute Yearbook*, 20:35–46.

Gross, Walter. 1959. "The Zionist Students' Movement." *Leo Baeck Institute Yearbook*, 4:143–65.

Grunwald, Max. 1936. *History of the Jews in Vienna*. Philadelphia: Jewish Publication Society of America.

Gurian, Waldemar. 1946. "Antisemitism in Modern Germany." In Pinson, *Essays on Antisemitism*, pp. 218–66.

Gutman, Yisrael, and Livia Rothkirchen (eds.). 1976. *The Catastrophe of European Jewry*. Jerusalem: Yad Vashem.

Gutman, Yisrael, and Cynthia Hanft (eds.). 1979. *Patterns of Jewish Leadership in Nazi Europe*. Jerusalem: Yad Vashem.

Guttman, Alexander. 1977. *The Struggle over Reform in Rabbinic Literature: During the Last Century and a Half*. New York: World Union for Progressive Judaism.

Guttman, J. 1972. "The Fate of European Jewry in the Light of the Nuremberg Documents." In Fishman (ed.), *Studies*, pp. 339–53.

Hagen, William W. 1980. *Germans, Poles and Jews: The Nationality Conflict in the Prussian East, 1772–1914*. Chicago: University of Chicago Press.

Hager-Halivni, Tzipora. 1979. "The Birkenau Revolt: Poles Prevent a Timely Insurrection." *Jewish Social Studies* 21, (Spring):123–54.

Halevy, Zvi. 1976. *Jewish Schools under Czarism and Communism*. New York: Springer Library.

Halperin, Adam. 1976. "Betar's Role in the Warsaw Ghetto Uprising." In Gutman and Rothkirchen (eds.), *The Catastrophe*, pp. 549–58.

Halpern, Ben. 1969. *The Idea of the Jewish State*. 2d ed. Cambridge: Harvard University Press.

Hamerow, Thomas S. 1958. *Restoration, Revolution, Reaction: Economics and Politics in Germany, 1815–1871*. Princeton: Princeton University Press.

Hamilton, Richard F. 1982. *Who Voted For Hitler?* Princeton: Princeton University Press.

Harris, James. 1975. "Eduard Lasker: The Jew as National German Politician." *Leo Baeck Institute Yearbook*, 20:151–77.

Heberle, Rudolf. 1970. *From Democracy to Nazism: A Regional Case Study of Political Parties in Germany*. New York: Grosset and Dunlap.

Hechter, Michael. 1975. *Internal Colonialism: The Celtic Fringe in British National Development, 1536–1966*. Berkeley: University of California Press.

Heller, Celia S. 1980. *On the Edge of Destruction: Jews of Poland Between the Two World Wars*. New York: Schocken.

Helmreich, William. 1982. *The World of the Yeshiva*. New York: Free Press.

Hersch, Liebman. 1949. "Jewish Migrations during the Last Hundred Years." In *The Jewish People, Past and Present*. New York: Central Yiddish Cultural Organization.

Herscher, Uri. 1981. *Jewish Agricultural Utopias in America, 1880–1910*. Detroit: Wayne State University Press.

Hertz, J. S. 1972. "The Bund's Nationality Program and Its Critics in the Russian, Polish and Austrian Socialist Movements." In Fishman (ed.), *Studies*, pp. 80–94.

Hertzberg, Arthur. 1968. *French Enlightenment and the Jews*. New York: Schocken.

——— (ed.). 1975. *The Zionist Idea: A Historical Analysis and Reader*. New York: Atheneum.

Hertzberg, Steven. 1978. *Strangers Within the Gate: The Jews of Atlanta, 1814–1915*. Philadelphia: Jewish Publication Society.

Heschel, A. J. 1972. "The Eastern European Era in Jewish History." In Fishman (ed.), *Studies*, pp. 3–23.

Hilberg, Raul. 1967. *The Destruction of the European Jews*. Chicago: Quadrangle Books.

Hirschberg, Alfred. 1962. "Ludwig Hollaender, Director of the CV." *Leo Baeck Institute Yearbook* 7:39–74.

Hobsbawm, Eric. 1962. *The Age of Revolution, 1789–1848*. New York: Mentor.

———. 1979. *The Age of Capital, 1848–1875*. New York: Mentor.

Horowitz, Dan, and Moshe Lissak. 1977. "Ideology and Politics in the Yishuv." Jerusalem Quarterly 2 (Winter):12–26.

———. 1978. *The Origins of the Israeli Polity*. Chicago: University of Chicago Press.

Howe, Irving. 1976. *The World of Our Fathers*. New York: Simon and Shuster.

Hundert, Gershon David. 1978. *Security and Dependence: Perspectives on Seventeenth-Century Polish-Jewish Society Gained through a Study of Jewish Merchants in Little Poland*. Ph.D. diss., Columbia University.

Huntington, Samuel. 1968. *Political Order in Changing Societies*. New Haven: Yale University Press.

Hyman, Paula. 1979. *From Dreyfus to Vichy: The Remaking of French Jewry, 1906–1939*. New York: Columbia University Press.

———. 1981. "Jewish Fertility in Nineteenth Century France." In Ritterband (ed.), *Modern Jewish Fertility*, pp. 78–93.

———. 1983. "Changes in Rural Jewish Communities: Alsatian Towns and Villages in the

Nineteenth Century." Paper presented at Conference on Jewish Settlement and Community in the Modern Western World. City University of New York, Graduate Center, March.

Israel Statistical Abstracts. 1982. Jerusalem: Central Bureau of Statistics.

Jacobs, Dan, and E. Paul (eds.). 1981. *Studies of the Third Wave: Recent Migration of Soviet Jews to the United States.* Boulder, Colo.: Westview Press.

Janowsky, Oscar I. 1933. *The Jews and Minority Rights (1898–1919).* New York: Columbia University Press.

Jarret, Charles. 1978. "The Impact of Geographical Mobility on Jewish Community Participation: Disruptive or Supportive." *Contemporary Jewry* 4 (Spring/Summer): 9–20.

Jelinek, Y. 1974. "The Vatican, the Catholic Church, the Catholics and the Persecution of the Jews during World War II: The Case of Slovakia." In Vago and Mosse (eds.), *Jews and Non-Jews,* pp. 221–56.

Jewish People, Past and Present, The. 1949. New York: Central Yiddish Cultural Organization.

Jews of Czechoslovakia, The. 1968. Vol. 1. Philadelphia: Jewish Publication Society.

Jews of Czechoslovakia, The. 1971. Vol. 2. Philadelphia: Jewish Publication Society.

Jick, Leon. 1976. *The Americanization of the Synagogue, 1820–1870.* Hanover, N.H.: Universities Press of New England.

Jochmann, Werner. 1975. "The Jews and German Society in the Imperial Era." *Leo Baeck Institute Yearbook*, 20:5–11.

Johnpoll, Bernard K. 1967. *The Politics of Futility: The General Jewish Workers Bund of Poland, 1917–1943.* Ithaca: Cornell University Press.

Joseph, Samuel. 1914. *Jewish Immigration to the United States from 1881 to 1910.* New York: Columbia University Studies in the Social Sciences, no. 145.

Jung, Leo. (ed.) 1953. *Jewish Leaders (1750–1940).* New York: Bloch.

Kann, Robert A. 1974. *A History of the Hapsburg Empire 1526–1918.* Berkeley: University of California Press.

Kaplan, Marion A. 1979. *The Jewish Feminist Movement in Germany: The Campaign of the Judischer Frauenbund, 1904–1938.* Westport, Conn.: Greenwood Press.

Karbach, Oscar. 1974. "The Founder of Modern Political Antisemitism: Georg von Schonerer." in Duker and Ben-Horin, (eds.), *Emancipation and Counter-Emancipation,* pp. 323–56.

Kass, Drora, and Seymour M. Lipset. 1982. "Israeli Immigrants in America." In Sklare (ed.), *Understanding American Jewry.*

Katsch, Abraham (trans. and ed.). 1973. *The Warsaw Diary of Chaim A. Kaplan.* New York: Collier.

Katz, Elihu. 1973. "Culture and Communication in Israel." *Jewish Journal of Sociology* 15 (June): 5–22.

Katz, Jacob. 1971. *Tradition and Crisis: Jewish Society at the End of the Middle Ages.* New York: Schocken.

———. 1972. *Emancipation and Assimilation: Studies in Modern Jewish History.* Westmead, England: Gregg International Publishers.

——— (ed.). 1974. *The Role of Religion in Modern Jewish History.* Cambridge, Mass.: Association for Jewish Studies.

———. 1975. "Was the Holocaust Predictable?" *Commentary* (May): 41–48.

———. 1978. *Out of the Ghetto.* New York: Schocken.

———. 1980. *From Prejudice to Destruction: Anti-Semitism, 1700–1933.* Cambridge: Harvard University Press.

Katzburg, Nathaniel. 1966. "The Jewish Congress of Hungary: 1868–1869." In Braham (ed.), *Hungarian Jewish Studies*, 1:137–70.

————. 1969. "Hungarian Jewry in Modern Times: Political and Social Aspects." In Braham (ed.), *Hungarian Jewish Studies*, 2:137–70.

————. 1974. "The Jewish Question in Hungary during the Inter-War Period—Jewish Attitudes." In Vago and Mosse (eds.), *Jews and Non-Jews*, pp. 113–24.

————. 1981. *Hungary and the Jews: Policy and Legislation 1920–1943*. Ramat-Gan, Israel: Bar-Ilan University Press.

Kermish, Joseph. 1976. "The Warsaw Ghetto Uprising in the Light of a Hitherto Unpublished Official German Report." In Gutman and Rothkirchen (eds.), *The Catastrophe* pp. 559–82.

Kessner, Thomas. 1977. *The Golden Door: Italian and Jewish Mobility in New York City 1880–1915*. New York: Oxford University Press.

Kestenberg-Gladstein, Ruth. 1968. "The Jews between Czechs and Germans in the Historic Lands, 1848–1918." In *The Jews of Czechoslovakia*, 1:21–71.

Klaff, Vivian. 1973. "Ethnic Segregation in Urban Israel." *Demography* 10 (May): 161–84.

————. 1977. "Residence and Integration in Israel." *Ethnicity*, vol. 4.

Klein, Dennis. 1979. "Assimilation and the Demise of the Liberal Political Tradition in Vienna: 1860–1914." In Bronsen (ed.), *Jews and Germans*, pp. 234–61.

Kligsberg, Moshe. 1974. "The Jewish Youth Movement in Interwar Poland (A Sociological Study)" (Yiddish). In Fishman (ed.) *Studies on Polish Jewry*, pp. 137–228.

Knodel, John E. 1974. *The Decline of Fertility in Germany, 1871–1939*. Princeton: Princeton University Press.

Kober, Adolf. 1948. *History of the Jews in Cologne*. Philadelphia: Jewish Publication Society of America.

Kobler, Franz. 1976. *Napoleon and the Jews*. New York: Schocken.

Kobrin, Frances, and Calvin Goldscheider. 1978. *The Ethnic Factor in Family Structure and Mobility*. Cambridge: Ballinger Press.

Kochan, Lionel (ed.). 1970. *The Jews in Soviet Russia since 1917*. London: Oxford University Press.

Kohn, Moshe M. (ed.). 1971. *Jewish Resistance during the Holocaust*. Jerusalem: Yad Vashem.

Kolatt, Israel. 1977. "*Eretz Israel* Socialism and International Socialism." *Jerusalem Quarterly* 3 (Spring): 51–73.

Koralnik, I. 1928. "Demographic Changes among East European Jewry" (Yiddish). In Lestchinsky (ed.), *Essays*, pp. 215–21.

Korzec, Pavel. 1974. "Antisemitism in Poland as an Intellectual, Social and Political Movement" (Yiddish). In Fishman (ed.), *Studies on Polish Jewry*, pp. 12–104.

Kranzler, George. 1961. *Williamsburg*. New York: Feldheim Books.

Kuznets, Simon. 1960. "Economic Structure and Life of the Jews." In Finkelstein (ed.), *The Jews*, pp. 1597–1666.

————. 1972. *Economic Structure of the Jews*. Jerusalem: Hebrew University, Institute of Contemporary Jewry.

Lamberti, Marjorie. 1972. "The Prussian Government and the Jews: Official Behavior and Policy-Making in the Wilhelmine Era." *Leo Baeck Institute Yearbook*, 17:5–17.

————. 1978. *Jewish Activism in Imperial Germany*. New Haven: Yale University Press.

Landes, David. 1974. "The Jewish Merchant." *Leo Baeck Institute Yearbook*, 19:11–23.

Laquer, Walter. 1972. *A History of Zionism*. New York: Holt, Rinehart and Winston.

Laslett, Peter. 1971. *The World We Lost: England before the Industrial Age*. New York: Scribners.

Laszlo, Erno. 1966. "Hungarian Jewry: Settlement and Demography, 1735 to 1910." In Braham (ed.), *Hungarian Jewish Studies*, 1:61–136.

Lazerwitz, Bernard. 1978. "An Estimate of a Rare Population Group: The United States Jewish Population." *Demography* 15 (August): 389–94.

Lee, Lloyd E. 1980. *The Politics of Harmony: Civil Service, Liberalism, and Social Reform in Baden, 1800–1850*. Newark: University of Delaware Press.

Leifer, Eric. 1981. "Competing Models of Political Mobilization: The Role of Ethnic Ties." *American Journal of Sociology* 87 (July):23–47.

Lestchinsky, Jacob. 1922. *The Jewish People in Numbers* (Yiddish). Berlin: Klal-Ferlag.

———— (ed.). 1928a. *Essays on Economics and Statistics* (Yiddish). Berlin: Jewish Social Science Institute.

————. 1928b. "The Migrations of Jews during the Last Hundred Years" (Yiddish). In Lestchinsky (ed.), *Essays*, pp. 1–64.

————. 1928c. "The Occupation and Social Structure of Central and Eastern European Jews." In Lestchinsky (ed.), *Essays*, pp. 193–210.

————. 1931. *The Economic Classes of Polish Jewry* (Yiddish). Berlin: no publ.

————. 1932. *Das Wirtschaftliche Schicksal des Deutschen Judentums*. Berlin: Schriften der Zentralwohlfartsstelle der Deutsche Juden und der Haupstelle fur Judische Wanderfursorge.

————. 1960. "Jewish Migrations, 1840–1956." In Finkelstein (ed.), *The Jews*, pp. 1536–96.

————. 1971"The Industrial and Social Structure of the Jewish Population of Interbellum Poland." In Fishman (ed.), *Studies*, pp. 107–33.

Levin, Nora. 1977. *While Messiah Tarried: Jewish Socialist Movements, 1871–1917*. New York: Schocken.

Levitats, Isaac. 1943. *The Jewish Community in Russia, 1772–1844*. New York: Columbia University Press.

Levy, Marion, Jr. 1966. *Modernization and the Structure of Society*, Vols. 1–2. Princeton: Princeton University Press.

Levy, Richard S. 1975. *The Downfall of the Anti-Semitic Political Parties in Imperial Germany*. New Haven: Yale University Press.

Lewis, Robert A., Richard Rowland, and Ralph S. Clem. 1966. *Nationality and Population Change in Russia and the USSR: An Evaluation of Census Data, 1897–1970*. New York: Praeger.

Lidtke, Vernon. 1980. "Social Class and Secularization in Imperial Germany: The Working Classes." *Leo Baeck Institute Yearbook*, 25:21–40.

Lieberman, Samuel, and M. Weinfeld. 1978. "Demographic Trends and Jewish Survival." *Midstream* (October): 9–19.

Lieberson, Stanley. 1980. *A Piece of the Pie*. Berkeley: University of California Press.

Liebman, Arthur. 1979. *Jews and the Left*. New York: Wiley.

Liebman, Charles. 1976. *The Ambivalent American Jew*. Philadelphia: Jewish Publication Society.

Lifschutz, Ezekiel. 1974. "Selected Documents Pertaining to Jewish Life in Poland 1919–1939" (Yiddish). In Fishman (ed.), *Studies on Polish Jewry*, pp. 277–94.

Linfield, Henry S. 1927. *The Communal Organizations of the Jews of the United States*. New York: American Jewish Committee.

Lipset, Seymour Martin. 1963. *Political Man*. New York: Anchor.
————. 1970. *Revolution and Counterrevolution*. New York: Anchor.
Lissak, Moshe. 1972. "Continuity and Change in the Voting Patterns of Oriental Jews." In Arian (ed.), *The Elections in Israel*, pp. 264–77.
Low, Alfred D. 1979. *Jews in the Eyes of the Germans: From the Enlightenment to Imperial Germany*. Philadelphia: Institute for the Study of Human Issues.
Lowenstein, Steven W. 1976. "The Pace of Modernization of German Jewry in the Nineteenth Century." *Leo Baeck Institute Yearbook*, 21:41–56.
————. 1981a. "The 1840s and the Creation of the German-Jewish Religious Reform Movement." In Mosse et al., *Revolution and Evolution*, pp. 255–97.
————. 1981b. "Voluntary and Involuntary Limitation of Fertility in Nineteenth Century Bavarian Jewry." In Ritterband (ed.), *Modern Jewish Fertility*, pp. 94–111.
Lowenthal, Marvin (trans. and ed.). 1962. *The Diaries of Theodor Herzl*. New York: Grosset and Dunlap.
Lumer, Hyman, 1974. *Lenin on the Jewish Question*. New York: International Press.
McCagg, William O., Jr., 1972. *Jewish Nobles and Geniuses in Modern Hungary*. New York: Columbia University Press.
McClelland, Charles. 1980. *State, Society and University in Germany, 1700–1914*. Cambridge: Cambridge University Press.
Maczak, Antoni. 1982. "The Structure of Power in the Commonwealth of the Sixteenth and Seventeenth Centuries." In Federowicz (ed.), *A Republic of Nobles*, pp. 113–34.
Magill, Stephen. 1979. "Defense and Introspection: Germany Jewry, 1914." In Bronsen (ed.), *Jews and Germans*, pp. 209–33.
Mahler, Raphael. 1946. "Antisemitism in Poland." In Pinson (ed.), *Essays on Antisemitism*, pp. 145–72.
————. 1971. *A History of Modern Jewry, 1780–1815*, New York: Schocken.
Maier, Joseph, and C. Waxman (eds.). 1983. *Ethnicity, Identity, and History*. New Brunswick, N.J.: Transaction.
Maimon, Solomon. 1967. *An Autobiography*. New York: Schocken.
Malino, Frances. 1978. *The Sephardic Jews of Bordeaux: Assimilation and Emancipation in Revolutionary and Napoleonic France*. University, Ala.: University of Alabama Press.
Malino, Frances, and Phyllis Cohen Albert (eds.). 1982. *Essays in Modern Jewish History*. Rutherford, N.J.: Fairleigh Dickinson University Press.
Mandel, N. 1974-75. "Ottoman Policy and Restrictions on Jewish Settlement in Palestine: 1881–1908. Parts I and II." *Middle Eastern Studies* (October and January).
Marcus, Jacob R. 1972. *Israel Jacobson: The Founder of the Reform Movement in Judaism*. Cincinatti: Hebrew Union College.
Marmorstein, Emile. 1969. *Heaven at Bay: The Jewish Kulturkampf in the Holy Land*. London: Oxford University Press.
Marrus, Michael R. 1971. *The Politics of Assimilation: A Study of the Jewish Community at the Time of the Dreyfus Affair*. Oxford: Clarendon Press.
Marton, Ernest (Erno). 1966. "The Family Tree of Hungarian Jewry." In Braham (ed.), *Hungarian Jewish Studies*, 1:1–60.
Matras, Judah. 1973a. "Israel's New Frontier: The Urban Periphery." In Curtis and Chertoff (eds.), *Israel: Social Structure and Change*.
————. 1973b. "On Changing Matchmaking, Marriage and Fertility in Israel." *American Journal of Sociology* 79 (September): 364–88.

Matras, Judah, and Dov Weintraub. 1976. "Ethnic and Other Primordial Differentials in Intergenerational Mobility in Israel." Paper presented to ISA Stratification and Mobility Seminar, Jerusalem.

Mayer, Milton. 1955. *They Thought They Were Free*. Chicago: University of Chicago Press.

Medding, Peter J. 1972. *Mapai in Israel: Political Organization and Government in a New Society*. Cambridge: Cambridge University Press.

Medvedev, Roy A. 1971. *Let History Judge: The Origins and Consequences of Stalinism*. New York: Vintage.

Melzer, Emanuel. 1977. "Relations between Poland and Germany and Their Impact on the Jewish Problem in Poland (1935–38)." *Yad Vashem Studies* 12:193–229.

Mendelsohn, Ezra. 1970. *Class Struggle in the Pale*. New York: Cambridge University Press.

———. 1972. "The Russian Jewish Labor Movement and Others." In Fishman (ed.), *Studies*, pp. 95–106.

———. 1974 "The Dilemma of Jewish Politics in Poland: Four Responses." In Vago and Mosse (eds.), *Jews and Non-Jews*, pp. 203–220.

———. 1979. "Jewish Leadership between the Two World Wars." In Gutman and Hanft (eds.), *Patterns of Jewish Leadership*, pp. 1–13.

———. 1981. *Zionism in Poland: The Formative Years, 1915–1926*. New Haven: Yale University Press.

———. 1983. *The Jews of East Central Europe between the World Wars*. Bloomington, Ind.: Indiana University Press.

Mendelssohn, Moses. 1969. *Jerusalem and Other Jewish Writings*. New York: Schocken.

Mendes-Flohr, Paul R., and Jehuda Reinharz (eds.). 1980. *The Jew in the Modern World: A Documentary History*. New York: Oxford University Press.

Menes, A. 1972. "The Am Oylom Movement." in Fishman (ed.), *Studies*, pp. 155–79.

Merkl, Peter H. 1975. *Political Violence under the Swastika: 581 Early Nazis*. Princeton: Princeton University Press.

Meyer, Michael A. 1967. *The Origins of the Modern Jew: Jewish Identity and European Culture in Germany, 1749–1824*. Detroit: Wayne State University Press.

———. 1971. "Jewish Religious Reform and Wissenschaft des Judentums: The Positions of Zunz, Geiger and Frankel." *Leo Baeck Institute Yearbook*, 16:19–41.

———. 1974. "Universalism and Jewish Unity in the Thought of Abraham Geiger." In Katz (ed.), *The Role of Religion*, pp. 91–104.

———. 1979. "The Religious Reform Controversy in the Berlin Jewish Community, 1814–1823." *Leo Baeck Institute Yearbook*, 24:139–56.

———. 1980. "The Orthodox and the Enlightened—an Unpublished Contemporary Analysis of Berlin Jewry's Spiritual Condition in the Early Nineteenth Century." *Leo Baeck Institute Yearbook*, 25:101–30.

Miller, J. 1970. "Soviet Theory on the Jews." In Kochan (ed.), *The Jews in Soviet Russia*, pp. 44–61.

Milward, Alan S., and S. B. Saul. 1977. *The Development of the Economies of Continental Europe 1850–1914*. Cambridge: Harvard University Press.

Minchinton, Walter. 1973. "Patterns of Demand 1750–1914." In Cipolla (ed.), *The Emergence of Industrial Societies,* pp. 77–186.

Minzin, I. 1928. "School Enrollment of Russian and Polish Jews" (Yiddish). In Lestchinsky (ed.), *Essays*, pp. 240–48.

Mishkinsky, Moshe (ed.). 1976. *Gal-Ed: On the History of the Jews in Poland* (Hebrew). Tel-Aviv: Society for Historical Research on Polish Jewry.

Moore, Deborah Dash. 1981. *At Home in America: Second Generation New York Jews*. New York: Columbia University Press.

Mork, Gordon R. 1977. "German Nationalism and Jewish Assimilation—the Bismark Period." *Leo Baeck Institute Yearbook,* 22:81–91.

Moskovits, Aron. 1964. *Jewish Education in Hungary, 1848–1948*. New York: Bloch.

Mosse, George L. 1964. *The Crisis of German Ideology: Intellectual Origins of the Third Reich*. New York: Grosset and Dunlap.

———. 1970. *Germans and Jews*. New York: Grosset and Dunlap.

———. 1978. *Toward the Final Solution: A History of European Racism*. New York: Howard Fertig.

Mosse, Werner E. 1979. "Judaism, Jews and Capitalism—Weber, Sombart and Beyond." *Leo Baeck Institute Yearbook*, 24:3–16.

Mosse, Werner E., Arnold Pauker, Reinhard Rurup (eds.), 1981. *Revolution and Evolution: 1848 in German-Jewish History*. Tubingen: J. C. B. Mohr.

Mostov, Stephen G. 1978. "A Sociological Portrait of German Jewish Immigrants in Boston: 1845–1861." *Association of Jewish Studies* 3:14–157.

———. 1981. "A 'Jerusalem' on the Ohio: The Social and Economic History of Cincinnati's Jewish Community, 1840—1875." Ph.D. diss., Brandeis University.

Newman, William, and Peter Halvorson. 1979. "American Jews: Patterns of Geographic Distribution and Change, 1952–1971." *Journal for the Scientific Study of Religion* 18 (June): 183–93.

Nielsen, Francois. 1980. "The Flemish Movement in Belgium after World War II: A Dynamic Analysis." *American Sociological Review* 45 (February): 76–94.

Nini, Y. 1981. "Immigration and Assimilation: On Yemenite Jews." *Jerusalem Quarterly* 21 (Fall): 85–98.

Nolte, Ernst. 1966. *Three Faces of Fascism*. New York: Holt, Rinehart and Winston.

Nossig, Alfred. 1887. *Materialen zur Statistik des Judischen Stammes*. Vienna: Bei Carl Konegen.

———(ed.). 1903. *Judische Statistik*. Berlin: Judischer Verlag.

Nove, A., and J. A. Newth. 1970. "The Jewish Population: Demographic Trends and Occupational Patterns." In Kochan (ed.) *The Jews in Soviet Russia*, pp. 125–58.

Nussbaum, Daniel. 1978. "Social Justice and Social Policy in the Jewish Tradition: The Satisfaction of Basic Human Needs in Poznan in the 17th and 18th Centuries." Ph.D. diss., Brandeis University.

Pennar, Jaan, Ivan I. Bakalo, and George Z. F. Bereday. 1971. *Modernization and Diversity in Soviet Education with Special References to Nationality Groups*. New York: Praeger.

Penniman, Howard R. (ed.). 1979. *Israel at the Polls*. Washington, D.C.: American Enterprise Institute.

Peres Y., and R. Katz. 1981. "Stability and Centrality: The Nuclear Family in Modern Israel, *Social Forces* 59 (May): 687–704.

Perspectives on German-Jewish History in the 19th and 20th Century, Jerusalem: Leo Baeck Institute; and Jerusalem: Academic Press.

Petuchowski, Jacob I. 1964. "Manuals and Catechisms of the Jewish Religion in the Early Period of Emancipation." Altmann (ed.), *Studies*, pp. 47–64.

———. 1968. *Prayerbook Reform in Europe: The Liturgy of European Liberal and Reform Judaism*. New York: World Union for Progressive Judaism.

———. (ed.). 1975. *New Perspectives on Abraham Geiger*. Cincinatti: Hebrew Union College Press.

Philippson, Johanna. 1962. "The Philippsons, German Jewish Family, 1775–1933." In *Leo Baeck Institute Yearbook*, 7:95–118.

Pinson, Koppel S. (ed.). 1946. *Essays on Antisemitism*. New York: Conference on Jewish Relations.

———. 1974. "Arkady Kremer, Vladimir Medem, and the Ideology of the Jewish 'Bund.' " In Duker and Ben-Horin (eds.), *Emancipation and Counter-Emancipation*, pp. 283–322.

Plaut, W. Gunther. 1963. *The Rise of Reform Judaism: A Source Book of Its European Origins*. New York: World Union for Progressive Judaism.

———. 1965. *The Growth of Reform Judaism: American and European Sources until 1948*. New York: World Union for Progressive Judaism.

Poliakov, Leon. 1974. *The Aryan Myth: A History of Racist and Nationalist Ideas in Europe*. New York: Basic Books.

Poll, Solomon. 1969. *The Hasidic Community of Williamsburg*. New York: Schocken.

Polonsky, Antony. 1972. *Politics in Independent Poland, 1921–1939*. Oxford: Clarendon Press.

Poppel, Stephen M. 1976. *Zionism in Germany, 1897–1933*. Philadelphia: Jewish Publication Society.

Pridham, Geoffrey. 1973. *Hitler's Rise to Power: The Nazi Movement in Bavaria 1923–1933*. New York: Harper Torchbooks.

Pulzer, P. G. J. 1964. *The Rise of Political Anti-Semitism in Germany and Austria*. New York: Wiley.

———. 1979. "Jewish Participation in Wilhelmine Politics." In Bronson (ed.), *Jews and Germans*, pp. 78–99.

———. 1980. "Why was There a Jewish Question in Imperial Germany." *Leo Baeck Institute Yearbook*, 25:133–46.

Rabinowicz, Aharon Moshe. 1969. "The Jewish Minority." In *The Jews of Czechoslovakia*, 1:155–266.

———. 1971. "The Jewish Party," In *The Jews of Czechoslovakia*, 2:253–346.

Rabinowicz, Harry M. 1965. *The Legacy of Polish Jewry*. New York: Thomas A. Yoseloff.

Rabinowitch, A., and J. Rabinowitch. 1972. *Revolution and Politics in Russia*. Bloomington, Ind.: Indiana University Press.

Ragins, Sanford. 1980. *Jewish Responses to Anti-Semitism in Germany, 1870–1914*. Cincinnati: Hebrew Union College Press.

Raphael, Marc Lee. 1975. *Jews and Judaism in a Midwestern Community: On Columbus, Ohio, Jews*. Columbus: Ohio Historical Society.

Reichman, Eva G. 1951. *Hostages of Civilization: The Social Sources of National Socialist Anti-Semitism*. Boston: Beacon Press.

Reinharz, Jehuda. 1975. *Fatherland or Promised Land: The Dilemma of the German Jew, 1893–1914*. Ann Arbor: University of Michigan Press.

Rezler, Julius. 1980. "Economic and Social Differentiation and Ethnicity." In Sugar (ed.), *Ethnic Diversity and Conflict*, pp. 279–345.

Richarz, Monika. 1975. "Jewish Social Mobility in Germany during the Time of Emancipation (1790–1871)." *Leo Baeck Institute Yearbook*, 20:69–78.

————. 1981. "Emancipation and Continuity: German Jews in the Rural Economy." In Mosse et al. (eds.), *Revolution and Evolution*, pp. 95–115.

Ringer, Fritz. 1979. *Education and Society in Modern Europe*. Bloomington: Indiana University Press.

Rischin, Moses. 1962. *The Promised City: New York's Jews 1870–1914*. Cambridge: Harvard University Press.

Ritterband, Paul (ed.) 1981. *Modern Jewish Fertility*. Leiden: E. J. Brill.

Robinson, Geroid Tangueray. 1972. *Rural Russia under the Old Regime*. Berkeley: University of California Press.

Robinson, Jacob. 1976. "The Holocaust." In Gutman and Rothkirchen (eds.), *The Catastrophe*, pp. 243–82.

Roos, Hans. 1966. *A History of Modern Poland*. New York: Knopf.

Rosenbloom, Noah H. 1976. *Tradition in an Age of Reform: The Religious Philosophy of Samson Raphael Hirsch*. Philadelphia: Jewish Publication Society.

Rosenkranz, Herbert. 1967. "The Anschluss and the Tragedy of Austrian Jewry 1934–1945." In Fraenkel (ed.), *The Jews of Austria*, pp. 479–526.

Rosensaft, Menachem Z. 1976. "Jews and Antisemites in Austria at the End of the Nineteenth Century." *Leo Baeck Institute Yearbook*, 21:57–86.

Rosenthal, Erich. 1961. "Jewish Fertility in the United States." *Eugenics Quarterly* 8 (December): 198–217.

Rossi, Mario. 1974. "Emancipation of the Jews of Italy." In Duker and Ben Horin (eds.), *Emancipation and Counter-Emancipation*, 205–35.

Rotenstreich, Nathan. 1959. "For and Against Emancipation: The Bruno Bauer Controversy." *Leo Baeck Institute Yearbook*, 4:3–36.

————. 1963. *The Recurring Pattern: Studies in Anti-Judaism in Modern Thought*. London: Weidenfeld and Nicholson.

Rothenberg, J. 1970. "Jewish Religion in the Soviet Union." In Kochan (ed.), *The Jews in Soviet Russia*, pp. 159–87.

Rothkirchen, Livia. 1968. "Slovakia: II, 1918–1938." In *The Jews of Czechoslovakia*, 1:85–124.

Rothschild, Joseph. 1981–82. "Ethnic Peripheries versus Ethnic Cores: Jewish Political Strategies in Interwar Poland." *Political Science Quarterly* (Winter): 591–606.

Rowe, Leonard. 1974. "Jewish Self-Defence: A Response to Violence" (Yiddish). In Fishman (ed.), *Studies on Polish Jewry*, pp. 105–49.

Rozenblit, Marsha. 1983. "Social Mobility and Ethnic Assimilation in the Jewish Neighborhoods of Vienna, 1867–1914." Paper presented at Conference on Jewish Settlement and Community in the Modern Western World. City University of New York, Graduate Center, March.

Rubinow, Isaac. 1975 [1907]. *Economic Condition of the Jews in Russia*. New York: Arno.

Rudavsky, David. 1967. *Modern Jewish Religious Movements: A History of Emancipation and Adjustment*. New York: Behrman House.

Rude, George. 1972. *Europe in the Eighteenth Century: Aristocracy and the Bourgeois Challenge*. New York: Praeger.

Ruppin, Arthur. 1904. *Die Juden der Gegenwart*. Berlin: Calvary.

————. 1934. *The Jewish Fate and Future*. London: MacMillan.

————. 1973 [1943]. *The Jews in the Modern World*. New York: Arno.

Rurup, Reinhard. 1969. "Jewish Emancipation and Bourgeois Society." *Leo Baeck Institute Yearbook*, 14:67–91.

———. 1975a. "Emancipation and Crisis—the 'Jewish Question' in Germany, 1850–1890." *Leo Baeck Institute Yearbook,* 20:13–26.

———. 1975b. "German Liberalism and the Emancipation of the Jews." *Leo Baeck Institute Yearbook,* 20:59–60.

———. 1981. "The European Revolution of 1848 and Jewish Emancipation." In Mosse et al., *Revolution and Evolution,* pp. 1–53.

Sawyer, Thomas. 1979. *The Jewish Minority in the Soviet Union.* Boulder, Colo.: Westview.

Schapiro, Leonard. 1964. *The Communist Party of the Soviet Union.* New York: Vintage.

———. 1974. "The Jewish Anti-Fascist Committee and Phases of Soviet Anti-Semitic Policy during and after World War II." In Vago and Mosse (eds.), *Jews and Non-Jews,* pp. 283–300.

Schappes, Morris (ed.) 1950. *A Documentary History of the Jews in the United States.* New York: Citadel Press.

Schiff, Gary S. 1977. *Tradition and Politics: The Religious Parties of Israel.* Detroit: Wayne State University Press.

Schindler, Peter. 1972. *Responses of Hassidic Leaders and Hassidim during the Holocaust in Europe, 1939–1945,* Ph.D. diss., New York University.

Schmelz, U. O. 1971. *Infant and Early Childhood Mortality among the Jews of the Diaspora.* Jerusalem: Hebrew University, Institute of Contemporary Jewry.

———. 1981. "Jewish Survival: The Demographic Factors." *American Jewish Yearbook* 81:61–117.

———. 1982. "Die Demographische Entwicklung der Juden in Deutschland von der Mitte des 19. Jahrhunderts bis 1933." *Zeitschrift fur Bevolkerungswissenschaft* 1:31–72.

Schmelz, U. O., and S. Della Pergola. 1982. "World Jewish Population Estimates." *American Jewish Yearbook.* 82:277–90.

———. 1983. "The Demographic Consequences of U.S. Jewish Population Trends." *American Jewish Yearbook,* 83:141–87.

Schmidt, H. D. 1962. "Chief Rabbi Nathan Adler (1803–1890)—Jewish Educator from Germany." *Leo Baeck Institute Yearbook,* 11:289–311.

Schmidtbauer, Peter. 1980. "Households and Household Forms of Viennese Jews in 1857." *Journal of Family History* (Winter): 375–89.

Schochat, Azriel. 1974. "Jews, Lithuanians and Russians, 1939–1941." In Vago and Mosse (eds.), *Jews and Non-Jews,* pp. 301–14.

Scholem, Gershom. 1979. "On the Social Psychology of Jews in Germany: 1900–1933." In Bronsen (ed.), *Jews and Germans,* pp. 9–32.

Schorsch, Ismar. 1972. *Jewish Reactions to German Anti-Semitism, 1870–1914.* New York: Columbia University Press.

———. 1977. "From Wolfenbuttel to Wissenschaft: The Divergent Paths of Isaak Markus Jost and Leopold Zunz." *Leo Baeck Institute Yearbook,* 21:109–28.

———. 1980. "The Religious Parameters of Wissenschaft—Jewish Academics at Prussian Universities." *Leo Baeck Institute Yearbook* 25:3–21.

———. 1981. "Emancipation and the Crisis of Religious Authority: The Emergence of the Modern Rabbinate." In Mosse et al., *Revolution and Evolution,* pp. 205–47.

Schreiber, Emanuel. 1892. *Reformed Judaism and Its Pioneers.* Spokane: Spokane Printing.

Schwab. Herman. n.d. *The History of Orthodox Jewry in Germany.* London: Mitre.

Schwarcz, Moshe. 1971. "Religious Currents and General Culture." *Leo Baeck Institute Yearbook,* 16:3–18.

Schwarz, Egon. 1979. "Melting Pot or Witch's Cauldron? Jews and Anti-Semites in Vienna at the Turn of the Century." In Bronsen (ed.), *Jews and Germans*, pp. 262–87.

Schwarz, Robert. 1967. "Antisemitism and Socialism in Austria 1918–26." In J. Fraenkel (ed.), *The Jews of Austria*, pp. 445–66.

Schwarzfuchs, Simon. 1979. *Napoleon, the Jews and the Sanhedrin*. London: Routledge and Kegan Paul.

Seeliger, Herbert. 1958. "Origin and Growth of the Berlin Community." *Leo Baeck Institute Yearbook*, 3:159–68.

Segal, Simon. 1938. *The New Poland and the Jews*. New York: Lee Furman.

Seliktar, Ofira. 1978. "Electoral Behavior in Israel: Political Cleavages in a Nation in Making." Haifa University, Department of Political Science. Mimeo.

Seton-Watson, H. 1974. "Two Contrasting Policies toward Jews: Russia and Hungary." In Vago and Mosse (ed.), *Jews and Non-Jews*, pp. 99–112.

Shapiro, Yonathan. 1971. *The Leadership of the American Zionist Organization*. Urbana: University of Illinois Press.

————. 1976. *The Formative Years of the Israeli Labor Party*. Beverly Hills, Calif.: Sage.

————. 1980a. "Generational Units and Intergenerational Relations in Israeli Politics." In Arian (ed.), *Israel*, pp. 161–79.

————. 1980b. *The Party System and Democracy in Israel*. Tel-Aviv University, Department of Sociology. Mimeo.

Sheehan, James J. 1978. *German Liberalism in the Nineteenth Century*. Chicago: University of Chicago Press.

Shofer, Lawrence. 1979. "The History of European Jewry: Search for a Method." *Leo Baeck Institute Yearbook*, 19:17–36.

————. 1981. "Emancipation and Population Change." In Mosse et al. *Revolution and Evolution*, pp. 63–89.

Shulvass, Moses A. 1971. *From East to West: The Westward Migration of Jews from Eastern Europe during the Seventeenth and Eighteenth Centuries*. Detroit: Wayne State University Press.

Simon, Walter, 1971. "The Jewish Vote in Austria." *Leo Baeck Institute Yearbook*, 16:97–122.

Singer, I. J. 1959. *The Brothers Ashkenazi*. New York: Knopf.

Sklare, Marshall. 1971. *America's Jews*. New York: Random House,

———— (ed.). 1974. *The Jew in American Society*. New York: Behrman House.

———— (ed.). 1982. *Understanding American Jewry*. New Brunswick, N.J.: Transaction Books.

Sklare, Marshall, and J. Greenblum. 1967. *Jewish Identity on the Suburban Frontier*. New York: Basic Books.

Sloan, Jacob. 1958. *The Journal of Emanuel Ringelblum*. New York: McGraw-Hill.

Smelser, Neil. 1969. "Mechanism of Change and Adjustment to Change." In W. Faunce and W. Form (eds.), *Comparative Perspectives on Industrial Society*, Boston: Little, Brown.

Smooha, Sammy. 1978. *Israel: Pluralism and Conflict*. Berkeley: University of California Press.

Sole, Aryeh. 1969. "Subcarpathian Ruthenia: 1918–1938." In *The Jews of Czechoslovakia*, 1:125–54.

Soliday, Gerald Lyman. 1974. *A Community in Conflict*. Hanover, N.H.: Brandeis University Press.

Solzhenitzyn, Aleksandr I. 1973. *The Gulag Archipelago*. Vols. 1–2. New York: Harper and Row.

Sorkin, David Jan. 1983. *Ideology and Identity: Political Emancipation and the Emergence of a Jewish Sub-Culture in Germany*. Ph.D. diss., University of California, Berkeley.

Spilerman, S., and J. Habib. 1976. "Development Towns in Israel." *American Journal of Sociology* 81 (November): 781–812.

Stachura, Peter D. 1975. *Nazi Youth in the Weimar Republic*. Santa Barbara, Calif.: Clio Books.

Stein, Siegfried, and Raphael Loewe (eds.). 1979. *Studies in Jewish Religious and Intellectual History*. University, Ala.: University of Alabama Press.

Steinberg, Stephen. 1974. *The Academic Melting Pot*. New York: Carnegie Foundation.

———. 1981. *The Ethnic Myth*. New York: Atheneum.

Stone, Daniel. 1976. *Polish Politics and National Reform, 1775–1788*. New York: Columbia University Press.

Stone, J. (ed.). 1979. *Internal Colonialism*. Special issue of *Ethnic and Racial Studies*, vol. 2, no. 3 (July).

Straus, Raphael. 1939. *History of the Jews of Regenburg and Augsberg*. Philadelphia: Jewish Publication Society.

Strauss, Herbert. 1966. "Pre-Emancipation Prussian Policies towards the Jews." *Leo Baeck Institute Yearbook*, 11:107–36.

Sugar, Peter F. (ed.). 1980. *Ethnic Diversity and Conflict in Eastern Europe*. Santa Barbara, Calif.: ABC-Clio.

Szajkowski, Zosa. 1959. *Autonomy and Communal Jewish Debts during the French Revolution of 1789*. New York: Alexander Kohut Memorial Foundation.

———. 1970. *Jews and the French Revolutions of 1789, 1830 and 1848*. New York: Ktav.

———. 1974. "Secular versus Jewish Religious Jewish Life in France." In Katz (ed.), *The Role of Religion*, pp. 109–25.

Tal, Uriel. 1976. "Anti-Christian Anti-Semitism." In Gutman and Rothkirchen (eds.), *The Catastrophe*, pp. 90–126.

———. 1981. "On the Structures of Political Theology and Myth in Germany Prior to the Holocaust." In Bauer and Rotenstreich (eds.), *The Holocaust*, pp. 43–76.

Talmon, Jacob L. 1976. "Mission and Testimony: The Universal Significance of Modern Anti-Semitism." In Gutman and Rothkirchen (eds.), *The Catastrophe*, pp. 127–76.

Tama, M. Diogene. 1807. *Transactions of the Parisian Sanhedrin*. London: Charles Taylor.

Tartakower, Arieh. 1967. "Jewish Migratory Movements in Austria in Recent Generations." in Fraenkel (ed.), *The Jews of Austria*, pp. 285–310.

Tcherikover, E. 1972. "Jewish Immigrants to the United States, 1881–1900." In Fishman (ed.), *Studies*, pp. 180–99.

Thernstrom, Stephan, et al. 1980. *Harvard Encyclopedia of American Ethnic Groups*. Cambridge: Harvard University Press.

Thomas, William I., and Florian Znaniecki. 1918. *The Polish Peasant in Europe and America*. Vols. 1–5. Boston: Richard G. Badge, Gorham Press.

Thompson, E. P. 1968. *The Making of the English Working Class*. London: Pelican.

Tobias, Henry J. 1972. *The Jewish Bund in Russia From Its Origins to 1905*. Stanford: Stanford University Press.

Toury, Jacob. 1968. "Organizational Problems of German Jewry: Steps towards the Establishment of a Central Organization (1902–1933)." *Leo Baeck Institute Yearbook*, 13:57–90.

———. 1971. "Jewish Manual Labour and Emigration—Records from Bavarian Districts." *Leo Baeck Institute Yearbook*, 16:45–62.

——. 1977a. "Types of Jewish Municipal Rights in German Townships—the Problem of Local Emancipation." *Leo Baeck Institute Yearbook*, 22:55–81.

——. 1977b. *Soziale und Politische Geschichte der Juden in Deutschland, 1847–1871*. Dusseldorf: Droste Verlag.

Trunk, Isaiah. 1972. *Judenrat*. New York: MacMillan.

——. 1974. "Economic Antisemitism in Poland between the Wars" (Yiddish). In Fishman (ed.), *Studies on Polish Jewry*, pp. 3–98.

Tucker, Robert C. (ed.). 1977. *Stalinism*. New York: Norton.

Vago, Bela. 1974. "The Attitude toward the Jews as a Criterion of the Left-Right Concept." In Vago and Mosse (eds.), *Jews and Non-Jews*, pp. 21–50.

——. 1981. "Contrasting Jewish Leaderships in Wartime Hungary and Rumania." In Bauer and Rotenstreich (eds.), *The Holocaust*, pp. 133–54.

Vago, Bela, and George L. Mosse (eds.). 1974. *Jews and Non-Jews in Eastern Europe, 1918–1945*. New York: Wiley.

Venturi, Franco. 1960. *Roots of Revolution*. New York: Grosset and Dunlap.

Viereck, Peter. 1965. *Meta-politics: The Roots of the Nazi Mind*. New York: Capricorn.

Vishniak, Mark. 1946. "Antisemitism in Tsarist Russia." In Pinson (ed.), *Essays on Antisemitism*, pp. 121–44.

Vital, David. 1976. *The Origins of Zionism*. New York: Oxford University Press.

——. 1982. *Zionism: The Formative Years*. Oxford: Clarendon Press.

Volkov, Shulamit. 1978. "Antisemitism as a Cultural Code: Reflections on the History and Historiography of Antisemitism in Imperial Germany." *Leo Baeck Institute Yearbook*, 24:25–46.

Walinsky, Louis (ed.). 1981. *Issues Facing World Jewry: A Report of the International Economic and Social Commission of the World Jewish Congress*. Washington, D.C.: Hershel Shanks.

Walk, Joseph. 1961. "The Torah Va'Avodah Movement in Germany." *Leo Baeck Institute Yearbook*, 6:236–56.

——. 1979. "Profile of a Local Zionist Association 1903–1904." *Leo Baeck Institute Yearbook*, 24–369–74.

Walker, Mack. 1971. *German Home Towns: Community, State, and General Estate, 1648–1871*. Ithaca: Cornell University Press.

Wandycz, Piotr S. 1974. *The Lands of Partitioned Poland, 1795–1918*. Seattle: University of Washington Press.

Wasserstein, Bernard. 1979. *Britain and the Jews of Europe: 1939–1945*. Oxford: Clarendon Press.

Waxman, Chaim. 1982. "The Family and the American Jewish Community on the Threshold of the 1980s." In Sklare (ed.), *Understanding American Jewry*.

Weber, Eugen. 1976. *Peasants into Frenchmen: The Modernization of Rural France 1870–1914*. Stanford: Stanford University Press.

——. 1980. "Modern Anti-Semitism." In Friedlander and Morton, (eds.), *The Holocaust*, pp. 37–52.

Weinberg, David H. 1977. *A Community on Trial: The Jews of Paris in the 1930s*. Chicago: University of Chicago Press.

Weiner, Max (ed.). 1962. *Abraham Geiger and Liberal Judaism*. Philadelphia: Jewish Publication Society.

Weinryb, Bernard D. 1946. "The Economic and Social Background of Modern Anti-Semitism." In Pinson (ed.), *Essays on Antisemitism*, pp. 17–34.

———. 1970. "Eastern European Jewry (since the Partitions of Poland, 1772–95)." In Finkelstein (ed.), *The Jews*, pp. 343–98.

———. 1973. *The Jews of Poland*. Philadelphia: Jewish Publication Society of America.

Weizmann, Chaim. 1966. *Trial and Error*. New York: Schocken.

White, Dan S. 1976. *The Splintered Party: National Liberalism in Hessen and the Reich, 1867–1918*. Cambridge: Harvard University Press.

Whiteside, Andrew G. 1975. *The Socialism of Fools: Georg Ritter von Schonerer and Austrian Pan-Germanism*. Berkeley: University of California Press.

Wiesel, Elie. 1969. *Night*. New York: Avon.

Wildman, Allan K. 1972. "Russian and Jewish Social Democracy." In Alexander and Janet Rabinowitch (eds.), *Revolution and Politics in Russia*, pp. 75–87.

Willner, Dorothy. 1969. *Nation-Building and Community in Israel*. Princeton: Princeton University Press.

Wilson, Nelly. 1978. *Bernard Lazare: Antisemitism and the Problem of Jewish Identity in Late Nineteenth Century France*. Cambridge: Cambridge University Press.

Wolf, Lucian (ed.). 1912. *The Legal Sufferings of the Jews in Russia*. London: Unwin.

Wyczanski, Andrzej. 1982. "The Problem of Authority in Sixteenth Century Poland: An Essay in Reinterpretation." In Federowicz (ed.), *A Republic of Nobles*, pp. 96–108.

Wynot, Edward D., Jr. 1974. *Polish Politics in Transition: The Camp of National Unity and the Struggle for Power, 1935–1939*. Athens: University of Georgia Press.

Yahil, L. 1974. "Madagascar—Phantom of a Solution for the Jewish Question." In Vago and Mosse (eds.), *Jews and Non-Jews*, pp. 315–34.

Yancey, W., et al. 1976. "Emergent Ethnicity: A Review and Reformulation." *American Sociological Review* 41:391–402.

Zander, Freidrich Hermann. 1937. *Die Verbreitung der Juden in der Welt*. Berlin: Kammerer Verlag.

Zarchin, Michael. 1939. *Jews in the Province of Posen*. Philadelphia: Dropsie College.

Zborowski, Mark, and Elizabeth Herzog. 1952. *Life Is with People: The Culture of the Shtetl*. New York: Schocken.

Zimmels, H. J. 1977. *The Echo of the Nazi Holocaust in Rabbinic Literature*. New York: Ktav.

Zucker, Norman. 1973. *The Coming Crisis in Israel*. Cambridge: M.I.T. Press.

Zuckerman, Alan S. 1982. "New Approaches to Political Cleavage: A Theoretical Introduction." *Comparative Political Studies* 15 (July): 131–41.

———. 1984. "The Limits of Political Behavior: Individual Calculations and Survival during the Holocaust." *Political Psychology*, vol. 5 (January).

Zuckerman, Yitzhak. 1976. "The Jewish Fighting Organization—Z.O.B.—Its Establishment and Activities." In Gutman and Rothkirchen (eds.), *The Catastrophe*, pp. 518–48.

Zureik, Elias. 1979. *The Palestinians in Israel: A Study in Internal Colonialism*. London: Routledge and Kegan Paul.

Author Index

Subject Index

Abba of Hlusk, 27

Aden, 203

Agricultural settlement: America, 124–25. *See also* Kibbutz; Moshav

Agudah, 110, 112–13, 117, 134, 240

Ahdut Ha'Avodah, 206. *See also* Israel: mass politics

Alexander II, 57, 123. *See also* Romanovs

Algeria, 208, 210

Aliya: American, 176; Fifth, 201; First, 196, Fourth, 200; Second, 191, 197; Third, 200. *See also* Israel: immigration to Alsace (-Lorraine), 12, 15–17, 35, 36, 39, 55, 72

America. *See* American Jewish Community; United States

American Croatians, 166

American Finns, 166

American Greeks, 166

American Hungarians, 166

American immigrants, Jewish and non-Jewish, 158–59

American Israelis, 175

American Italians, 166

American Jewish community: and anti-Semitism, 157, 169; credit system in, 160–61, 170; divorce in, 176; Eastern European immigration, 162–65, 226; economic concentration, 166–69, 172, 183–85, 225–26; emigration from, 175–76; English language, 168; family, 167, 169–72, 176–80, 184, 224–26; fertility of, 177–79; formation of, 157–71; generational change, 169–71; Germans in, 158–62; immigration patterns, 157–64, 174–76, 226; income, 168; intermarriage, 159, 171–74, 178–81, 184, 224–25; marriage patterns, 176–77; migration, 182–83, 224; minority status, 158; mortal-ity, 174; occupations, 160, 166–68, 172, 183–85, 224–26; organizational structure, 159, 161, 169–70, 173, 175, 181, 185–88; perspectives on assimilation, 185–88, 223, 224–46, 235; politics of, 157, 172, 176, 185, 226; population growth, 158–59, 162, 165, 173–76, 179, 181, 225; religious changes, 161, 164, 172, 184–87, 225–26; residential distribution, 159–60, 164–66, 168–69, 172, 174, 181–83, 224–26; return migration, 162; transformation of, 181–85, 188

American Jewish Year Book, 159, 170, 173

American Poles, 166

American Russians, 166

American Slovenians, 166

American Zionist Federation, 195

American Zionists, 170

Am Haolam, 125

Amsterdam, 15, 44

Ancona, 40

Anti-Semitism; 6, 11, 39, 45–46, 49, 55, 80, 81, 111, 121, 127, 157, 169, 223, 225, 231, 237–39; in America, 157, 169; and competi-tion, 141–42; and the Holocaust, 136–49; political, 136–44; and political parties, 139–40; rise of, 138–44

Augsburg, 16, 47

Auschwitz, 146. *See also* Final Solution; Holocaust

Austria, 15, 34, 40, 46, 51, 77, 81–83, 86, 107, 112, 132, 140, 141, 145–7, 167, 201

Autoemancipation, 119. *See also* Pinsker

Baden, 47, 62, 72

Baer, Israel, 44

Balfour Declaration, 199, 205–6. *See also* Palestine